RHS
PLANTS
— FOR —
PLACES

A DORLING KINDERSLEY BOOK

Dorling Kindersley

LONDON, NEW YORK, SYDNEY,
DELHI, PARIS, MUNICH and JOHANNESBURG

WRITERS **Lin Hawthorne, Simon Maughan**
PROJECT EDITOR **Simon Maughan**
ART EDITOR **Ann Thompson**
MANAGING EDITOR **Anna Kruger**
MANAGING ART EDITOR **Lee Griffiths**
DTP DESIGN **Louise Waller**
PRODUCTION **Liz Cherry, Mandy Inness**

First edition published in Great Britain in 2001 by
Dorling Kindersley Limited
9 Henrietta Street
Covent Garden, London WC2E 8PS

2 4 6 8 10 9 7 5 3

A CIP catalogue record for this book is available from
the British Library.

ISBN 0 7513 0983 4

Colour reproduction by GRB Editrice Srl. Italy.
Printed and bound in Italy by Lego.

see our complete
catalogue at
www.dk.com

CONTENTS

USING THE GUIDE

THIS RHS BOOK is a handy pocket-sized guide that will help in choosing plants for specific conditions or places in the garden.

PLANTS FOR PLACES

Once you have identified the areas in your garden for which you need plants, turn to the relevant chapter where you will find a "shopping list" of suitable choices. Knowing which plant is most likely to succeed in a particular place will lessen the chances of disappointing results and allow you to plan planting schemes with confidence. Your needs may be practical, such as plants for a damp, shady site (*see p.238*), or you may be looking for plants that will add structure to the garden such as architectural specimens (*see p.472*) or flowers to attract wildlife (*see p.494*).

Even the smallest garden can offer several different planting options: perhaps a shaded area, which may be predominantly dry or damp, as well as a need for climbers with, say, containers for added interest. To arrive at a "wish list" of plants you will often have to refer to two or more chapters and you will find that many plants are suitable for more than one place. For example, rosemary can be clipped to make a low hedge (*see p.162*) but also suits coastal gardens and hot, dry sites. Other uses are listed in the text relating to a particular plant.

SYMBOLS USED

♥ The RHS Award of Garden Merit

SOIL MOISTURE PREFERENCES/TOLERANCES
◊ Well-drained soil
◑ Moist soil
● Wet soil

SUN/SHADE PREFERENCES/TOLERANCES
☀ Full sun
◐ Partial shade, either dappled shade or shade for part of the day
☀ Full shade
NB Where two symbols appear from the same category, the plant is suitable for a range of conditions.

HARDINESS RATINGS
❋ Plants requiring the protection of a heated glasshouse over winter but may be placed outdoors in sheltered sites in summer.
❋❋ Plants that survive outside in mild regions or in favoured sites, or those that, in temperate countries, are usually grown outside in summer but need frost-protection over winter.
❋❋❋ Fully hardy plants.
f Fragrant flowers or aromatic leaves.

KNOW YOUR SOIL

THE SOIL IN YOUR GARDEN has a strong influence on the plants that are likely to thrive there, so it is important to identify its type before you make any decisions on what to grow. It is always better and easier to choose plants to suit the soil than to try to alter the conditions to suit the plant. Plants put in unsuitable soils struggle to survive, are a waste of money and will only be a disappointment.

WHAT SOIL IS THAT?

In most soils, the relative proportion of clay, sand, and silt particles influence its physical and chemical nature. The main exception is peaty soil, which is dark in colour and rich in organic matter. Peaty soils are derived from sedges or mosses, which have decomposed in waterlogged conditions. They are acidic and moisture-retentive, providing ideal conditions for acid-loving plants like rhododendrons (*see p.92*).

There are laboratories that will analyse your soil for a fee, but you can get a good assessment of your soil type simply by looking at its colour and feeling the texture. Begin by rubbing a small amount of moist soil between your fingers. Clay soils easily form a cohesive ball that holds its shape when moulded, developing a shiny surface when smoothed. They are fertile, but are slow to warm in spring, sticky, and slow-draining after rain, baking hard in dry weather. Silty soils feel silky or soapy, and are easily compacted. Sandy soils feel gritty and will not stick together to form a ball. They are light and free-draining, and quick to warm in spring, but they will need frequent irrigation and feeding. Chalky soils are alkaline, usually pale in colour and stony, with chunks of flint or chalk visible on the surface. They are often shallow and sometimes sticky.

The ideal soil type is a loamy one, which has an approximately equal mixture of clay, silt, and sand. This much-envied combination gives the very best combination of good drainage and moisture- and nutrient-retention. Loamy soils suit the widest possible range of plants. If you are not blessed with a loamy soil, a sure way to improve any soil is to introduce plenty of well-rotted organic matter.

ACID AND ALKALINE SOILS

The soil's pH value is a measure of its acidity or alkalinity and also influences the range of plants that can be grown. pH is measured on a scale of 1–14, with the neutral point being pH 7. Below pH 7, soils become progressively more acid, and above, increasingly limy or alkaline. The most accurate way to gauge soil pH is using a pH-testing kit or electronic meter; both are inexpensive, easy to use, and available from garden centres. You can get a rough idea of your soil pH by observing the type of plants

ACID TEST

Like all rhododendrons, deciduous, fragrant R. luteum *needs acid soil.*

that succeed in your area. For example, if rhododendrons thrive in neighbouring gardens, and hydrangeas have clear blue flowers, it indicates that the local soil is acidic. If nearby hydrangeas are pink, the soil will be near neutral or slightly alkaline. The vast majority of plants thrive in soils that are neutral or nearly so, and a great number tolerate slightly alkaline or slightly acid soils.

SUN AND SHADE

ALL PLANTS NEED light to manufacture food, although they vary considerably in their tolerance of shade. Choosing the best aspect to suit an individual plant is crucial if it is to produce healthy and sustained growth. Many plants, however, are flexible about the amount of light they need. A particular specimen may prefer full sun, but it may still grow reasonably well in light, dappled shade, perhaps flowering a little less profusely and producing slightly lankier stems. Conversely, a shade-loving plant may tolerate full sun, but only in a site where the soil remains moist during the growing season.

GARDEN OBSERVATIONS

Surveying areas of light and shade in the garden is not a technical task – you could even do it on a warm,

A PLACE IN THE SUN
Many plants such as daisy-flowered anthemis and oriental poppies produce their finest displays if given a sunny site.

sunny day from the vantage point of a deck chair. The aim is simply to observe which areas of the garden are in sun or shade, and how this changes through the day as the sun moves across the sky. Take account of the fact that the sun is lower in winter and casts longer shadows, but bear in mind that trees may be leafless and cast less shade through the winter.

LEVELS OF SUN AND SHADE

It is helpful to categorize sunny and shady areas so that you can choose plants to fit the site.

FULL SUN: This category includes areas that are open to the sun for most of the day and are not subject to shade from nearby trees or buildings. Generally, they suit most plants that are grown for their flowers or fruits, since flower and consequent fruit production demands considerable energy. The sun and the warmth it gives also helps to ripen woody growth, and ripe growth bears the most flowers and fruits.

PARTIAL SHADE: Areas shaded by buildings or vegetation may actually receive between two and six hours of sun during the day as the sun moves across the sky. In these conditions, only the most committed sun- or shade-loving plants will fail to thrive. In many cases, partially shaded sites may actually prove to be advantageous to the gardener, especially if it protects both flowers and foliage from the scorching heat of the midday sun in summer.

LIGHT, DAPPLED SHADE: This is the sort of shade cast by the open canopies of deciduous trees like birches, robinias, and flowering cherries. They create a moving patchwork of light and shade, which alters with the sun's daily course. Seasonal variation is dramatic here; shade is relatively deep when the trees are in leaf, but it is almost non-existent in winter when the sun is low in the sky. These are admirable spots for woodland plants in the summer and for early spring bulbs that finish blooming before the leafy canopy finally closes over.

DEEP SHADE: This category defines areas where tall buildings or dense vegetation – most typically of evergreen plants – block the light for much or all of the day during the growing season. Little or no sunlight reaches the ground, but ther are some ferns and other woodland plants that thrive in these conditions.

WORKING WITH THE SITE

THERE ARE many suggestions in this book for plants that thrive in a variety of locations, some of which are quite taxing on plants, such as damp or dry places in shade, coastal gardens, exposed sites, and hot and sunny areas prone to drought. While there are plants to suit even the most stressful conditions, there is much that the gardener can do to make such conditions more hospitable. The optimistic gardener will always seek to turn apparent disadvantage into positive advantage.

TOUGH SITES

Exposed and coastal gardens can be among the most difficult for vegetation. Both sites experience strong winds and, by the sea, the gales carry salt spray and scouring airborne sand. Here, conditions can be improved by planting windbreaks or wind-filtering hedges (*see pp.118, 138, 166*) to create a gentler microclimate within the garden. In coastal areas, this makes an almost magical difference to the types of plant that will thrive there. Given shelter, coastal gardens can be extremely mild, enjoying balmy humidity and a high degree of frost protection by virtue of their proximity to a large body of water, which cools down more slowly than land. Slightly tender plants may often be grown without winter protection. Inland exposed gardens do not benefit from the ameliorating effect of the sea and unless windbreaks are planted few plants will survive.

Hot, dry sites can be hard on plants too, since they have to put up with an almost continual shortage of water during summer, unless the gardener takes steps to remedy this. Of course, choosing drought-tolerant plants is the first and best approach, but if the soil's capacity to retain moisture is improved, many plants will give their spectacular best in such sunny, warm conditions. Dig copious amounts of well-rotted organic matter into the soil, and mulch deeply around the plants. Try to make sure that you supply water by the most economical means, such as using trickle irrigation. Sun and warmth ripen the growth of woody plants, and ripe wood – replete with ample food reserves – not only flowers and fruits more freely, but it is also more resistant to winter cold.

FROST POCKETS AND SHADE

Frost pockets can be dealt with by choosing the hardiest plants and avoiding those that emerge very early in the year. Mulch deeply in autumn to insulate the plant roots from the worst of the cold, and even if the first shoots are bitten by frost, new shoots will follow.

Shade can only really be considered a disadvantage when it is really deep or accompanied by poor, dry soil. The more experienced a gardener becomes, the more shade is seen as an opportunity to grow some or the world's most beautiful woodland flora. These plants cannot tolerate unrelenting sunshine. While there may not be a wealth of highly coloured flowers to choose from, there are many that deserve cultivation for their luscious foliage alone, or for their characteristically pale flowers, which become positively luminous in the gloom.

IDEAL HOME
A pocket in a wall is the perfect place for Erigeron karvinskianus.

PLANTS FOR CLAY SOILS

THE NEW GARDENER often views a heavy clay soil with despair, because it is slow to warm in spring, poorly drained, and backbreaking to dig. It is also prone to compaction when walked on, impossibly sticky when wet, and as hard as brick when dry. Such inhospitable conditions can test even the most durable of plants as well as the patience of most gardeners, but these drawbacks are far from insurmountable. Once improved, by careful digging and the use of soil additives, clay can prove the most fertile of soils. Clay benefits from a remarkable ability to retain nutrients and water, so it is rich in the ingredients needed for good plant growth.

CHOOSING PLANTS

With time, a little work, and good management, an enormous range of plants will thrive in clay. They may be slow to get going, but once they are established they can attain their maximum dimensions.

Realistically, it takes several seasons to create the perfect growing medium, however, and the keen gardener may wish to delay planting until it is achieved. Choosing plants that either thrive in, or at least tolerate, heavy clay soil is a sensible starting point. This way, you will not waste money and be disappointed by failure, and the plant roots will do much to improve drainage and aeration as they penetrate the soil. The plants included in this chapter tolerate, or positively thrive in, soils that are heavy and slow-draining. Regard them as a starting point for creating a beautiful garden full of scent and colour; they will form the backbone of a garden, which will become more diverse as the soil conditions improve.

IMPROVING CLAY SOILS

A clay soil can be improved by a variety of techniques. Firstly, it can be dug over in autumn, with the clods left exposed through winter. As soil water freezes and thaws, it expands, breaking up the clods to create a more open structure. Avoid undoing the good work by treading on and compacting the soil. Delay planting until spring to reduce the damaging effects of cold, wet soil, which cause fragile new roots to rot; they will establish better in summer. Digging in coarse grit will also open up the structure, especially if it is incorporated along with copious quantities of relatively low-nutrient organic matter — in the form of garden compost, composted bark, well-rotted manure, or leafmould. Apply these materials as an autumn or spring mulch on cultivated soils and let the worms do the work of gradually mixing it. Lime can be applied to cause tiny clay particles to clump together into crumbs. This crumb structure improves aeration and water percolation and makes it easier for roots to penetrate. It can make soil more alkaline, however, and may damage roots if overdone, especially on limy soils – in this case, use gypsum, which causes clumping without affecting alkalinity.

AESCULUS HIPPOCASTANUM ♀

The horse chestnut is a vigorous, spreading tree, valued for its dense, conical 'candles' of creamy white flowers in early summer. Spiny fruits that enclose shiny brown conkers follow in autumn. The palmately divided, dark green leaves flush red, yellow, and rich brown before falling. An excellent specimen tree for larger gardens. Prune in winter, when fully dormant, if necessary. It tolerates chalky soils (see p.64).

ALSO RECOMMENDED: *'Baumannii'* ♀ *has double flowers and does not bear fruit;* A. × carnea *'Briotii'* ♀ (see p.120).

☼ ◐ ❊❊❊　　　　**Deciduous tree**
‡ 25m (80ft) ↔ 20m (70ft)

JUGLANS NIGRA ♀

The black walnut has a wide-spreading crown of aromatic, dark green leaves, and it makes an excellent, long-lived specimen tree. Its edible nuts need long summers to ripen fully, so a hot, dry site is desirable (see p.190). Walnuts do not transplant well, so set in their final position when no more than 60cm (24in) tall. Pruning should be done in late summer to avoid bleeding of the sap.

ALSO RECOMMENDED: J. regia ♀ *is the common walnut with smaller leaves, which are purple-flushed when young.*

☼ ◐◐ ❊❊❊　　　　**Deciduous tree**
‡ 30m (100ft) ↔ 20m (70ft)

+ LABURNOCYTISUS *'Adamii'*

An unusual small tree with curiously beautiful flowers that hang from its branches in spring. It bears pea-like flowers in separate clusters in three colours: purple, yellow, and pink-purple with a yellow flush. A fine specimen for small gardens, it looks especially effective when grown in groups. Keep pruning to a minimum, but remove any shoots that arise from below the graft joint.

☼ ◊ ❋ ❋ ❋ **Deciduous tree**

‡ 8m (25ft) ↔ 6m (20ft)

MAGNOLIA ✕ SOULANGEANA

It is the huge, goblet-shaped, pink, violet, or white flowers that are treasured on this shrubby tree, and they emerge with the new leaves in late spring. Preserve them from frost damage by growing as a specimen in a sheltered niche or by training the plant against a warm wall (*see p.280*). It withstands urban pollution and tolerates acid soils (*see p.92*).

ALSO RECOMMENDED: *'Lennei'* ♀ *has deep pink-purple, white-centred flowers; 'Rustica Rubra'* ♀ *has deep purplish red flowers.*

☼ ◊ ❋ ❋ ❋ **Deciduous tree**

‡ 6m (20ft) ↔ 6m (20ft)

MALUS *'John Downie'* ♛

This vigorous tree has beautiful white flowers in late spring and bears orange-red crab apples in autumn. The bright green leaves darken as they mature. An ideal small garden tree that produces its best fruits and flowers when planted in full sun. It also grows in chalky soils (*see p.64*).

ALSO RECOMMENDED: *M. × zumi 'Golden Hornet' ♛ bears pink-flushed white flowers in late spring, followed by yellow crab apples that persist well into winter.*

☼ ◐ ◊◊ ❀❀❀　　**Deciduous tree**
↕ 10m (30ft) ↔ 6m (20ft)

POPULUS TREMULA *'Pendula'*

The weeping aspen is a fine specimen tree for small gardens, with pendent branches clothed in leaves that tremble and rustle in the breeze; they are bronzed when young and butter yellow in autumn. It bears a profusion of elegant, purple-grey catkins in late winter. Also tolerant of sandy and acid soils (*see pp.38, 92*), and coastal and exposed gardens (*see pp.118, 166*). Plant all poplars well away from drains or foundations. Needs minimal pruning.

ALSO RECOMMENDED: *P. alba (see p.169); P. nigra 'Italica' ♛, the Lombardy poplar, is narrowly columnar to 30m (100ft) tall.*

☼ ◊ ❀❀❀　　**Deciduous tree**
↕ 6m (20ft) ↔ 8m (25ft)

QUERCUS ROBUR
F. FASTIGIATA

This narrow and upright form of the
English oak is a rugged-looking tree
with fissured, grey-brown bark. It is
densely furnished with the characteristic
dark green, round-lobed oak leaves.
Acorns appear from the end of summer.
It is best as a specimen tree in a large
garden. Also suitable for acid soils (*see
p.92*), exposed and coastal gardens
(*see pp.118, 166*), and hot, dry sites
(*see p.190*).

ALSO RECOMMENDED: *'Concordia' is a
smaller, rounded tree with bright yellow
young foliage, which turns to green.*

☼ ☀ ◊ ❄ ❄ ❄   **Deciduous tree**
‡ 15m (50ft) ↔ 12m (40ft)

TAXODIUM DISTICHUM ♀

This shapely, conical conifer is an ideal
specimen tree, especially for very wet
sites (*see p.372*); at the edge of water,
it produces knee-like, protuberant aerial
roots. The narrow, pale green leaves
are late to emerge in spring and turn
brilliant shades of russet brown in
autumn. Hanging, red male cones
emerge in winter. It grows in most wet
or moist ground, including acid soils (*see
p.92*). Little or no pruning is required.

ALSO RECOMMENDED: *The shoots of
'Nutans' ♀ become pendent when mature.*

☼ ☀ ◊◊ ❄ ❄ ❄   **Deciduous tree**
‡ 25m (80ft) ↔ 8m (25ft)

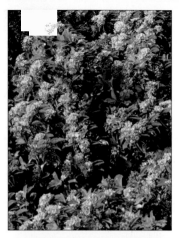

KALMIA LATIFOLIA ♥

A dense bush valued for its long-lasting display of pale to deep pink, occasionally white flowers that open from crimped, dark pink or red buds from late spring to midsummer. Equally at home in a shrub border or woodland garden, it flowers best in sun in reliably moist soil, which must be lime-free (*see p.92*). Deadhead regularly, and remove any dead wood and over-long shoots in spring.

ALSO RECOMMENDED: *'Ostho Red' ♥ is similar but has pale pink flowers opening from bright red buds.*

☀ ☀ ◊ ❋ ❋ ❋   **Evergreen shrub**
‡↔ 3m (10ft)

NEILLIA THIBETICA

The gracefully arching, zig-zagging branches of this shrub bear dense clusters of bell-shaped, rose-pink flowers at their tips in early summer. It is perfect for either mixed and shrub borders or a woodland garden. It forms thickets by suckering, so is useful for barrier plantings. Trim after flowering. Also tolerant of chalky, acid, and permanently moist soils (*see pp.64, 92, 372*).

ALSO RECOMMENDED: *N. sinensis has dense clusters of pale pink to white flowers in late spring and early summer.*

☀ ☀ ◊◊ ❋ ❋ ❋   **Deciduous shrub**
‡↔ 2m (6ft)

OXYDENDRON ARBOREUM

The sorrel tree is a large shrub, valued for its colourful autumn foliage and late summer flowers; the two displays sometimes coincide. The elliptical and finely toothed, glossy dark green leaves turn to brilliant shades of red, yellow, and purple before they fall, and the small, fragrant white flowers are produced in large clusters that droop from the branches. For the best autumn tints, grow on an acid soil (*see p.92*). Suitable for wild areas (*see p.494*).

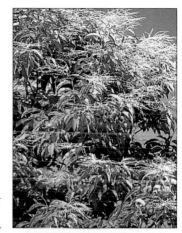

:::: ☼ ☀ ◐ ❀ ❀ ❀ *f*   **Deciduous shrub**
‡ 10–15m (30–50ft) ↔ 8m (25ft)

PYRACANTHA *'Mohave'*

This firethorn makes a bushy plant, admired for its short clusters of small white flowers in early summer and its bright red berries, which persist well into winter and are a food source for birds (*see p.494*). The leaves are glossy dark green. It is ideal in a shrub border or against a wall (*see pp.262, 280*); its spiny branches make for a good boundary hedge (*see p.138*). If winters are severe, choose a site that is sheltered from cold, drying winds.

ALSO RECOMMENDED: *'Golden Charmer'* (see p.159); *'Soleil d'Or'* (see p.269); *'Watereri'* ♥ (see p.505).

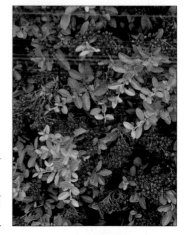

☼ ☀ ◐ ❀ ❀   **Evergreen shrub**
‡ 4m (12ft) ↔ 5m (15ft)

SAMBUCUS RACEMOSA
'Plumosa Aurea'

Delicately cut, golden leaves make this plant a fine focal point in a mixed or shrub border, or as a specimen in a woodland garden. Cut the stems back hard in early spring for the best foliage effect. If unpruned, creamy white flowers appear in spring and give rise to red berries that attract birds (*see p.494*). Tolerant of chalky and permanently moist soils (*see pp.64, 372*). May scorch in full sun.

ALSO RECOMMENDED: *'Sutherland Gold'* ♀ *is less liable to sun scorch; 'Tenuifolia'* ♀ *is shorter with finely cut green leaves.*

☀ ◐ ◊◑ ❀❀❀   **Deciduous shrub**
↕↔ 3m (10ft)

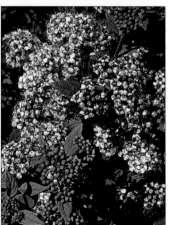

SPIRAEA JAPONICA
'Little Princess'

A low but wide-spreading shrub, forming a dense mound of small, dark green leaves, that makes good ground cover (*see p.304*). In mid- to late summer, it bears a profusion of rose-pink flowers. Ideal for edging a sunny border or for a rock garden. Tolerant of chalky soils (*see p.64*) and urban pollution. Cut back to a low, permanent framework in spring.

ALSO RECOMMENDED: *'Goldflame'* ♀ *is taller with bronze young leaves that turn bright yellow, then green with the arrival of the flowers; 'Nana'* ♀ *is more compact.*

☀ ◊ ❀❀❀   **Deciduous shrub**
↕ 50cm (20in) ↔ 1m (3ft)

SYRINGA VULGARIS *'Congo'*

This densely flowered form of the common lilac bears conical clusters of fragrant, lilac-purple flowers in early summer above heart-shaped, dark green leaves. Like other lilacs, it also thrives on well-drained soils, including shallow chalk (*see p.64*), and it tolerates coastal sites (*see p.166*) and urban pollution. A fine backdrop for a shrub or mixed border, or in a wildlife garden (*see p.494*). Little pruning is necessary.

ALSO RECOMMENDED: *'Andenken an Ludwig Späth'* ♥ *has dark purple-red flowers; those of 'Charles Joly'* ♥ *are double and deep purple.*

☼ ◊ ❀ ❀ ❀ *f*   **Deciduous shrub**
↕↔ 7m (22ft)

THUJA OCCIDENTALIS *'Hetz Midget'*

This slow-growing, dwarf variant of white cedar has yellowish green, scale-like leaves, which are fruit scented when bruised. It forms a spherical bush and is good for a rock garden or for providing strong contrasts of form in a conifer collection. Tolerant of most well-drained soils including chalk (*see p.64*). Provide shelter from cold, drying winds.

ALSO RECOMMENDED: *'Caespitosa' has bluish foliage, making a bun-shaped bush to 30cm (12in) tall; 'Golden Globe' makes a golden yellow sphere to 1m (3ft) tall.*

☼ ◊ ❀ ❀ ❀   **Evergreen shrub**
↕↔ 80cm (32in)

WEIGELA FLORIDA
'Foliis Purpureis' ♀

This compact bush has arching shoots bearing generous clusters of funnel-shaped, dark pink flowers with pale insides in late spring and early summer. The foliage is bronze-green. It is ideal for a shrub or mixed border in an urban garden. Prune out some older branches at ground level each year after flowering. Also suitable as a hedge plant (*see p.138*), and it tolerates chalky soils (*see p.64*).

ALSO RECOMMENDED: *W. 'Florida Variegata' ♀ is twice the size with white-margined, greyish green leaves.*

☼ ◊ ✿✿✿ **Deciduous shrub**
‡ 1m (3ft) ↔ 1.5m (5ft)

HUMULUS LUPULUS 'Aureus' ♀

The golden hop is grown for its prettily lobed, bright golden yellow foliage, which will twine over a fence or trellis, or up into a small tree. Hanging clusters of papery, cone-like, greenish yellow flowers appear in autumn, and they dry well for garlands and swags. It can be grown on a partially shaded wall (*see p.262*), but leaf colour is best in full sun. Give the twining stems support, and cut back any dead growth to ground level in early spring.

ALSO RECOMMENDED: *H. lupulus, the traditional hop, is similar, but with pale green leaves.*

☼☀ ◊◊ ✿✿✿ **Climber**
‡ 6m (20ft)

VITIS COIGNETIAE ♀

This vigorous, woody-stemmed climber
has large, heart-shaped leaves, which
turn bright red in autumn; the colour
is best in full sun. It climbs using its
tendrils and is ideal for clothing a warm
wall (*see p.280*), pergola, or large tree;
if pegged down it also makes good
ground cover (*see p.304*). It tolerates
sandy and slightly alkaline soils
(*see pp.38, 64*). Prune in midwinter.

ALSO RECOMMENDED: *V. vinifera*
'Purpurea' ♀ (see p.303).

☼ ◑ ◊ ❀ ❀ ❀   **Climber**
‡ 15m (50ft)

ACONITUM × CAMMARUM
'BICOLOR' ♀

Arching branches of hooded, blue and
white flowers appear on this upright
plant from mid- to late summer, well
above the deeply lobed, glossy dark
green leaves. It needs staking. Good for
late colour in herbaceous or mixed
borders, and it will tolerate full sun
where soils are reliably moist. All parts
are highly toxic if ingested.

ALSO RECOMMENDED: *A. 'Bressingham*
Spire' ♀ *has deep violet flowers; 'Newry*
Blue' has dense spires of mid blue flowers

◑ ◊ ❀ ❀ ❀   **Perennial**
‡ 1.2m (4ft) ↔ 30cm (12in)

ARUNCUS DIOICUS

Goatsbeard forms clumps of rich green, fern-like foliage, from which loose and arching clusters of creamy or greenish white flowers emerge in the first half of summer. A graceful woodland plant that also suits damp shade (*see p.238*) and permanently moist soils (*see p.372*), such as around the edge of a pond. Cut spent flower stems back hard in autumn.

ALSO RECOMMENDED: *'Kneiffii' has very finely divided leaves and cream flowers;* A. aethusifolius *is more compact with leaves that turn yellow in autumn.*

☼ ◑ ◔◔ ❋❋❋ **Perennial**

↕ 2m (6ft) ↔ 1.2m (4ft)

ASTER NOVI-BELGII *'Jenny'*

This Michaelmas daisy is grown for its sprays of daisy-like, red-purple and yellow flowers, which appear from late summer to mid-autumn above stout clumps of mid-green leaves. This is a useful plant for a perennial border; feed and water it well in spring and summer for best results. Mildew may be a problem if conditions become too dry. Also good for wildlife areas (*see p.494*).

ALSO RECOMMENDED: *'Alice Haslam' has rose-red flowers; those of 'Audrey' are lavender-blue; 'Fellowship' has large, double, deep pink flowers; 'Little Pink Beauty' has soft pink flowers.*

☼ ◑ ◔◔ ❋❋❋ **Perennial**

↕ 1.5m (5ft) ↔ 60cm (24in)

ASTILBE *'Deutschland'*

Branching, feathery spires of many tiny,
creamy white flowers rise above the
dense mass of finely divided, bright
green leaves in late spring and early
summer on this versatile, clump-
forming perennial. It is ideal for damp
borders (*see p.238*), woodland gardens,
and waterside plantings (*see p.372*).
Divide the clumps every few years to
maintain vigorous growth.

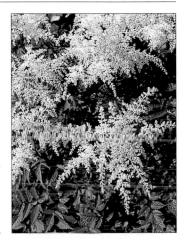

ALSO RECOMMENDED: A. × arendsii
'Fanal' ♥ *has long-lived, deep crimson
plumes;* A. × crispa *'Perkeo'* ♥ (see p.377).

☼ ◐▲ ❋❋❋   **Perennial**
‡ 50cm (20in) ↔ 30cm (12in)

ASTRANTIA MAJOR

Ground-level clumps of deeply lobed
leaves give rise to tall stems in early
and midsummer, topped by small,
green or pink, sometimes deep purple-
red flowers. They are good for dried
flower arrangements (*see p.524*). In
a suitable position, such as damp
woodland (*see p.238*) or anywhere with
moist soil (*see p.372*), the plant will
self-seed and form clumps. The leaves
die down in winter.

ALSO RECOMMENDED: *'Hadspen Blood' has
dark red flowers; 'Sunningdale Variegated'* ♥
has cream-margined leaves and pink flowers.

☼☼ ◐▲ ❋❋❋   **Perennial**
‡ 30–90cm (12–36in) ↔ 45cm (18in)

CAMPANULA LATILOBA
'Hidcote Amethyst' ♛

A clump-forming bellflower with cup-shaped, pale amethyst blooms that appear against mid-green foliage in the second half of summer. An ideal border perennial that can also be naturalized in a wildlife garden (*see p.494*) or in gaps in paving (*see p.348*); the delicate flowers are best preserved in partial shade. Cut back after flowering to encourage further blooms. Also good for chalky soils and hot, dry sites (*see pp.64, 190*)

ALSO RECOMMENDED: *'Percy Piper'* ♛ *has rich violet-blue flowers;* C. latifolia *'Brantwood' is upright with violet flowers.*

☼ ◐ ◊◊ ❀ ❀ ❀　　　　　**Perennial**
‡ 90cm (36in) ↔ 45cm (18in)

CAREX OSHIMENSIS
'Evergold' ♛

This evergreen sedge forms a low tussock of narrow, dark green leaves, each with a broad, creamy yellow central stripe. Brown flower spikes appear in mid- and late spring above the foliage. Tolerant of more freely drained soils than many sedges and is suitable for a mixed border or a sunny container (*see p.412*).

ALSO RECOMMENDED: C. morrowii *'Fisher's Form' is slightly less hardy to frost and grows to 50cm (20in) tall with cream-striped, dark green leaves.*

☼ ◐ ◊◊ ❀ ❀ ❀　　　　　**Perennial**
‡ 30cm (12in) ↔ 35cm (14in)

CENTAUREA MACROCEPHALA

This stout knapweed with robust stems
bears rich yellow flowers in mid- and
late summer. The bases of these thistle-
like blooms are fringed with shiny
brown bracts. The leaves are soft and
mid-green. Bees and butterflies are
drawn to the bright flowers, which
makes this plant suitable for a
wildlife garden (*see p. 494*) as well
as a traditional border. Tolerant of
coastal sites (*see p.106*).

ALSO RECOMMENDED: *C. simplicicaulis
grows to 25cm (10in) tall, has rose-pink
flowers in early summer, and needs full
sun and well-drained soil.*

☼ ◑ ◊◑ ❉ ❉ ❉   **Perennial**
‡ 1.5m (5ft) ↔ 60cm (24in)

EUPATORIUM RUGOSUM

White snakeroot forms clumps of
purple-tinged, stiffly upright stems,
which are topped by domed clusters of
pink, pinkish purple, or creamy white
flowers from midsummer to early
autumn. Whorls of coarse, purplish
green leaves decorate the stems.
Suitable for a reliably moist border (*see
p.372*) or woodland garden (*see p.238*).
It tolerates chalky soils (*see p.64*).

ALSO RECOMMENDED: *E. album
'Braunlaub' bears brown-flushed young
leaves and brown-tinged flowers.*

☼ ◑ ❉ ❉ ❉   **Perennial**
‡ 1.5–1.8m (5–6ft) ↔ 60cm (24in)

FILIPENDULA PURPUREA ♔

An upright, clump-forming plant that looks well planted in groups to form drifts of elegant, dark green foliage. Feathery clusters of red-purple flowers are carried above the leaves on purple-tinged stems in summer. Suitable for a waterside planting or bog garden (*see p.372*), it can also be naturalized in damp woodland (*see p.238*).

ALSO RECOMMENDED: *f.* albiflora *has white flowers;* 'Elegans' *has greenish yellow leaves.*

☼ ◑ ◖◗ ❀ ❀ ❀   **Perennial**
‡ 1.2m (4ft) ↔ 60cm (24in)

HELENIUM 'Moerheim Beauty'

From early to late summer, this robust and upright, undemanding perennial bears a succession of rich, coppery red, daisy-like blooms with dark brown centres; they are attractive to bees (*see p.494*) and good for cutting (*see p.524*). Deadhead regularly and divide the clumps every third year to maintain vigour. Also suitable for containers in sun (*see p.412*).

ALSO RECOMMENDED: *'Butterpat' bears golden flowerheads from midsummer;* 'Wyndley' (*see p.85*).

☼ ◖◗ ❀ ❀ ❀   **Perennial**
‡ 90cm (36in) ↔ 60cm (24in)

HELIOPSIS HELIANTHOIDES
'Sommersonne'

Also sold as 'Summer Sun', the bright,
golden yellow daisy flowers of this
vigorous perennial are borne from
midsummer to early autumn, making
it invaluable in a sunny border. A
little unobtrusive support and regular
deadheading improves the display, and
dividing the clumps every third year
will maintain vigour.

ALSO RECOMMENDED: *'Goldgefieder'* ♀
*has double, bright yellow flowerheads with
green centres.*

☼ ◊◊ ❄ ❄ ❄   **Perennial**
↕ 90cm (36in) ↔ 60cm (24in)

HEMEROCALLIS
'Stella de Oro' ♀

With dense clumps of bright green
leaves, this elegant daylily makes good
ground cover (*see p.304*), especially
in permanently moist soil (*see p.372*).
The bright yellow flowers are borne
repeatedly from early summer. Ideal
at the front of a sunny border or in
a sunny container (*see p.412*).

ALSO RECOMMENDED: *'Gentle Shepherd' is
taller, spreads more widely, and bears ivory
white flowers; 'Stafford' is also taller and has
star-shaped scarlet flowers.*

☼ ◊ ❄ ❄ ❄   **Perennial**
↕ 30cm (12in) ↔ 45cm (18in)

HOSTA VENTRICOSA ♥

This plantain lily forms dense mounds of broad, shiny dark green, overlapping leaves with slightly wavy margins. Spires of bell-shaped, deep purple flowers arch above the luxuriant foliage in late summer. Good at the front of a mixed border, but also suitable for containers (*see p.448*), as ground cover under deciduous trees (*see p.326*), or in permanently moist soils (*see p.372*). Shelter from cold winds.

ALSO RECOMMENDED: *var.* aureomaculata *has yellow-splashed leaves; those of H. 'Aureo-marginata' ♥ are margined yellow.*

☀◐ ◊ ❀❀❀ **Perennial**
‡ 50cm (20in) ↔ 1m (3ft)

HOUTTUYNIA CORDATA

In damp shade, at the margins of streams or ponds, or in shady containers (*see pp.238, 372, 448*), the blue-green, heart-shaped leaves of this vigorous, spreading plant make excellent ground cover (*see p.326*). Tiny white flowers appear in spring. Protect roots of plants grown in wet soils with a winter mulch in cold areas.

ALSO RECOMMENDED: *'Chameleon' (syn. 'Tricolor') spreads less vigorously and has variegated leaves in shades of pale yellow, green, and red.*

☀◊◐ ❀❀❀ **Perennial**
‡ 15–30cm (6–12in) ↔ indefinite

HYACINTHOIDES NON-SCRIPTA

Bluebells are perfect for naturalizing in grass, in a wildlife area (*see p.494*), or in a damp woodland garden (*see p.238*). Although they prefer moist soils, they tolerate dry shade (*see p.216*) and are good for underplanting a shrub border. The spires of scented, soft violet-blue flowers are borne in spring and look best in massed plantings; leave dead flowers in place, and they will self-seed where conditions suit. Plants bulbs in autumn.

ALSO RECOMMENDED: *H. hispanica is more robust with denser flower spikes.*

:☼: :●: ◐ ❀ ❀ ❀ *f*   **Perennial**
‡ 20–40cm (8–16in) ↔ 8cm (3in)

KIRENGESHOMA PALMATA ♀

A handsome, upright perennial with broad, lobed, pale green leaves. In late summer and early autumn, these are topped by loose clusters of nodding, pale yellow flowers, which are sometimes called nodding wax bells. It brings a gentle elegance to a cool and damp, shady border (*see p.238*), and it thrives in acid soils (*see p.92*). Shelter from wind, and enrich the planting site with leaf mould.

:☼: ◐ ❀ ❀ ❀   **Perennial**
‡ 60–120cm (24–48in) ↔ 75cm (30in)

MONARDA *'Mahogany'*

This bergamot forms clumps of dark green, aromatic leaves on upright stems. From midsummer to early autumn, a profusion of rich red, shaggy flowerheads appear, making a colourful addition to any herbaceous or mixed border. Since the flowers are also very attractive to bees, bergamots suit wildlife gardens (*see p.494*). Protect from excessive winter wet.

ALSO RECOMMENDED: *'Beauty of Cobham'* ♥ *has pale pink flowers; those of* 'Cambridge Scarlet' ♥ *are scarlet-red;* 'Croftway Pink' ♥ (see p.517).

☼ ◐ ◊◊ ❀ ❀ ❀ *f*   **Perennial**

‡ 90cm (36in) ↔ 45cm (18in)

PERSICARIA CAMPANULATA

This knotweed is grown for its display of small, white or pink, fragrant flowers, which appear on upright stems in loose clusters from midsummer to early autumn. The plant forms a clump of spreading, slender and wiry stems with bright green leaves. An undemanding plant for a border, as ground cover (*see pp.304, 326*), or in containers (*see pp.412, 448*). Also good in cracks between paving or in permanently moist soils (*see pp.348, 372*).

ALSO RECOMMENDED: *'Rosenrot' is more upright in habit with deep pink flowers;* 'Southcombe White' has white flowers.

☼ ◐ ◊ ❀ ❀ ❀ *f*   **Perennial**

‡↔ 90cm (36in)

POLEMONIUM CARNEUM

An upright perennial with dense clumps of decorative, divided leaves that are topped in early summer by loose clusters of shallowly bell-shaped flowers in pale pink, yellow, or sometimes deep purple or lavender. Remove dead flowerheads for a second, later flush of flowers. Grow in a border or wildlife garden (see p.494).

ALSO RECOMMENDED: *P. caeruleum has violet-blue flowers and reaches 90cm (36in) tall; f. album has white flowers; P. pauciflorum has pale yellow, red-flushed flowers.*

☼☀☽ ◐◊ ✽✽✽　　　　**Perennial**

↕ 10–40cm (4–18in) ↔ 20cm (8in)

POLYGONATUM HIRTUM

Solomon's seals are valued for their fresh green foliage and tubular flowers. From late spring to midsummer, this species carries a few hanging, green-tipped, greenish white flowers from the axil of each leaf. Spherical black fruits follow. A favourite plant for a dry, shady border (see p.216). Cut old stems back in winter when the plant is dormant.

ALSO RECOMMENDED: *P. × hybridum 'Striatum' is shorter with late spring flowers and cream-striped leaves.*

☼☀ ◐◊ ✽✽✽　　　　**Perennial**

↕ 1.2m (4ft) ↔ 60cm (24in)

PULMONARIA
'Sissinghurst White' ♀

Slowly spreading to form a carpet of dark green, white-spotted leaves, this plant is spangled in spring with a mass of pure white flowers, which open from pale pink buds. Excellent as ground cover beneath shrubs or in a woodland garden (*see p.326*); it is best in shade but tolerates full sun. Also suitable for a wildlife garden (*see p.494*). Divide and replant clumps every few years.

ALSO RECOMMENDED: P. angustifolia ♀ *bears deep blue flowers*; P. longifolia *has deep blue-purple flowers from late winter.*

☼ ◐ ◊ ❀ ❀ ❀   **Perennial**
‡ 30cm (12in) ↔ 45cm (18in)

RODGERSIA AESCULIFOLIA ♀

The deeply crinkled, horse-chestnut-like leaves of this architectural plant (*see p.472*) form a foil for the plumes of tiny, pink or white, star-shaped flowers, which appear in midsummer. It makes excellent ground cover (*see pp.304, 326*), especially for permanently moist soil (*see p.372*) or in a damp, shady border (*see p.238*). Also suitable for a container in shade (*see p.448*).

ALSO RECOMMENDED: R. pinnata 'Superba' ♀ (see p.391); R. sambucifolia *has white or pink flowers in early to midsummer.*

☼ ◐ ◊◊ ❀ ❀ ❀   **Perennial**
‡ to 2m (6ft) ↔ 1m (3ft)

SANGUISORBA CANADENSIS

The Canadian burnet produces fluffy, long-stemmed spikes of tiny white flowers in midsummer and autumn, above a clump of divided, dark green leaves. It is perfect for naturalizing in permanently moist soils (*see p.372*). The long-lived flowers, which open from the bottom of the spike upwards, are excellent for cutting (*see p.524*).

ALSO RECOMMENDED: S. obtusa *is shorter, to 60cm (24in), and has nodding spikes of pink flowers.*

☼ ◐◖ ❋❋❋   **Perennial**
‡ 2m (6ft) ↔ 1m (3ft)

SCROPHULARIA AURICULATA 'Variegata'

The variegated water figwort forms a mound of wrinkled green leaves that are boldly splashed with cream; the bright variegation is maintained even in deep shade. An ideal marginal plant, it thrives in permanently moist soils and shallow water (*see pp.372, 394*); it also suits a damp wildlife area (*see p.494*) or woodland garden. Cut the flowerheads off as they form to keep clumps neat and to maintain variegation.

☼ ◐◖ ❋❋❋   **Perennial**
‡↔ 90cm (36in)

SILPHIUM PERFOLIATUM

The cup plant forms a clump of resinously aromatic, triangular leaves and bears branching heads of yellow daisy flowers from midsummer to autumn. They attract a variety of pollinating insects, which makes this plant ideal for naturalizing in a wildlife garden (*see p.494*). It also tolerates chalky and permanently moist soils (*see pp.64, 372*).

ALSO RECOMMENDED: S. laciniatum, *the compass plant, is taller with nodding heads of yellow flowers that always face east.*

☼ ◑ ◊ ❀ ❀ ❀ *f*　　　**Perennial**

↕ 2.5m (8ft) ↔ 1m (3ft)

SOLIDAGO *'Golden Wings'*

With broad heads of golden yellow flowers borne from late summer to early autumn, this vigorous plant is ideal for late colour at the back of a mixed or herbaceous border; it will also naturalize in a wildlife area (*see p.494*) or woodland garden. The flowers are excellent for cutting (*see p.524*). This plants also tolerates sandy soils and maritime conditions (*see pp.38, 166*).

ALSO RECOMMENDED: *'Goldenmosa'* ♀ *is more compact, with yellow flowerheads; 'Crown of Rays' is shorter still with radiating golden yellow flowerheads.*

☼ ◊◊ ❀ ❀ ❀　　　**Perennial**

↕ 2m (6ft) ↔ 90cm (36in)

THELYPTERIS PALUSTRIS

The marsh fern is a spreading plant and forms substantial clumps of arching, finely divided, pale green fronds with deeply lobed segments. It thrives in permanently moist soils (*see p.494*), where it is ideal as ground cover (*see pp.304, 326*), such as at the edge of a pond. It grows well in full sun or shade, but will only produce spores in good light. It may be invasive.

☼ ☼ ◊▲ ❁ ❁ ❁   **Perennial fern**
‡ 60cm (24in) ↔ 1m (3ft)

THERMOPSIS RHOMBIFOLIA

An upright, unbranched plant with pretty, laburnum-like, mid-green leaves clothed in silky silver hair. The short spires of soft yellow flowers in early summer are attractive to bees. This spreading plant is worth naturalizing in a wildlife area (*see p.494*) or woodland garden, although it may be invasive.

ALSO RECOMMENDED: T. villosa *is taller with downy yellow flowers in late spring and early summer.*

☼ ☼ ◊▲ ❁ ❁ ❁   **Perennial**
‡ 90cm (36in) ↔ 60cm (24in) or more

PLANTS FOR SANDY SOILS

Sandy soils are a joy to work. They are well-aerated and very free-draining, and unlike clay soils, they can be worked at almost any time of year without harming the structure. As a rule, if you can walk on the bare earth without it sticking to your boots, it is safe to dig, and all a sandy soil will need is the lightest of cultivations before it is planted. Sandy soils also warm quickly in spring, giving plants a head start into growth.

There is a price to pay for such a plethora of advantages, however. Sandy soils are generally very hungry and thirsty, as a result of being open and free-draining. Water is lost rapidly both by evaporation from the surface and drainage, and as the water drains away, it takes dissolved plant nutrients with it. Organic matter also degrades rapidly, which compounds the loss of nutrients.

SPECIAL PLANTS
Plants that thrive on sandy soils include many annuals that are either tolerant of, or adapted to

survival on, low-nutrient soils, and they are often accustomed to drought in their natural habitat. For example, the foxtail lily (see p.55) grows in the dry, stony hills of Afghanistan, and its thick, fleshy roots have evolved to conserve what little moisture they can find. Sun loving helianthemums (see pp.46, 72, 351) naturally dwell in dry, rocky places and on sand dunes, and their small, tough, often white-hairy leaves conserve vital moisture while deflecting the sun's burning rays. Many such plants have a waxy, bluish bloom to their foliage, another method of conserving water. The beauty of their foliage is often one of their most enduring features and can be used to create exciting mixtures of colours and textures. In the race to set seed before conditions become too dry, many plants also flower freely and attract pollinating insects with exuberant colours and fragrances. Some plants may even flower themselves to death if they exhaust the soil nutrients in the process.

CULTIVATION TIPS

If you garden on sand, be prepared to apply well-rotted, nutrient-rich organic matter, such as well-rotted manure or garden compost, on an annual basis, and to give additional plant food in the form of a balanced, preferably slow-release, fertilizer. Organic matter will be most effective if applied as a mulch, 5–10cm (2–4in) thick, to previously weeded ground. There is little point in digging organic matter and nutrients deep into sandy soil as this will damage the structure you are trying to improve. The natural actions of rainfall and beneficial soil organisms will carry them down to the plant roots where they are needed. A mulch also helps to reduce evaporation of water from the soil surface and to avoid extreme fluctuations in temperature, which may harm the roots. A ground-covering carpet of evergreen foliage will also help (see pp.304, 326), particularly in winter, when increased rainfall leads to a greater leaching of nutrients.

Betula ermanii

Erman's birch is a conical tree with rough, warty shoots and pinkish or creamy white bark. Long, yellow-brown catkins open as the foliage emerges in spring; the dark green leaves turn yellow in autumn before they fall. Like most birches, this tree is an excellent landscape tree planted alone or in clumps. Also tolerant of clay and acid soils (*see pp.12, 92*).

ALSO RECOMMENDED: B. pendula *'Tristis'* ♥ (see p.474); B. utilis *'Jermyns'* ♥ (see p.121).

☼ ◊ ❄❄❄   **Deciduous tree**
‡ 20m (70ft) ↔ 12m (40ft)

Castanea sativa *'Albomarginata'*

This vigorous, broadly columnar tree has toothed, glossy dark green leaves margined with cream. In summer, it produces creamy white, catkin-like flowers in large clusters; these are followed by edible fruits – sweet chestnuts – in autumn. A good specimen for larger gardens. Little pruning is required. Best in slightly acid soils (*see p.92*).

ALSO RECOMMENDED: *'Aspleniifolia' has deeply cut leaves; 'Marron de Lyon' is grown for its fruit.*

☼◑ ◊ ❄❄❄   **Deciduous tree**
‡ 30m (100ft) ↔ 15m (50ft)

CERCIS SILIQUASTRUM ♈

The Judas tree is a handsome, broad tree. It bears clusters of pea-like, bright pink flowers on the previous year's wood either before or with the heart-shaped leaves in mid spring. The foliage is bronze when young, maturing to dark blue-green, then to yellow in autumn. Flowering is best after a long, hot summer. Also good for chalky soils (*see p.64*) and hot, dry sites (*see p.190*). Prune young trees to a balanced shape in early summer.

ALSO RECOMMENDED: C. canadensis *'Forest Pansy'* ♈ *has dark red purple leaves*

☼☀ ◊◊ ❀❀❀ **Deciduous tree**
↕↔ 10m (30ft)

ROBINIA PSEUDOACACIA *'Frisia'* ♈

This variety of black locust is a fast-growing, broadly columnar tree much admired for its gentle yellow-green foliage, which is golden yellow when young and orange-yellow in autumn. Hanging clusters of small white flowers appear sparsely in summer. The stems are spiny. When young, maintain a single trunk by removing competing stems as soon as possible. Do not prune once established. Also suitable for chalky soils (*see p.64*).

ALSO RECOMMENDED: R. hispida ♈ (see p.296).

☼ ◊◊ ❀❀❀ **Deciduous tree**
↕ 15m (50ft) ↔ 8m (25ft)

BALLOTA PSEUDODICTAMNUS ♀

A low subshrub that forms mounds of aromatic, yellow-grey-green foliage on upright, white-woolly stems. Whorls of small, white or pinkish white flowers, each enclosed by a pale green funnel, are borne in early summer. It is ideal for a sunny border. Cut back in early spring to keep plants compact. Protect from excessive winter wet.

ALSO RECOMMENDED: *B. acetabulosa is slightly larger with purple-pink flowers in mid- and late summer.*

☼ ◊ ✿ ✿ ✿ *f*   **Evergreen shrub**
‡ 45cm (18in) ↔ 60cm (24in)

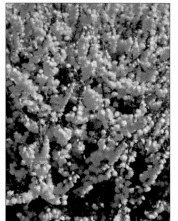

CALLUNA VULGARIS
'Kinlochruel' ♀

A distinctive heather with double white flowers in long clusters that are borne very freely from midsummer to late autumn. It forms a spreading mound of bright green foliage, which turns to bronze during winter. Hundreds of different cultivars exist, most of which make good ground cover on acid soils (*see pp.92, 304*). They also suit wildflower gardens (*see p.494*).

ALSO RECOMMENDED: *'Wickwar Flame' ♀ has gold leaves, which turn red in winter.*

☼ ◊ ✿ ✿ ✿   **Evergreen shrub**
‡ 25cm (10in) ↔ 40cm (16in)

CERATOSTIGMA WILLMOTTIANUM ♥

Chinese plumbago is valued for its long-lasting display of pale to mid-blue flowers from late summer; autumn flowers appear at the same time as the diamond-shaped, mid-green leaves turn to blazing red. It dies right back in cold winters, but usually regenerates in spring. Grow in a sheltered mixed border. It also tolerates urban pollution and chalky soils (see. p.64).

ALSO RECOMMENDED: *C. plumbaginoides* ♥ *is a shorter perennial form with bright blue flowers and crimson leaves in autumn.*

☼ ◊ ❀ ❀ ❀   **Deciduous shrub**
‡ 1m (3ft) ↔ 1.5m (5ft)

CISTUS × SKANBERGII ♥

A beautiful and compact rock rose that bears small clusters of pale pink blooms in profusion throughout summer. They are saucer-shaped with crinkled petals and a central boss of gold stamens – similar to single rose flowers. The narrow, slightly wavy-margined leaves are grey-green. Good for sunny shrub borders or containers, against warm walls, or in hot, dry sites (see pp.190, 280. 412).

ALSO RECOMMENDED: *C. × cyprius* ♥ *has white flowers with crimson marks at the petal bases and is twice the size; C. × purpureus* ♥ *has dark pink flowers.*

☼ ◊ ❀ ❀   **Evergreen shrub**
‡ 75cm (30in) ↔ 90cm (36in)

CONVOLVULUS CNEORUM ♛

This small, rounded bush bears masses of funnel-shaped, sparkling white flowers with yellow centres from late spring and into summer. They stand out against the dark silvery green, narrow leaves. Excellent as a largish plant in a rock garden or on a sunny bank. In areas with cold, wet winters, grow in a container (*see p.412*) and move into a cool greenhouse in winter. Trim back after flowering, if necessary.

ALSO RECOMMENDED: C. sabatius ♛
(see p.432).

☼ ◊ ❋ ❋　　　　**Evergreen shrub**
‡ 60cm (24in) ↔ 90cm (36in)

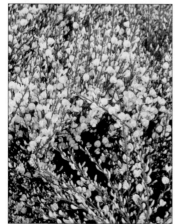

CYTISUS × PRAECOX *'Warminster'* ♛

Warminster broom has slender, arching green branches, wreathed in fragrant, pea-like, creamy yellow flowers in spring. It suits a shrub border or large rock garden, hot, dry sites (*see p.190*), and warm walls (*see p.280*). Pinch out branch tips to promote bushy growth. Cut shoots back by up to two-thirds after flowering; do not cut into old wood. Also tolerant of clay and acid soils (*see pp.12, 92*) and coastal conditions (*see p.166*).

ALSO RECOMMENDED: *'Allgold'* ♛ *has deep yellow flowers.*

☼ ◊ ❋ ❋ ❋ *f*　　　　**Deciduous shrub**
‡ 1.2m (4ft) ↔ 1.5m (5ft)

ERICA AUSTRALIS ♛

Unlike many heathers, the Spanish heath is a relatively tall and upright shrub. It bears masses of bell-shaped, purplish pink flowers from mid-spring to early summer against a backdrop of fine, needle-like, dark green foliage. Grow in a heather garden or among other shrubs. Prone to damage by wind or snow; cut back damaged growth after flowering. Also good for acid soils (*see p.92*).

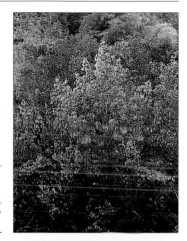

ALSO RECOMMENDED: *'Mr Robert'* ♛ *produces white flowers. 'Riverslea'* ♛ *bears lilac-pink flowers.*

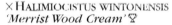

:☼: ◊ ❀ ❀   **Evergreen shrub**
‡ 2m (6ft) ↔ 1m (3ft)

× HALIMIOCISTUS WINTONENSIS *'Merrist Wood Cream'* ♛

A spreading shrub that bears rose-like, creamy yellow flowers with red bands and yellow centres against greyish foliage in late spring and early summer. Good for a raised bed or rock garden, or for the front of a mixed border. It also suits warm walls, hot, dry sites, and containers (*see pp.190, 280, 412*). It may perish during cold winters if not sheltered from excessive rain. Pruning is rarely needed.

ALSO RECOMMENDED: × *H. sahucii* ♛ *is more compact with pink flowers in summer.*

:☼: ◊ ❀ ❀   **Evergreen shrub**
‡ 60cm (24in) ↔ 90cm (36in)

HEBE CUPRESSOIDES
'Boughton Dome' ♀

This dwarf shrub is grown for its neat shape and dense, cypress-like foliage, which forms a pale green dome. Flowers are infrequent. An excellent addition to a rock garden, giving a topiary effect without any clipping. It also thrives in coastal gardens (*see p.166*) and can be grown as a low hedge (*see p.138*).

ALSO RECOMMENDED: H. albicans ♀ *forms a compact mound of grey-green foliage to 60cm (24in) tall, and white flowers appear from early to midsummer.*

☼ ◐ ◊◊ ❀ ❀ ❀   **Evergreen shrub**
‡ 30cm (12in) ↔ 60cm (24in)

HELIANTHEMUM
'Raspberry Ripple'

This rock rose is a spreading shrub with greyish green leaves that bears a profusion of saucer-shaped white flowers with irregular, purple-pink centres. They open in succession from late spring to summer. It suits a rock garden and makes good ground cover, especially in hot, dry sites (*see pp.190, 304*). Grow in neutral to alkaline soil (*see p.64*).

ALSO RECOMMENDED: *'Rhodanthe Carneum' ♀ (see p.72); 'Wisley Primrose' ♀ has pale yellow flowers; those of 'Wisley White' are creamy white.*

☼ ◊ ❀ ❀ ❀   **Evergreen shrub**
‡ 20cm (8in) ↔ 30cm (12in)

HIBISCUS SYRIACUS
'Woodbridge' ♀

A fast-growing, upright shrub that bears large, deep rose-pink flowers from late summer to mid-autumn. They have maroon blotches around the centres and stand out against the dark green leaves. Valued for its late season of interest. In cold areas, it may flower better against a warm wall (*see p.280*). Prune young plants to encourage branching; keep this to a minimum once established. It also suits chalky soils and hot, dry sites (*see pp.64, 190*).

ALSO RECOMMENDED: *'Oiseau Bleu'* ♀ *(syn. 'Blue Bird') has lilac-blue flowers.*

☼ ◐◖ ❀❀❀   **Deciduous shrub**
‡ 3m (10ft) ↔ 2m (6ft)

LAVANDULA STOECHAS
SUBSP. PEDUNCULATA ♀

French lavender is a small, neat shrub, which blooms from spring to summer. Dense spikes of tiny, fragrant, dark purple flowers, each spike topped by distinctive long bracts, are carried on upright stalks above the narrow, woolly, silver-grey leaves. Effective in sheltered shrub borders, hot and dry sites, rock gardens, and wild areas (*see pp.190, 494*). The flower stalks are good for cutting (*see p.524*). It can also be clipped as a hedge (*see p.138*).

ALSO RECOMMENDED: *'Kew Red' has red flowers; f. leucantha has white flowers.*

☼ ◊ ❀❀ *f*   **Evergreen shrub**
‡↔ 60cm (24in)

LAVATERA *'Kew Rose'*

This pink-flowered mallow is a small shrub with purplish shoots and grey-green leaves. Its bright sprays of large flowers appear over a long season throughout summer. A fine, fast-growing but short-lived plant for a shrub border or coastal garden (*see p.166*). In areas prone to severe frost, grow against a warm wall (*see p.280*).

ALSO RECOMMENDED: *'Barnsley'* ♀ *has red-eyed white flowers; 'Bredon Springs'* ♀ *has dusky pink flowers; those of 'Burgundy Wine'* ♀ *are rich deep pink; 'Rosea'* ♀ *also has deep pink flowers.*

LESPEDEZA THUNBERGII ♀

The bush clover is a small shrub with arching shoots and divided, blue-green leaves. A profusion of purple-pink, pea-like flowers are borne in pendent spikes in early autumn. Good for late colour in a sunny mixed border. In cold areas, the top growth may be cut back by frost, but it will regenerate in spring. Cut back to a low, permanent framework in spring.

ALSO RECOMMENDED: *L. bicolor has dark green leaves and purple-pink flowers in mid- to late summer.*

☼ ◊ ✿✿✿   **Deciduous shrub**
‡ 2m (6ft) ↔ 3m (10ft)

PEROVSKIA *'Blue Spire'* ♀

This easily grown, upright subshrub,
valued for its foliage and flowers,
suits a mixed or herbaceous border. Its
branching, airy spikes of tubular, violet-
blue flowers are borne in profusion
during late summer and early autumn
above the aromatic, silvery grey, deeply
cut leaves. Prune back hard each spring
to a low framework for vigorous, bushy
growth. Also tolerates coastal conditions
(*see p.166*), chalky soils (*see p.64*),
and hot, dry sites (*see p.190*).

ALSO RECOMMENDED: *'Hybrida' has
darker flowers.*

☼ ◊ ❀❀❀ *f*   **Deciduous shrub**
‡ 1.2m (4ft) ↔ 1m (3ft)

PHLOMIS FRUTICOSA ♀

Jerusalem sage is an aromatic, greyish
leaved shrub that forms a fine foil
for dark or purple-leaved plants in a
shrub or mixed border. From early to
midsummer, it bears whorls of deep
golden yellow flowers; it blooms later
if hard pruned in spring to achieve the
best foliage effects. Tolerates hot, dry
sites (*see p.190*), chalky soils (*see p.64*),
and coastal exposure (*see p.166*), but it
can suffer in cold, wet winters.

ALSO RECOMMENDED: *P. chrysophylla* ♀
*as grey-green leaves, turning golden in late
summer; P. italica is slightly less cold-tolerant
and has silver-grey leaves and pink flowers.*

☼ ◊ ❀❀❀   **Evergreen shrub**
‡ 1m (3ft) ↔ 1.5m (5ft)

SALIX EXIGUA

One of the most elegant willows, the coyote willow has slender stems bearing long, narrow, grey-green leaves, which are densely covered in silky, silver hair when young. This thicket-forming shrub bears grey-yellow catkins in spring. It makes a fine specimen and a beautiful backdrop for purple- or dark-leaved plants in a shrub border. Needs little or no pruning. It tolerates coastal conditions (*see p.166*), and clay and permanently moist soils (*see pp.12, 372*).

ALSO RECOMMENDED: *S. gracilistyla is slightly smaller; 'Melanostachys' ♀ has unusual black catkins with red anthers.*

☼ ◊ ❀ ❀ ❀   **Deciduous shrub**
‡ 4m (12ft) ↔ 5m (15ft)

SANTOLINA PINNATA 'Sulphurea'

A dense and rounded, small shrub that is grown chiefly for its finely cut, aromatic, bright green leaves, although prominent pale yellow flowers appear at the tips of slender stems from midsummer. Useful for filling gaps in a sunny border; its bushy habit can also be trimmed to form a low hedge (*see p.138*). Remove old flowers in autumn and cut back straggly plants in spring. Tolerant of chalky soils (*see p.64*).

ALSO RECOMMENDED: *'Edward Bowles' has greyish foliage and cream flowers.*

☼ ◊ ❀ ❀ ❀ *f*   **Evergreen shrub**
‡ 60cm (24in) ↔ 1m (3ft)

ECCREMOCARPUS SCABER ♀

The Chilean glory flower is a fast-growing, scrambling climber with clusters of brilliant orange-red, tubular flowers throughout summer. Grow as a short-lived perennial to decorate an arch, pergola, or large shrub. Choose a sheltered, sunny site, and cut the stems back to within 30–60cm (12–24in) of the base in spring. In frost-prone areas, grow as a trailing annual. Also good for hot, dry sites (*see p.190*).

ALSO RECOMMENDED: *f.* aureus *has gold flowers; f.* carmineus *has red flowers.*

☀ ◊◊ ❄❄   **Climber**
‡ 3–5m (10–15ft), sometimes more

ROSA *'American Pillar'*

A rambling rose that is easily trained onto a sunny wall (*see p.280*), pergola, or up into a tree. Its large clusters of carmine-red, single flowers with white eyes are quite sensational when seen to full effect in midsummer. The mid-green foliage is leathery and glossy. The majority of roses do not thrive on sandy soils, preferring more moisture-retentive conditions. This one also tolerates partial shade.

ALSO RECOMMENDED: *'Chaplin's Pink Climber' has bright pink flowers; 'Zéphirine Drouhin' ♀ is thornless with very fragrant, deep pink flowers.*

☀☀ ◊◊ ❄❄❄   **Climber**
‡ 5m (15ft) ↔ 4m (12ft)

ACHILLEA FILIPENDULINA
'Gold Plate' ♡

This strong-growing yarrow forms clumps of luxuriant, greyish, fern-like foliage. Flat-headed clusters of bright golden yellow flowers are borne on tall stems from early summer to autumn. Good for cutting (*see p.524*), and tolerant of hot, dry sites (*see p.190*) and chalky soils (*see p.64*). Grow in a mixed or herbaceous border or as ground cover (*see p.304*). Contact with the foliage may aggravate skin allergies.

ALSO RECOMMENDED: *'Cloth of Gold' has light green leaves and deeper flowers.*

☼ ◊◖ ❁ ❁ ❁   **Perennial**
‡ 1.2m (4ft) ↔ 45cm (18in)

ARTEMISIA PONTICA ♡

An evergreen, upright artemisia that is valued for its dense dome of aromatic and feathery, silver-green leaves. Greyish yellow flowerheads appear in early summer. An excellent ground-cover plant for poor soils in full sun (*see p.304*). Cut back to the ground in autumn. Its vigorous spread can be invasive. Tolerant of coastal conditions (*see p.166*) and hot, dry sites (*see p.190*).

ALSO RECOMMENDED: *A. absinthium 'Lambrook Silver' ♡ has silver foliage and spreads less vigorously – good in a herbaceous border.*

☼ ◊ ❁ ❁ ❁ ❁ *f*   **Perennial**
‡ 40–80cm (16–32in) ↔ indefinite

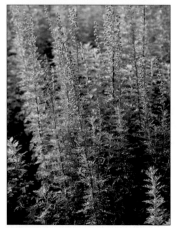

COREOPSIS VERTICILLATA

This pretty tickseed bears a mass of starry, daisy-like yellow flowers throughout summer, above finely divided, feathery, bright green foliage. The flowers are good for cutting (*see p.524*) and are attractive to bees (*see p.494*). It also tolerates chalky soils (*see p.64*) and can be grown in a sunny container (*see p.412*), or mixed or herbaceous border.

ALSO RECOMMENDED: *'Moonbeam' has lemon-yellow flowerheads.*

☼ ☀ ◊ ❀ ❀ ❀   **Perennial**
‡ 60–80cm (24–32in) ↔ 45cm (18in)

CRAMBE CORDIFOLIA ♔

This imposing perennial forms a clump of large and puckered, bristly, dark green leaves and bears airy sprays of small, honey-scented, creamy white flowers, which form a gauzy screen, from late spring to midsummer. The whole plant dies back by late summer. An architectural plant for the back of a sunny border that tolerates coastal sites (*see pp.166, 472*). The flowers are attractive to bees (*see p.494*).

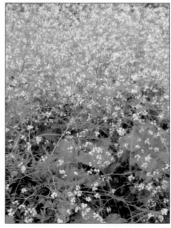

ALSO RECOMMENDED: C. maritima (see p.183).

☼ ☀ ◊ ❀ ❀ ❀   **Perennial**
‡ 2.5m (8ft) ↔ 1.5m (5ft)

DICTAMNUS ALBUS ♥

Burning bush is an aromatic plant with divided, leathery, lemon-scented leaves. It bears spires of white, or palest pink flowers with very long stamens and darker veins in early summer. In hot, still weather, as the seedheads ripen, the aromatic oils vaporize and surround the plant, and they can be ignited. It tolerates chalky soils (*see p.64*) and hot, dry places (*see p.190*).

ALSO RECOMMENDED: *var.* purpureus ♥ *has purple-mauve flowers with darker veins.*

☼ ◐ ◊ ❀❀❀❀ *f*　　　**Perennial**
‡ 40–90cm (16–36in) ↔ 60cm (24in)

ECHINOPS SPHAEROCEPHALUS

This majestic globe thistle forms a clump of spiny, divided, grey-green leaves. From mid- to late summer, it produces branching spires of spherical, silver-grey flowerheads on stout grey stems. Excellent as a focal plant in a mixed or herbaceous border. The flowerheads are popular with bees and birds, and with flower arrangers (*see pp.494, 524*). It tolerates chalky soils and hot, dry places (*see pp.64, 190*).

ALSO RECOMMENDED: E. ritro '*Veitch's Blue*' (see p.207).

☼ ◐ ◊ ❀❀❀　　　**Perennial**
‡ 2m (6ft) ↔ 90cm (36in)

EREMURUS ROBUSTUS

The foxtail lily bears imposing spires of pale pink flowers, which appear in early and midsummer. They make this fleshy rooted perennial an ideal focal plant in a sunny border. Its narrow, grass-like leaves wither by flowering time. Mulch with garden compost in autumn, avoiding the crown. Good for cutting (*see p.524*) and tolerant of chalky soils (*see p.64*).

ALSO RECOMMENDED: *E.* himalaicus *is shorter with white flowers from late spring.*

☼ ◊ ❀ ❀ ❀   **Perennial**
↕ 3m (10ft) ↔ 1.2m (4ft)

ERIOPHYLLUM LANATUM

The woolly sunflower displays a profusion of bright yellow, daisy-like flowers throughout summer, above clumps of white-woolly, silver-grey leaves. It needs sharp drainage and is tolerant of poor soils and hot, dry sites (*see p.190*). Grow on a sunny bank, a dry border, or between paving crevices (*see p.348*). Position with care in a rock garden; it may overwhelm smaller plants.

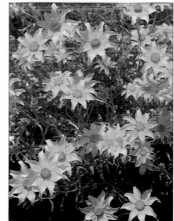

☼ ◊ ❀ ❀ ❀   **Perennial**
↕↔ 20–60cm (8–24in) or more

ERYNGIUM × TRIPARTITUM ♔

This plant forms a mound of lobed, few-spined, glossy dark green leaves. From midsummer to autumn, it bears branched heads of small, almost spherical, violet-blue flowers, each with a ruff of narrow, grey-blue bracts beneath; they are good for cutting and drying (*see p.524*). Tolerant of chalky soils (*see p.64*), and coastal and hot, dry and sites (*see pp.166, 190*).

ALSO RECOMMENDED: E. bourgatii (*see p.208*); E. variifolium *has white-marbled leaves and blue-violet flowers.*

☼ ◊ ❀❀❀ **Perennial**
‡ 60–90cm (24–36in) ↔ 50cm (20in)

LIMONIUM PLATYPHYLLUM

Sea lavender attracts bees and butterflies (*see p.494*) with its airy clusters of tiny, papery, lavender-blue flowers in mid- to late summer. They are good for cutting and drying (*see p.524*) and are borne on wiry stems above rosettes of leathery, dark green leaves. Suitable for a mixed border or gravel plantings, especially in coastal or hot, dry sites (*see pp.166, 190*).

ALSO RECOMMENDED: 'Violetta' *has blue-violet flowers;* L. bellidifolium *is much shorter, suitable for border edging in sharply drained soil.*

☼ ◊ ❀❀❀ **Perennial**
‡ 60cm (24in) ↔ 45cm (18in)

LUPINUS *'The Chatelaine'*

The stately, pink-and-white-flowered spires of this lupin, which rise above a mound of palmate, mid-green leaves, are excellent for lending height and colour to a mixed or herbaceous border from early to midsummer. Lupins are generally short-lived, but last longest in slightly acid to neutral soils (*see p.92*) with good drainage. Good for cutting (*see p.524*). Protect from slugs.

ALSO RECOMMENDED: *'Chandelier' has creamy yellow flowers; 'Lulu' is shorter with flowers in a mixture of pinks, reds, blues, purples, and whites. 'The Governor' has blue and white flowers.*

☼ ◊ ✳ ✳ ✳   **Perennial**
‡ 90cm (36in) ↔ 75cm (30in)

LYCHNIS × ARKWRIGHTII *'Vesuvius'*

This clump-forming perennial has lance-shaped, dark maroon leaves that form a perfect foil for the cross-shaped, brilliant orange-scarlet flowers that are borne from early to midsummer. Good for a sunny, mixed or herbaceous border, especially those with a hot-coloured theme. Often short-lived.

ALSO RECOMMENDED: L. coronaria (see p.318).

☼ ◐ ◊ ✳ ✳ ✳   **Perennial**
‡ 45cm (18in) ↔ 30cm (12in)

NERINE BOWDENII ♥

This is one of the best late-flowering bulbs. In autumn, it bears open sprays of trumpet-shaped, bright pink flowers with curled, wavy-edged petals. The strap-like, fresh green leaves appear after the display, at the base of the plant. Provide a deep, dry mulch in winter; in areas prone to heavy frosts, grow at the base of a warm, sunny wall (*see p.280*), in a hot, dry site (*see p.190*), or as pot plant (*see p.412*). The scented flowers are good for cutting (*see p.524*).

ALSO RECOMMENDED: *'Alba' has white or very pale pink flowers; 'Mark Fenwick' has pink flowers on dark stalks.*

☼ ◊ ❀❀❀ *f*   **Perennial bulb**
‡ 45cm (18in) ↔ 12–15cm (5–6in)

OENOTHERA MACROCARPA ♥

Ozark sundrops produces a long succession of cup-shaped, golden yellow flowers from late spring to early autumn. They appear above a mat of trailing, red-tinted stems and green foliage. It makes good ground cover (*see p.304*), especially in gravel or scree gardens, and in coastal and hot, dry sites (*see pp.166, 190*). Tolerant of poor and stony soils.

ALSO RECOMMENDED: O. fruticosa *'Fyrverkeri' ♥ is taller and more upright with clusters of bright yellow flowers.*

☼ ◊ ❀❀❀   **Perennial**
‡ 15cm (6in) ↔ 50cm (20in)

ORNITHOGALUM UMBELLATUM

The star of Bethlehem produces clumps of grass-like leaves, which wither as the starry white flowers open in early summer. Vigorous and suitable for naturalizing in short turf, it is especially effective in gravel plantings. It thrives in sunny or partially shaded sites (*see p.216*) and hot, dry places (*see p.190*). Plant bulbs in autumn.

ALSO RECOMMENDED: *O. nutans* ♥ *also has white flowers. O. oligophyllum has white petals, green on the insides.*

☀ ☼ ◊ ❀ ❀ ❀   **Perennial bulb**
‡ 10–30cm (4–12in) ↔ 10cm (4in)

PARAHEBE PERFOLIATA ♥

Digger's speedwell has a spreading habit and bears short spikes of saucer-shaped blue flowers in late summer. The bluish or greyish, evergreen, overlapping leaves are oval and slightly leathery. Suitable for gaps in old walls or in a rock garden; it needs an open, sunny site. Provide shelter from cold, drying winds in frost-prone climates.

ALSO RECOMMENDED: *P. hookeriana is a mat-forming species with white to lavender-blue flowers in summer.*

☀ ◊ ❀ ❀   **Perennial**
‡ 60–75cm (24–30in) ↔ 45cm (18in)

PETRORHAGIA SAXIFRAGA ♀

The creeping, wiry stems of the tunic flower root to form mats of grass-like, rich green leaves that are spangled throughout summer with many tiny, white or pink flowers. It thrives in poor soils and makes good ground cover for a sunny bank (*see p.304*), or at the top of a wall or raised bed. It also suits a rock garden. Grow in any poor to moderately fertile, well-drained soil

ALSO RECOMMENDED: *'Rosette' is more compact with double pink flowers.*

☼ ◊ ❀ ❀ ❀   **Perennial**
‡ 10cm (4in) ↔ 20cm (8in)

PHLOX BIFIDA

Sand phlox makes good ground cover for rock gardens or sunny banks (*see p.304*). Mounds of grassy, dark green foliage are studded with a profusion of starry, fragrant, lavender-blue to white flowers from spring to early summer. Grow in gritty or poor, well-drained soil in sun, or in dappled shade in areas with low rainfall. Thrives in hot, dry sites (*see p.190*) and in paving crevices (*see p.348*).

ALSO RECOMMENDED: *'Colvin's White' has white flowers;* P. douglasii *is slightly larger with white, lavender-blue, or pink flowers.*

☼ ◊ ❀ ❀ ❀ *f*   **Perennial**
‡ 20cm (8in) ↔ 15cm (6in)

POTENTILLA NEPALENSIS
'Miss Willmott' ♀

A summer-flowering, clump-forming plant that carries its loose clusters of small pink blooms with cherry red centres on wiry, red-tinged stems. The leaves are divided and mid-green. A colourful perennial for a cottage-style planting or at the front of a hot and sunny, herbaceous border (see p.190). Tolerant of clay soils (see p.12).

ALSO RECOMMENDED: *'Roxana' has copper-pink flowers with red centres.*

☼ ◐ ◊ ❄ ❄ ❄   **Perennial**
‡ 30–45cm (12–18in) ↔ 60cm (24in)

SALVIA OFFICINALIS 'Tricolor' ♀

This variegated sage is a low, shrubby perennial suitable for a sunny border or wildlife garden (see p.494). Its woolly, grey-green leaves with cream and pink markings combine well with the short spikes of early to midsummer, lilac-blue flowers. The colourful foliage is aromatic and is used in cooking; it will add interest to a herb garden. Trim to shape each year after flowering. Tolerant of chalky soils (see p.64) and hot, dry sites (see p.190).

ALSO RECOMMENDED: *'Icterina' ♀ has yellow and green leaves; 'Purpurascens' ♀ bears red-purple young leaves.*

☼ ◐ ◊◊ ❄ ❄ ❄ *f*   **Perennial**
‡ 80cm (32in) ↔ 1m (3ft)

STROBILANTHES ATROPURPUREA

This upright, branching plant forms a dense, basal clump of deeply veined, dark green leaves and produces spikes of hooded, 2-lipped, indigo or purple flowers along the length of the stems in summer. Excellent for a sunny, mixed or herbaceous border, but it must have good drainage. Protect the crowns with a dry winter mulch.

☼ ◊ ❀❀❀   **Perennial**
‡ 1.2m (4ft) ↔ 1m (3ft)

TANACETUM PARTHENIUM

Once introduced to the garden, feverfew becomes a permanent fixture with its copious self-seeding. The aromatic, fresh green leaves form a bright foil for the white, daisy-like flowers, which are produced through summer. Suitable for edging in borders and herb gardens. It tolerates most well-drained soils including chalky ones (*see p.64*).

ALSO RECOMMENDED: *'Aureum' has golden leaves and single white flowerheads.*

☼ ◊ ❀❀❀ *f*   **Perennial**
‡ 45–60cm (18–24in) ↔ 30cm (12in)

TULIPA HAGERI *'Splendens'*

A bulbous perennial that bears large, star-shaped flowers on upright stems from early spring. They are crimson-scarlet with brownish red insides and are carried singly or in clusters of up to four. The basal leaves are lance-shaped and light green. After flowering, remove spent blooms, but allow the foliage to die back naturally. Suitable for a rock garden, hot and dry site, or in a container (*see pp.190, 412*). Plant bulbs in autumn.

ALSO RECOMMENDED: *T.* saxatilis *has pink to lilac-purple flowers in late spring.*

☼ ◊ ✽ ✽ ✽   **Perennial bulb**
‡ 35cm (14in)

VERBASCUM OLYMPICUM

The towering, white-woolly, yellow-flowered spires that arise like candelabra from the large, basal rosette of silver-white leaves make this verbascum one of the finest of architectural plants (*see p.412*). It thrives in hot, dry sites (*see p.190*) and is set off to brilliant effect in gravel plantings. It often dies after flowering, but it self-seeds freely. Tolerant of chalky soils (*see p.64*).

ALSO RECOMMENDED: *V.* bombyciferum ♀ *is slightly shorter; 'Silver Lining', often grown as an annual, is densely silver-woolly.*

☼ ◊ ✽ ✽ ✽   **Perennial**
‡ 2m (6ft) ↔ 60cm (24in)

PLANTS FOR CHALK & LIMESTONE SOILS

MANY OF THE world's favourite plants occur naturally on chalk or limestone soils, so the choice of plants for the gardener who is presented with these conditions is huge. They include pinks (*see p.82*), clematis (*see p.76*), and many of the jewel-like alpine plants found growing on the limestone mountains of Europe and Asia.

Soils over chalk or limestone are almost invariably alkaline in nature, but they can also be very fertile if they are deep and rich in organic matter – a wealth of plants thrive and give their ornamental best on such soils. Their growth is not entirely limited by the soil's alkalinity, but chiefly by its ability to hold moisture. Therefore, plants like the Madonna lily (*see p.490*) will grow well on alkaline soils, as long as they are rich in well-rotted organic matter.

Alkalinity, however, does exclude a small proportion of plants. In particular, it will not be possible to grow committed acid-lovers like rhododendrons (*see pp.108, 160, 243, 454*).

SHALLOW SOILS ON CHALK

If the soil over chalk or limestone is very shallow, the chief problem – even for lime-tolerant plants – is rapid drainage, which can lead to very hot and dry soil conditions in summer. For these sites, many of the plants listed for sandy soils, hot and dry sites, and coastal conditions will thrive, provided that they do not also demand an acid soil (see pp.38, 190, 166). Plants like *Crocus* 'E.A. Bowles' (see p.81) or *Pulsatilla vulgaris* (see p.89) are so well-adapted to free-draining, alkaline conditions that they may rot and die in deep and moist, fertile soils, rich in organic matter. Deep or very sticky chalk and limestone soils need to be treated as for clay soils (see p.12).

WORKING CHALKY SOILS

Shallow chalk soils are generally light and easy to work at almost any time of year, but because they drain so quickly, they often lack organic matter and plant nutrients; both are leached or washed away by natural rainfall.

Apply a well-rotted organic matter, such as leafmould, manure, or garden compost as a deep, annual mulch to help build their levels in the soil. Organic matter helps to retain moisture and nutrients, and it keeps the plant roots cool. It also helps to counteract the effects of the soil's alkalinity. If this is done regularly and over many seasons, it will eventually build up a useful depth of soil. In consequence, the range of plants that can be grown successfully will expand.

The addition of well-rotted organic matter can also help to reduce the problem of yellowing leaves, which some plants experience in alkaline soils. Even some fairly lime-tolerant plants, such as *Chaenomeles speciosa* 'Moerloosei' (see p.264) begin to show these symptoms after several seasons of growth due to vital nutrients, including iron, being "locked up" by the soil's alkaline chemistry. A simple remedy is to apply sequestered iron annually as new growth begins in spring.

ARBUTUS UNEDO ♀

The strawberry tree has a spreading crown of glossy deep green foliage and attractive, rough and shredding, red-brown bark. Hanging clusters of small, urn-shaped, white or pink-tinged flowers open during autumn as the previous season's strawberry-like red fruits open; they are not palatable. Keep pruning to a minimum. Excellent for a large, sheltered shrub border. It also suits acid soils (*see p.92*).

ALSO RECOMMENDED: *'Elfin King' is compact and flowers and fruits freely when small; f.* rubra ♀ *has dark pink flowers.*

☼ ◊ ✤ ✤ ✤   **Evergreen tree**
‡↔ 8m (25ft)

CHAMAECYPARIS LAWSONIANA *'Intertexta'* ♀

This variant of Lawson's cypress makes a distinctive specimen tree with a conical crown of drooping branchlets bearing flattened sprays of dark blue-grey, scale-like foliage. It forms a strong leading shoot naturally, seldom needing formative pruning. The strongest growth occurs on moist but well-drained, neutral to slightly acid soils (*see p.92*).

ALSO RECOMMENDED: *'Kilmacurragh' ♀ has bright green foliage on upswept branchlets; 'Lanei Aurea' ♀ has golden yellow foliage.*

☼ ◊ ✤ ✤ ✤   **Evergreen tree**
‡ 25m (80ft) ↔ 5m (15ft)

FRAXINUS ORNUS ♥

The manna ash forms a rounded crown of divided, dark green leaves that turn dark purple before falling in autumn. In spring and early summer, it produces dense clusters of many tiny, fragrant, creamy white flowers. A shapely specimen tree that thrives in fertile, well-drained or even hot and dry, chalky or acid soils (*see pp.64, 92, 190*). Needs little pruning; cut out any badly placed or crossing shoots in winter.

ALSO RECOMMENDED: *F. americana* '*Autumn Purple*' *and F. angustifolia* '*Flame*' *have red-purple autumn colour.*

☼ ◊ ❄❄❄ *f*   **Deciduous tree**
‡↔ 15m (50ft)

MORUS NIGRA ♥

Black mulberry makes a picturesque, gnarled tree with age, forming a broad crown of large, heart-shaped leaves. Tiny green flowers in spring give rise to edible, juicy black fruits, which attract birds (*see p.494*). It tolerates coastal sites (*see p.166*) and urban pollution. This long-lived tree needs minimal pruning, in late autumn or early winter if necessary; it bleeds sap if pruned at other times.

ALSO RECOMMENDED: *M. alba bears less palatable, white then red fruits;* '*Pendula*' *is a small, weeping tree.*

☼ ◊◊ ❄❄❄   **Deciduous tree**
‡↔ 10m (30ft)

PINUS NIGRA ♀

The Austrian pine has dense, spreading branches and deeply fissured, greyish, dark brown, or black bark. It forms a dark green, domed canopy of paired, needle-like leaves. The pine cones are yellow-brown. This tree also grows in clay soils (*see p.12*) and is tolerant of coastal exposure (*see p.166*).

ALSO RECOMMENDED: *subsp.* laricio ♀, *the Corsican pine, is narrower with grey-green needles.*

☼ ◊ ❀ ❀ ❀   **Evergreen tree**
‡ 30m (100ft) ↔ 6–8m (20–25ft)

PRUNUS *'Pink Perfection'* ♀

One of the most reliably floriferous of flowering cherries, this spreading tree bears a profusion of double, rose-pink flowers in heavy, drooping clusters amid bronzed young leaves in late spring. Effective as a single specimen and fabulous in groves or avenues, it is relatively easy to grow. Keep pruning to a minimum; remove dead or diseased wood in summer.

ALSO RECOMMENDED: *'Accolade'* ♀ *has pale pink flowers in early spring.*

☼ ◊ ❀ ❀ ❀   **Deciduous tree**
‡↔ 8m (25ft)

BUDDLEJA LINDLEYANA

A slightly arching, late-flowering shrub with dark green foliage that is suitable for a mixed or shrub border. Its tapering spikes of dark violet flowers nod from the branches in late summer. Prune branches hard in early spring to encourage a tidy shape. In areas with heavy frosts, it will fare better against a warm wall (*see p.280*).

ALSO RECOMMENDED: *B. globosa* ♀ *has round clusters of orange-yellow flowers in early summer. B. salviifolia has pale blue, fragrant flowers in late autumn.*

☼ ◊ ❄❄   **Deciduous shrub**
↕↔ 2m (6ft)

CEANOTHUS *'Autumnal Blue'* ♀

A vigorous Californian lilac that bears its brilliant and profuse display of dense, rich sky-blue flowerheads from late summer to autumn. They are complemented by the glossy dark green leaves. It suits a sheltered border, but may perform better against a warm wall in cold areas (*see p.280*). Trim to shape after flowering.

ALSO RECOMMENDED: *C. × delileanus 'Gloire de Versailles'* ♀ *is deciduous and hardier with pale blue flowers from midsummer to autumn.*

☼ ◊ ❄❄   **Evergreen shrub**
↕↔ 3m (10ft)

CORNUS MAS ♥

The Cornelian cherry makes a fine specimen plant for late winter colour when small clusters of yellow flowers appear in profusion on the bare branches. The oval, dark green leaves turn red-purple in autumn, giving a display at the same time as the fruits ripen to bright red. Also suitable for a woodland garden. Keep pruning to a minimum.

ALSO RECOMMENDED: *'Aurea' has yellow young leaves; 'Variegata' ♥ is compact with white leaf margins and abundant fruit.*

☀☀ ○ ❄❄❄ **Deciduous shrub**
↕↔ 5m (15ft)

COTINUS COGGYGRIA *Purpureus Group*

This smoke bush has oval, light green leaves, which turn to orange then red in autumn. Smoke-like plumes of tiny, purplish pink flowers are produced on older wood, but only in areas with long, hot summers. Good in a shrub border or as a specimen tree. Cut back hard to a framework each spring for the best foliage effect.

ALSO RECOMMENDED: *'Royal Purple' ♥ bears dark red-purple foliage, turning scarlet in autumn; C. 'Grace' ♥ has purple leaves, turning brilliant red in autumn.*

☀☀ ○○ ❄❄❄ **Deciduous shrub**
↕↔ 5m (15ft)

COTONEASTER STERNIANUS ♀

A graceful shrub with arching branches that bear clusters of pink-tinged white flowers in summer. A profusion of large, orange-red berries follow in autumn, which attract birds (*see p.494*) and contrast well with the glossy grey-green foliage. It is good grown as a hedge (*see p.138*). Trim lightly after flowering, if necessary.

ALSO RECOMMENDED: C. cashmiriensis ♀ (see p.306); C. frigidus (see p.218), C. horizontalis ♀ (see p.265); C. lacteus ♀ (see p.149).

☼ ◐ ◊ ❅ ❅ ❅   **Evergreen shrub**
↕↔ 3m (10ft)

DEUTZIA CRENATA '*Nikko*'

This spreading shrub is among the smallest of the deutzias. It has rich green leaves, which turn red-purple in autumn, and produces clusters of starry white flowers in summer. Excellent for a rock garden or for the front of a shrub border. Cut back flowered shoots to strong buds after flowering.

ALSO RECOMMENDED: D. gracilis (see p.128); D. × rosea *has white flowers that are flushed with pink.*

☼ ◊ ❅ ❅ ❅   **Deciduous shrub**
↕ 60cm (24in) ↔ 1.2m (4ft)

HELIANTHEMUM 'Rhodanthe Carneum' ♚

This long-flowering rock rose, also sold as 'Wisley Pink', is a low and spreading bush. Pale pink, saucer-shaped flowers with yellow centres appear from late spring to summer amid narrow, grey-green leaves. Good in a rock garden, raised bed, or mixed border. Trim after flowering. Also good for sandy soils (*see p.38*) and ground cover (*see p.304*).

ALSO RECOMMENDED: *'Fire Dragon'* ♚ (syn. *'Mrs Clay'*) *has vivid orange-red flowers;* *'Henfield Brilliant'* ♚ *has brick-red flowers;* *'Raspberry Ripple'* (see p.46).

☼ ◊ ❀❀❀ **Evergreen shrub**
‡ 30cm (12in) ↔ 45cm (18in) or more

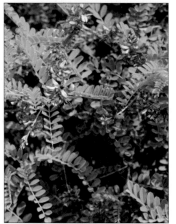

INDIGOFERA HETERANTHA ♚

A spreading plant with arching stems that is valued for its pretty, pea-like flowers and grey-green foliage. It carries dense, more-or-less upright clusters of small, purple-pink flowers from early summer to autumn. In cold climates, it is best trained against a warm wall (*see p.280*). Cut all stems to just above ground level in early spring. Also suitable for a sunny shrub border.

ALSO RECOMMENDED: I. amblyantha ♚ *bears spikes of pink flowers.*

☼ ◊ ❀❀❀ **Deciduous shrub**
‡↔ 2–3m (6–10ft)

KOLKWITZIA AMABILIS
'Pink Cloud' ♀

This beauty bush is well-known for its abundant clusters of bell-shaped, bright deep pink flowers with yellow throats, which appear during late spring and early summer. It grows vigorously and has arching stems clothed with dark green leaves. Excellent for a shrub border or as a specimen plant. Let young plants develop without pruning, then thin out some old stems each year after flowering.

☼ ◊ ❋ ❋ ❋   **Deciduous shrub**
‡ 3m (10ft) ↔ 4m (12ft)

OSMANTHUS × BURKWOODII ♀

A dense, rounded shrub with leathery, dark green leaves that bears profuse clusters of sweetly fragrant, tubular white flowers in spring. An ideal shrub as a backdrop in a mixed border or as a specimen in a woodland garden. It can be hard pruned and makes a very attractive flowering hedge (*see p.138*), which can be trimmed after flowering. It tolerates urban pollution.

ALSO RECOMMENDED: O. delavayi ♀ (see p.221); O. heterophyllus *has holly-like leaves and flowers in late summer.*

☼ ☀ ◊ ❋ ❋ ❋ *f*   **Evergreen shrub**
‡↔ 3m (10ft)

PHILADELPHUS MICROPHYLLUS

This compact mock orange is an
upright shrub with peeling, chestnut-
brown bark. It bears a profusion of
single, highly scented white flowers in
early and midsummer. Ideal for a mixed
border in smaller gardens, it associates
well with roses and is easy to grow on
most well-drained soils. Its tolerance
of pollution makes it well-suited to
city gardens. Good for cut flowers (*see
p.524*). Cut one in four flowered
stems back to ground level after flowering.

ALSO RECOMMENDED: P. coronarius
'*Variegatus*' ♀ (see p.156); P. '*Manteau
d'Hermine*' ♀ has double, creamy flowers.

☼ ◊ ❋ ❋ ❋ *f*　　**Deciduous shrub**
↕↔ 1m (3ft)

POTENTILLA FRUTICOSA
'Red Ace'

A compact and densely rounded shrub
that has dark green foliage and rose-
like, vermilion-red flowers from spring
to autumn. It makes good ground cover
(*see p.304*) or low hedging (*see p.138*),
especially in coastal sites (*see p.166*).
It also suits a mixed border. Trim after
flowering. The flowers tend to fade
in full sun.

ALSO RECOMMENDED: '*Abbotswood*' ♀
has white flowers; those of '*Katherine
Dykes*' ♀ are canary yellow; '*Tangerine*' ♀
has yellow flowers, tinted orange-red.

☼ ☼ ◊ ❋ ❋ ❋　　**Deciduous shrub**
↕ 1m (3ft) ↔ 1.5m (5ft)

SYRINGA × PERSICA ♀

The Persian lilac is a robust and stocky shrub that bears small but fragrant purple flowers in dense clusters in late spring. Tolerant of pollution, it is ideal for city gardens that are too confined for the common lilac (*S. vulgaris*). Its flowers are good for cutting (*see p.524*). It makes a fine informal hedge (*see p.138*), needing only a light trim after flowering.

ALSO RECOMMENDED: *'Alba'* ♀ *has white flowers*; S. pubescens *'Superba'* ♀ (*see p.165*); S. vulgaris *'Congo'* (see p.21).

☼ ◊ ❀ ❀ ❀ *f*　　　**Deciduous shrub**
↔ 2m (6ft)

CAMPSIS RADICANS

The common trumpet creeper is a vigorous climber with fine autumn colour, bearing clusters of trumpet-like, orange to red flowers at the branch tips from late summer. They look striking against the dark green foliage. Grow in a sheltered site against a wall, fence, or pillar, or up into a tree; it may need support, and in cold areas, a warm wall is best (*see p.280*). Prune branches while they are bare in late winter.

ALSO RECOMMENDED: *f.* flava ♀ (*syn. 'Yellow Trumpet'*) *has yellow flowers*; C. × tagliabuana *'Madame Galen'* ♀ *has salmon-red flowers*.

☼ ◊◊ ❀ ❀　　　**Climber**
↕ 10m (30ft) or more

CLEMATIS *'The President'* ♥

This early-flowering clematis is valued for its showy, early summer display of large, rich purple blooms with silvery undersides and red anthers. It is vigorous and flowers freely, making it ideal for covering a featureless or unattractive wall (*see pp.262, 280*). Allowed to grow through a deciduous shrub, it may flower before the host comes into leaf. Keep the roots shaded.

ALSO RECOMMENDED: *'Bill MacKenzie'* ♥ (see p.299); *C. montana* (see p.274); *'Nelly Moser'* ♥ (see p.273); *C. rehderiana* ♥ (see p.300); *C. tangutica* (see p.508).

☀️◐ ◊◊ ❄❄❄　　　**Climber**
‡ 3m (10ft)

JASMINUM NUDIFLORUM ♥

This mound-forming winter jasmine displays its cheerful yellow flowers on bare green branches in late winter. It is grown to best effect if tied to a framework on a warm, sunny wall (*see p.280*), but tolerates most aspects except those facing east. If allowed to sprawl unsupported, it makes good ground cover (*see p.304*). Cut back after flowering; the flowers are good for cutting (*see p.524*).

ALSO RECOMMENDED: *'Aureum' has gold-blotched leaves that are almost yellow.*

☀️◐ ◊ ❄❄❄　　　**Climber**
‡↔ 3m (10ft)

PARTHENOCISSUS HENRYANA ♥

Virginia creepers are prized for their colourful autumn foliage. The white-veined leaves of this one, however, are impressive from the moment they emerge in spring to the time they turn bright red and drop in autumn. The summer flowers are insignificant. Train over a wall or a strongly built fence (*see pp.262, 280*) and prune in autumn; young stems may need support. Leaf colour is best in deep or partial shade. Good for wildlife gardens (*see p.494*).

ALSO RECOMMENDED: *P.* quinquefolia ♥ *has brilliant red autumn foliage;* *P.* tricuspidata ♥ (*see p.277*).

☼ ☀ ◊◊ ❋ ❋ ❋   **Climber**
↕ 10m (30ft)

ROSA *'Albertine'* ♥

This vigorous, very thorny rambler bears a mass of scented, fully double, soft salmon-pink blooms in midsummer. They are displayed to perfection on purple-flushed stems against glossy dark green leaves. An excellent specimen for a pergola; it blooms well trained on trellis on a warm, sunny wall (*see p.280*). Prune after flowering.

ALSO RECOMMENDED: *'Albéric Barbier'* ♥ *has double white flowers and tolerates shaded walls; 'François Juranville' ♥ bears apple-scented, pale salmon-pink flowers over long periods.*

☼ ◊ ❋ ❋ ❋ ❋ *f*   **Climber**
↕ 5m (15ft) ↔ 4m (12ft)

ALYSSUM WULFENIANUM

This evergreen plant forms mounds of grey- or white-hairy leaves and bears sweetly scented, pale yellow flowers in abundance in early summer. A fine rock-garden plant that also suits paving crevices and the tops of dry stone walls (*see p.348*). It tolerates hot, dry sites (*see p.190*) and most well-drained soils. Trim after flowering to keep compact.

ALSO RECOMMENDED: A. montanum *'Berggold' forms mats with golden yellow flowers;* A. spinosum *'Roseum'* ♀ *is mound-forming and shrubby with rose-pink flowers.*

☼ ◊ ✽✽✽ *f*   **Perennial**

‡ 10–15cm (4–6in) ↔ 50cm (20in)

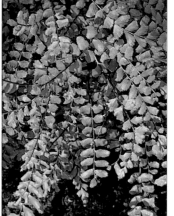

ASPLENIUM TRICHOMANES ♀

The maidenhair spleenwort is a short fern that occurs naturally on limestone outcrops, so it is perfectly suited to alkaline conditions. It bears tufts of narrow, dark green fronds, which are divided into many rounded leaflets with glossy black or dark brown stalks. Very suitable for wall and paving crevices (*see p.348*) and rock gardens.

ALSO RECOMMENDED: A. scolopendrium ♀ (see p.225).

☼ ◊◊ ✽✽✽   **Perennial fern**

‡ 15cm (6in) ↔ 20cm (8in)

BERGENIA CILIATA

The large and rounded, paddle-shaped leaves of this fleshy plant form elegant, mid-green clumps at ground level. White or pinkish white flowers enliven the display from early spring. Mulch the plants in autumn; the foliage may die back in frosty areas. Suitable as ground cover (*see pp.304, 326*) and tolerant of exposed sites (*see p.118*), permanently moist soils (*see p.372*), and damp or dry shade (*see pp.216, 238*).

ALSO RECOMMENDED: *f.* ligulata *has very pale pink flowers;* B. *'Morgenröte'* ♀ *(syn. 'Morning Red')* (see p.333).

☼ ◐ ◌◌ ❊ ❊ ❊   **Perennial**
‡ 30cm (12in) ↔ 45cm (10in)

CAMPANULA PUNCTATA

This bellflower forms clumps of dark green leaves. It produces short clusters of hanging, bell-shaped, creamy white to dusky pink flowers on upright stems in early summer; they colour better if the plant is grown in shade. Cut back after flowering to encourage further blooms. Suitable for a border.

ALSO RECOMMENDED: C. *'Birch Hybrid'* ♀ (see p.358); C. carpatica *'Bressingham White'* (see p.359); C. glomerata *'Superba'* ♀ (see p.313); C. isophylla ♀ (see p.430); C. lactiflora *'Prichard's Variety'* ♀ (see p.532); C. latiloba *'Hidcote Amethyst'* ♀ (see p.26).

☼ ◐ ◌◌ ❊ ❊ ❊   **Perennial**
‡ 30cm (12in) ↔ 40cm (16in)

CHIONODOXA FORBESII

Glory of the snow produces a sheaf of narrow leaves topped by clusters of white-centred, starry, clear blue flowers in early spring. It is ideal for early colour in a rock garden or for naturalizing beneath trees and shrubs. It self-seeds freely to form extensive colonies. Plant bulbs in autumn.

ALSO RECOMMENDED: *'Pink Giant' has white-eyed, pink flowers; C. sardensis ♀ has slightly pendent, deep clear blue flowers.*

☼ ◊ ❄❄❄ **Perennial bulb**
‡ 10–20cm (4–8in) ↔ 3cm (1¼in)

COLCHICUM AUTUMNALE

The meadow saffron has weatherproof, goblet-shaped pink flowers, which arise in autumn, before the large, lance-shaped leaves emerge in winter or early spring. Grow at the front of a border, at the foot of rockwork in a rock garden, or naturalize in turf. All parts are highly toxic if ingested. Plant corms in summer.

ALSO RECOMMENDED: *'Album' has white flowers; 'Pleniflorum' has double, pinkish lilac flowers; C. agrippinum ♀ (see p.360).*

☼ ◊◊ ❄❄❄ **Perennial corm**
‡ 10–15cm (4–6in) ↔ 8cm (3in)

CROCUS CHRYSANTHUS
'E.A. Bowles' ♥

Spring-flowering crocuses are
indispensable dwarf perennials, since
they bring early colour to the garden.
This one, like other *C. chrysanthus*
cultivars, is among the earliest to
flower. The flowers are rich lemon-
yellow with purple feathering on the
outer petals. Very effective in drifts
at the front of a mixed or herbaceous
border, naturalized in turf, or in a
rock garden. Plant bulbs in autumn.

ALSO RECOMMENDED: *'Cream Beauty'* ♥ *has
cream flowers; 'Ladykiller'* ♥ *has white flowers
with purple marks; C. corsicus* ♥ *(see p.361).*

☼ ◊ ❄ ❄ ❄   **Perennial bulb**
‡ 8cm (3in) ↔ 5cm (2in)

DELPHINIUM TATSIENENSE

A delicate variation on the more
common theme of the familiar, tall
spires of hybrid delphiniums, this is a
far more modest plant with clusters of
elf-cap-shaped, bright cornflower-blue
flowers with hooded eyes and azure
tips. They appear during the first half of
summer against deeply divided, lobed
leaves. Suitable for a rock garden or at
the front of a border. It does not need
to be staked. The flowers can be cut
for indoor arrangements *(see p.524).*

ALSO RECOMMENDED: D. grandiflorum
'Blue Butterfly' (see p.534).

☼ ◊◊ ❄ ❄ ❄   **Perennial**
‡ 20–60cm (8–24in) ↔ 30cm (12in)

DIANTHUS *'Bovey Belle'* ♀

The double, clove-scented, deep pink flowers of this modern pink are borne in profusion throughout summer above a mound of narrow, blue-grey leaves. The stiff-stemmed blooms are excellent as cut flowers (*see p.524*). Grow in a mixed or herbaceous border; they associate well with roses.

ALSO RECOMMENDED: *'Doris'* ♀ *has pale pink flowers with dark pink centres; 'Haytor White'* ♀ *has white flowers; 'Houndspool Ruby'* ♀ *has rose-pink blooms with currant red centres; 'La Bourboule'* ♀ (see p.361); D. subacaulis (see p.314).

☼ ◊ ❀ ❀ ❀ *f*   **Perennial**
‡ 25–45cm (10–18in) ↔ 40cm (16in)

DICENTRA SPECTABILIS ♀

Bleeding heart is an elegant, late-spring-flowering plant for a damp, shady border (*see p.238*) or woodland garden. The red-pink flowers are heart-shaped and hang in rows from long, arching stems; they contrast vividly against the hummock of bright green, deeply cut foliage. The plant usually dies back after flowering. Also suitable for acid soils (*see p.92*).

ALSO RECOMMENDED: *'Alba'* ♀ *has white flowers; D. 'Stuart Boothman'* ♀ *has pink flowers and greyish foliage; D. 'Bacchanal'* (see p.336); D. cucullaria (see p.229).

☼ ☀ ◊ ❀ ❀ ❀   **Perennial**
‡ to 1.2m (4ft) ↔ 45cm (18in)

DORONICUM *'Miss Mason'* ♀

A spreading plant with dense, basal clumps of heart-shaped leaves that are almost covered, from spring to early summer, by golden yellow daisy flowers, which are held well above the foliage. Suits a mixed or herbaceous border and can be naturalized in a woodland garden. It tolerates clay soils (*see p.12*), and the flowers are good for cutting (*see p.524*).

ALSO RECOMMENDED: D. × excelsum *'Harpur Crewe' has golden yellow flowers*, D. pardalianches (see p.534).

☀ ◐ ◊ ❄❄❄   **Perennial**
↕↔ 60cm (24in)

ERODIUM MANESCAUI

Through summer and into autumn, this clump-forming perennial bears its geranium-like, bright magenta-purple flowers above basal clumps of softly hairy, divided leaves. Ideal for a rock garden, raised bed, or at the front of a mixed or herbaceous border. Grow in very well-drained, neutral to alkaline soil. It self-seeds freely.

ALSO RECOMMENDED: E. chrysanthum *has silver-green leaves and sulphur yellow flowers*; E. glandulosum ♀ *is smaller with lilac-pink flowers*.

☀ ◊ ❄❄❄   **Perennial**
↕ 20–45cm (8–18in) ↔ 20cm (8in)

ERYSIMUM *'Bredon'* ♀

The bright, chrome-yellow flowers of this shrubby evergreen appear from spring to early summer above a mound of grey-green foliage. Grow at the front of a mixed or herbaceous border in poor- or not-too-fertile, well-drained soil. Trim after flowering to keep compact. Also suitable for hot, dry sites (*see p.190*) and sunny containers (*see p.412*).

ALSO RECOMMENDED: *'Butterscotch' has orange-yellow flowers; 'Constant Cheer'* ♀ *has dusky orange-red flowers that age to purple; 'John Codrington' has pale yellow flowers shaded brown and purple.*

☼ ◊ ❃ ❃ ❃   **Perennial**

‡ 30cm (12in) ↔ 45cm (18in)

FRANCOA SONCHIFOLIA

This plant is named bridal wreath for its tall spires of pink flowers that appear from midsummer. They are good for cutting (*see p.524*). The crinkled green leaves form rosettes at ground level. Suitable for border edging or in a woodland garden, so long as it is sheltered from winter wet. It survives hard frosts for short periods only.

ALSO RECOMMENDED: F. ramosa *has white flowers with dark pink markings.*

☼☀ ◊◊ ❃ ❃   **Perennial**

‡ 60–90cm (24–36in) ↔ 45cm (18in)

HELENIUM *'Wyndley'*

From early to late summer, this robust, upright and undemanding perennial bears a succession of rich yellow blooms with orange-brown centres and irregular shades of dark orange; they are excellent for cutting (*see p.524*) and attract to bees (*see p.494*). Deadhead regularly and divide every third year to maintain vigour. It also tolerates clay soils (*see p.12*).

ALSO RECOMMENDED: *'Coppelia'* has copper-orange, brown-centred flowerheads, *'Moerheim Beauty'* (see p.28), *'Rotgold'* (syn. *'Red and Gold'*) has brown-centred flowerheads in shades of red and gold.

☼ ◊◊ ✳ ✳ ✳   **Perennial**
‡ 80cm (32in) ↔ 60cm (24in)

HERMODACTYLUS TUBEROSUS

The widow iris is notable for the sombre, but nonetheless elegant combination of yellow-green and velvety dark brown in its iris-like, fragrant spring blooms. Give it a prominent place in a mixed or herbaceous border, or allow it to naturalize freely in grass. It also grows as an early flowering container plant (*see p.412*). It must have sharp drainage and protection from excessive summer rain. It thrives – and flowers most freely – in hot, dry soils (*see p.190*). Plant tubers in autumn.

☼ ◊ ✳ ✳ ✳ *f*   **Perennial**
‡ 20–40cm (8–16in) ↔ 5cm (2in)

IRIS BUCHARICA ♚

This fast-growing, spring-flowering iris bears up to six golden yellow to white flowers on each stem; the most commonly available form has yellow and white flowers. The glossy, strap-shaped leaves die back after flowering. It must have good drainage and needs dry conditions when dormant after flowering. Plant bulbs in late summer or autumn.

ALSO RECOMMENDED: I. graeberiana *has blue flowers marked white and darker blue;* I. magnifica ♚ *has pale lilac flowers marked yellow and white.*

☼ ◊ ❀❀❀ **Perennial bulb**
‡ 20–40cm (8–16in) ↔ 12cm (5in)

KNAUTIA MACEDONICA

The deep purple-red, pincushion-like flowerheads of this clump-forming perennial are borne on slender, branching stems above greyish green leaves, from mid- to late summer. They suit wildflower borders (*see p.494*) or meadow plantings. Also useful for late colour in a cottage garden or herbaceous border. It self-seeds freely.

ALSO RECOMMENDED: K. arvensis, *the field scabious, is taller with pale bluish lilac flowers, and it may also be naturalized in meadow plantings.*

☼ ◊ ❀❀❀ **Perennial**
‡ 60–80cm (24–32in) ↔ 45cm (18in)

LATHYRUS VERNUS
'Alboroseus' ♥

This spring vetchling is a vigorous, clump-forming plant bearing very pretty, pink and white, pea-like flowers on upright stems well above the mid-green foliage in spring. Suitable for a rock garden or herbaceous border, and it can be naturalized in a woodland garden or rough grassland. It tolerates poor soils, but resents disturbance.

ALSO RECOMMENDED: L. vernus ♥ *has purplish blue flowers.*

☼☀ ◊ ❀❀❀ **Perennial**
↕ 20–45cm (8–18in) ↔ 45cm (18in)

MALVA MOSCHATA

Musk mallow is a bushy, woody-based plant with faintly musk-scented foliage. A long succession of showy, pale pink flowers is borne throughout summer; they are long-lasting and very pretty – ideal in a sunny, hot and dry, wildflower or herbaceous border (*see p.190*). It may be short-lived, but it self-seeds freely. Tolerant of poor soils and urban pollution.

ALSO RECOMMENDED: *f.* alba ♥ *has white flowers;* M. sylvestris *'Primley Blue'* (see p.539).

☼ ◊ ❀❀❀ **Perennial**
↕ to 90cm (36in) ↔ 30cm (12in)

NARCISSUS CANTABRICUS

This early-spring-flowering hoop-petticoat daffodil bears delicate white flowers, which are perfect in a rock garden and exquisite when naturalized in fine turf. This species needs very well-drained soil and warm, dry conditions during summer. Plant bulbs in autumn.

ALSO RECOMMENDED: *N. jonquilla* ♀ *has heads of up to five scented, golden yellow flowers with tiny cups and pointed perianth segments; N. romieuxii* ♀ *has pale yellow, hoop-petticoat flowers.*

☀ ◊ ❀ ❀ ❀   **Perennial bulb**
‡ 15–20cm (6–8in) ↔ 5cm (2in)

PAEONIA MLOKOSEWITSCHII ♀

The Caucasian peony is an upright perennial with large, bowl-shaped, lemon-yellow flowers in late spring and early summer amid bluish green foliage. Each leaf is divided into nine red-margined leaflets, and the flowers are followed by seed pods that split open when ripe. A fine addition to a mixed, herbaceous, or shrub border.

ALSO RECOMMENDED: P. delavayi ♀ (see p.243); P. lactiflora 'Sarah Bernhardt' ♀ (see p.541).

☀ ☀ ◊◊ ❀ ❀ ❀   **Perennial**
‡↔ 65–90cm (26–36in)

PLATYCODON GRANDIFLORUS ♀

The balloon flower forms clumps of
purplish green foliage from which
emerge clusters of large, purple to
violet-blue flowers in late summer. They
are borne on upright stems, which may
need support, and the flowers open
from balloon-shaped buds. Suitable for
a rock garden or herbaceous border; do
not allow the soil to dry out. Established
plants resent disturbance. The flowers
are good for cutting (*see p.524*).

ALSO RECOMMENDED: *'Apoyama'* ♀ *has
deep violet flowers; 'Fuji Pink' has pink
flowers; those of 'Mariesii'* ♀ *are violet-blue.*

☼ ◐ ◊ ❁ ❁ ❁   **Perennial**
↕ to 60cm (24in) ↔ 30cm (12in)

PULSATILLA VULGARIS ♀

The nodding, silky-hairy flowers of the
pasque flower are deep to pale purple
or occasionally white; they rise above
the feathery foliage in spring and are
followed by silky seedheads. Ideal for
a rock garden, scree or gravel plantings,
or for paving crevices (*see p.348*), and it
can be naturalized in turf. The flowers
are attractive to bees (*see p.494*). It
resents disturbance.

ALSO RECOMMENDED: *'Alba'* ♀ *has white
flowers; var.* rubra *has plum-red flowers.*

☼ ◊ ❁ ❁ ❁   **Perennial**
↕ 10–20cm (4–8in) ↔ 20cm (8in)

RUDBECKIA 'Herbstsonne'

A robust, clump-forming plant for bold, back-border placement. It bears daisy-like, bright yellow flowerheads with protruding, cone-shaped green centres from midsummer to autumn. The plant is an imposing specimen when naturalized in a woodland garden. It tolerates clay soil (*see p.12*) and is a good source of cut flowers (*see p.524*). Also sold as Autumn Sun.

ALSO RECOMMENDED: R. fulgida *var.* deamii ♥ *is shorter with orange-yellow and dark brown flowers;* R. 'Goldquelle' ♥ (see p.543).

☼ ◑ ◊◊ ❀❀❀   **Perennial**
‡ 2m (6ft) ↔ 90cm (36in)

SAXIFRAGA 'Tumbling Waters' ♥

A slow-growing, white-flowered saxifrage that forms large and clustered rosettes of narrow, lime-encrusted, silvery green leaves at ground level. In spring, long and arching flowering stems arise from the centres of these leafy rosettes. Flowers will not appear for the first few years. Suitable for a rock garden or trough with shelter from excessive winter wet.

ALSO RECOMMENDED: 'Southside Seedling' ♥ has red-spotted white flowers.

☼ ◊ ❀❀❀   **Perennial**
‡ 45cm (18in) ↔ 30cm (12in)

SIDALCEA *'Elsie Heugh'*

This prairie mallow bears its spires of satiny, purple-pink flowers with pretty, fringed petals over long periods in summer, above a mound of lobed, glossy bright green leaves. Grow in a mixed or herbaceous border; the flowers are good for cutting (*see p.524*), and deadheading encourages a second flush of bloom.

ALSO RECOMMENDED: *'Croftway Red' has rich red-pink blooms; 'Rose Queen' is taller with large, pink flowers; 'Sussex Beauty' has clear pink flowers; 'William Smith'* ♥ *has deep pink flowers.*

◐ ☀ ◊ ❀ ❀ ❀　　　　　**Perennial**
‡ 90cm (36in) ↔ 45cm (18in)

VERBASCUM *'Gainsborough'* ♥

A short-lived plant that is much admired for its grand appearance and long flowering season. Throughout summer, it bears spires of saucer shaped, soft yellow, purple-marked flowers above a rosette of grey-green leaves arranged around the base of the stem. A very beautiful plant for a hot and dry, sunny, herbaceous or mixed border (*see p.190*). Suitable for a wildlife garden (*see p.494*).

ALSO RECOMMENDED: *'Cotswold Beauty'* ♥ *has peachy pink flowers; 'Mont Blanc' has pure white flowers; 'Pink Domino'* ♥ *has rose-pink flowers.*

☀ ◊ ❀ ❀ ❀　　　　　**Perennial**
‡ 1.2m (4ft) ↔ 30cm (12in)

PLANTS FOR ACID SOILS

THE MAJORITY OF acid-loving plants are originally from woodland areas, and they prefer a cool, more or less shady environment and a soil that is leafy, humus-rich, and moist but well-drained. In nature, such soils are fairly fertile because nutrients are annually replenished by the recycling of fallen leaves. If you are one of the lucky few to be blessed with such gardening conditions, all you really have to do is choose, plant, and admire your handiwork.

There are also many acid-loving plants that need or tolerate more open sites in sun, such as witch alder (*see p.103*), *Lithodora diffusa* 'Heavenly Blue' (*see p.104*), and most heathers (*see pp.42, 45, 102, 173, 306, 418*). Provided that the soil is not excessively acid – perhaps on the acid side of neutral – a huge range of plants are likely to thrive, excluding only those that positively demand alkaline conditions. Plan a display that lasts through the year, with woodland gems that flower in spring or early summer, followed by plants that bloom later in the year. You can also enjoy creating blazing tapestries of autumn colour using plants like maples (see pp.94, 95), *Amelanchier lamarckii* (see p.95), or *Enkianthus cernuus* var *rubens* (see p.102), as their foliage tints are at their best on acid soils.

KEEP THE SOIL FERTILE

Relatively few acid-lovers thrive in poor, acid soils. There are exceptions, however, such as bog rosemary (see p.99), brooms (see pp.44, 198, 350), heathers (see pp.42, 45, 102, 173, 306, 418), and vacciniums (see pp.109, 376, 456), which are found in the wild on wind-blasted heath and moorland. If you garden on peaty soil, the range of plants grown is usually limited by low fertility, so additional nutrients, preferably in the form of slow-release fertilizers, are needed to extend the range. If the soil is very acid, it may fail to support even the most dedicated acid-lovers; in this case, careful liming can moderate the acidity. Adding organic matter to an already peaty soil may appear paradoxical, but it has value, as it adds a modicum of nutrients and improves drainage and moisture retention. Peaty soils are often poorly drained and can be difficult to wet again if allowed to dry out. Acidic clay or sandy soils also benefit from such treatment.

ACID-LOVERS IN CONTAINERS

Plants that thrive on acid soils, like azaleas and rhododendrons (see pp.108, 160, 243, 454), often have such delicate glamour that gardeners yearn to grow them, even if they have totally unsuitable, alkaline soils. The best solution in this case is to choose small or dwarf cultivars of the plant in question and grow them in tubs or other containers filled with lime-free or ericaceous compost. Alternatively, create a raised bed on top of perforated polythene, which will allow drainage, and fill it with acid soil. Be prepared to top-dress annually with more of the same.

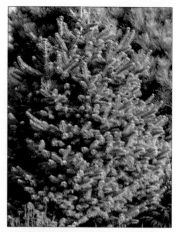

ABIES LASIOCARPA
'Arizonica Compacta'

A compact and slow-growing form of the corkbark fir that develops into a small and densely foliaged, conical to oval tree with soft, corky bark. The blue-grey leaves give this tree a distinctive colour. The upward-pointing fir cones are dark purple and ripen to brown. Grow in a shrub border or as a specimen tree.

ALSO RECOMMENDED: *A. koreana (see p.496); A. nordmanniana ♀ is a columnar tree to 40m (130ft) tall with glossy foliage.*

☼ ◑◊ ✿✿✿　　　**Evergreen tree**
↕ 3–5m (10–15ft) ↔ 2–3m (6–10ft)

ACER JAPONICUM
'Aconitifolium' ♀

This Japanese maple forms a bushy tree and bears deeply lobed, mid-green leaves, which turn brilliant dark red in autumn. It flowers very freely, producing upright clusters of conspicuous, reddish purple flowers in spring, followed by winged fruits. In cold areas, provide a thick mulch around the base. Remove badly placed branches in autumn only.

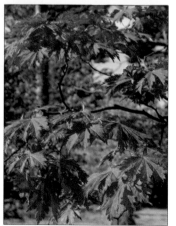

ALSO RECOMMENDED: *'Vitifolium' ♀ has shallowly lobed leaves.*

☼ ◊ ✿✿✿　　　**Deciduous tree**
↕ 5m (15ft) ↔ 6m (20ft)

ACER PALMATUM
'Bloodgood' ♥

The delicate, divided leaves of this small and graceful Japanese maple are dark red-purple and turn brilliant red in autumn. A fine specimen for a sheltered site in a small garden; it is also suitable for growing in containers (*see p.412*). Prune in winter only when young, to remove any badly placed shoots.

ALSO RECOMMENDED: *f.* atropurpureum *has red-purple leaves that turn to bright red;* 'Burgundy Lace' ♥ *has deeply cut, dark red-purple leaves;* Dissectum Atropurpureum *Group have finely divided, dark red-purple leaves.*

☼☀ ◊ ❀❀❀   **Deciduous tree**
↕↔ 5m (15ft)

AMELANCHIER LAMARCKII ♥

Juneberry is an upright, multi-stemmed shrubby tree, which lends interest with its bronzed new leaves in spring and brilliant red and gold autumn colour. The white flowers in hanging clusters that appear in spring are followed by purple-black fruits, which attract birds (*see p.494*). A fine specimen that forms its shape naturally, needing only minimal winter pruning. It will also grow as a hedge (*see p.138*).

ALSO RECOMMENDED: *A.* canadensis *bears white flowers in upright clusters;* A. × grandiflora 'Ballerina' ♥ *is more spreading with arching flower clusters.*

☼☀ ◊◊ ❀❀❀   **Deciduous tree**
↕ 10m (30ft) ↔ 12m (40ft)

EUCRYPHIA × INTERMEDIA 'Rostrevor' ♀

Glistening white, cup-shaped flowers festoon this narrowly upright tree from late summer to autumn, and they are attractive to bees (*see p.494*). With its glossy dark green leaves, it makes an elegant specimen in any site that is sheltered from cold, drying winds. It grows best with its roots in shade and top-growth in sun. Only minimal pruning is required.

ALSO RECOMMENDED: E. glutinosa ♀ *is deciduous with orange-red autumn colour and is more tolerant of exposure;* E. × nymansensis 'Nymansay' ♀ *is taller.*

☼ ◊◊ ❀❀❀ **Evergreen tree**
‡ 10m (30ft) ↔ 6m (20ft)

NOTHOFAGUS × ALPINA

This fast-growing, broadly conical southern beech, also known as *N. procera* of gardens, has beech-like leaves, which are bronze when young, maturing to fresh green, and assuming glorious red, orange, and yellow tints before they fall in autumn. A fine specimen tree for larger gardens. It needs little pruning; cut out crossing or badly placed shoots in winter.

ALSO RECOMMENDED: N. antarctica *is smaller and often multi-stemmed;* N. obliqua *is taller with smaller leaves.*

☼ ◊◊ ❀❀❀ **Deciduous tree**
‡ 25m (80ft) ↔ 15m (50ft)

NYSSA SINENSIS ♥

The Chinese tupelo is a conical
tree valued for its colourful foliage.
The leaves are bronze when young,
maturing to dark green in summer,
turning to brilliant shades of orange,
red, and yellow in autumn before they
fall. The flowers are inconspicuous.
Ideal as a specimen tree near water,
but choose a site that is sheltered from
cold, drying winds. Thin out crowded
branches in late winter.

ALSO RECOMMENDED: N. sylvatica ♥ *is
very similar but reaches 20m (70ft) in height.*

☼ ◐ ◊◐ ❄❄❄   **Deciduous tree**
‡↔ 10m (30ft)

PSEUDOLARIX AMABILIS ♥

The golden larch, although initially
slow-growing, makes a beautiful
specimen tree for larger gardens.
The open, broadly conical crown of
branches, which have purple-tipped
shoots, bears soft, fresh green, needle-
like leaves; they turn glorious shades
of orange and gold in autumn. In
spring, it bears catkin-like male flowers,
and the female cones are spiky and
egg-shaped. It needs a warm, sunny
site and deep, fertile soil; in cold areas,
select a site with shelter from spring
frosts. Areas with long, hot summers
are the most suitable.

☼ ◊ ❄❄❄   **Deciduous tree**
‡ 15–20m (50–70ft) ↔ 12m (40ft)

STEWARTIA MONADELPHA

In midsummer, this elegant, slow-growing tree bears camellia-like, crystalline white flowers with a boss of violet anthers. The glossy dark green leaves turn deep orange and red in autumn and, at maturity, the bark is patterned grey and red-brown. A fine specimen for a woodland garden. Prune only to remove badly placed or damaged branches when dormant in winter.

ALSO RECOMMENDED: S. ovata *is a large shrub*; S. pseudocamellia ♥ *has a tiered habit and is a smaller tree.*

☼ ◐ ◊ ❀ ❀ ❀   **Deciduous tree**
↕ 25m (80ft) ↔ 8m (25ft)

STYRAX JAPONICUS ♥

The Japanese snowbell is a small and graceful tree with glossy leaves that turn red and yellow in autumn. In midsummer, it is festooned with delicate, bell-shaped white flowers, which hang beneath the branches. Suitable for a woodland garden or a shrub border in dappled shade. Choose a site with some shelter from cold, drying winds. Prune only to remove badly placed branches in winter.

ALSO RECOMMENDED: S. hemsleyanus ♥ *is more columnar in habit*; S. obassia ♥ *is taller with more rounded leaves and fragrant flowers.*

☼ ◐ ◊◊ ❀ ❀ ❀   **Deciduous tree**
↕ 10m (30ft) ↔ 8m (25ft)

ANDROMEDA POLIFOLIA
'Compacta' ♥

Bog rosemary forms a compact mound of wiry stems clothed in narrow and leathery, dark green leaves. In spring and early summer, it bears urn-shaped, light pink flowers. Excellent for a rock or woodland garden, or for a moist shady border (*see p.238*), it tolerates full sun where soils remain reliably moist. Good as ground cover (*see pp.304, 326*). Trim after flowering.

ALSO RECOMMENDED: *A. polifolia is larger; 'Macrophylla' ♥ is also smaller with larger flowers.*

☼ ☀ ◐ ❀ ❀ ❀ **Evergreen shrub**
‡ 40cm (16in) ↔ 60cm (24in)

CAMELLIA JAPONICA
'Lady Vansittart'

An upright shrub with dark green, leathery foliage. In the early part of spring, it is covered by masses of saucer-shaped, semi-double white flowers with rose-pink stripes or specks. Good for the back of a border or as a specimen shrub, sheltered from cold, drying winds. Mulch around the base in winter, and prune young plants to shape after flowering. Also good for containers in shade (*see p.448*) and protected, north-facing walls (*see p.262*).

ALSO RECOMMENDED: *'Adolphe Audusson' ♥ (see p.450); 'Elegans' ♥ has pink flowers.*

☼ ◐ ◐◐ ❀ ❀ ❀ **Evergreen shrub**
‡ 9m (28ft) ↔ 8m (25ft)

CASSIOPE LYCOPODIOIDES ♔

A heather-like shrub with scale-like, dark green leaves that forms a low and dense, ground-covering mat (*see pp.304, 326*). In late spring, it is clothed by upright spikes of red-stemmed, narrowly bell-shaped white flowers. Good for a rock or woodland garden, or a cool, shady border; it tolerates sun if the soil remains moist. It can also be grown in a wide, shallow pot (*see p.448*). Trim after flowering.

ALSO RECOMMENDED: *C. 'Edinburgh' ♔ is more upright with green-stemmed flowers; C. 'Randle Cooke' ♔ has taller-stemmed flowers in late spring.*

☼ ☀ ◐ ❄ ❄ ❄   **Evergreen shrub**
‡ 8cm (3in) ↔ 45cm (18in)

CELMISIA WALKERI

The arching, spreading branches of this low-growing plant bear rosettes of narrow, leathery, dark green leaves at their tips; they are white and woolly beneath. In early summer, it produces a mass of daisy-like, yellow-centred white flowers. Good for a rock garden or a damp border; celmisias dislike hot sun and grow best in areas with cool, moist summers. Trim after flowering.

ALSO RECOMMENDED: *C. bellidioides is a mat-forming perennial with white flowerheads; C. semicordata has rosettes of silky, hairy leaves and white flowers.*

☼ ☀ ◐◐ ❄ ❄ ❄   **Evergreen shrub**
‡↔ 30cm (12in)

DESFONTAINIA SPINOSA ♀

This dense bush has a holly-like appearance, but unlike holly, showy hanging flowers are borne from midsummer to late autumn. These tubular blooms are red with yellow tips and appear amid the spiny, glossy dark green leaves. Choose a cool shrub border in dappled shade with shelter from cold, drying winds, such as against a north-facing wall (*see p.262*). It tolerates more open situations in areas of high rainfall. Trim in early

☀ ◑ ◊◊ ❄ ❄   **Evergreen shrub**
↕↔ 2m (6ft)

EMBOTHRIUM COCCINEUM

The Chilean firebush is a bushy and upright shrub with narrow, shiny dark green leaves. In early summer, it bears clusters of showy, tubular, flaming scarlet flowers that stand out brilliantly if the shrub is grown as a specimen in the dappled shade of a woodland garden. Grow in the protection of a wall (*see pp.262, 280*) as it must have shelter from cold, drying winds. Needs minimal pruning.

ALSO RECOMMENDED: '*Norquinco*' ♀ *is slightly hardier.*

☀☀ ◑ ◊ ❄ ❄ ❄   **Evergreen shrub**
↕ 10m (30ft) ↔ 5m (15ft)

ENKIANTHUS CERNUUS
F. RUBENS ♀

A bushy plant with clusters of bright green leaves that assume dark red-purple tints before falling in autumn. The hanging clusters of bell-shaped, rich red flowers, which are delicately toothed at the mouth, are borne in late spring and early summer. Grow as a specimen in a woodland garden or in shrub border. If the soil is reliably moist, it thrives in sun and will produce its best autumn colour there.

ALSO RECOMMENDED: *E. campanulatus* ♀ *is taller with pink-veined cream flowers and scarlet leaves in autumn.*

☼ ☀ ◐ ❄ ❄ ❄   **Deciduous shrub**
↕↔ 2.5m (8ft)

ERICA CINEREA *'Romiley'*

This form of bell heather produces spires of magenta flowers from early summer to autumn above a dense clump of narrow, dark green leaves. Good ground cover (*see p.304*) for a shrub border, rock garden, or when grown in a tapestry with other heathers. It associates well with dwarf conifers. Trim after flowering to keep compact. Tolerant of exposure (*see p.118*), and the flowers attract bees (*see p.494*).

ALSO RECOMMENDED: *'Eden Valley'* ♀ *has lavender-pink flowers; 'Pink Ice'* ♀ *has pink flowers and bronzed winter foliage.*

☼ ◑ ❄ ❄ ❄   **Evergreen shrub**
↕ 25cm (10in) ↔ 55cm (22in)

FOTHERGILLA GARDENII

Witch alder makes a dense bush with
spikes of bottlebrush-like, fragrant
white flowers on the bare branches in
spring. It is also valued for its blaze of
autumn foliage; the glossy dark green
leaves turn orange, yellow, and red
before they fall. An attractive addition
to a shrub border or light woodland.
Very little pruning is required.

ALSO RECOMMENDED: *'Blue Mist' has
bluish foliage; F. major* ♀ *is very similar but
larger and with slightly later spring flowers.*

☀ ◊◊ ❋❋❋ *f*   **Deciduous shrub**
↕↔ 1m (3ft)

HAMAMELIS *'Brevipetala'*

Whether grown in woodland, in a
shrub border, or as a specimen, this
graceful witch hazel brings welcome
scent and colour in winter with its
spidery yellow flowers that spangle the
bare branches. In autumn, the leaves
turn gold before falling. It also tolerates
deep soil over chalk (*see p.64*). Pruning
is best kept to a minimum, although
the flowering branches are good for
cutting (*see p.524*).

ALSO RECOMMENDED: H. × intermedia
'Arnold Promise' ♀ *has larger yellow
flowers; 'Diane'* ♀ *has dark red flowers;*
H. mollis ♀ *has yellow flowers.*

☀◑ ◊ ❋❋❋ *f*   **Deciduous shrub**
↕↔ 4m (12ft)

KALMIA ANGUSTIFOLIA ♛

The sheep laurel is a tough, rabbit - proof bush grown for its spectacular, rounded clusters of small, pink to deep red, sometimes white flowers. They appear in early summer amid the dark green leaves. Useful for a shrub border or rock garden, it naturally forms a mound; prune after flowering, if necessary. Mulch in spring with leaf mould or pine needles. It will tolerate full sun if the soil is kept moist, and it is suitable for a container (*see p.448*).

ALSO RECOMMENDED: *f.* rubra *has dark red flowers;* K. latifolia ♛ (see p.18).

☀ ◐ ❋ ❋ ❋   **Evergreen shrub**
‡ 60cm (24in) ↔ 1.5m (5ft)

LITHODORA DIFFUSA *'Heavenly Blue'* ♛

A spreading bush, sometimes sold as *Lithospermum* 'Heavenly Blue', that grows flat along the ground. Rich blue, funnel-shaped flowers are borne in profusion from late spring and on into summer. The leaves are dark green and hairy. Suitable for an open position in a rock garden or raised bed. Trim lightly after flowering.

ALSO RECOMMENDED: L. oleifolia ♛ *has sky-blue flowers in early summer.*

☀ ◐ ❋ ❋ ❋   **Evergreen shrub**
‡ 15cm (6in) ↔ 60cm (24in) or more

MAGNOLIA LILIIFLORA
'Nigra' ♥

A dense, summer-flowering shrub
bearing goblet-shaped, deep wine-
red, fragrant flowers amid dark green
leaves. Plant as a specimen or among
other shrubs and trees. Unlike many
magnolias, it begins to flower when
quite young. Provide a mulch in early
spring, and prune young plants in
midsummer to encourage a good shape.

ALSO RECOMMENDED: M. campbellii
(see p.478); M. grandiflora *'Goliath'* ♥
(see p.283); M. × soulangeana (see p.15).

☼ ☀ ◐◐ ✿✿✿ *f* **Deciduous shrub**
↕ 3m (10ft) ↔ 2.5m (8ft)

MITRARIA COCCINEA

A weakly scrambling shrub with scarlet
flowers over a long period from late
spring to autumn. They contrast well
with the glossy dark green foliage and
are followed by fleshy berries. Keep
the roots cool and shaded, and allow
the top to grow into the sun. An easy
plant to grow in a woodland garden
or sheltered shrub border where it will
trail along the ground, spill over banks,
or climb through a trellis. It will also
cascade from a container or hanging
basket in shade (*see p.448*). Trim in
spring, if necessary.

☼ ☀ ◐◐ ✿✿ **Evergreen shrub**
↕ 2m (6ft)

PHYLLODOCE × INTERMEDIA *'Drummondii'*

A bushy, low-spreading plant with stems that are densely clothed in narrow, glossy dark green leaves. In a rock garden, peaty soil, or shady border, it makes good ground cover (*see p.326*). In spring, red stems bear clusters of nodding, narrowly bell-shaped, rich pink flowers. Trim after flowering to keep it dense and neat.

ALSO RECOMMENDED: *P. caerulea ♀ has purplish pink flowers; P. empetriformis has purple-pink to rose-red flowers.*

☼ ◑ ❄❄❄   **Evergreen shrub**
‡ 15–23cm (6–9in) ↔ 35cm (14in)

PICEA ABIES *'Ohlendorffii'*

This very slow-growing form of the Norway spruce makes a densely foliaged, rounded bush. It narrows to a more conical shape with age and has dark green, forward-pointing, needle-like leaves. Very little pruning is necessary.

ALSO RECOMMENDED: *P. abies, the traditional Christmas tree, grows to 40m (130ft) tall; 'Nidiformis' ♀ grows slowly to 1.5m (5ft) tall with a spreading habit;* P. mariana *'Nana' ♀ (see p.423);* P. omorika *♀ (see p.479).*

☼ ◐◑ ❄❄❄   **Evergreen shrub**
‡ 3m (10ft) ↔ 3–4m (10–12ft)

PIERIS FORMOSA
'Wakehurst' ♥

This upright shrub is valued for its
brilliant red young foliage, which fades
to pink and matures to dark green. Also
attractive are the large, slightly drooping
clusters of small, fragrant white flowers
in spring. Suitable for a woodland
garden or shrub border, but it may
not survive in areas with cold winters
where it must be sheltered from cold
winds. Trim lightly after flowering.

ALSO RECOMMENDED: *P. 'Forest Flame' ♥
is similar; P. japonica 'Little Heath' ♥
(see p.453).*

☼ ◑ ◊◑ ❄ ❄ ❄ *f*   **Evergreen shrub**
‡ 60cm (24in) ↔ 30cm (12in)

PINUS SYLVESTRIS
'Gold Coin' ♥

A dwarf and slow-growing cultivar of
the Scots pine that forms a rounded
bush with bright golden yellow, needle-
like foliage. It is suitable for small
gardens and can be grown in a rock
garden or as a specimen in a large
container (*see p.412*). This shrub also
tolerates exposed sites (*see p.118*)
and sandy soils (*see p.38*).

ALSO RECOMMENDED: *Aurea Group ♥
are a selection of trees to 15m (50ft) tall,
with green foliage that turns to golden
yellow in winter.*

☼ ◊ ❄ ❄ ❄   **Evergreen shrub**
‡ ↔ 2m (6ft)

RHODODENDRON LUTEUM ♚

This azalea makes an open shrub with
mid-green, bristly, deciduous leaves.
In late spring and early summer, trusses
of up to a dozen funnel-shaped, sticky
and sweetly scented yellow flowers
cover the plant. Unlike many
rhododendrons, it grows best in direct
sun. Little or no pruning is required.

ALSO RECOMMENDED: R. *Blue Diamond
Group* (see p.160); R. *'Homebush'* ♚ (see
p.454); R. *'Polar Bear'* ♚ (see p.243).

◐ ◊◊ ❋❋❋ *f*   **Deciduous shrub**
↕↔ 4m (12ft)

SKIMMIA JAPONICA *'Rubella'* ♚

A tough male plant that bears dark red
flower buds in autumn and winter, which
open in spring as fragrant heads of white
flowers. The dome of oval leaves have
red rims. No berries are produced, but
it will pollinate female skimmias nearby.
It tolerates coastal areas (*see p.166*),
urban pollution, and dry shade (*see
p.216*), and it can be pot-grown (*see
p.448*). Requires little pruning, but cut
back any shoots that spoil the shape.

ALSO RECOMMENDED: *'Nymans'* ♚ *is female
with red berries; 'Robert Fortune'* ♚ *is a
hermaphrodite;* S. × confusa *'Kew Green'* ♚
(see p.455); S. japonica (see p.223).

◐☀ ◊ ❋❋❋ *f*   **Evergreen shrub**
↕↔ to 6m (20ft)

VACCINIUM VITIS-IDAEA
Koralle Group ♔

This group of wide-spreading cowberries forms a mat of small and leathery, dark green leaves, which is spangled with dense, nodding spikes of bell-shaped white flowers in spring and early summer. The shiny red fruits that follow are borne very freely. Excellent ground cover for peaty soils in woodland or shrub borders (*see pp.304, 326*). Also suitable for sandy soils (*see p.38*). Trim to shape in spring, if necessary.

ALSO RECOMMENDED: *var.* minus *is smaller with pink flowers;* V. corymbosum ♔ (see p.376); V. glaucoalbum ♔ (see p.456).

☼ ◐ ◑ ❄ ❄ ❄   **Evergreen shrub**
↕ 25cm (10in) ↔ indefinite

ZENOBIA PULVERULENTA

The slender and spreading, arching shoots of this shrub are clothed in narrowly oval, bluish green leaves. At the stem tips, in early to midsummer, it produces upright clusters of fragrant, nodding, bell-shaped white flowers. An attractive specimen for a woodland garden or damp, shady border (*see p.238*). It tolerates sun where soils remain reliably moist and may be semi-evergreen in a warm, sheltered site. To keep it compact, cut the stems back to strong buds after flowering.

☼ ◐ ❄ ❄ ❄ ❄ *f*   **Deciduous shrub**
↕ 2m (6ft) ↔ 1.5m (5ft)

Bulbinella hookeri

This sturdy perennial for a rock garden or peaty soil forms dense clumps of narrow and succulent, grass-like foliage. From spring to summer, spikes of golden yellow flowers appear on top of tall, upright stems above the foliage. In frost-prone areas, provide a thick mulch of leaf mould in winter.

☼◑ ◊◊ ❄❄   **Perennial**
‡ 60cm (24in) ↔ 30cm (12in)

Deschampsia flexuosa 'Tatra Gold'

This evergreen grass forms a mound of arching threads of yellow-green leaves. In early to midsummer, it bears airy heads of tiny bronze flowers on slender, wavy stalks. May be cut for fresh or dried flower arrangements (*see p.524*). Suits a mixed border or woodland garden. Remove old flowerheads as new growth appears in spring.

ALSO RECOMMENDED: D. flexuosa *is slightly taller with blue-green leaves and glistening, silver-tinted, purple or brown flowers;* D. cespitosa *'Goldtau' (syn. Golden Dew) (see p.228).*

☼◑ ◊ ❄❄❄   **Perennial**
‡ 50cm (20in) ↔ 30cm (12in)

DIANELLA TASMANICA

This plant forms clumps of long and arching, grass-like foliage from which rise branching sprays of star-shaped, lavender-blue to violet flowers with pale yellow anthers. These are borne on upright stems in early summer, and persistent, glossy deep blue berries follow. An enchanting plant for a woodland garden or warm, sheltered border in mild areas.

ALSO RECOMMENDED: D. caerulea *has blue, blue-green, or white flowers.*

☀ ◐ ◊ ❁ ❁   **Perennial**
‡ 1.2m (4ft) ↔ 45cm (18in)

GENTIANA SINO ORNATA ♔

This autumn-flowering gentian bears its trumpet-shaped, deep bright blue flowers, striped darker blue and palest green, above mats of trailing shoots carrying rosettes of narrow, dark green leaves. Ideal for a rock garden or the front of a damp, lightly shaded border (see p.238). It grows well in paving crevices (see p.348).

ALSO RECOMMENDED: G. *'Inverleith'* ♔ *has pale blue flowers with dark blue stripes;* G. × macaulayi *'Kingfisher' is more compact.*

☀ ◊ ❁ ❁ ❁   **Perennial**
‡ 5–7cm (2–3in) ↔ 30cm (12in)

IRIS INNOMINATA

This iris produces a clump of evergreen, very narrow, deep green leaves and bears cream, yellow, or purple to lavender-blue flowers in early summer. It suits a herbaceous border, and its tendency to spread makes it good for ground cover (*see p.304*). Mulch with garden compost in spring, and divide clumps every few years to maintain vigour.

ALSO RECOMMENDED: I. douglasiana ♀ *has flowers in shades of purple, blue, or white; those of* I. tenax *come in lavender-blue, yellow, and cream.*

☼☀◑ ○ ❄❄❄ **Perennial**
‡ 15–25cm (6–10in) ↔ 30cm (12in)

LEIOPHYLLUM BUXIFOLIUM ♀

Sand myrtle is an upright to mat-forming, shrubby evergreen grown for its glossy dark green foliage and its abundance of star-shaped, pinkish white flowers, which appear in late spring and early summer. The leaves tint bronze in winter. A good, free-flowering underplanting perennial for a border or woodland garden. Protect form cold, drying winds. Trim after flowering, as it tends to spread widely.

☼☀ ○○ ❄❄❄ **Perennial**
‡ 30–60cm (12–24in) ↔ 60cm (24in) or more

LILIUM SUPERBUM ♛

The maroon-spotted orange flowers of
the American turkscap lily, which rise
on sturdy, purple-spotted stems in late
summer and autumn, are spectacular
if grouped in large clumps at the back
of a border or in a woodland garden.
Grow in deep, fertile, humus-rich soil,
siting the roots in shade and the tops
in sun. Plant bulbs in autumn.

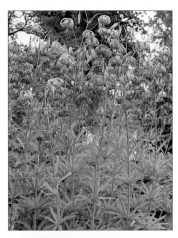

ALSO RECOMMENDED: L. martagon
*has pink to purplish red flowers in early
and midsummer;* L. Bellingham Group ♛
*have yellow to orange and red, brown
spotted flowers in early and midsummer.*

☼☀ ◊ ✻✻✻   **Perennial bulb**
‡ 1.5–3m (5–10ft) ↔ 30cm (12in)

MECONOPSIS NAPAULENSIS

This tall, evergreen poppy is worth
growing for its overwintering, basal
rosettes of large, tawny-hairy leaves
alone. From spring to midsummer, it
bears branched stems of dusky pink, red,
or purple poppy flowers. It dies after
flowering. Best in leafy, humus-rich
soil in areas with cool, damp summers.

ALSO RECOMMENDED: M. betonicifolia ♛
has sky-blue flowers in early summer;
M. grandis ♛ *has deep rich blue to purplish
red flowers in early summer.*

☼ ◊◊ ✻✻✻   **Perennial**
‡ 2.5m (8ft) ↔ 60–90cm (24–36in)

NOMOCHARIS PARDANTHINA

The nodding, white or pink flowers of this slender, elegant plant are borne in early summer above whorls of narrow stem leaves. An ideal companion for rhododendrons, because it enjoys cool, damp conditions in partial shade, as found in woodland or shady borders (*see p.238*). It withstands sun in areas with cool summers where the soil remains moist. Plant bulbs in winter or spring. Protect from slugs.

ALSO RECOMMENDED: N. aperta *is shorter with pale pink, purple-spotted flowers.*

☼ ◐ ◗ ❊ ❊ ❊   **Perennial**
‡ 90cm (36in) ↔ 10cm (4in)

PHLOX ADSURGENS
'Wagon Wheel'

This woodland phlox has trailing stems and forms a mound of light to mid-green foliage, which is covered by salmon-pink flowers in late spring and early summer. The petals are very narrow, resembling the spokes of a wheel. Also useful for ground cover in shade (*see p.326*).

ALSO RECOMMENDED: 'Red Buttes' has *deep pink flowers.*

☼ ◐ ◗ ❊ ❊ ❊   **Perennial**
‡↔ 30cm (12in)

PODOPHYLLUM HEXANDRUM

The deeply lobed, purple-splashed leaves of this spreading perennial emerge fully after the cup-shaped, white or pale pink flowers have completed their spring and summer display. The plum-like red fruits that follow, though ornamental, are very toxic if ingested. Grow in damp, leafy soil in a woodland garden or shady border (*see p.238*). Tolerates permanently moist soils (*see p.372*).

ALSO RECOMMENDED: *P. peltatum has leaves that are well-developed when it bears its fragrant, white or pink flowers – the fruits are yellow-green.*

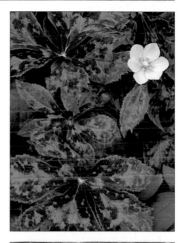

:☼: ◑: ◊◊ ❀❀❀　　**Perennial**
‡ 45cm (18in) ↔ 30cm (12in)

SEMIAQUILEGIA ECALCARATA

This delicate, usually short-lived plant carries clusters of diminutive, gracefully nodding, bell-shaped flowers in shades of dusky pink to purple-red in early summer; they are held above finely divided, fresh green leaves. A perfect plant for a sheltered niche in a rock garden. It grows well if it has some midday shade. Protect from slugs.

:☼: ◑: ◊ ❀❀❀　　**Perennial**
‡ 30cm (12in) ↔ 20cm (8in)

SMILACINA RACEMOSA ♈

False spikenard is a beautiful plant for a woodland garden or shady border, forming clumps of luxuriant, pale green leaves. Dense and upright, feathery spikes of creamy white, often green-tinged flowers arise from the clumps in late spring. These are occasionally followed by red berries. The foliage fades to yellow in autumn. Good as ground cover in shade (*see p.326*).

ALSO RECOMMENDED: S. stellata *is shorter with smaller and less feathery flower spikes.*

☼ ◑ ◊ ✳ ✳ ✳ **Perennial**

‡ 90cm (36in) ↔ 60cm (24in)

TRICYRTIS FORMOSANA ♈

The toad lily is an upright plant with unusual flowers, and it would suit a shady border or open woodland garden. Its white, purple-spotted, star-shaped flowers appear in early autumn on zig-zagging, softly hairy stems above dark green, stem-clasping leaves. Where there is unlikely to be deep snow cover, choose a sheltered site and provide a deep winter mulch.

ALSO RECOMMENDED: T. hirta *is similar with flowers from late summer.*

☼ ◑ ◊ ✳ ✳ ✳ **Perennial**

‡ 80cm (32in) ↔ 45cm (18in)

TRILLIUM ERECTUM ♛

Stinking benjamin is a vigorous, upright perennial bearing whorls of broadly oval leaves atop sturdy stems. In spring, funnel-shaped, deep red-purple flowers appear just above them. Ideal for damp, shady borders (*see p.238*) or woodland gardens. Mulch annually with leafmould to maintain optimum soil conditions. Protect from slugs.

ALSO RECOMMENDED: *f. albiflorum has white flowers. T. grandiflorum ♛ is shorter with more prominent white flowers.*

☀ ◐ ◐ ❄ ❄ ❄　　　**Perennial**

‡ 50cm (20in) ↔ 30cm (12in)

UVULARIA GRANDIFLORA ♛

Large merrybells forms slow-spreading clumps of slender, upright stems, which bear bell-shaped yellow flowers in late spring. Like the mid green leaves, they hang downward gracefully. An excellent plant for a shady border or woodland garden. Protect young plants from slugs and snails.

ALSO RECOMMENDED: *var. pallida has pale yellow flowers.*

☀ ◐ ◐◐ ❄ ❄ ❄　　　**Perennial**

‡ 75cm (30in) ↔ 30cm (12in)

PLANTS FOR EXPOSED SITES

GARDENS THAT SUFFER extreme
exposure present some of
the most difficult conditions
for plants, the most detrimental
feature being the force of the
wind. Exposed gardens may be
lashed by salt-laden coastal gales
(*see p.166*), laid bare to the full
brunt of the weather on a
blasted hillside, or on flat, open
land denuded of tree cover and
hedges. High winds loosen plant
roots, break fragile stems and
shoots, and scorch foliage when
the leaves lose water faster than
they can replace it from the soil.

Some beautiful gardens,
however, are sited in exposed
locations, and the secret of their
success is due largely to the
creation of shelter belts or
wind-filtering hedges around
their margins (*see p.138*).
Explore beyond the perimeter
of such exposed gardens on a
windy day, and compare the
conditions outside and within;
you will clearly feel just how
effective a windbreak can
be in creating a sheltered
microclimate on the leeward
side. With such shelter in place,

the range of plants that can be grown within the garden is so much wider – in fact, the choice is about the same as in a more naturally sheltered spot. If you have an exposed garden, therefore, your first priority is to alleviate the full force of the wind's chill blast.

WINDBREAK PLANTS

The choice of windbreak or hedging material is more important in cold, exposed gardens than elsewhere, because the sheltering plants themselves must be very tough if they are to grow well enough to fulfil their function. Hawthorn (*see pp. 123, 141*) makes some of the most resilient hedging, while Scots pines, sycamores (*see p. 168*), poplars (*see pp. 16, 169*), and willows (*see p. 162*) are ideal windbreak material, not least because their flexible stems go with the flow, rather than crack in the teeth of the gales.

Even tough plants benefit from some protection in their early years, in the form of temporary, artificial shelter, such as wattle fencing, windbreak netting, or plastic tree shelters. Once the plants are established, the shelter can be removed.

THE REST OF THE GARDEN

In the lee of a windbreak, tough evergreen shrubs can be planted to further cut down the force of the wind and provide a background for the garden proper. This secondary defence should include leathery leaved shrubs, such as *Prunus laurocerasus* 'Zabeliana' (*see p. 131*) and *Viburnum rhytidophyllum* (*see p. 134*). In more open areas, use lower-level plantings of small-leaved, ground-hugging plants, such as those that grow naturally on heathland or tundra. These include *Ledum groenlandicum* (*see p. 129*), *Arctostaphylos* x *media* 'Wood's Red' (*see p. 127*), or heather (*see p. 102*). If you site the more robust plants carefully, they will begin to create sheltered niches within the garden as they grow. This creates more choice and will ultimately allow you to grow more delicate plants.

ACER PLATANOIDES
'Crimson King' ♥

This Norway maple is a fast-growing
tree with a crown of deep red-purple
leaves divided into several pointed
lobes. The leaves turn to red in
autumn. Clusters of reddish yellow
flowers clothe the bare branches in
spring. Tolerant of most soils, including
those on chalk (*see p.64*), and urban
pollution. Remove badly placed or
unhealthy growth in late autumn
to midwinter only.

ALSO RECOMMENDED: *'Drummondii'* ♥
*is tougher with cream-margined green
leaves;* A. campestre ♥ (*see p.496*).

☀️◐ ◊◊ ❄❄❄   **Deciduous tree**
‡ 25m (80ft) ↔ 15m (50ft)

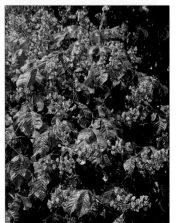

AESCULUS × CARNEA *'Briotii'* ♥

This cultivar of the red horse chestnut
is a spreading tree, admired in early
summer for its large, upright cones of
dark red flowers. They are followed
by round, spiny fruits. The dark green
leaves are divided into several leaflets.
A tree for large gardens only. Remove
dead, damaged, or badly placed
branches during winter.

ALSO RECOMMENDED: *'Plantierensis'* has
bigger flower clusters and shiny foliage.

☀️◐ ◊◊ ❄❄❄   **Deciduous tree**
‡ 20m (70ft) ↔ 15m (50ft)

ALNUS GLUTINOSA '*Imperialis*' ♥

This curious form of the common alder has deeply dissected, mid-green leaves. Groups of yellow-brown catkins are seen in late winter, followed by small, oval cones in summer. This beautiful foliage tree is not as tough as the species, but it is particularly good close to water as it tolerates poor, wet soils (*see p.372*). If necessary, prune in autumn after the leaves have fallen.

ALSO RECOMMENDED: A. glutinosa *with oval leaves is a better choice for a cold, windy site;* A. incana (see p.140).

☼ ◐ ❀ ❀ ❀   **Deciduous tree**
‡ 26m (80ft) ↔ 5m (15ft)

BETULA UTILIS '*Jermyns*' ♥

West Himalayan birch trees should be grown where winter sun will illuminate the white, smooth, and peeling bark, which is particularly brilliant in this variety. Catkins are a feature in early spring, and the dark green leaves turn to rich golden yellow in autumn. Remove any damaged or dead wood in late autumn.

ALSO RECOMMENDED: B. ermanii (see p.40), B. nigra ♥, *and* B. papyrifera *are all very hardy and good planted in clumps in exposed sites.*

☼ ◐ ❀ ❀ ❀   **Deciduous tree**
‡ 15m (50ft) ↔ 7.5m (23ft)

CHAMAECYPARIS PISIFERA *'Filifera Aurea'* ♥

A broad conifer that develops into a conical tree with flattened sprays of golden green-yellow foliage. The fronds arch gracefully and are sometimes covered with small green cones, which ripen to brown. An excellent specimen tree that requires no regular pruning. The species is tougher and better as a windbreak; both are tolerant of permanently moist soils (*see p.372*).

ALSO RECOMMENDED: C. obtusa *and* C. pisifera *both make excellent windbreaks and can be trimmed as hedges.*

☼ ◖◗ ❋ ❋ ❋   **Evergreen tree**
‡ 12m (40ft) ↔ 5m (15ft)

CORNUS FLORIDA *'Cherokee Chief'* ♥

The flowering dogwood makes a beautiful tree with broad, mid-green leaves. These turn scarlet and purple in autumn before they fall. Dark ruby pink flowers appear late the following spring, and if the summer is hot enough, they may be succeeded by a scattering of red berries. A good specimen tree that needs little pruning.

ALSO RECOMMENDED: C. alternifolia *'Argentea'* ♥ (see p.476).

☼ ☀ ◗ ❋ ❋ ❋   **Deciduous tree**
‡ 6m (20ft) ↔ 8m (25ft)

CRATAEGUS LAEVIGATA
'Paul's Scarlet' ♔

Midland hawthorn or may is a small
and thorny tree with a rounded crown.
This cultivar is valued for its abundant
clusters of double, dark pink flowers,
which appear in late spring amid the
glossy green leaves. Red berries ripen
in autumn. Hawthorns are extremely
hardy and also tolerate urban pollution
and coastal sites (*see p.166*). Prune after
flowering; it is easily trimmed as a
hedge (*see p.138*).

ALSO RECOMMENDED: C. monogyna
(see p.141); *'Rosea Flore Pleno'* ♔ *is also
pink-flowered.*

☀ ◑ ◊◐ ❄❄❄ **Deciduous tree**
↕↔ 8m (25ft)

CRYPTOMERIA JAPONICA
'Cristata'

This narrow and conical conifer is a
cultivated form of the Japanese cedar,
and it is also sold as 'Sekka-sugi'. It has
slender, feathery sprays of deep green
leaves and a neat growth habit that
needs little or no formal pruning.
All cryptomerias are tolerant of chalky
soils (*see p.64*).

ALSO RECOMMENDED: C. japonica ♔ *is the
one to plant as a windbreak or hedge.*

☀ ◑ ◊ ❄❄❄ **Evergreen tree**
↕ 8m (25ft) ↔ 5m (15ft)

FRAXINUS EXCELSIOR 'Jaspidea' ♥

The yellowish foliage of this common ash make it a popular alternative to the species, which has dark green leaves. 'Jaspidea' is vigorous, and its broad crown of foliage is yellow in spring, darkening to pale green in summer, then fading to yellow again before falling in autumn. An excellent specimen tree, which also suits coastal gardens (*see p.166*) and chalky soils (*see p.64*). Prune in winter, if necessary.

ALSO RECOMMENDED: F. excelsior ♥ *makes a better windbreak; 'Pendula' ♥ has weeping branches.*

☼ ◊◊ ❁❁❁　　**Deciduous tree**

‡ 30m (100ft) ↔ 20m (70ft)

LABURNUM × WATERERI 'Vossii' ♥

A tough tree suitable for small gardens, this laburnum bears long, hanging clusters of golden yellow, pea-like flowers in late spring. The leaves are deep green. It can also be trained on an arch, pergola, or tunnel framework. All parts are toxic if eaten. Prune in winter or early spring, if necessary, and remove any growth that appears from the base of the trunk.

ALSO RECOMMENDED: L. alpinum *'Pendulum' is similar with weeping branches.*

☼ ◊ ❁❁❁　　**Deciduous tree**

‡↔ 8m (25ft)

PSEUDOTSUGA MENZIESII *VAR.* GLAUCA

The blue Douglas fir is a cone-shaped tree with a bluish tinge to its dark green foliage. It makes an imposing specimen tree. The bark is scaly and dark grey, maturing to red-brown. The needle-like leaves are arranged in two ranks along the shoots. Protect from cold winds when young with a screen of plastic, fleece, or hessian. Little pruning is required.

ALSO RECOMMENDED: P. menziesii ♥ *has dark green foliage.*

☼ ◊ ❀ ❀ ❀   **Evergreen tree**
‡ 25–50m (80–160ft) ↔ 6–10m (20–30ft)

PYRUS SALICIFOLIA *'Pendula'* ♥

The silvery grey leaves of the weeping pear are willow-like, and the spring display of small, creamy white flowers is followed by green ornamental pears in autumn. A fine tree that also tolerates pollution and is suitable for a small or urban garden.

ALSO RECOMMENDED: P. calleryana *'Chanticleer'* ♥ *has dark green foliage, which reddens in autumn, and brown fruits.*

☼ ◊ ❀ ❀ ❀   **Deciduous tree**
‡ 8m (25ft) ↔ 6m (20ft)

SORBUS AUCUPARIA

Rowan or mountain ash is a good tree for cold exposed areas and to plant in clumps to make a windbreak. It has a crown of dark green leaves that colour to red or yellow in autumn. Flat-headed clusters of white flowers appear in late spring, and these are followed later in the season by orange-red, inedible berries. It is also suitable for a small, urban garden or wildlife area (*see p.494*), and is tolerant of acid soils (*see p.92*). Prune in winter, if necessary.

ALSO RECOMMENDED: S. aria, *whitebeam, is similar.*

☼ ◑ ◊ ❊ ❊ ❊   **Deciduous tree**
‡ 15m (50ft) ↔ 7m (22ft)

TILIA CORDATA ♥

The small-leaved lime has a reasonably broad crown of rounded, dark green leaves, which turn yellow in autumn. With age, the smooth, silvery grey bark becomes fissured and the tree becomes more conical. Grow in clumps or as a specimen tree. Suitable for a wildlife garden as the small, pale yellow summer flowers are attractive to bees (*see p.494*). Prune badly placed growth in winter.

ALSO RECOMMENDED: T. × euchlora ♥ *is rounded and is unaffected by aphids;* T. platyphyllos *is taller with larger leaves.*

☼ ◑ ◊ ❊ ❊ ❊   **Deciduous tree**
‡ 15m (50ft) ↔ 8m (25ft)

ARCTOSTAPHYLOS × MEDIA
'Wood's Red'

This dwarf, pink-flowered form of the common bearberry is a very low and spreading shrub, which may form a mat of small and leathery, dark green leaves. Its flowers appear in summer and are followed in autumn by large, shiny red berries. Suitable for ground cover in open windswept areas in sun or partial shade (*see pp.304, 326*). Tolerant of acid soils (*see p.92*).

ALSO RECOMMENDED: A. uva-ursi *is similar but hardier.*

☼ ◐ ◊◊ ❀❀❀   **Evergreen shrub**
‡ 10cm (4in) ↔ 50cm (20in)

BERBERIS × STENOPHYLLA
'Corallina Compacta' ♥

While *Berberis stenophylla* is a large, arching shrub, ideal for exposed places as an informal hedge (*see p.138*), this cultivar of it is tiny and more suited to a rock garden. It bears spine-tipped, deep green leaves on arching, spiny stems. Many small, orange-yellow flowers appear in spring, followed by inedible, blue-black berries. Cut back hard after flowering.

ALSO RECOMMENDED: B. thunbergii ♥ *is also good as hedging;* B. × ottawensis *is very tough and intruder-proof.*

☼ ◊ ❀❀❀   **Deciduous shrub**
‡↔ 30cm (12in)

CORNUS ALBA *'Kesselringii'*

Red-barked dogwoods are usually grown for the winter effect of their colourful bare young stems, which are blackish purple in this variety. Small clusters of creamy white flowers appear from late spring amid oval, dark green leaves, which turn red and purple in autumn. Plant in clumps by water (*see p.372*) where the winter stems show up well. Cut back hard and feed every spring for the best stem colour, although this will be at the cost of the flowers.

ALSO RECOMMENDED: *'Sibirica'* ♀ *has bright red shoots;* *'Spaethii'* ♀ *has yellow-margined leaves.*

☼ ◊◊ ❋❋❋   **Deciduous shrub**
‡↔ 3m (10ft)

DEUTZIA GRACILIS

A graceful bush whose appearance belies its toughness. It has bright green foliage and bears its slender clusters of star-like, fragrant white flowers from spring to early summer. It has an upright, slightly spreading habit and is suitable for a mixed shrub border. Prune back after flowering.

ALSO RECOMMENDED: D. *'Mont Rose'* ♀ *has purple-pink flowers in early summer;* D. scabra (see p.150) *is tougher.*

☼ ◊ ❋❋❋ *f*   **Deciduous shrub**
‡↔ 1m (3ft)

LEDUM GROENLANDICUM

Labrador tea makes a rounded, white-flowering bush, a bit like a dwarf rhododendron. It is very hardy to frost. At the tips of the wiry, rusty stems in late spring, small flowers are borne in rounded clusters, which contrast with the dark green, aromatic leaves. This is a compact shrub for a cool position and combines well with heathers as it is also tolerant of acid soils (*see p.92*). Trim after flowering, if necessary.

☼ ◑ ◊ ❄ ❄ ❄ *f*   **Evergreen shrub**
‡ 90cm (36in) ↔ 1.2m (4ft)

LONICERA TATARICA

This deep green, upright bush with white to pink or red flowers in late spring and early summer looks good in a mixed shrub barrier and can be grown as a hedge (*see p.138*). The tubular flowers absolutely cover the plant, and they are followed by red to deep yellow berries. Trim or prune after flowering.

ALSO RECOMMENDED: *'Hack's Red' has very deep purple-red flowers.*

☼ ◑ ◊ ❄ ❄ ❄   **Deciduous shrub**
‡ 4m (12ft) ↔ 2.5m (8ft)

MAHONIA AQUIFOLIUM *'Smaragd'*

This popular variety of Oregon grape is a low-growing shrub with stiff and spiny, dark green leaves. These turn brownish purple in winter. Large clusters of bright yellow flowers open in spring, followed by small, blue-black berries. Only tolerant of sun in reliably moist soil. It can be grown as ground cover in shade (*see p.326*) if sheared close to the ground every two years.

ALSO RECOMMENDED: *'Apollo'* ♀ *has golden yellow flowers; the young leaves of* *'Orange Flame'* *are rusty orange.*

☼ ◐ ◊◊ ❀❀❀　　**Evergreen shrub**
‡ 60cm (24in) ↔ 1m (3ft)

PINUS MUGO *'Mops'* ♀

This dwarf pine is a small, round bush with scaly grey bark and thick, upright branches. The shoots are covered with long, dark to bright green needles and the occasional dark brown pine cone; these take a few years to ripen. Effective in a large rock garden or, where space allows, planted in groups. Very little pruning is required.

ALSO RECOMMENDED: *Tall pines like* P. nigra *are very wind tolerant and ideal for windbreaks if you have the space.*

☼ ◊ ❀❀❀　　**Evergreen shrub**
‡ 1m (3ft) ↔ 2m (6ft)

PRUNUS LAUROCERASUS
'Zabeliana'

This short and spreading cherry laurel is
an evergreen shrub with dense, glossy
dark green foliage. Abundant spikes of
white flowers are borne in spring and
often again in autumn. Conical red
fruits follow and ripen to black. Plant
in groups as a low hedge (*see p.138*) or
to cover bare ground (*see p.304*). Prune
in late spring or early summer to restrict
size. *P. laurocerasus* ♀ can be planted as
a second line of defence in a windbreak.

ALSO RECOMMENDED: P. laurocerasus *and*
P. lusitanica *made good infillers between*
windbreak trees (see p.118).

☼ ◐◖ ❀❀❀   **Evergreen shrub**
‡ 1m (3ft) ↔ 2.5m (8ft)

ROSA PIMPINELLIFOLIA *'Plena'*

The Scots or burnet rose has a dense,
spreading habit with very thorny and
prickly stems. It has small, fern-like,
dark green foliage, and this is covered
with creamy white double flowers
in early summer; purplish black hips
follow. The leaves turn to russet brown
in autumn. Prune out some older stems
after flowering, if necessary. Also good
as a hedge or ground cover (*see pp.138,
304*), or in a wildlife garden (*see p.494*).
The species is tougher.

ALSO RECOMMENDED: R. rugosa (see
p.178).

☼ ◐◖ ❀❀❀   **Deciduous shrub**
‡ 1m (3ft) ↔ 1.2m (4ft)

SAMBUCUS NIGRA
'Guincho Purple' ♥

This elder is an upright shrub with dark green leaves that turn black-purple then red in autumn. In early summer, musk-scented flowers are borne in flattened clusters, followed in late summer by small black berries. Elders are ideal to plant round the perimeter of a new garden because they establish quite quickly. They also tolerate hard pruning in winter. *S. nigra* and *S. racemosa* are particularly good for providing sanctuary in wildlife gardens (*see p.494*).

ALSO RECOMMENDED: S. racemosa *is hardier with some lovely foliage forms.*

☼ ◐ ◊ ❀❀❀   **Deciduous shrub**
↕↔ 6m (20ft)

SPIRAEA NIPPONICA
'Snowmound' ♥

This fast-growing and spreading, flowering shrub makes an invaluable contribution to any shrub border. It has arching, reddish green stems, which bear tidy clusters of densely packed, tiny white flowers in midsummer. The foliage is bright green when young and darkens with age. Cut back flowered stems in autumn.

ALSO RECOMMENDED: S. japonica *is bushy with pink or white flowers in late summer.*

☼ ◊ ❀❀❀   **Deciduous shrub**
↕↔ 1.2–2.5m (4–8ft)

THUJA OCCIDENTALIS 'Rheingold' ♀

This bushy and spreading, slow-growing conifer is valued for its golden foliage, which has a pink tinge when young and turns bronze in winter. Small cones are carried amid the sprays of apple-scented, scale-like leaves. Trim in spring and late summer. Also suitable for hedging (*see p.138*) and for large containers in sun (*see p.412*). Protect from cold winds when young.

ALSO RECOMMENDED: *'Holmstrup'* ♀ *makes a dense, cone-shaped shrub to 4m (12ft) tall; T. plicata 'Atrovirens'* ♀ *is the one to choose for a really tough hedge or screen.*

☼ ◊◐ ❄❄❄   **Evergreen shrub**
‡ 1–2m (3–6ft) ↔ 3–5m (10–15ft)

ULEX EUROPAEUS

Gorse is a very spiny shrub with rigid, dark green shoots. It is impenetrable with an upright to rounded shape. Yellow flowers appear sparsely through the year, but the main flush is seen in spring; brown-black seed pods follow. Suitable for a first defence against wind, especially in coastal areas, or as an intruder-proof hedge (*see p.138*). Tolerant of poor, sandy and acid soils (*see pp.38, 92*) and hot and dry, sunny sites (*see p.190*). Trim after flowering.

ALSO RECOMMENDED: *'Flore Pleno'* ♀ *has double flowers and no seed pods, thus is better for gardens.*

☼ ◊ ❄❄❄   **Evergreen shrub**
‡ 2.5m (8ft) ↔ 2m (6ft)

VIBURNUM RHYTIDOPHYLLUM

The leatherleaf viburnum is named for its characteristic foliage, which is dark green and deeply veined. It grows quickly and is decorated every spring with domed heads of creamy white flowers, which form at the ends of the branches. Planted in groups, shiny red, inedible berries often follow, and they darken to black with age. Keep pruning to a minimum. It will tolerate chalky soils (*see p.64*).

ALSO RECOMMENDED: V. lantana, *the wayfaring tree, is deciduous with white flowers followed by red, then black berries.*

☼ ◐ ◊◗ ❄ ❄ ❄　　**Evergreen shrub**
‡ 5m (15ft) ↔ 4m (12ft)

ASTER ALPINUS ♀

This spreading, low-growing aster suits the front of a border, a rock garden, or a wildlife area (*see p.494*). In the first half of summer, it bears a mass of daisy-like, purplish blue or pinkish purple flowerheads with deep yellow centres. These are borne on upright stems above the deep green leaves. Provide a mulch after cutting back in autumn. Also good for hot, dry sites (*see p.190*).

ALSO RECOMMENDED: *'Dunkle Schöne' (syn. 'Dark Beauty') has deep purple flowers; those of 'White Beauty' are white.*

☼ ◊ ❄ ❄ ❄　　**Perennial**
‡ 25cm (10in) ↔ 45cm (18in)

CORNUS CANADENSIS ♥

The creeping dogwood is a superb ground-cover plant for a shady shrub border or woodland garden (*see p.326*) below wind-breaking shrubs and trees. In late spring and early summer, flower clusters with prominent, shining white bracts appear above the oval, bright green leaves, and these are followed by glossy red berries. Also tolerant of acid soils (*see p.92*)

☀ ◐ ❀❀❀   **Perennial**

‡ 15cm (6in) ↔ indefinite

LATHYRUS LATIFOLIUS ♥

The everlasting or perennial pea is a clambering plant, which needs support. It bears pink-purple, pea-like flowers and is ideal for growing through shrubs or over a bank. Its blooms appear in clusters from summer to early autumn amid the blue-green foliage; the seeds are inedible. Cut back to ground level in spring and pinch out the shoot tips of new spring growth to encourage bushiness. It resents disturbance. Also good for shady walls (*see p.262*).

ALSO RECOMMENDED: *'Rosa Perle'* ♥ *has pink flowers; those of 'White Pearl'* ♥ *are white.*

☀☀ ◐ ❀❀❀   **Perennial**

‡ 2m (6ft) or more

LYSIMACHIA NUMMULARIA *'Aurea'* ♥

Golden creeping Jenny is a rampant and sprawling plant, which makes an excellent mat of golden yellow ground cover (*see pp.304, 326*). The bright yellow summer flowers further enhance the foliage colour. It tolerates light foot traffic and permanently moist soils (*see p.372*).

ALSO RECOMMENDED: L. nummularia *has green foliage.*

☼ ◐ ◊ ❋ ❋ ❋　　　**Perennial**
‡ 5cm (2in) ↔ indefinite

MOLINIA CAERULEA *SUBSP.* ARUNDINACEA

Purple moor grass forms tall tussocks of dark green leaves from which gently arching spikes of purple flowers appear for a long season from spring to autumn on tall, light brown stems. *M. caerulea* is one of the toughest ornamental grasses and forms a fine architectural plant (*see p.472*) for a border or a woodland garden. Clay and acid to neutral soils are tolerated (*see pp.12, 92*).

ALSO RECOMMENDED: *'Karl Foerster' is similar; 'Sky Racer' has golden foliage.*

☼ ◐ ◊ ❋ ❋ ❋　　　**Perennial**
‡ 1.5m (5ft) ↔ 40cm (16in)

PHALARIS ARUNDINACEA *VAR.* PICTA

Gardeners' garters is a clump-forming grass with narrow, white-striped, evergreen leaves. Tall plumes of pale green flowers that fade as they mature are borne on upright stems during the first months of summer. It is good as ground cover (*see p.304*) or in permanently moist soils (*see p.372*), but it can be invasive; lift and divide regularly to control spread. Cut back in early summer to encourage fresh growth.

ALSO RECOMMENDED: *'Feesey' is less invasive with purple-flushed flowers.*

☀ ◐ ◊ ❄ ❄ ❄　　　　　**Perennial**
↕ 1m (3ft) ↔ indefinite

VERONICA SPICATA *'Rotfuchs'*

A red-flowered speedwell that forms mats of hairy leaves. Its upright spikes of star-like flowers emerge from early to late summer. The bright flower display is ideal for a rock garden, or a mixed border; choose a site that is sheltered from winter wet. Most other speedwells have blue flowers. It is also good in coastal gardens (*see p.166*) and chalky soils (*see p.64*). Sometimes sold as Red Fox.

ALSO RECOMMENDED: *'Heidekind' is a silvery plant with dark pink flowers; subsp. incana ♀ is also silver with blue flowers.*

☀ ◊ ❄ ❄ ❄　　　　　**Perennial**
↕↔ 30cm (12in)

PLANTS FOR HEDGES

THE MAIN REASONS for planting a hedge are to define boundaries within and around the garden and to create a sense of security. By using evergreens, you can create privacy, too. There are also less obvious benefits. Perhaps the most important is wind protection. Unlike solid barriers, such as walls, which create turbulence on their leeward side, a hedge filters wind and slows it down over a distance of up to ten times the height of the hedge. When wind hits a solid barrier, it speeds up as it passes over, creating fast eddies on the far side.

Hedges are also used to keep children and pets safely inside a garden. Planting against a chain-link fence sunk into the ground prevents pets from squeezing through any gaps at the base. Hedges can also be used to frame views or screen unwanted ones, and – if prickly plants are chosen – to deter unwanted visitors. There are many types of plants to choose from, for both formal or informal styles, and all will need to be kept attractive and constrained in height and spread by regular clipping.

CHOOSING A HEDGE

A boundary hedge is one of the garden's most permanent and prominent features. Dark hedges like yew (see p 144), for example, form a quiet backcloth to brilliantly coloured borders, while flowering and fruiting hedges of mixed native species entice birds and other wildlife into the garden. Choose plants appropriate for your climate, site, and soil, and consider the desired height and spread. Fast-growing species achieve quick results, but they need frequent clipping to keep them in good shape once established. In the long term, slower-growing plants tend to make a denser, lower maintenance feature.

GROWING A HEDGE

Cultivate the site thoroughly before planting, to a width of 60–90cm (24–36in). Space plants 30–60cm (12–24in) apart, giving the more decorative species the wider spacing. Early training is vital to form a hedge that is dense at the base. Most evergreens and conifers need no initial pruning, allowing the leading shoots to grow to the desired height. For deciduous species, shorten weak shoots by two-thirds of their length, and strong shoots by up to one third to encourage bushy growth. Continue to prune until the desired size and shape is established, then clip regularly at the recommended time to keep growth dense and healthy. The hedge should be wider at the base than at the top.

MAINTAINING FERTILITY

Every time you clip a hedge, you remove some of its food reserves. If plants are to maintain good growth, they should be fed every few years with a balanced fertilizer in spring or after clipping. Also remember to keep the base of the hedge free from weeds, which will compete for water and nutrients. After weeding, mulch with organic matter in spring to suppress weeds and reduce moisture loss from the soil.

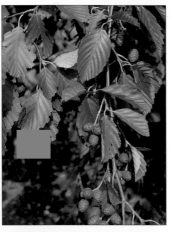

ALNUS INCANA

Grey alder is a large, broad, conical tree with oval, dark green leaves and brown male catkins in winter and early spring. Female catkins, borne on the same plant, develop into small, woody fruits resembling fir cones; these persist for some months. It makes a good boundary hedge for moist sites and should be trimmed in autumn. Tolerant of a wide range of soil conditions including wet sites (*see p.372*). As a tree, it can be grown as a windbreak (*see p.118*).

ALSO RECOMMENDED: *Unclipped, 'Aurea', reaches 10m (30ft) tall and has pale green foliage; A. glutinosa is similar.*

☼ ◊ ❋ ❋ ❋　　　　**Deciduous tree**
‡ 20m (70ft) ↔ 10m (30ft)

CARPINUS BETULUS ♛

Hornbeam makes an excellent medium to tall boundary hedge with a beech-like appearance, although the oval leaves are a duller green and sharply toothed. In autumn, the foliage turns to yellow then brown; if trimmed in late summer, a large proportion of the crisp dead leaves are retained throughout winter and maintain privacy. Also suitable for a stilted hedge. It does especially well on chalky soils (*see p.64*). Established hedges tolerate hard pruning if renovation is necessary.

ALSO RECOMMENDED: *C. caroliniana, the American hornbeam, is similar.*

☼ ◑ ◊ ❋ ❋ ❋　　　　**Deciduous tree**
‡ 25m (80ft) ↔ 20m (70ft)

CORYLUS MAXIMA *'Purpurea'* ♀

This purple-leaved selection of the filbert has larger leaves than the common hazel (*C. avellana*) and also produces edible nuts. Purplish yellow male catkins hang from the branches in early spring. It makes a multi-stemmed shrub. It can be grown as a formal or informal hedge, which should be lightly trimmed late each summer. Suitable as a boundary.

ALSO RECOMMENDED: *C.* avellana *and C.* maxima *have green leaves that turn yellow in autumn.*

☼ ◐ ○ ✷ ✷ ✷   **Deciduous tree**
‡ 6m (20ft) ↔ 5m (15ft)

CRATAEGUS MONOGYNA

The common hawthorn makes a fine and cost-effective hedge plant that thrives under all but the wettest soil conditions. Its deterrent thorns make it good as a boundary, and it withstands severe and coastal gales (*see pp.118, 166*). The glossy leaves are attractively lobed, and spectacular white flowers appear in late spring to be followed by glossy dark red haws. Trim hedges at any time but after flowering is best. Excellent for rural and wildlife gardens (*see p.494*).

ALSO RECOMMENDED: *C.* laevigata *is very similar.*

☼ ◐ ○◐ ✷ ✷ ✷   **Deciduous tree**
‡ 10m (30ft) ↔ 8m (25ft)

× CUPRESSOCYPARIS LEYLANDII *'Castlewellan'*

A slower growing, yellow-foliaged form of the notoriously vigorous Leyland cypress, which will grow very quickly to a great height if left untrimmed. It makes an excellent, dense hedge or windbreak (*see p.118*), which tolerates a wide range of soils and situations, but it should not be planted unless it will be regularly trimmed. It will take a great deal of moisture from the soil. Unsuitable for small gardens.

ALSO RECOMMENDED: × C. leylandii *is more vigorous with dark green foliage, and it should be planted with great caution.*

☼☀ ◊ ❄❄❄   **Evergreen tree**
‡ 25m (80ft) ↔ 5m (15ft)

CUPRESSUS MACROCARPA *'Goldcrest'* ♛

This golden yellow-leaved form of the Monterey cypress is a popular conifer for trimming into a formal hedge. It grows quickly and is useful for mild coastal gardens (*see p.166*). The lemon-scented foliage is best trimmed in late summer. Protect very young plants from frost.

ALSO RECOMMENDED: C. macrocarpa *has bright green foliage;* C. sempervirens *has dark grey-green foliage.*

☼ ◊ ❄❄❄   **Evergreen tree**
‡ 5m (15ft) ↔ 2.5m (8ft)

FAGUS SYLVATICA ♔

The common beech makes a fine, medium or tall hedge suitable for a boundary and is relatively inexpensive. The leaves are silky haired and pale green at first, becoming dark green and glossy, then golden yellow in autumn. Like hornbeam, beech hedges will retain their attractive, brown, crispy and dried out leaves through winter if trimmed in late summer. Suitable for chalky soils (*see p.64*)

ALSO RECOMMENDED: *Atropurpurea Group, the copper beech, has purple leaves.*

☼ ◐ ◊ ❀ ❀ ❀   **Deciduous tree**
↕ 25m (80ft) ↔ 15m (50ft)

LAURUS NOBILIS ♔

The bay laurel has glossy dark green, aromatic foliage. It is long-lived in fertile, moist soil and is a fine choice for hedging and topiary work. The flowers are insignificant. Trim to shape with secateurs during summer, taking care not to shred the large, oval leaves. Bay is susceptible to severe frost, so it is best planted in mild areas or as an internal hedge; specimen plants benefit from wall protection in exposed areas. Also useful for containers (*see pp.412, 448*).

ALSO RECOMMENDED: *'Aurea' ♔ has glossy golden yellow leaves.*

☼ ◐ ◊◊ ❀ ❀ ❀ *f*   **Evergreen tree**
↕ 12m (40ft) ↔ 10m (30ft)

TAXUS BACCATA ♥

Yew is a well-proven, coniferous hedge plant with small and linear, dark green leaves borne on green shoots. Small red fruits may appear at the end of summer, although these are usually clipped off. All parts of the plant are toxic except for the red, fleshy covering of the seeds. An excellent choice for topiary. It will grow in dry shade (*see p.216*) and tolerates chalky soils (*see p.64*). It is one of the few conifers that can be cut back hard and recover. Trim in late summer or early autumn.

ALSO RECOMMENDED: T. cuspidata, *the Japanese yew, is hardier.*

☀ ◑ ◐◊ ❀ ❀ ❀   **Evergreen tree**
‡ 6m (20ft) ↔ 4m (12ft)

THUJA PLICATA *'Stoneham Gold'* ♥

This short variety of western red cedar is amenable to trimming into a low, formal hedge. It has aromatic leaves borne in graceful, hanging sprays, which are bright gold when young, becoming dark green as they age. Grow in any deep, well-drained soil and provide shelter from winds, especially when young. Trimming should be done in spring or preferably late summer.

ALSO RECOMMENDED: T. occidentalis, T. plicata, *and its cultivar 'Atrovirens'* ♥ *are more vigorous and better for tall hedges.*

☀ ◐◊ ❀ ❀ ❀ *f*   **Evergreen tree**
‡↔ 2m (6ft)

TSUGA CANADENSIS

The eastern hemlock is a fast-growing conifer with glossy green, narrow, needle-like leaves arranged in two ranks along the branch tips. Like other hemlocks, it is tolerant of shade, but it will not grow well in alkaline soils. As a hedge, it suits formal trimming during summer. If allowed to grow, it forms a tall, conical tree.

ALSO RECOMMENDED: *'Jeddeloh' ℗ is very compact, to 1.5m (5ft) tall, with bright green foliage; T. heterophylla ℗, the western hemlock, will make a tall hedge.*

☼ ◐ ◊◗ ❋❋❋   **Evergreen tree**
↕ 25m (00ft) ↔ 10m (30ft)

ULMUS PARVIFOLIA

The Chinese elm has leathery, glossy green foliage that turns yellow or red in late autumn or early winter. It makes a reliable hedge plant, showing resistance to Dutch elm disease, and should be trimmed in autumn. Untrimmed specimens are of poor form and bear very small red flowers from late summer; green winged fruits follow in late autumn.

ALSO RECOMMENDED: U. pumila *also shows resistance to Dutch elm disease.*

☼ ◐ ◊ ❋❋❋   **Deciduous tree**
↕ 18m (60ft) ↔ 8–12m (25–40ft)

AUCUBA JAPONICA

Spotted laurel is a rounded bush, which, when planted closely, makes a natural hedge. The leaves are glossy deep green. If a male plant is grown among females, the latter bear bright red berries from late summer into winter. It tolerates most soils, is good in dry shade (*see p.216*), and suits containers (*see pp.412, 448*). Prune shoots with secateurs in spring to keep the hedge in shape.

ALSO RECOMMENDED: *'Crotonifolia'* ♀ *and 'Gold Dust' are both females with yellow-spotted leaves; 'Crassifolia' is a male with dark green foliage.*

☼☀ ◊◊ ❀❀❀ **Evergreen shrub**
‡↔ 3m (10ft)

BERBERIS JULIANAE

An evergreen berberis that can be grown as either a formal or informal hedge. The foliage is glossy deep green with strongly spined margins, and small yellow flowers decorate the bush in late spring; black berries follow. Its dense, very spiny growth makes it ideal as a perimeter hedge. Trim in summer; it can be pruned hard for containment.

ALSO RECOMMENDED: *B. darwinii* ♀ *has orange flowers; B. × stenophylla* ♀ *has deep yellow flowers; B. verruculosa* ♀ *is similar but about half the size.*

☼☀ ◊ ❀❀❀ **Evergreen shrub**
‡↔ 3m (10ft)

BERBERIS THUNBERGII
'Dart's Red Lady'

This dense and very spiny shrub makes an impenetrable boundary hedge with dramatic autumn colour when the very dark red-purple foliage turns to bright red. Small, pale yellow flowers are borne in spring, followed by glossy red berries. It can be grown as a formal or informal hedge. Trim after flowering.

ALSO RECOMMENDED: *'Aurea'* has bright yellow young foliage; *'Rose Glow'* ♥ has red-purple, white-flecked leaves and is more tolerant of shade.

☼ ☀ ◊ ✿ ✿ ✿   **Deciduous shrub**
‡ 1m (3ft) or more ↔ 2.5m (8ft)

BRACHYGLOTTIS *'Sunshine'* ♥

This low-growing shrub with white-hairy leaves is well-tried as a low-maintenance screen. It produces an abundance of bright yellow daisy flowers from summer to autumn and is a suitable choice for hedging in seaside gardens (*see p.166*). It grows well as an informal hedge, if trimmed in spring, but it can also be pruned back hard, preferably with secateurs, at the same time of year for a more formal look. It tolerates hot and dry, sunny sites (*see p.190*).

☼ ◊ ✿ ✿ ✿   **Evergreen shrub**
‡ 1.5m (5ft) ↔ 2m (6ft) or more

BUXUS SEMPERVIRENS �

Box is very tolerant of clipping, and well-proven as hedging, edging, and topiary. It has small, glossy green leaves, although many foliage forms exist. Trim hedges once a year in summer. Clip topiary twice a year from late spring to summer. Encourage new growth with a dressing of fertilizer and a surface mulch. Also good for chalky soils (*see p.64*) and in shady containers (*see p.448*).

ALSO RECOMMENDED: *'Marginata' is similar; 'Suffruticosa'* ♑ *is slow-growing and ideal for edging;* B. microphylla *also grows slowly and is best in partial shade.*

☼ ☀ ◊ ✻✻✻   **Evergreen shrub**
↕↔ 5m (15ft)

CHAMAECYPARIS PISIFERA *'Boulevard'* ♑

This blue-green form of the Sawara cypress is a large, coniferous shrub or tree with dense fans of aromatic, scale-like foliage. It is suitable for training into a formal hedge if trimmed closely from spring to autumn; do not cut into older wood as it will not resprout. It grows well on acid to neutral soils (*see p.92*), but tolerates chalk (*see p.64*).

ALSO RECOMMENDED: *'Filifera Aurea'* ♑ *has dark green foliage;* C. lawsoniana *'Green Hedger'* ♑ *and 'Pembury Blue'* ♑ *both make reliable hedges.*

☼ ◊ ✻✻✻ *f*   **Evergreen shrub**
↕ 10m (30ft) ↔ 5m (15ft)

COTONEASTER LACTEUS ♛

There are many cotoneasters suitable
for hedging, and this one is an
excellent choice. It has dense growth
with tough, dark green leaves, white-
felted on the undersides. White flowers
are followed by large clusters of brick
red berries, which persist into winter.
It benefits from light trimming in winter
to maintain a formal shape.

ALSO RECOMMENDED: *C. divaricatus*
is deciduous with pink flowers and good
autumn leaf colour; C. franchetii is similar
with pinkish flowers; C. frigidus (see p.218).

☼ ◐ ◊ ❋ ❋ ❋   **Evergreen shrub**
↕ ↔ 4m (12ft)

DEUTZIA LONGIFOLIA 'Veitchii' ♛

This spreading shrub with greyish green
foliage can be grown as an informal,
summer-flowering screen. The deep
lilac-pink, starry blooms are carried
during the first half of summer at the
ends of arching branches. Trim back
after flowering. Most deutzias
are also suitable for shrub borders.

ALSO RECOMMENDED: D. longifolia
has white flowers.

☼ ◐ ◊◊ ❋ ❋ ❋   **Deciduous shrub**
↕ 2m (6ft) ↔ 3m (10ft)

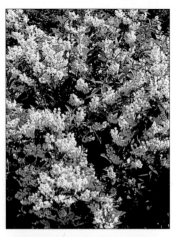

DEUTZIA SCABRA

An easily grown and well-tried, upright, summer-flowering, informal hedge plant. Dense, upright clusters of white, sometimes pink-tinged, honey-scented flowers are borne in the first half of summer amid the dark green foliage. The mature shoots have attractive peeling bark. Prune to thin out the older stems immediately after flowering.

ALSO RECOMMENDED: *'Pride of Rochester' has double flowers;* D. gracilis (see p.128) *makes a dwarf hedge, but it is less hardy.*

☼ ◐◊ ❀❀❀ *f*   **Deciduous shrub**
↕ 3m (10ft) ↔ 2m (6ft)

ESCALLONIA *'Langleyensis'* ♥

This small-leaved shrub produces abundant clusters of miniature, rose-pink flowers from early summer. It thrives in relatively mild, coastal sites (*see p.166*) as a formal or informal hedge, a windbreak, or in a shrub border. Clip annually for a formal shape in spring. In frost-prone areas inland, it is suitable for an internal hedge as long as the site is sheltered from cold winds. It can rob the surrounding soil of moisture and nutrients.

ALSO RECOMMENDED: *'Donard Seedling'* (see p.173); E. rubra *and its cultivars are excellent hedging subjects.*

☼ ◊ ❀❀❀   **Evergreen shrub**
↕ 2m (6ft) ↔ 3m (10ft)

EUONYMUS ALATUS ♥

The winged spindle makes a dense informal hedge with a spectacular display of foliage and fruits in autumn. At this time, the small, purple and red, poisonous fruits split to reveal orange seeds as the oval, deep green leaves turn to bright scarlet. The flowers are much less significant. Trim lightly after flowering. For the best autumn display, grow in full sun.

ALSO RECOMMENDED: *'Compactus' ♥ grows to 1m (3ft) tall*, E. fortunei *'Silver Queen' ♥ (see p.219) and* E. japonicus *are both evergreen.*

☼ ☀ ◊ ❀ ❀ ❀   **Deciduous shrub**
‡ 2m (6ft) ↔ 3m (10ft)

FORSYTHIA × INTERMEDIA 'Lynwood' ♥

This bushy and vigorous plant with finely toothed leaves makes a good flowering hedge of medium height. Its striking, bright yellow flowers bring the garden to life in early spring; they are good for cutting (*see p.524*) and emerge on the bare brown branches before the leaves. Prune or trim after flowering. A reliable shrub that looks good underplanted with spring bulbs. Flowering is less profuse in partial shade.

ALSO RECOMMENDED: *'Spectabilis' is similar;* F. suspensa *♥ (see p.267).*

☼ ☀ ◊ ❀ ❀ ❀   **Deciduous shrub**
‡ ↔ 3m (10ft)

FUCHSIA *'Riccartonii'* ♀

This popular fuchsia hybrid is an upright shrub with bronze-tinged, dark green foliage. It carries its characteristic red and purple flowers right through summer; they are small and delicate, and hang like earrings from the graceful branches. A beautiful low to medium hedge that is at its best in mild-climate areas, especially by the sea (*see p.166*), but it will usually regenerate from the base even after severe frosts. Prune back hard in spring.

ALSO RECOMMENDED: *'Genii'* ♀ *and 'Mrs Popple'* ♀ *are both shorter, about 1m (3ft) tall; F. magellanica (see p.174).*

☼ ☀ ◊◊ ❄❄   **Deciduous shrub**
↕ 2–3m (6–10ft) ↔ 1–2m (3–6ft)

GRISELINIA LITTORALIS *'Variegata'*

A dense and attractive shrub that carries glossy leaves variegated with irregular creamy white margins and grey-green streaks. It responds well to trimming with secateurs in spring, and it thrives in coastal gardens (*see p.166*) where it is one of the quickest hedges to establish. If necessary, cut back hard from time to time to reduce spread.

ALSO RECOMMENDED: *G. littoralis* ♀ *has plain, apple-green leaves and makes a smarter, more formal, medium to tall hedge.*

☼ ◊ ❄❄❄   **Evergreen shrub**
↕ 8m (25ft) ↔ 5m (15ft)

HEBE *'White Gem'*

A rounded, tidy shrub that is suitable for low hedging. It has densely packed, deep green leaves and is covered by short spikes of white flowers from early summer. In mild regions, all hebes are worth considering as hedges, doing best on moist soil in full sun; they are good in coastal sites (*see p.166*). They regrow well from older wood – useful when renovating. Each year, prune lightly in spring or after flowering.

ALSO RECOMMENDED: *H. albicans* ♥ (*see p.46*), *H. brachysiphon, and H. rakaiensis* ♥ *are similar;* H. salicifolia *forms a taller hedge, to 2m (6ft), with pale blue summer flowers.*

☼ ◐ ◊◊ ❉❉❉   **Evergreen shrub**
↕ 75–100cm (30–39in) ↔ 1m (3ft)

HIPPOPHAE RHAMNOIDES ♥

Sea buckthorn is a spiny shrub with long and narrow, silvery green leaves. It produces tiny yellow-green flowers in spring, with male and female flowers on separate plants; if both are grown, female plants bear small, bright orange berries in autumn, which remain on the bush in winter. Very tolerant of salt-laden winds and also suitable as a windbreak for coastal gardens (*see p.166*); it remains hardy inland. Trim shoots lightly in late summer to maintain a formal shape.

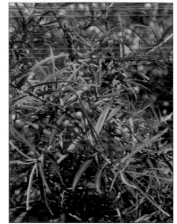

☼ ◊◊ ❉❉❉   **Deciduous shrub**
↕↔ 6m (20ft)

HYDRANGEA MACROPHYLLA
'Générale Vicomtesse de Vibraye' ♥

A rounded shrub with large, oval leaves that bears big, spherical heads of flowers from midsummer. Like most hydrangeas, the flower colour is influenced by soil acidity; on acid soils (*see p.92*) the flowers are pale blue, ranging through to pink on more chalky soils (*see p.64*). A good ornamental hedge of medium height that needs to be pruned in late autumn. Suitable for coastal sites.

ALSO RECOMMENDED: *'Mariesii Perfecta'* ♥ *(syn. 'Blue Wave') has flat flowerheads; 'Madame Emile Mouillère'* ♥ *has white flowers.*

☼☼ ◐ ◊ ❋❋❋   **Deciduous shrub**

‡ 2m (6ft) ↔ 2.5m (8ft)

ILEX AQUIFOLIUM
'Golden van Tol'

This female holly is fairly slow-growing, but it makes a very good, dense hedge. The yellow-margined leaves have few spines. In informal hedges, plant in an occasional male holly for the red berries, which attract birds (*see p.494*) and can persist into winter. Trim hedges regularly in summer. Also suitable for exposed and coastal sites (*see pp.118, 166*).

ALSO RECOMMENDED: I. × altaclerensis *and* I. aquifolium ♥ *make excellent medium to tall formal hedges with plain green leaves; both have many cultivars also suitable for hedging.*

☼☼ ◐ ◊ ❋❋   **Evergreen shrub**

‡ 4m (12ft) ↔ 3m (10ft)

LAVANDULA ANGUSTIFOLIA 'Hidcote' ♀

English lavender is compact with aromatic, greyish leaves. It is valued for its dense spikes of fragrant, dark purple midsummer flowers. Lavender does well on a wide range of soils and is ideal as a low hedge or edging. Trim below the flowering spikes in early spring, but do not cut into old wood. Replace hedges when they become woody and straggly. Good for hot and dry sites, as edging for paths and patios, and in wildlife gardens (*see pp.190, 348, 494*).

ALSO RECOMMENDED: *'Loddon Pink' has soft pink flowers;* L. dentata (*see p.200*).

☼ ◊ ❀ ❀ ❀ *f*   **Evergreen shrub**
‡ 60cm (24in) ↔ 75cm (30in)

LIGUSTRUM SINENSE

Privets are widely grown as medium to tall hedges. They are ideal for formal hedging and topiary if repeatedly clipped in summer. This one is tough, fast-growing, and good in well drained soil. Cut it hard in spring to renovate or restore its shape, and to keep the hedge within bounds. Clipping up to three or four times a year is necessary to keep a neat shape and to remove the white, unpleasantly scented flowers. It may shed its leaves in harsh winters.

ALSO RECOMMENDED: *'Variegatum' is best in full sun;* L. lucidum ♀ (*see p.194*); L. ovalifolium *and* L. vulgare *are similar.*

☼ ◑ ◊ ❀ ❀ ❀   **Evergreen shrub**
‡↔ 4m (12ft)

LONICERA NITIDA
'Baggesen's Gold' ♇

This form of shrubby honeysuckle is a foliage plant with tough shoots and small yellow-green leaves. *L. nitida* is green-leaved and also excellent for hedging. Both grow quickly and must be trimmed hard up to three or four times each summer to avoid a straggly appearance. This tolerance of clipping makes it good for simple topiary. If it becomes unkempt or bare at the base, cut it down to within 15cm (6in) of ground level.

ALSO RECOMMENDED: *'Silver Beauty' has cream-variegated leaves; 'Maigrün (syn. Maygreen) has pale then dark green leaves.*

☼ ☀ ◊ ❀ ❀ ❀   **Evergreen shrub**
‡ 3.5m (11ft) ↔ 3m (10ft)

PHILADELPHUS CORONARIUS
'Variegatus' ♇

This upright shrub makes a wonderful informal hedge on account of its small bunches of intensely fragrant, pure white, saucer-shaped flowers, which are borne in early summer. The leaves are an added attraction with broad white margins. Remove one in four flowered shoots at ground level after flowering.

ALSO RECOMMENDED: *'Aureus' ♇ has lime-green to golden leaves, which are better in part shade; P. 'Belle Etoile' ♇ and 'Manteau d'Hermine' ♇ (see p.74) are similar.*

☼ ☀ ◊ ❀ ❀ ❀ *f*   **Deciduous shrub**
‡ 2.5m (8ft) ↔ 2m (6ft)

PHYLLOSTACHYS BAMBUSOIDES *'Allgold'*

The giant timber bamboo has thick and shiny, rich golden yellow canes, which can be used to good effect as a screening hedge. The leaves are glossy and dark green with the occasional yellow stripe. Suitable for a woodland garden in dappled shade. It has very vigorous roots, so plant it in a trench lined with concrete slabs, or equivalent, to prevent unwanted spread.

ALSO RECOMMENDED: *P. aurea* ♥ *has brownish yellow canes and golden green leaves; P. nigra* ♥ *has dark green leaves and arching canes, which age to black.*

☼ ◐ ◊◊ ❄❄❄   **Evergreen bamboo**
‡ 3–0m (10–25ft) ↔ indefinite

PITTOSPORUM TENUIFOLIUM ♥

A fast-establishing, large shrub that is much valued for its tough, wavy-edged, glossy green leaves. Insignificant flowers appear from late spring. Trim hedges to shape in spring and again in autumn. It is especially good as a windbreak in mild coastal gardens (*see p.166*), but it may not survive in areas with harsh winters. The foliage is good for cutting (*see p.524*).

ALSO RECOMMENDED: *'Irene Paterson'* ♥ *has white-speckled leaves; 'Silver Queen'* ♥ *has greyish leaves with irregular white margins.*

☼ ◐ ◊◊ ❄❄   **Evergreen shrub**
‡ 4–10m (12–30ft) ↔ 2–5m (6–15ft)

PONCIRUS TRIFOLIATA

Japanese bitter orange is a formidable, thorny shrub with thick green stems armed with sharp spines. The leaves, made up of three leaflets, are dark green, turning yellow in autumn. Fragrant, cup-shaped white flowers are produced in spring with a second flush in autumn. Orange-like, inedible fruits follow. Cut young plants hard to help them establish bushy growth, trimming more established hedges twice in summer.

☼ ◊ ❀❀❀ *f*   **Deciduous shrub**
↕↔ 5m (15ft)

PRUNUS LUSITANICA *'Variegata'*

This variegated form of Portugal laurel makes a relatively slow-growing but dense hedge with slender spikes of small, fragrant white flowers in early summer. The oval, glossy dark green leaves are narrowly margined with white. Purple berries appear later in the season. Prune to shape with secateurs in spring.

ALSO RECOMMENDED: P. laurocerasus ♥ *and* P. lusitanica ♥ *have plain dark green leaves and both make excellent hedges and windbreaks.*

☼ ◊◊ ❀❀❀   **Evergreen shrub**
↕↔ to 20m (70ft)

PRUNUS SPINOSA *'Purpurea'*

Blackthorn is a dense and thorny shrub, which makes a good protective barrier and tolerates hard trimming at any time. This red-leaved variety bears small pink flowers in early spring, before the leaves appear, followed by very dark blue fruits – sloes. These persist until winter, during which time the foliage has turned purple and fallen.

ALSO RECOMMENDED: *P. spinosa makes a good stockproof hedge for a rural garden, it has green leaves and white flowers; P. cerasifera also has green leaves and white flowers, followed by plum-like, red or yellow fruits.*

☼ ◐◗ ❄❄❄　　　　**Deciduous shrub**
↕ 5m (15ft) ↔ 4m (12ft)

PYRACANTHA *'Golden Charmer'*

Spiny pyracanthas are excellent as a vandal-resistant barrier hedge and attract nesting birds (*see p.494*). This one has golden yellow autumn berries. Profuse clusters of tiny white flowers appear in early summer against the glossy dark green leaves. Also suitable for clay soils (*see p.12*) and for covering sunny or shady walls (*see pp.262, 280*). Trim in early summer.

ALSO RECOMMENDED: *'Mohave'* (see p.20); *'Soleil d'Or'* (see p.270); *'Teton' has yellow-orange berries; 'Watereri'* ♀ (see p.500).

☼◐ ◐ ◗ ❄❄❄　　　**Evergreen shrub**
↕↔ 3m (10ft)

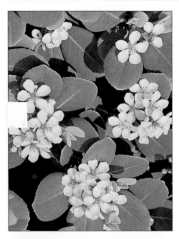

Rhaphiolepis umbellata ♀

A dense and slow-growing shrub suitable for hedging in mild areas only. It has tough and toothed, large, deep green leaves. It bears tight clusters of white flowers, which are sometimes tinted pink, in early summer, and they are followed by bronze-black fruits. Trim to shape after flowering. In cold areas, it is best planted as a specimen in an enclosed garden, protected border, or against a sunny wall (*see p.280*).

ALSO RECOMMENDED: *R. × delacourii grows to 2m (6ft) tall with pink flowers, and is also for mild areas only.*

☼ ◊◊ ❄❄   **Evergreen shrub**
↕↔ 1.5m (5ft)

Rhododendron *Blue Diamond Group*

Many evergreen rhododendrons make spectacular hedges on moist but well-drained, acid to neutral soils (*see p.92*). There is an immense range available, and it may be worth seeking the advice of a nearby nursery for a cultivar that grows well in your locality. The Blue Diamond Group rhododendrons have a compact habit and produce trusses of violet-blue flowers amid the relatively small leaves in late spring.

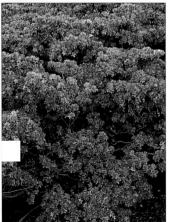

ALSO RECOMMENDED: *R. ponticum is a vigorous species, to 8m (25ft) tall, with large leaves and mauve-lilac flowers in late spring.*

☼ ◊◊ ❄❄❄   **Evergreen shrub**
↕↔ 1.5m (5ft)

RIBES SANGUINEUM 'Brocklebankii' ♥

This upright shrub is valued for its bright yellow-green, hairy leaves, and it makes an attractive informal hedge within the garden. A fine display of deep pink flowers in hanging clusters appears through spring. Flowering currants establish well on most soils; the majority do well in full sun, but this slow-growing form displays better foliage in partial shade, including dry shade (see p.216). Trim after flowering.

ALSO RECOMMENDED: *'King Edward VII' and 'Pulborough Scarlet'* ♥ *have dark red flowers; R. alpinum 'Aureum'* (see p.222).

☼ ☀ ◊ ❄ ❄ ❄   **Deciduous shrub**
↕↔ 1.2m (4ft)

ROSA *Chinatown* ♥

Many roses succeed as hedges, and this one is particularly vigorous, easy to grow, and resistant to disease. Clusters of large and rounded, double yellow flowers are borne from summer to autumn amid the glossy dark green leaves. They are suffused with pink and carry a heavy scent. Prune this shrub rose lightly when dormant, removing some of the oldest stems at the base each year.

ALSO RECOMMENDED: *R. × alba 'Alba Maxima'* ♥ *has sweetly fragrant, double white flowers; R. rubiginosa* ♥ *has single pink flowers; R. rugosa* (see p.178).

☼ ◊◊ ❄ ❄ ❄ *f*   **Deciduous shrub**
↕ 1.2m (4ft) ↔ 1m (3ft)

ROSMARINUS OFFICINALIS

The upright shoots of rosemary bear narrow and aromatic leaves, useful in cooking. Pale blue flowers appear along the stems in spring and autumn. Informal hedges require minimal pruning; it can be grown formally if clipped once or twice during summer. Otherwise, grow as an edging or in a herb garden. Also suitable for coastal and hot, dry sites (*see pp.166, 190*), and containers (*see p.412*). Best in mild or protected gardens as a decorative internal low hedge.

ALSO RECOMMENDED: *'Miss Jessopp's Upright'* ♥ *is strong-growing and upright; the flowers of 'Tuscan Blue' are dark blue.*

☼ ◊ ❀ ❀ *f*   **Evergreen shrub**
↕↔ 1.5m (5ft)

SALIX PURPUREA

The purple osier is notable for its arching, red-tinged shoots and dark bluish green leaves. Slender, silvery green catkins are seen in early spring before the first leaves. Willows will succeed on wet sites (*see p.372*), but never plant them close to drains or building foundations. Cut back to the base each year when dormant for a temporary screen, or allow to grow up as a tall windbreak (*see p.118*).

ALSO RECOMMENDED: S. alba *and its coloured-stem forms, like subsp.* vitellina ♥ *and 'Britzensis'* ♥ *(see p.375), are tall and vigorous, good as an external shelter hedges.*

☼ ◊ ❀ ❀ ❀   **Deciduous shrub**
↕↔ 5m (15ft)

SANTOLINA CHAMAECYPARISSUS 'Lemon Queen'

This compact cotton lavender makes a low hedging subject, suitable for border edging, with slender, aromatic, greyish leaves. It bears small, button-like, lemon-yellow flowers from midsummer. Trim after flowering to remove straggly shoots, or before flowering for the best foliage, and cut back hard every few years in spring to rejuvenate. Also suits coastal and hot, dry sites (*see pp.166, 190*).

ALSO RECOMMENDED: *S. chamaecyparissus* ♡ *is just as good; 'Pretty Carol' and 'Small-Ness' are even more compact; S. pinnata 'Sulphurea' (see p.50)*

☼ ◊ ❀❀❀   **Evergreen shrub**
↕↔ 60cm (24in)

SEMIARUNDINARIA FASTUOSA ♡

Narihira bamboo is a very tall and upright bamboo, forming dense clumps of smooth green canes with plum-purple and brown stripes. The glossy foliage is borne mostly at the top of the canes. Where a tall screen is required, this bamboo makes an interesting option. Suitable for woodland gardens. It has vigorous roots, so plant it in a trench lined with concrete slabs, or equivalent, to limit its spread.

☼☀ ◊◊ ❀❀❀   **Evergreen bamboo**
↕ 7m (22ft) ↔ 2m (6ft) or more

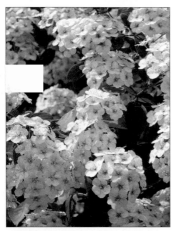

SPIRAEA × VANHOUTTEI ♛

This spiraea makes a bushy informal flowering hedge with dark green foliage. It bears masses of white flowers along the arching shoots during early summer. After flowering, prune the flowered shoots back to a strong bud, and cut a number of older shoots out at ground level. It suits clay soils and exposed sites (*see pp.12, 118*).

ALSO RECOMMENDED: S. *'Arguta'*, *bridal wreath*, *is similar*; S. japonica *'Little Princess'* (*see p.20*); S. nipponica *'Snowmound'* ♛ (*see p.132*).

☼ ◐◑ ❀❀❀   **Deciduous shrub**
‡ 2m (6ft) ↔ 1.5m (5ft)

SYMPHORICARPOS ALBUS *VAR.* LAEVIGATUS

Snowberry is a densely upright, robust shrub with rounded, dark green leaves. It carries tiny pink flowers in summer, followed by eye-catching, pure white berries in autumn. It grows on a wide range of sites but can be invasive, so it is best as a boundary, where it could be included in a mixed hedge. Prune selectively to the base in early spring. Tolerant of urban pollution, exposed sites, and dry shade (*see pp.118, 216*).

ALSO RECOMMENDED: S. × doorenbosii *'White Hedge'* (*see p.224*).

☼☀ ◐ ❀❀❀   **Evergreen shrub**
‡↔ 2m (6ft)

SYRINGA PUBESCENS
'Superba' ♀

A bushy lilac with glossy dark green
leaves that makes a fine informal
flowering hedge. Its red-green young
shoots ripen through summer to bear
conical clusters of fragrant, purple-lilac
flowers the following spring. Minimal
pruning is required, after flowering if
necessary, it tolerates the occasional
hard prune to rejuvenate. Tolerant of
clay and chalky soils (*see pp.12, 64*).

ALSO RECOMMENDED: *'Miss Kim'* ♀ *is
much more compact, to 2m (6ft) tall; S ×
persica* ♀ (*see p.75*).

☼ ◊◊ ❄❄❄ *f*　　**Deciduous shrub**
↕↔ 6m (20ft)

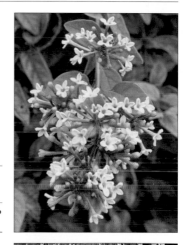

TEUCRIUM FRUTICANS

Tree germander is suitable as a low
evergreen hedge for mild areas or
edging within a sheltered garden. The
greyish green, aromatic leaves are held
on white woolly shoots, and if it is not
trimmed in spring, light blue flowers
emerge in summer. Prune in spring
or trim to a formal shape in summer.

ALSO RECOMMENDED: T. × lucidrys *(syn.
T. chamaedrys) wall germander, is hardier
with dark green foliage and red, pink,
purple, or white flowers, but better as
border edging as it grows to just 60cm
(24in) tall;* T. polium (*see p.352*).

☼ ◊ ❄❄ *f*　　**Evergreen shrub**
↕ 60–100cm (24–39in) ↔ 4m (12ft)

PLANTS FOR COASTAL GARDENS

O<small>N A SUNNY</small> summer's day, with a balmy breeze blowing offshore, it is easy to view the prospect of gardening on the coast with rose-tinted spectacles. In reality, many of the plants that grow there must be exceptionally tough to survive. Not only do they often have to contend with severe winter gales, but also with the quantities of scorching salt spray that high winds bring with them, often several miles inland. Nevertheless, the proximity to the sea reduces

the incidence of hard frosts, and light levels and humidity are often higher than inland. In coastal gardens, many slightly tender plants will thrive when they might otherwise fail in gardens even a few miles from the protective effects of the sea.

WINDBREAKS FOR SHELTER
The advantages of coastal gardens are magnified if the garden is surrounded by a windbreak to alleviate the worst effects of salt-laden winds (*see also Plants for Exposed*

Sites, p.118). On the coast, it is common to see even notably tough trees like hawthorn (*see pp.123, 141*) and sycamore wind-trained into gnarled and stunted – though picturesque – versions of their inland counterparts. Planted as windbreaks, even a relatively low, wind-filtering barrier can provide shelter in its lee for five times its height. With such shelter in place, the range of plants that can be grown is greatly extended.

In a new garden, creating or planting a windbreak should be the first priority. A fence of woven hazel or willow hurdles, for example, will give temporary shelter until a living windbreak grows tall enough to be useful. A driftwood fence can be effective, as it is attractive and perfectly appropriate to its setting. Although a wall is better than nothing, solid barriers should be avoided as they create problems; instead of filtering the wind, the wind surmounts them and creates turbulence on the leeward side, which can cause damage.

MARITIME PLANTS

Many of the plants that succeed in coastal sites have special adaptations that enable them to shrug off the worst effects of wind and salt spray. Plants like *Eucalyptus gunnii* (*see p.168*), *Olearia nummularifolia* (*see p.176*), or *Phillyrea latifolia* (*see p.177*) have tough, leathery leaves, while others, like *Anaphalis margaritacea* (*see p.182*), have leaves with a protective covering of fine hair, which limits salt damage and helps conserve moisture. Some, like ground-hugging *Alchemilla conjuncta* (*see p.181*), survive simply by keeping their heads down. You can also be sure that any plant with "littoralis" (meaning "of the shore") or "maritima" in its name – *Griselinia littoralis* (*see p.152*) and *Crambe maritima* (*see p.183*), for example – will be in its element in a coastal garden. Listings of suitable plants often seem limited, but by observing the native flora and the successes in other people's plots, you will find many more, often surprising, survivors.

ACER PSEUDOPLATANUS *'Simon-Louis Frères'*

This compact sycamore is a slow-growing, round-headed tree with five-lobed leaves, which are pink when young, later turning creamy green with white speckles. It tolerates a range of soils, including clay and chalk (*see pp.12, 64*), urban pollution, and exposure (*see p.118*). Remove dead or badly placed growth from late autumn to midwinter only.

ALSO RECOMMENDED: *'Brilliantissimum'* ♀ *has bright pink young leaves, which age to green; 'Leopoldii'* ♀ *has pink young leaves, later green with yellow and pink speckles.*

☀ ☀ ◊ ❄ ❄ ❄   **Deciduous tree**
‡↔ 10m (30ft)

EUCALYPTUS GUNNII ♀

The cider gum is a tall tree with peeling, pale green, grey and pink bark, and narrow grey-green leaves. If hard-pruned, it produces attractive, rounded, blue-grey juvenile leaves, which are good for cutting (*see p.524*). Grow in neutral to acid soil (*see p.92*) with shelter from cold, dry winds, as it is not reliably hardy. Cut all shoots back to the base or to a short trunk annually in early spring for the best foliage effect.

ALSO RECOMMENDED: E. coccifera ♀, E. globulus ♀, *and* E. pauciflora *subsp.* niphophila ♀ *all respond well to pruning to maintain distinctive juvenile foliage.*

☀ ◊ ❄ ❄ ❄   **Evergreen tree**
‡ 10–25m (30–80ft) ↔ 15m (50ft)

POPULUS ALBA

This tough tree makes an excellent windbreak in exposed, coastal gardens (*see p.118*); the silvery white undersides of its lobed, dark green leaves are revealed as the branches move in the breeze. It tolerates urban pollution and any but waterlogged soils, including dry or chalky ones (*see pp.64, 190*). It needs little pruning, in winter if necessary. Site at least 30m (100ft) away from drains or foundations.

ALSO RECOMMENDED: *f.* pyramidalis *is pyramidal in shape;* 'Raket' *is smaller and narrowly conical;* 'Richardii' ♥ *is smaller with golden leaves.*

☼ ◑◐ ❄ ❄ ❄   **Deciduous tree**

‡ 20–40m (70–130ft) ↔ 15m (50ft)

ARGYRANTHEMUM FRUTESCENS

A close relative of the chrysanthemum, this small bush of divided, bright green leaves gives an abundant display of white and yellow, daisy-like flowers all year round. Cultivated varieties extend the colour range to deep pink and yellow. In frost-prone areas, it can either be grown as temporary plant for a summer border or grown in a container (*see p.412*), which should be moved under cover in winter.

ALSO RECOMMENDED: *A.* 'Cornish Gold' ♥ *has yellow flowers;* 'Mary Wootton' *has pale pink flowers;* 'Vancouver' ♥ (*see p.416*).

☼ ◑ ❄   **Evergreen shrub**

‡↔ 70cm (28in)

ATRIPLEX HALIMUS

Tree purslane is a dense and bushy foliage plant with leathery grey leaves; it is very tolerant of coastal or dry and windy situations (*see p.118*), and it is a good choice for a hedge in such areas (*see p.138*). The flowers are of little ornamental value. Lightly trim damaged shoots in early spring. It can also be grown as part of a shrub border.

☼ ◊ ❀ ❀　　　　　**Evergreen shrub**
‡ 2m (6ft) ↔ 2.5m (8ft)

BUPLEURUM FRUTICOSUM

This spreading, slender-stemmed shrub has leathery, deep sea-green leaves and forms a dense mound that is clothed in rounded heads of tiny yellow flowers from midsummer to autumn. It is good ground cover (*see p.304*) for a shrub or mixed border, and in cold areas, grows best against a warm, sunny wall (*see p.280*). It tolerates urban pollution. Prune to remove badly placed or damaged shoots in mid- to late spring.

☼ ◊ ❀ ❀ ❀　　　　**Evergreen shrub**
‡ 2m (6ft) ↔ 2.5m (8ft)

CASSINIA LEPTOPHYLLA
SUBSP. VAUVILLIERSII

This rounded bush has small, leathery, dark green leaves arranged on white, sticky-hairy shoots. The honey-scented white flowers of midsummer attract bees (*see p.494*). Grow in a shrub border; it associates well with heathers. Trim after flowering to keep the shape compact.

ALSO RECOMMENDED: *The stem and leaf undersides of var. albida are silvery white; subsp. fulvida has yellow stems and dark green leaves, which are yellow beneath.*

☼ ◊ ❀ ❀ ❀   **Evergreen shrub**
↕ ↔ 3m (10ft)

CHAMAEROPS HUMILIS ♥

The dwarf fan palm is a bushy plant, as it produces several shaggy, fibrous stems from the base. They are topped by broad, blue- or grey-green, fan-like leaves with spiny stalks. Unspectacular flowers appear from spring. It will only survive short spells just below freezing, so in areas prone to heavy frosts, it is best grown in a cool greenhouse or in a sunny container outdoors, which can be moved under cover in winter (*see p.412*).

☼ ☀ ◊ ❀   **Evergreen palm**
↕ 2–3m (6–10ft) ↔ 1–2m (3–6ft)

COLUTEA ARBORESCENS

The bladder senna is a very tough specimen for a shrub or mixed border. It tolerates urban pollution, poor soils, and exposure (*see p.118*), and thrives on dry, sunny banks (*see p.190*). During summer, above divided, bright green foliage, it bears clusters of yellow, pea-like flowers followed by translucent, bladder-like seed pods. It may be cut back hard in winter or early spring to renovate or keep compact.

ALSO RECOMMENDED: *C. × media has orange-brown flowers; C. orientalis has copper-red flowers marked with yellow.*

☼ ◊ ❁ ❁ ❁   **Deciduous shrub**
↕↔ 3m (10ft)

COROKIA × VIRGATA

This upright bush with glossy dark green foliage is treasured for its small and star-shaped, fragrant yellow flowers and colourful orange or yellow fruits. The blooms are displayed in late spring, and the berries colour in autumn. Grow as a specimen plant in a sheltered shrub border or against a warm wall (*see p.280*). Trim after flowering.

ALSO RECOMMENDED: *'Bronze King' has bronze-tinted foliage; 'Yellow Wonder' is vigorous with golden fruit; C. cotoneaster is more tangled, like a cotoneaster.*

☼ ◊ ❁ ❁ ❁ *f*   **Evergreen shrub**
↕↔ 3m (10ft)

ERICA ARBOREA *VAR.* ALPINA ♀

The tree heath is much larger than other heathers, and this form is shorter than the species. Its upright branches are covered by small, honey-scented white flowers from late winter to spring, and the needle-like leaves are dark green. This specimen plant suits sandy soils (*see p.38*), and unlike most heathers, both chalky and acid soils (*see pp.64, 92*). Cut young plants back hard in early spring to promote bushiness.

ALSO RECOMMENDED: *Alben's Gold* ♀ *has golden foliage, but rarely flowers;* 'Estrella Gold' ♀ *bears white flowers above lime-green foliage, tipped bright yellow.*

☼ ◊ ❀ ❀ ❀ *f*   **Evergreen shrub**
‡ 2m (6ft) ↔ 85cm (34in)

ESCALLONIA *'Donard Seedling'*

A compact shrub that carries dense, glossy dark green foliage. During the first half of summer, a profusion of small, pink-flushed white flowers appear on the arching branches. Suitable for a shrub border, it can also be grown as a hedge (*see p.138*) or as a windbreak (*see p.118*). Trim after flowering.

ALSO RECOMMENDED: *'C.F. Ball' carries red flowers; 'Iveyi'* ♀ *bears fragrant, pure white flowers; 'Langleyensis'* ♀ *(see p.150).*

☼ ◊ ❀ ❀ ❀   **Evergreen shrub**
‡↔ 2.5m (8ft)

EUPHORBIA MELLIFERA

Honey spurge is an attractive shrub with long and narrow, gentle green leaves. It is named for its rounded, honey-scented brown flowerheads, which appear at the ends of the stout shoots in late spring. It forms a grand feature plant, which also suits sandy soils and hot, dry sites (*see p.38, 190*). Choose a sheltered position. Prune after flowering, if necessary, but wear gloves as the sap irritates skin.

ALSO RECOMMENDED: E. characias (see p.482); E. × martinii ♀ *grows 1m (3ft) tall and wide with spikes of yellow-green, red-eyed flowers from spring to summer.*

☼ ◊ ❋ ❋　　　　　**Evergreen shrub**
‡ 2m (6ft) or more ↔ 2.5m (8ft)

FUCHSIA MAGELLANICA

A hardy fuchsia with a profusion of hanging, red and purple flowers through summer. Useful in mixed borders or against a warm wall (*see p.280*). Provide a winter mulch. In cold areas, the top growth will perish; cut back in spring, and it will regrow. Good for informal hedging in frost-free areas (*see p.138*).

ALSO RECOMMENDED: *var.* molinae (syn. 'Alba') *has very pale pink flowers;* F. 'Riccartonii' ♀ (see p.152).

☼ ☀ ◊◊ ❋ ❋　　　　　**Deciduous shrub**
‡↔ 3m (10ft)

HEBE *'Autumn Glory'*

A small bush that carries a long display of dark purple-blue flowers from midsummer to early winter. They are small and borne in short, dense spikes. The bronze shoots are covered with dark green, red-margined leaves. Useful as hedging and as ground cover (*see p.138, 304*) if sheltered from cold winds. No regular pruning is necessary.

ALSO RECOMMENDED: *'Great Orme'* ♀ (see p.503); H. cupressoides *'Boughton Dome'* ♀ (see p.46).

☼ ◑ ◊◊ ❋ ❋ **Evergreen shrub**
‡ 60cm (24in) ↔ 90cm (36in)

JUNIPERUS COMMUNIS *'Compressa'* ♀

This slow-growing, dwarf form of the common juniper forms a dense shrub shaped like a tiny tree. It is suitable for a rock garden with its deep to blue-green, aromatic sprays of foliage. Small berries remain on the plant for three years, ripening from green through cloudy blue to black. Little or no pruning is needed.

ALSO RECOMMENDED: *'Hibernica'* ♀ is *more vigorous, reaching 3–5m (10–15ft); 'Sentinel' is vigorous, to 1.5m (5ft).*

☼ ◑ ◊ ❋❋❋ *f* **Evergreen shrub**
‡ 80cm (32in) ↔ 45cm (18in)

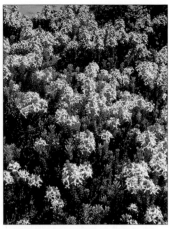

OLEARIA NUMMULARIIFOLIA

Daisy bush is suitable for shrub borders and informal hedging (*see p.138*). Its golden shoots are clothed in small, round, dark green leaves that are white-to yellow-woolly beneath. The fragrant, white and yellow, daisy-like flowers of midsummer attract bees (*see p.494*). It thrives in most fertile, well-drained soils, including chalky ones (*see p.64*). Shelter from cold, dry winds and trim in spring; it tolerates hard pruning.

ALSO RECOMMENDED: O. × haastii *is similar;* O. macrodonta ♀ *is taller with spiny, holly-like leaves.*

☼ ◊ ❄❄❄ ƒ   **Evergreen shrub**
↕↔ 2m (6ft)

OZOTHAMNUS ROSMARINIFOLIUS

A compact shrub with rosemary-like, dark green foliage that is woolly beneath. Fragrant white flowerheads emerge from red buds in early summer, and they are carried in dense clusters at the ends of the upright stems. Suitable for a shrub border. Trim after flowering.

ALSO RECOMMENDED: *'Silver Jubilee'* ♀ *has silvery grey foliage;* O. ledifolius ♀ *has scented leaves and yellow-green shoots.*

☼ ◊ ❄❄❄ ƒ   **Evergreen shrub**
↕ 2–3m (6–10ft) ↔ 1.5m (5ft)

PHILLYREA LATIFOLIA

A dense, rounded shrub or small tree with oval, glossy dark green leaves that makes a fine backdrop in a shrub or mixed border. It is also useful for informal hedging (*see p.138*); trim after flowering. In late spring, inconspicuous but very fragrant, greenish white flowers appear, followed by spherical, blue-black fruits. In cold areas, it flowers and fruits more freely against a warm, sunny wall (*see p.280*). Suitable for most well-drained soils. Also sold as *P. media*.

ALSO RECOMMENDED: *P. angustifolia is shorter, to 3m (10ft), with narrower leaves.*

:☼: ◐ ◊ ❋ ❋ ❋ *f*   **Evergreen shrub**
‡↔ 9m (28ft)

ROMNEYA COULTERI 'White Cloud'

This vigorous tree poppy is actually a small shrub with grey-green foliage and showy white flowers through summer. They are large and sweetly fragrant with a prominent boss of golden yellow stamens. Choose a site sheltered from strong, cold winds, and provide a deep, dry mulch in winter; frost may damage the top growth. Grow in a border or against a sunny wall (*see p.280*). It spreads quickly once established.

ALSO RECOMMENDED: *The spread of* R. coulteri ♀ *is less vigorous.*

:☼: ◊ ❋ ❋ *f*   **Deciduous shrub**
‡ 1–2.5m (3–8ft) ↔ indefinite

ROSA RUGOSA

The Japanese or hedgehog rose is a dense and very prickly shrub, which can make a vigorous flowering hedge for cold, exposed areas (*see pp.118, 138*). It is decorative for most of the year, starting with the fragrant, deep pink, yellow-centred flowers from summer to autumn. Tomato-like, orange-red hips follow, and in autumn, the leathery, dark green leaves fade to deep yellow. Also suitable for wild areas (*see p.494*). Trim after flowering.

ALSO RECOMMENDED: *'Alba'* ♥ *has white flowers; those of 'Rubra'* ♥ *are purple-red.*

☼ ◐◊ ❀❀❀ *f*   **Deciduous shrub**
‡↔ 1–2.5m (3–8ft)

SALIX RETICULATA ♥

This diminutive willow has trailing branches bearing rounded, deeply veined, dark green leaves, which are white-hairy beneath. In spring, it bears upright, pink-tipped catkins, and these are a useful source of pollen for emerging bumblebees (*see p.494*). Excellent ground cover (*see p.304*) for the front of a border or rock garden. It tolerates poor soils.

ALSO RECOMMENDED: *S. retusa has glossy mid-green leaves and grey catkins; S. serpyllifolia has small, dark green leaves and silky grey-green catkins.*

☼ ◊ ❀❀❀   **Deciduous shrub**
‡ 8–10cm (3–4in) ↔ 30cm (12in)

SPARTIUM JUNCEUM ♛

Spanish broom is an upright bush with dark blue-green shoots, which are almost leafless. Masses of fragrant, pea-like, rich yellow flowers appear at the stem tips from early summer to autumn, followed by brown seed pods. Particularly useful on poor, sandy soils, in hot, dry shrub borders, and against warm, sunny walls (*see pp.38, 190, 280*). Cut young plants back by half in spring to promote bushiness.

☼ ◊◊ ❄ ❄ ❄ *f*   **Evergreen shrub**
↕↔ 3m (10ft)

TAMARIX RAMOSISSIMA *'Pink Cascade'*

Tamarisks are versatile shrubs bearing billowing branches of feathery foliage. This one produces clouds of pink flowers in summer and autumn, adding to the general effect. It is also suitable as a windbreak hedge in coastal areas (*see pp.118, 138*) but requires shelter from cold, drying winds if grown inland. It can become straggly if not hard pruned regularly to shape in early spring. Tolerant of sandy soils (*see p.39*).

ALSO RECOMMENDED: T. tetrandra ♛ *is shorter and flowers in spring.*

☼ ◊ ❄ ❄ ❄   **Deciduous shrub**
↕ 60cm (24in) ↔ 1m (3ft)

BILLARDIERA LONGIFLORA 🏆

The climbing blueberry is a twining climber with narrow, deep green leaves grown for its pendulous, cream flowers in summer and big, deep purple-blue, edible berries, which follow. It tolerates poor, neutral to acid soils (*see p.92*). Choose a sheltered site, training its wiry stems against a warm or cold wall (*see pp.262, 280*), or over a structure or into nearby shrubs. If the top growth is damaged, it may regenerate from its robust root system.

☼ ◐ ◊◊ ❊❊   **Climber**
↕ 2–3m (6–10ft)

TROPAEOLUM TUBEROSUM 'Ken Aslet' 🏆

A colourful climber with bright orange-yellow flowers amid lobed, greyish green leaves from midsummer to autumn. It is ideal for growing over a fence, trellis, or non-flowering shrub, and it will trail over a bank or dry wall. In cold areas, lift the tubers and store them in a frost-free place until the following spring; otherwise, cover them with a dry winter mulch.

ALSO RECOMMENDED: T. majus *'Alaska'* (see p.447).

☼ ◊◊ ❊   **Climber**
↕ 2–4m (6–12ft)

AGAPANTHUS *'Blue Giant'*

One of the hardiest of the African blue lilies, this is a useful plant in the late summer border. It is vigorous and forms clumps of strap-shaped leaves. From the centre of these clumps emerge stout, upright stems, which bear round heads of bell-shaped, bright violet-blue flowers in the second half of summer. Also good for large containers in sun (*see p.412*).

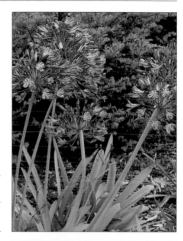

ALSO RECOMMENDED: *'Bressingham White'* has pure white flowers.

☼ ◐ ❈ ❈ ❈   **Perennial**

↕ 1.2m (4ft) ↔ 60cm (24in)

ALCHEMILLA CONJUNCTA

This low, spreading plant is valued for its rounded, lobed leaves, which are finely silver-hairy beneath, and for the summer-long display of tiny, yellow-green flowers; deadhead these to prevent self-seeding and for cut flowers (*see p.524*). It makes restrained ground cover (*see p.304*) in a rock garden or at the front of a border. It also tolerates clay and chalky soils (*see pp.12, 64*).

ALSO RECOMMENDED: A. alpina (see p.354); A. mollis ♀ (see p.311).

☼◐ ◐◐ ❈ ❈ ❈   **Perennial**

↕ 40cm (16in) ↔ 30cm (12in)

ANAPHALIS MARGARITACEA

A clump-forming, spreading plant that is valued in herbaceous borders for its mounds of grey-green, white-woolly leaves; it makes good ground cover (*see p.304*). White flowerheads appear in midsummer and autumn; they are excellent for cuttting and drying (*see p.524*), and they are favoured by bees and butterflies (*see p.494*).

ALSO RECOMMENDED: *A. triplinervis* ♀ *has narrower leaves; 'Sommerschnee'* ♀ *has brilliant white bracts.*

☼ ◑ ◊ ❀ ❀ ❀   **Perennial**
↕↔ 60cm (24in)

ARMERIA MARITIMA
'Vindictive' ♀

Sea thrift is a natural seaside plant, and it forms mounds of vary narrow, dark green leaves. This variety has fluffy, hemispherical heads of dark crimson flowers borne on the tips of stiff stems from late spring to summer. It is ideal for a rock garden, trough, or border front. It tolerates sandy soils and hot, dry sites (*see p.38, 190*), and the flowers attract bees and butterflies (*see p.494*).

ALSO RECOMMENDED: *'Alba' has small white flowerheads; 'Bloodstone' has dark, blood-red flowerheads.*

☼ ◊ ❀ ❀ ❀   **Perennial**
↕ 20cm (8in) ↔ 30cm (12in)

CICHORIUM INTYBUS

Chicory is a clump-forming plant with lance-shaped, basal leaves and leafy stems bearing clear blue, dandelion-like flowerheads in summer; they are attractive to bees (*see p.494*). Grow in a herbaceous or wildflower border, or in a herb garden, or naturalize in grass. It tolerates chalky soils (*see p.64*). Removed spent flowerheads to prevent excessive self-seeding.

ALSO RECOMMENDED: *f. album has white flowers; 'Roseum' has pink flowers.*

☼ ◊ ❀❀❀   **Perennial**
‡ 1.2m (4ft) ↔ 60cm (24in)

CRAMBE MARITIMA

Sea kale forms a sculptural mound of twisted, irregularly cut leaves, which are waxy blue-green. They die back after flowering, so associate with other, more arching plants to disguise any gaps. Stout shoots arise in early summer, bearing dense heads of small, honey-scented white flowers, which attract bees (*see p.494*). It tolerates poor, gravelly or sandy soils, and hot, dry sites (*see pp.38, 190*). Grow in a herbaceous border, or as a specimen in a gravel garden.

ALSO RECOMMENDED: *C. cordifolia* ♥ *is much taller* (see p.53).

☼ ◊ ❀❀❀   **Perennial**
‡ 75cm (30in) ↔ 60cm (24in)

CROCOSMIA *'Lucifer'* ♛

This dazzling, deep red crocosmia makes a fabulous midsummer display when its spikes of upward-facing flowers arch over the fans of bright green leaves. It is particularly effective at the edge of a shrub border or by a pool, and the flowers are good for cutting (*see p.524*). 'Lucifer' is a little hardier than other crocosmias. Plant corms in spring and cover with a dry mulch in winter.

ALSO RECOMMENDED: C. × crocosmiiflora *'Emily McKenzie' has bright orange flowers; 'Lady Hamilton' has golden flowers; 'Star of the East'* (see p.533).

☼ ◐ ◊◊ ❀❀❀   **Perennial corm**
‡ 1–1.2m (3–4ft) ↔ 8cm (3in)

DRABA MOLLISSIMA

This compact, rosette-forming evergreen forms a dense hummock of hairy and narrow, grey-green leaves. They are almost obscured in late spring by the tiny, cross-shaped, bright yellow flowers. It must have gritty, very sharply drained soil and will grow in shingle or gravel, or on top of a dry stone wall (*see p.348*). Where winters are wet, it is best to confine it to an alpine house; outdoors, protect it with an open-ended cloche.

ALSO RECOMMENDED: D. aizoides *forms slightly larger mounds of bristly, dark green leaves;* D. dedeana *has white flowers, flushed pale violet at the base.*

☼ ◊ ❀❀❀   **Perennial**
‡ 8cm (3in) ↔ 20cm (8in)

EPILOBIUM GLABELLUM

This semi-evergreen plant forms low mats of small and bronzed, dark green leaves. In summer, it bears branching spikes of creamy white or pink flowers. A good ground cover plant (*see pp.304, 326*) for a rock garden or damp, shady border (*see p.238*). It tolerates sun where soils are reliably moist, preferring some midday shade.

ALSO RECOMMENDED: *'Sulphureum' has pale yellow flowers;* E. crassum *has pink-veined white flowers.*

:☼: :☼: ◊◊ ❄ ❄ ❄   **Perennial**
↕↔ 20cm (8in)

ERIGERON *'Quakeress'*

This robust fleabane is popular for its lavish displays of daisy-like flowers during the first months of summer. They are pinkish white with yellow centres and appear in clusters above the clumps of greyish green leaves. Good in a border, and the flowers are ideal for cutting if picked when fully open (*see p.524*).

ALSO RECOMMENDED: *'Dunkelste Aller' (syn. 'Darkest of All') has dark violet, yellow-centred flowers.*

:☼: ◊ ❄ ❄ ❄   **Perennial**
↕ 60cm (24in) ↔ 45cm (18in)

ERYNGIUM × OLIVERIANUM ♀

This sea holly is a striking plant when naturalized in shingle or in a sunny, well-drained herbaceous border. In summer and autumn, branched flower stems rise above a mound of leathery, blue-green leaves, which are armed with triangular teeth. The flower stems, which cut and dry well (*see p.524*), are topped by rounded flowerheads with ruffs of spiny, grey-blue bracts. It tolerates sandy and chalky soils (*see pp.38, 64*) and hot, dry sites (*see p.190*).

ALSO RECOMMENDED: *E. alpinum* ♀ *has steel-blue flowerheads; E. giganteum* ♀ (see p.535); *E. × tripartitum* ♀ (see p.56).

☼ ◊ ❀ ❀ ❀   **Perennial**
‡ 90cm (36in) ↔ 45cm (18in)

GLACIUM FLAVUM

The yellow-flowered horned poppy produces a rosette of divided, blue-green leaves and branched stems of poppy-like flowers in summer. The long, horned seed pods that follow are decorative if cut and dried (*see p.524*). Good for a sunny border or gravel garden; it tolerates hot, dry sites (*see p.190*). Often grown as a biennial that may self-seed once established.

ALSO RECOMMENDED: *G. corniculatum has red flowers with a black spot at the base; G. grandiflorum has orange or crimson flowers.*

☼ ◊ ❀ ❀ ❀   **Perennial**
‡ 30–90cm (12–36in) ↔ 45cm (18in)

KNIPHOFIA *'Percy's Pride'*

This red hot poker bears tall, dense spikes of creamy yellow flowers in late summer and autumn above clumps of arching, grass-like leaves. The flowers attract bees (*see p.494*) and are good for cutting (*see p.524*). Grow in a herbaceous border and mulch in the first winter and whenever frosty weather threatens. Divide overcrowded clumps in late spring. It also tolerates sandy and chalky soils (*see pp.38, 64*).

ALSO RECOMMENDED: *'Bees' Sunset'* ♀ *has orange flowers; 'Green Jade' has pale green flowers; 'Little Maid'* ♀ *is smaller with ivory flowers; 'Royal Standard'* ♀ *(see p.536).*

:☼: ◐: ◊◊ ❀❀❀   **Perennial**
‡ 1.2m (4ft) ↔ 60cm (24in)

LYCHNIS FLOS-JOVIS

Flower of Jove forms a mat of grey-green leaves and a long display of pink, white, or scarlet flowers in summer. It is good for ground cover on hot, dry sites (*see pp.304, 190*) and ideal for a gravel garden or the front of a mixed or herbaceous border. It thrives in most well-drained sites, including poor, sandy, chalky, or acid soils (*see pp.38, 64, 92*). The seeds may self-sow.

ALSO RECOMMENDED: *'Hort's Variety' is compact with clear pink flowers; 'Nana' is even more compact; L. coronaria is taller (see p.318).*

:☼: ◊ ❀❀❀   **Perennial**
‡ 20–60cm (8–24in) ↔ 45cm (18in)

OSTEOSPERMUM JUCUNDUM ♥

Also known as *O. barberae*, this perennial is famous for its striking, mauve-pink, daisy-like flowers, which give a long display from late spring until autumn. The greyish leaves form clumps at ground level. A good-value plant for wall crevices or at the front a border. Remove dead flowers to promote flowering.

ALSO RECOMMENDED: *'Blackthorn Seedling'* ♥ *has dark purple flowers.*

☼ ◊ ❀ ❀ ❀   **Perennial**
‡ 10–50cm (4–20in) ↔ 50–100cm (20–39in)

PHORMIUM *'Dazzler'*

New Zealand flax is a striking plant with its spiky clumps of tough, evergreen leaves. In this variety, they are bronze with pink, red, and orange stripes. Dusky red flowers appear in summer on stout, upright spikes, which form seedheads for winter ornament. Choose a sheltered site and mulch deeply in autumn. It also makes a good architectural plant (*see p.472*).

ALSO RECOMMENDED: *'Yellow Wave'* ♥ *has yellow-green leaves;* P. tenax *Purpureum Group* ♥ *have deep copper-purple foliage.*

☼ ◊◊ ❀ ❀   **Perennial**
‡ 1m (3ft) ↔ 1.2m (4ft)

PHYSOSTEGIA VIRGINIANA *'Variegata'*

This variegated form of obedient plant forms an erect clump of long, narrow green leaves margined with white. The hooded, magenta-pink flowers, which appear from summer to autumn, are good for cutting (*see p.524*); they remain in a new position if moved on the stalks, hence the common name. Grow in a mixed or herbaceous border

ALSO RECOMMENDED: *P. virginiana has deep purple to bright lilac-pink flowers; 'Summer Snow' ♀ has white flowers; 'Vivid' ♀ has bright purple-pink flowers.*

☼ ◐ ◊ ❋ ❋ ❋   **Perennial**

‡ 1.2m (4ft) ↔ 60cm (24in)

POTENTILLA *'Gibson's Scarlet'* ♀

An attractive flowering perennial that should be used to add a bit of bold colour to a herbaceous border or rock garden in summer. It forms dense clumps of soft green, strawberry-like foliage, which is covered by very bright scarlet flowers in succession from early to late summer. Tolerant of hot and dry, sunny sites (*see p.190*).

ALSO RECOMMENDED: *'Monsieur Rouillard' has deep red flowers with yellow marks; 'William Rollison' ♀ has orange-red, semi-double flowers.*

☼ ◊ ❋ ❋ ❋   **Perennial**

‡ 45cm (18in) ↔ 60cm (24in)

PLANTS FOR HOT & DRY SITES

YOU MAY FIND that there are several sites in your garden where conditions get very hot and dry during summer. For example, steeply sloping, sunny banks where drainage is rapid, the base of sunny walls that are in a rain shadow, and virtually any sunny site protected from the worst effects of wind and rain by surrounding walls and fences where the soil is very sandy, stony, or shallow and chalky. All of these can prove difficult for any plant that is not adapted to cope. Hot, dry sites present a challenge to plant survival, not only because of the obvious lack of moisture needed for growth, but also because the leaves of many plants – even some committed sun-lovers – scorch in very hot sun, particularly where the water supply is short or unreliable.

PRACTICAL PLANTS

Many of the plants that will thrive in these conditions have characteristic features, which are as beautiful as they are practical. Grey- or silver-leaved plants like *Senecio viravira* (*see p.202*), and blue-leaved ones like *Leymus arenarius* (*see p.211*), are clothed in fine hair, or have a waxy surface bloom to deflect the burning rays of the sun. Plants with fragrant foliage, such as lavender (*see pp.47, 155, 200*), rosemary (*see p.162*), hyssop (*see p.504*), and *Phlomis purpurea* (*see p.201*), exude volatile oils, which form a haze around the plant and act as an aromatic "sun-block". Then there are succulent species of low, neat habit, like sempervivums (*see pp.323, 370, 438*) and sedums (*see pp.323, 369, 370, 520*), whose thick, fleshy leaves store water to prevent dehydration. Many bulbs, like *Amaryllis belladonna* (*see p.204*), demand a summer baking to enable their bulbs to ripen and so they can flower freely.

IMPROVING THE SITE

In exceptionally dry, free-draining soils, it is a good idea to incorporate some organic matter to aid water retention. Leafmould is an excellent form of organic matter for such sites, because it does not add too many nutrients; garden compost is also good. However, many heat- and sun-loving plants perform best on soils that are not too fertile. High nutrient levels can produce soft, sappy growth that is more susceptible to damage by cold and wet in winter, and it may induce plants to produce leafy growth at the expense of flowers.

A mulch of water-worn pebbles or gravel enhances this style of planting, forming beautiful tonal and textural contrasts, especially with grey-leaved plants. It also helps to suppress weeds and conserve soil moisture. As the soil water evaporates, it condenses on the cooler undersides of the stones and is recycled back into the soil. At the same time, it keeps the roots cool and the vulnerable neck of the plants clear of accumulated moisture, which helps prevent rotting. Crushed shells, a by-product of the shellfish industry, have a similar effect, and they are perfectly in keeping if used in coastal gardens.

CLADRASTIS KENTUKEA ♥

Also sold as *C. lutea*, yellow wood has a spreading crown of large, divided, light green leaves, which turn yellow in autumn. Hanging clusters of pea-like, scented white flowers emerge in early summer. A fine specimen tree for larger gardens, needing shelter from strong winds as the wood is brittle, and it flowers best in areas with long, hot summers. Prune after flowering or in winter when dormant to remove dead or badly placed growth only. It tolerates chalky soils (*see p.64*).

☼ ◊ ❀❀❀ *f*   **Deciduous tree**
‡ 12m (40ft) ↔ 10m (30ft)

EUCALYPTUS DALRYMPLEANA ♥

The columnar crown and creamy white bark of the mountain gum make it a fine specimen for larger gardens. It can be pruned hard each year to produce oval, blue-green juvenile leaves, which are valued by flower arrangers (*see p.524*); if unpruned, it bears narrow, bright green adult leaves. Choose a site sheltered from cold, dry winds. It tolerates chalky soils and coastal conditions (*see pp.64, 166*).

ALSO RECOMMENDED: E. parvifolia ♥ *has grey and white bark*; E. perriniana *has grey, yellow, green, and bronze bark.*

☼ ◊ ❀❀   **Evergreen tree**
‡ 20m (70ft) ↔ 8m (25ft)

FICUS CARICA

The common fig, with its spreading
crown of large, lobed leaves, makes
a very ornamental specimen. It is most
productive of ripe, juicy figs if grown
in a sheltered, sunny site with the
roots confined in not-to-fertile soil; they
are good in large tubs (*see p.412*). In
areas with cool summers, train against
a south-facing wall (*see p.280*) with
protection from severe winter frosts.
Remove wayward or crossing shoots
in late winter.

ALSO RECOMMENDED: *'Brown Turkey'* ♀,
'Brunswick', and *'White Marseilles'* are
the best cultivars for cooler climates.

☼ ◊ ❋ ❋ ❋   **Deciduous tree**
‡ 3m (10ft) ↔ 4m (12ft)

GLEDITSIA TRIACANTHOS
'Rubylace'

The divided leaves of this elegant,
broadly conical tree are rich bronze-red
on emergence, turning later to bronze
green. A useful specimen for large
gardens, tolerant of urban pollution,
with a canopy that is light enough to
permit underplanting. Prune from late
summer to midwinter only to cut out
diseased, damaged, or dead wood.

ALSO RECOMMENDED: G. triacanthos *has
dark green leaves that yellow in autumn;*
'Sunburst' ♀, *to 12m (40ft), has gold foliage.*

☼ ◊ ❋ ❋ ❋   **Deciduous tree**
‡ 30m (100ft) ↔ 20m (70ft)

LIGUSTRUM LUCIDUM ♀

Chinese privet is a small and conical, shrubby tree with lustrous, dark green leaves and open clusters of white flowers in late summer and autumn; in warm summers, they are followed by egg-shaped, blue-black fruits. A shapely specimen, good for a shrub border or for hedging (*see p.138*). Remove unwanted growth in winter; clip hedges twice in summer.

ALSO RECOMMENDED: *'Excelsum Superbum' ♀ has yellow-margined leaves; 'Tricolor' has green and greyish leaves with white margins, pink-flushed when young.*

☼ ☀ ◊ ❄ ❄ ❄   **Evergreen tree**
‡↔ 10m (30ft)

MAACKIA AMURENSIS

An open, spreading tree with a crown of divided, dark green leaves. In late summer, it produces upright clusters of white flowers, flushed palest slate-blue; it flowers even when young. An unusual specimen that is most easily grown as a multi-stemmed tree. Remove dead, diseased, or damaged growth between autumn and early spring. Grow in neutral to acid soil (*see p.92*).

ALSO RECOMMENDED: M. chinensis *has bluish young shoots and young leaves, which have a dense silver-silky down in spring.*

☼ ◊ ❄ ❄ ❄   **Deciduous tree**
‡ 15m (50ft) ↔ 10m (30ft)

PINUS ARISTATA

One of the most distinctive of small, slow-growing pines, the branches of the bristle cone pine are densely clothed in bright green, needle-like leaves, speckled with white resin. Egg-shaped brown cones have a bristle-like prickle on each scale, hence the common name. It tolerates exposed sites (*see p.118*) and grows best on neutral to acid soils (*see p.92*). An attractive specimen that may be used as a low windbreak. It rarely needs pruning.

ALSO RECOMMENDED: P. mugo *is smaller, with dense, dark green leaves;* P. pumila *'Glauca' ♀ has grey-blue leaves.*

☼ ◊ ❀ ❀ ❀   **Evergreen tree**
‡ 10m (30ft) ↔ 6m (20ft)

QUERCUS CANARIENSIS ♀

Algerian oak is a vigorous, broadly columnar tree with rugged black bark; it makes a fine specimen for larger gardens. Lobed, glossy bright green leaves turn yellow before falling, often remaining on the tree until midwinter. In autumn, acorns are borne in scaly cups. It tolerates clay and chalky soils (*see pp.12, 64*) and is best in deep, fertile soils. Little pruning is needed; cut out crossing or badly placed shoots in winter, if necessary.

ALSO RECOMMENDED: Q. ilex ♀, *the holm oak, is evergreen;* Q. macranthera *has large, deeply lobed leaves.*

☼ ◊ ❀ ❀ ❀   **Deciduous tree**
‡ 30m (100ft) ↔ 15m (50ft)

SOPHORA JAPONICA ♛

The Japanese pagoda tree forms a wide-spreading crown of finely divided, fresh green leaves, which turn yellow in autumn. At maturity, it bears hanging clusters of pea-like white flowers; they are profuse if summers are long and hot. Grow as a specimen tree and prune in winter only to remove dead, diseased, or damaged wood.

ALSO RECOMMENDED: *'Regent' starts to flower at a relatively young age.*

☀ ◊ ❀ ❀ ❀   **Deciduous tree**
‡ 30m (100ft) ↔ 20m (70ft)

UMBELLULARIA CALIFORNICA

California laurel is a low-branching and rounded tree with aromatic, glossy bright green leaves. It flowers most freely in a warm site with shelter from cold, dry winds; the waxy, creamy green flowers appear in late winter and early spring, followed by egg-shaped purple berries. An attractive specimen for any well-drained soil. Keep pruning to a minimum, since the aromatic oils released when the branches are cut can cause severe headaches. For mild, sheltered gardens only, as it is not reliably hardy to frost.

☀ ◊ ❀ ❀ ❀   **Evergreen tree**
‡ 18m (60ft) ↔ 12m (40ft)

CARAGANA ARBORESCENS
'Nana'

This dwarf pea tree has a dense and
curiously twisted habit with divided,
bright green leaves in congested
clusters on thorny stems. The pea-like
yellow flowers appear in late spring.
Plant in a shrub border or as a low
hedge (*see p.138*). It needs little or
no pruning, but if necessary, prune
in winter. It will grow in exposed
positions (*see p.118*).

ALSO RECOMMENDED: *C. arborescens
reaches 6m (20ft) tall; 'Lorbergii'* ♀ *is also
tall, with narrower leaflets; 'Pendula' is
a small and weeping form.*

☼ ◊ ❋ ❋ ❋   **Deciduous shrub**
‡ 1.5m (5ft) ↔ 1m (3ft)

CISTUS × ARGENTEUS
'Peggy Sammons' ♀

A rounded, bushy rock rose with grey
green leaves bearing profuse clusters of
pale purplish pink flowers in summer.
It suits sunny banks or borders, or large
rock gardens, and it will also grow in a
container (*see p.412*). Tolerant of chalky
soils and coastal gardens (*see pp.64,
166*). To keep it compact, trim lightly
after flowering. In areas with cold, wet
winters, grow at the base of a warm,
sunny wall (*see p.290*).

ALSO RECOMMENDED: *C. × purpureus* ♀
*has deep pink flowers; C. 'Silver Pink' has
silvery pink flowers with paler centres.*

☼ ◊ ❋ ❋   **Evergreen shrub**
‡↔ 1m (3ft)

CYTISUS MULTIFLORUS ♡

Portuguese broom is an upright shrub with narrow, simple or divided, dark green leaves. It bears clusters of pea-like white flowers along the length of the stems in spring and early summer. Grow in a shrub or mixed border in well-drained soil. Trim lightly after flowering; do not cut into old wood. Tolerates poor, acid soils and coastal conditions (*see pp.92, 166*).

ALSO RECOMMENDED: *C. 'Hollandia' ♡ has cream and dark pink flowers; 'Zeelandia' ♡ has cream and lilac-pink flowers – both reach 1.5m (5ft) tall by as much across.*

☼ ◊ ❀❀❀   **Deciduous shrub**
‡ 3m (10ft) ↔ 2.5m (8ft)

ERINACEA ANTHYLLIS ♡

Hedgehog broom forms a slow-growing mound of hard, spine-tipped, intricately branched stems clothed in small, dark green, divided leaves. In late spring and early summer, the bush is covered in pea-like, violet-blue flowers. This long-lived plant is ideal for a rock garden or scree bed, or for clothing a dry, sunny bank; it needs gritty, very well-drained soil. It is especially effective when cascading over the edge of a raised bed.

☼ ◊ ❀❀❀   **Evergreen shrub**
‡ 30cm (12in) ↔ 1m (3ft)

EURYOPS PECTINATUS ♀

This vigorous shrub with upright shoots
bears daisy-like, bright yellow flowers
against the deeply divided, grey-hairy
foliage from early summer and into
autumn. Keep it free from frost and
water sparingly in winter, and it may
continue to flower. Trim lightly after
flowering. In a container in sun (*see
p.412*), it can be moved under glass
during winter.

ALSO RECOMMENDED: E. acraeus ♀ *is
hardier* (see p.350).

☼ ◊ ❄   **Evergreen shrub**
↔ 1m (3ft)

GENISTA AETNENSIS ♀

From midsummer, the weeping, rush-
like branches of the Mount Etna broom
are wreathed in fragrant, bright yellow
pea flowers. A fine, large specimen
shrub or tree for a sunny bank or lawn.
It does best in poor, light and sandy,
well-drained soils (*see p.38*). Too much
pruning can spoil its weeping habit,
and do not cut into old wood. A good
architectural plant that will also grow
in coastal gardens (*see pp.166, 472*).

ALSO RECOMMENDED. G. hispanica *is
spiny* (see p.307); G. lydia ♀ *is short,
to 60cm (24in) tall, with yellow early
summer flowers.*

☼ ◊ ❄ ❄ *f*   **Deciduous shrub**
↔ 8m (25ft)

GREVILLEA *'Canberra Gem'* ♥

A spreading bush with narrow, spine-tipped, dark green leaves that are silky-hairy beneath. The waxy, pinkish red flowers appear between late winter and late summer in spidery clusters. Grow in well-drained, neutral to acid soil (*see p.92*); it tolerates sandy sites (*see p.38*). In cold areas, grow against a warm, sheltered wall (*see p.280*). Prune out dead or damaged wood in spring.

ALSO RECOMMENDED: G. rosmarinifolia ♥ *has cream, pink, or red flowers.* G. juniperina f. sulphurea ♥ *has yellow flowers.*

☼ ◊ ❀ ❀   **Evergreen shrub**
‡ 2–4m (6–12ft) ↔ 2–5m (6–15ft)

LAVANDULA DENTATA

This lavender is a fragrant shrub with dense spikes of mauve-blue, late summer flowers topped by purple bracts. It is suitable for most garden positions, and the soft, greyish foliage makes it particularly useful as an edging plant to lessen the harsh lines of paving (*see pp.138, 348*). Also good for cutting and drying (*see p.524*) or in sunny containers (*see p.412*). Grow against a warm wall in areas with harsh winters (*see p.280*).

ALSO RECOMMENDED: L. lanata ♥ *is shorter with dark purple flowers;* L. viridis *has white flowers and pale green leaves.*

☼ ◊ ❀ ❀ *f*   **Evergreen shrub**
‡ 1m (3ft) ↔ 1.5m (5ft)

PHLOMIS PURPUREA

This compact and upright shrub with leathery leaves on white-woolly shoots bears showy whorls of hooded, purple to pink flowers in summer. It is very effective when massed in a sunny border; in cold areas, it thrives best against a warm, sunny wall (*see p.280*). Tolerant of poor, sandy and chalky soils (*see pp.38, 64*). Prune back any weak or leggy stems in spring.

ALSO RECOMMENDED: *P. fruticosa* ♥ (*see p.49*); *P. cashmeriana has yellowish, grey-green leaves and lilac-purple flowers.*

☼ ◊ ❀❀   **Evergreen shrub**
‡↔ 60cm (24in)

RUTA GRAVEOLENS
Jackman's Blue ♥

Common rue forms a rounded bush of aromatic and decorative, greyish blue-green, lace-like leaves. Clusters of cup-shaped, yellow-green flowers are borne in summer; they are good for cutting (*see p.524*), although contact with the foliage may irritate skin. Ideal for a herbaceous or mixed border. Prune in spring or after flowering.

ALSO RECOMMENDED: *R. graveolens is less compact and the foliage less blue.*

☼◐ ◊ ❀❀❀   **Evergreen shrub**
‡↔ 60cm (24in)

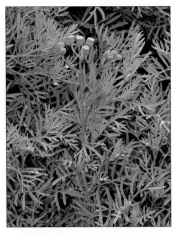

SENECIO VIRAVIRA ♥

The finely divided leaves of this shrubby plant lend striking foliage contrasts in a sunny border; they are bright, velvety, and silver-white. Many gardeners prefer to remove the pale yellow flowerheads, which appear from summer to autumn; trim lightly in early spring for the best foliage effects. It must have well-drained soil and a warm, sheltered site.

ALSO RECOMMENDED: S. cineraria *'Silver Dust'* ♥ (see p.425).

☼ ◊ ❀❀　　　　　**Evergreen shrub**
‡ 60cm (24in) ↔ 1m (3ft)

XANTHOCERAS SORBIFOLIUM ♥

The stout, upright shoots of this bush bear finely divided, glossy dark green leaves, which emerge in spring with the upright spikes of star-shaped white flowers. These are borne most profusely where summers are long and hot; training on a warm, sunny wall (*see p.280*) is recommended for cool areas. Good as a free-standing specimen, or in a shrub border in mild climates. Prune in winter only to remove damaged or badly placed shoots.

☼ ◊ ❀❀❀　　　　**Deciduous shrub**
‡ 4m (12ft) ↔ 3m (10ft)

ALLIUM CERNUUM

The nodding onion is one of many alliums that thrive in hot, dry sites. In summer, above a sheaf of narrow leaves, stiff stems appear bearing clusters of bell-shaped, mid- to deep pink flowers. Grouped together in a mixed or herbaceous border, they look especially lovely alongside grey-leaved plants. Plant bulbs in sandy soil in autumn (*see p.38*). Tolerant of coastal conditions (*see p.166*).

ALSO RECOMMENDED: A. caeruleum ♥ *has round heads of bright blue, starry flowers;* A. carinatum *subsp.* pulchellum ♥ *has rich purple, bell-shaped flowers.*

☼ ◊ ❀ ❀ ❀   **Perennial bulb**
‡ 30–60cm (12–24in) ↔ 5cm (2in)

ALLIUM FLAVUM ♥

This yellow-flowered onion, ideal for the front of a border, produces its loosely rounded flowerheads atop upright stems in summer. As they open, the flowers bend down towards the narrow, greyish leaves below. Plant bulbs in autumn, preferably in sandy soil (*see p.38*). Tolerant of coastal conditions (*see p.166*).

ALSO RECOMMENDED: A. karataviense ♥ *has round heads of pale pink flowers in summer;* A. schoenoprasum (see p.510).

☼ ◊ ❀ ❀ ❀   **Perennial bulb**
‡ 10–35cm (4–14in) ↔ 5cm (2in)

AMARYLLIS BELLADONNA

The fragrant, funnel-shaped pink blooms of this autumn-flowering plant appear atop stout, purple-flushed stems before the strap-shaped leaves. In warm areas, it is suitable for herbaceous or mixed borders; otherwise, it will grow at the base of a warm, sunny wall (*see p.280*). Provide some protection from frost and excessive rain in winter and when the plant is dormant. Plant bulbs just below the soil surface in late spring or summer in well-drained soil.

☼ ◊ ❀❀ *f*   **Perennial bulb**
‡ 75cm (30in) ↔ 10cm (4in)

AMSONIA ORIENTALIS ♥

The upright stems of this clump-forming plant carry willow-like, grey-green leaves. In early and midsummer, delicate clusters of many tiny, starry, violet-blue flowers appear. Grow at the front of a mixed or herbaceous border in well-drained soil; incorporating well-rotted organic matter to improve moisture retention will aid growth in very dry soils.

ALSO RECOMMENDED: A. tabernaemontana *is taller with pale blue flowers.*

☼ ◊ ❀❀❀   **Perennial**
‡ 50cm (20in) ↔ 30cm (12in)

ANTHEMIS TINCTORIA
'E.C. Buxton'

Pretty, lemon-yellow flowerheads are
produced throughout summer above a
mound of divided, greyish green leaves
on this clumping perennial. The flowers
are attractive to bees and good for
cutting (*see pp.494, 524*). Grow in a
mixed or herbaceous border; it also
thrives in sandy and chalky soils (*see
pp.38, 64*), and coastal sites (*see p.166*).
Cut back hard after flowering to
increase longevity.

ALSO RECOMMENDED: *'Kelwayi' has
clear yellow flowerheads; those of 'Sauce
Hollandaise' are pale cream.*

☼ ◊ ❋ ❋ ❋   **Perennial**

‡ 45–70cm (10–20in) ↔ 60cm (24in)

ANTHERICUM LILIAGO

St. Bernard's lily produces elegant
spires of delicate white flowers in late
spring and early summer above a sheaf
of grass-like leaves; these grow so
densely as to be useful for ground
cover (*see p.304*). It lends emphasis to
clump-forming plants in a herbaceous
border and can be naturalized in grass.
The flowers cut well (*see p.524*). It
will grow in coastal gardens (*see p.166*).

ALSO RECOMMENDED: *var.* major ♥ *has
larger, more open flowers; A. ramosum is
shorter and flowers from early summer.*

☼ ◊ ❋ ❋ ❋   **Perennial**

‡ 60–90cm (24–36in) ↔ 30cm (12in)

ASPHODELINE LUTEA

Yellow asphodel produces a clump of narrow, blue-green leaves, which are an attractive feature before the dense, leafy spires of fragrant, starry yellow flowers appear in late spring. Grow in a border, where it is especially effective with grey- or silver-leaved plants, or on a dry, grassy bank. It must have a warm site and deep, well-drained soil; sandy ground is suitable (*see p.38*). Both flowers and seedheads are good for cutting (*see p.524*).

ALSO RECOMMENDED: *A. liburnica has pale yellow flowers in summer; A. taurica has white flowers.*

☼ ◊ ✸✸✸ *f*   **Perennial**
‡ 1.5m (5ft) ↔ 30cm (12in)

BUPHTHALMUM SALICIFOLIUM

A good plant for attracting bees (*see p.494*), this robust perennial bears its daisy-like, deep yellow flowers from early summer to autumn. When cut, they last well in water (*see p.524*). The stems, with willow-like, dark green leaves, are rather lax, so space plants closely or provide unobtrusive support early in the season. Grow in a border or naturalize on a sunny bank. It thrives on poor soils.

☼☀ ◊ ✸✸✸   **Perennial**
‡ 60cm (24in) ↔ 45cm (18in)

CATANANCHE CAERULEA
'Major' ♥

A short-lived perennial with grassy leaves that bears cornflower-like, dark-centred, lilac-blue flowers. They have papery, silvery white bracts and appear from summer to autumn. It thrives in any well-drained site, including clay and chalky soils (*see pp.12, 64*). Good for cutting and drying (*see p.524*); it flowers most freely in its second year.

ALSO RECOMMENDED: *C. caerulea has blue to lilac-blue flowerheads; 'Bicolor' has white flowerheads with purple centres.*

☼ ◊ ❀ ❀ ❀   **Perennial**

↕ 50cm (20in) ↔ 30cm (12in)

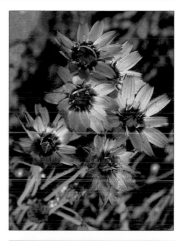

ECHINOPS RITRO
'Veitch's Blue'

The deep blue flowerheads of this globe thistle, borne in succession from late summer, attract pollinating insects and are good for cutting and drying (*see pp.494, 524*). With a basal mound of spiny, divided, white-cobwebbed leaves, it is an excellent specimen for a border with a grey- or silver-leaved theme. Best in poor, well-drained sites, it also tolerates sandy soils and coastal sites (*see pp.38, 166*).

ALSO RECOMMENDED: *E. bannaticus has blue-grey flowerheads; 'Taplow Blue' ♥ has bright blue flowerheads.*

☼ ◊ ◊ ❀ ❀ ❀   **Perennial**

↕ 90cm (36in) ↔ 45cm (18in)

ERYNGIUM BOURGATII

A good plant for attracting bees (*see p.494*), the blue-grey flowerheads of this spiny plant are surrounded by silver bracts. They appear from mid- to late summer above basal clumps of divided, dark green, silver-veined leaves. Grow in a herbaceous border or gravel garden; it tolerates sandy soils and coastal exposure (*see pp.38, 166*). The flowers are good for cutting and drying (*see p.524*).

ALSO RECOMMENDED: E. alpinum *'Amethyst'* has violet-blue flowerheads; those of E. planum *'Blauer Zwerg' (syn. 'Blue Dwarf')* are intense blue.

☼ ◊ ✱✱✱ **Perennial**
‡ 45cm (18in) ↔ 30cm (12in)

ERYSIMUM *'Bowles' Mauve'* ♥

This bushy, evergreen wallflower forms a round mound of narrow, grey-green leaves. For most of the year, it bears dense spikes of small, rich mauve flowers, most freely in spring and summer. It is ideal for growing on a sunny bank, at the front of a border, or on top of a dry stone wall (*see p.348*). Trim lightly after flowering to keep compact. It tolerates chalky soils (*see p.64*) and is often short-lived.

ALSO RECOMMENDED: E. linifolium *has lilac- to lavender-blue flowers and plain, grey-green leaves.*

☼ ◊ ✱✱ **Perennial**
‡ 75cm (30in) ↔ 60cm (24in)

FESTUCA GLAUCA
'Blaufuchs' ♛

The narrow, bright blue leaves of this
evergreen grass are its chief attraction.
It is excellent in a border or rock
garden as a foil to other plants. The
flower spikes are less significant. Divide
and replant clumps every two or three
years for the best foliage colour. Often
sold as 'Blue Fox'. It tolerates sandy
soils (*see p.38*) and can also be grown
as ground cover in sun (*see p.304*).

ALSO RECOMMENDED: *'Harz' has purple-
tipped, dark olive-green leaves; 'Seeigel'
(syn. Sea Urchin) has hair-fine, blue-green
foliage in a tight bun.*

☀ ◊ ❄ ❄ ❄ **Perennial**
‡ 30cm (12in) ↔ 25cm (10in)

FRITILLARIA IMPERIALIS

The stout stems of the crown imperial
arise in early summer to display
hanging, bell-shaped, orange, red,
or yellow flowers above whorls of
narrow, fresh green leaves. It is ideal
in a sunny border with fertile, well-
drained soil; plant where they can be
left undisturbed. The foxy scent can be
unpleasant at close range. Plant bulbs
in late summer. It tolerates shallow,
chalky soils (*see p.64*).

ALSO RECOMMENDED: *'Aurora' has
golden orange flowers; those of 'Lutea'
are yellow; 'Rubra' has red flowers.*

☀ ◊ ❄ ❄ ❄ **Perennial bulb**
‡ 1.5m (5ft) ↔ 30cm (12in)

GAILLARDIA *'Kobold'*

The brightly coloured, daisy-like flowerheads of this dwarf and bushy perennial bloom for a very long period, from early summer until the first frosts. It is good for a sunny border, especially one with a theme of hot colours, and is best on light, well-drained soils; it tolerates chalk (*see p.64*). The flowers are good for cutting (*see p.524*), which encourages further flowering. In cool climates, cut back in late summer – the new growth overwinters well.

ALSO RECOMMENDED: *'Burgunder' has wine-red flowerheads; those of 'Dazzler'* ♀ *are orange-red with yellow tips.*

☼ ◊ ❀ ❀ **Perennial**
‡ 30cm (12in) ↔ 45cm (18in)

GERANIUM CINEREUM *'Ballerina'* ♀

This low-growing, hardy geranium is useful at the front of a border, in a rock garden, or as ground cover (*see p.304*). From late spring into summer, a succession of light purple flowers with very dark veins open against the lobed, greyish foliage and face the sky. The soil must be sharply drained.

ALSO RECOMMENDED: *'Laurence Flatman' and subsp.* subcaulescens *are more vigorous;* G. dalmaticum ♀ (see p.363).

☼ ◊ ❀ ❀ ❀ **Perennial**
‡ 60cm (24in) ↔ 30cm (12in)

GERANIUM RENARDII ♥

In early summer, this low-growing plant bears violet-veined, white to pale lavender flowers. Often shy-flowering, it is more highly valued for the dense clumps of rounded, velvety, greyish green leaves, which form excellent ground cover at border fronts or in gravel gardens (*see p.304*). Best in poor, light, well-drained soils; it may self seed in ideal conditions.

ALSO RECOMMENDED: *'Whiteknights' has white, pale-blue-lilac-flushed flowers; G. × riversleaianum is more spreading with light pink to deep magenta flowers.*

☼ ◊ ❀ ❀ ❀   **Perennial**

‡↔ 30cm (12in)

LEYMUS ARENARIUS

One of the finest of the blue-leaved grasses, this spreading plant produces stiffly upright stems of tiny, blue-grey then buff coloured spikelets throughout summer; they are good for cutting and drying (*see p.524*). A fine architectural plant (*see p.472*) for specimen planting in gravel. It can be invasive, but it is suitable for a mixed or herbaceous border. Grow in sandy soil (*see p.38*). Cut down dead growth in autumn and, if necessary, divide mature plants when the soil has warmed up in spring.

☼ ◊ ❀ ❀ ❀   **Perennial**

‡ 1.5m (5ft) ↔ indefinite

LINARIA PURPUREA 'Canon Went'

This slender plant produces upright, wand-like stems clothed in greyish green leaves. They are topped by spikes of pale, dusky pink, two-lipped flowers throughout summer. An ideal choice for a cottage garden or herbaceous border. It self-seeds and comes true to type if isolated from the species. Grow in any light, well-drained soil; it tolerates sandy and chalky soils (*see pp.38, 64*).

ALSO RECOMMENDED: L. purpurea *has violet-purple flowers;* 'Springside White' *has white flowers.*

☼ ◊ ✽ ✽ ✽   **Perennial**
‡ 90cm (36in) ↔ 30cm (12in)

OENOTHERA SPECIOSA 'Rosea'

A vigorous evening primrose with rosettes of narrow leaves that spreads by means of runners; it makes good ground cover at the front of a border (*see p.304*). Scented, pink-flushed white flowers, veined with pink, appear in succession from summer to autumn; they remain open in daylight. Good in poor to moderately fertile, sandy soils (*see p.38*). It may be invasive.

ALSO RECOMMENDED: O. speciosa *has white flowers that may age to pink;* 'Pink Petticoats' *has pale pink, veined flowers.*

☼ ◊ ✽ ✽ ✽ *f*   **Perennial**
‡↔ 30cm (12in)

PAPAVER ORIENTALE *'Allegro'*

This oriental poppy forms a mound of bristly, divided leaves and, in late spring and early summer, produces bowl-shaped, satiny, vivid red-orange flowers, each with a black basal blotch. They are followed by characteristic poppy seed pods. Grow in any moderately fertile, well-drained site, including chalky soils (*see p.64*). Oriental poppies make spectacular plants for herbaceous borders.

ALSO RECOMMENDED: *'Black and White'* ♥ *has black-blotched white flowers; 'Mrs Perry'* ♥ *has pale salmon-pink flowers with blotches.*

☼ ◊ ❀ ❀ ❀   **Perennial**

‡ 45–90cm (18–36in) ↔ 60–90cm (24–36in)

PHORMIUM COOKIANUM *'Tricolor'* ♥

This striking perennial, very useful as a focal point in a border, forms arching clumps of strap-like, light green leaves to 1.5m (5ft) long; they are boldly margined with cream and red stripes. Tall spikes of tubular, pale green flowers emerge from the centre of the plant in summer. It is of borderline hardiness, so mulch deeply for winter. A fine architectural plant, which will grow in a large container (*see pp.412, 472*); It also tolerates coastal sites (*see p.166*).

ALSO RECOMMENDED: *'Cream Delight'* ♥ *is similar; P. 'Dazzler'* (see p.188).

☼ ◊◊ ❀ ❀ ❀   **Perennial**

‡ 0.6–2m (2–6ft) ↔ 0.3–3m (1–10ft)

TRITELEIA LAXA

This delicate plant with grassy leaves produces loose, showy clusters of pale to deep blue-purple flowers in early summer; the leaves usually wither by flowering time. It grows best in light, sandy soils (*see p.38*) and is very effective if grown *en masse* in a sunny, mixed or herbaceous border. It thrives in containers in sun (*see p.412*). Plant corms in autumn.

ALSO RECOMMENDED: T. hyacinthina *has white or pale blue flowers;* T. laxa *'Koningin Fabiola' (syn. Queen Fabiola) has purple-blue flowers.*

☼ ◊ ❀❀   **Perennial corm**
‡ 70cm (28in) ↔ 5cm (2in)

TULIPA PRAESTANS *'Unicum'*

Suitable for a raised bed or rock garden, this easy tulip produces several bright red flowers in the first half of spring. An appealing feature of this tulip is its large, variegated leaves, which have cream margins. It makes a superior display when planted in clusters. Tolerant of sandy soils (*see p.38*), and it can be grown in a sunny container (*see p.412*). Plant bulbs in late autumn.

ALSO RECOMMENDED: *'Fusilier' has bright orange-scarlet flowers;* T. *'Keizerskroon'* ♀ (see p.439); T. hageri *'Splendens'* (see p.63); T. *'Purissima'* ♀ (see p.545).

☼ ◊ ❀❀❀   **Perennial bulb**
‡ 30cm (12in)

VERBENA *'Peaches and Cream'*

A spreading plant with clusters of tiny summer to autumn flowers in pastel shades. They open pinky orange and fade through apricot to cream. It is often grown as an annual in a sunny border or container (*see p.412*), but it can be overwintered under glass in frost-prone areas.

ALSO RECOMMENDED: *'Homestead Purple'* has red-purple flowers; *'Silver Anne'* ♥ has pink flowers; *'Sissinghurst'* ♥ (see p.439); V. bonariensis *is hardier with purple flowers on stems to 2m (6ft) tall;* V. rigida ♥ has fragrant purple flowers.

☼ ◊ ❁ **Perennial**
‡ 45cm (18in) ↔ 30–50cm (12–20in)

YUCCA WHIPPLEI

This almost stemless yucca forms a dense rosette of rigid, narrow, grey-green leaves at ground level; they are sharply spine-tipped, so site with care. It is an impressive architectural plant for well-drained borders or gravel gardens (*see p.472*). When mature, it produces spectacular spires of fragrant, creamy white flowers in summer, after which the flowered clump will die. Grow in sandy soil (*see p.38*).

ALSO RECOMMENDED: Y. filamentosa *'Bright Edge'* ♥ (see p.483); Y. gloriosa ♥ *is twice as large and has blue-green leaves.*

☼ ◊ ❁ ❁ *f* **Perennial**
‡ 1m (3ft) ↔ 1.2m (4ft)

PLANTS FOR DRY SITES IN SHADE

THERE CAN BE no denying that the combination of shade and drought presents a challenge to plants, and even experienced gardeners may despair when faced with such a difficult site. Many plants thrive in damp shade, but few are able to tolerate the combined lack of light and moisture.

Dry shade often occurs in urban gardens at the base of a wall or side of a building that faces away from the direction of prevailing wind, and is therefore sheltered from rain. It is also evident beneath large, shallow-rooting trees, which create a rain shadow beneath their leaf canopies, further parched by the moisture-depleting effects of their questing roots. If the soil is also free-draining, as in sandy and shallow, chalky soils, the problems are exacerbated.

IMPROVE THE SOIL

As always, the first line of attack is to choose plants that are known to tolerate such sites, such as *Geranium phaeum* (see p.232) or *Liriope muscari* (see p.233), although much can be done to improve soil conditions so the range of survivors is extended. The most important action is to improve the moisture retention of the soil by incorporating plenty of well rotted organic matter, like farmyard manure, garden compost, composted bark, or leafmould. The same materials can also be applied as a mulch in autumn or spring, but it is vital to do this when the soil is already damp. If applied to dry soil, it prevents rainfall penetrating to the soil beneath thus making the problem worse. In the absence of natural rainfall, give the soil a thorough soaking before mulching.

Another trick is to excavate a wide planting hole and lining it with perforated polythene, which is especially effective under shallow-rooting trees like beech (see p.143). Mix the excavated soil with copious quantities of loam-based potting compost or well-rotted organic matter, then backfill with the improved soil.

PREPARE THE SITE

Establishing a carpet of drought-resistant ground cover, made up of plants like *Pachysandra terminalis* (see p.235) or *Tellima grandiflora* (see p.236), also helps to retain soil moisture by reducing surface evaporation. Planting through permeable, woven landscaping fabric (often sold as geotextile membrane), especially if used in combination with a mulch, gives them the best possible chance of establishing good cover. Bear in mind that in such testing conditions, even the toughest plants may not achieve their expected height and spread, so you may need to plant more closely than is usually recommended. It is also vital that new plantings are kept well-watered during the most vulnerable period before they develop a well-established root system. With shrubby plants, like *Elaeagnus* x *ebbingei* 'Gilt Edge' (see p.218), take the reduced vigour into account, so there should be little need to prune.

COTONEASTER FRIGIDUS

A spreading shrub that has matt green leaves, which turn yellow before falling. In summer, it is covered by clusters of cream flowers, followed in late summer and autumn by a profusion of bright red berries; these attract birds (*see p.494*). An easily grown, versatile shrub that can be clipped as a hedge (*see p.138*) or trained as a single-trunked tree. Tolerant of clay and chalky soils (*see pp.12, 64*).

ALSO RECOMMENDED: *'Cornubia'* ♥ *is similar;* C. horizontalis ♥ (see p.265); C. lacteus ♥ (see p.149); C. sternianus ♥ (see p.71).

☼ ◐ ◊ ❀ ❀ ❀   **Deciduous shrub**
↕↔ 10m (30ft)

ELAEAGNUS × EBBINGEI *'Gilt Edge'* ♥

This dense, fast-growing shrub is valued for its gold-margined, glossy green leaves; the creamy white flowers of autumn are fragrant but inconspicuous. Use in a shrub border or to brighten a dark corner. It may also be grown as informal hedging (*see p.138*); trim in late spring. Tolerant of exposed and coastal sites (*see pp.118, 166*). It provides cover for wildlife (*see p.494*).

ALSO RECOMMENDED: *'Coastal Gold' has golden yellow leaves with irregular green margins; 'Limelight' has silvery young leaves, maturing to yellow and pale green.*

☼ ◐ ◊ ❀ ❀ ❀ *f*   **Evergreen shrub**
↕↔ 4m (12ft)

EUONYMUS FORTUNEI
'Silver Queen' ♀

An upright or scrambling shrub with
white-margined, dark green leaves that
tinge pink in cold weather. The spring
flowers are insignificant. It makes good
ground cover (*see pp.304, 326*), can be
clipped as a hedge (*see p.138*), and will
climb against a lightly shaded wall (*see
p.262*), reaching 6m (20ft) tall. Grow
in any but waterlogged soil; it tolerates
coastal conditions and suits containers
(*see pp.166, 412, 448*). Trim in spring.

ALSO RECOMMENDED: *'Emerald 'n' Gold' ♀
has yellow edged leaves; Golden Prince (syn.
'Gold Tip') is compact with gold-tipped leaves.*

☼ ◐ ◊◊ ❀❀❀ **Evergreen shrub**
↕ 2.5m (8ft) ↔ 1.5m (5ft)

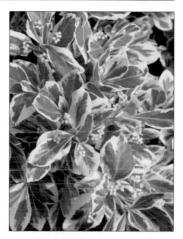

GARRYA ELLIPTICA

The silk tassel bush is a dense shrub
with dark sea-green, wavy-margined
leaves, glossy or matt. It is prized for
the grey catkins borne on male plants,
which may be up to 20cm (8in) long
and dangle in clusters through winter
and into spring; they make interesting
cut flowers (*see p.524*). It can be treated
as a hedge (*see p.138*) but is also fine
in a shrub border or against a wall (*see
pp.262, 280*). It tolerates coastal sites
(*see p.166*). Trim after flowering.

ALSO RECOMMENDED: *'James Roof' ♀
is noted for having the longest catkins.*

☼ ◐ ◊ ❀❀ **Evergreen shrub**
↕↔ 4m (12ft)

HEDERA HELIX *'Erecta'* ♥

Common ivy is typically a climbing plant, but this unusual form is used mostly as a shrub or as ground cover (*see pp.304, 326*), because the stiff stems are upright and self-supporting. The round-lobed leaves are dark green with prominent, pale green veins. Site in a shrub border or rock garden, or grow in a container (*see pp.412, 448*) or against a shady wall (*see p.262*). It tolerates chalky soils (*see p.64*).

ALSO RECOMMENDED: *'Congesta'* ♥ *is less vigorous and forms a tidy bush.*

☼ ☀ ◊◊ ❀ ❀ ❀   **Evergreen shrub**
↕ 1m (3ft)

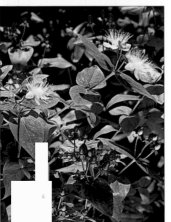

HYPERICUM × INODORUM *'Elstead'*

This vigorous shrub produces dense clumps of upright stems bearing aromatic, dark green leaves. The bright yellow flowers are borne at the stem tips in summer and autumn, followed by glossy red berries. Shear over in early spring to produce the densest ground cover (*see pp.304, 326*). Grow in any but waterlogged soil.

ALSO RECOMMENDED: H. androsaemum *'Albury Purple' has purple-flushed leaves and black fruits;* H. calycinum (*see p.328*).

☼ ☀ ◊◊ ❀ ❀ ❀   **Deciduous shrub**
↕↔ 1.2m (4ft)

KERRIA JAPONICA
'Golden Guinea' ♥

A suckering shrub that has glossy green, cane-like stems and neatly toothed, bright green leaves. It bears large and single, sunshine yellow flowers during spring, making a cheerful and reliable, early-flowering shrub for a border or woodland garden, or against a partially shaded wall (*see p.262*). Cut flowered canes back to different levels to obtain blooms at varying heights. It tolerates clay soils (*see p.12*).

ALSO RECOMMENDED: *'Picta' has cream-margined, grey-green leaves; 'Pleniflora'* ♥ *is taller with double, pompon-like flowers.*

☀ ☀ ◗ ❀ ❀ ❀   **Deciduous shrub**
‡ 2m (6ft) ↔ 2.5m (8ft)

OSMANTHUS DELAVAYI ♥

The arching branches of this rounded shrub bear small, glossy dark green leaves. Sweetly scented, pure white flowers appear in mid- to late spring. It thrives in most, fertile, well-drained soils, including those on chalk (*see p.64*). A fine specimen for a border or for training against a partially shaded wall (*see p.262*); it can also be grown as a hedge (*see p.138*). Prune to shape after flowering; trim hedges in summer.

ALSO RECOMMENDED: *O.* decorus *has larger leaves; O.* × burkwoodii ♥ *(see p.73).*

☀ ☀ ◗ ❀ ❀ ❀   **Evergreen shrub**
‡ 2–6m (6–20ft) ↔ 4m (12ft)

RIBES ALPINUM *'Aureum'*

A neat and adaptable currant bush with dense growth that is clothed by beautiful, bright yellow-green, lobed leaves, which colour better in light, dappled shade. The foliage is accompanied by flowers of a similar colour in spring. Bunches of scarlet berries follow if a male form is growing nearby. Trim after flowering; it may be clipped as a hedge (*see p.138*).

ALSO RECOMMENDED: *R. alpinum has mid-green foliage and is better for heavy shade.*

☼ ☀ ◊ ❄ ❄ ❄   **Deciduous shrub**
↕↔ 1.5m (5ft)

RUSCUS HYPOGLOSSUM

The tough, glossy green leaves of this small shrub are actually modified stems, and – on female plants only – they bear ornamental red berries from autumn to winter. The flowers are insignificant, although plants of both sexes are needed if the females are to bear fruit. Cut out any dead stems in spring. It can be grown as ground cover (*see p.326*).

ALSO RECOMMENDED: *R. aculeatus, butcher's broom, is taller.*

☼ ☀ ◊◊ ❄ ❄ ❄   **Evergreen shrub**
↕ 45cm (18in) ↔ 1m (3ft)

SARCOCOCCA CONFUSA ♥

Christmas box is a dense, rounded shrub with small, dark green leaves, making good ground cover (*see p.326*). It is noted for the intense winter fragrance of its honey-scented white flowers – best appreciated near a frequently used door or entrance. Small, glossy black fruits follow. It can be pruned hard in late spring and makes a fine low hedge (*see p.138*). Grow in any fertile, well-drained soil, including those on chalk (*see p.64*). It tolerates urban pollution.

ALSO RECOMMENDED: *S.* hookeriana *var.* digyna ♥ *is similar but more compact; var.* humilis (see p.244).

☼ ◐ �○�○ ❄❄❄ *f*　　**Evergreen shrub**
‡ 2m (6ft) ↔ 1m (3ft)

SKIMMIA JAPONICA

This tough, rounded shrub bears heads of dark red flower buds in autumn and winter, which open in spring as cream flowers; red berries follow on female plants, so long as males grow nearby. They contrast well with the glossy deep green, leathery, red-rimmed leaves. Tolerant of urban pollution, coastal sites, and damp, acid soils (*see pp.92, 166, 238*). Little pruning is required. It will grow in a container (*see p.448*).

ALSO RECOMMENDED: *Fragrans* ♥ *is male; subsp.* reevesiana *has both male and female flowers on one plant;* 'Rubella' ♥ (see p.108); 'Veitchii' *is female.*

☼ ◐ ◐ ◯◯ ❄❄❄　　**Evergreen shrub**
‡↔ to 6m (20ft)

SYMPHORICARPOS × DOORENBOSII *'White Hedge'*

This snowberry is a vigorous, suckering shrub with upright stems and oval, dark green leaves. In summer, it bears clusters of white flowers, followed by white berries, which attract birds (*see p.494*). As informal hedging (*see p.138*), it can be trimmed in winter. Its spread may become invasive.

ALSO RECOMMENDED: *'Mother of Pearl' is arching with pink-flushed white fruit; S. albus var. laevigatus (see p.164).*

☼☀ ◊◊ ✷✷✷　　**Deciduous shrub**
‡ 1.5m (5ft) ↔ indefinite

HOLBOELLIA CORIACEA

A twining climber with ornamental, evergreen leaves, divided into three dark green leaflets. In a sheltered site, it can be trained up into a small tree, or onto a support or wall (*see pp.262, 280*). Two types of small, bell-shaped flowers emerge in spring: sprays of mauve male flowers at the tips of the previous year's growth and clusters of purple-flushed, greenish white female flowers at the base of new growth. Sausage-shaped purple fruits follow infrequently. It may be rampant in favourable conditions.

ALSO RECOMMENDED: *the leaves of H. latifolia are divided into more leaflets.*

☼☀ ◊ ✷✷　　**Climber**
‡ 7m (22ft)

AJUGA REPTANS *'Multicolor'*

The dark bronze-green leaves of this evergreen perennial are attractively marked with deep pink and cream. It is a good choice for ground cover (*see pp.304, 326*), spreading freely by means of rooting stems. Spikes to 15cm (6in) tall of dark blue flowers appear in early summer. Invaluable for border edging under shrubs and perennials, and in wall and paving crevices (*see p.348*). Tolerant of clay and damp soils (*see pp.12, 238*).

ALSO RECOMMENDED: *'Burgundy Glow'* ♥ *has silvery leaves with deep red tints; 'Catlin's Giant'* ♥ *(see p.354); 'Pink Elf' has pink flowers on stems 5cm (2in) tall.*

☀ ◐ ◊◊ ❁❁❁　　　　**Perennial**

↕ 15cm (6in) ↔ 1m (3ft)

ASPLENIUM SCOLOPENDRIUM ♥

The hart's tongue fern forms a crown of tongue-shaped, leathery, bright green, undivided fronds to 40cm (16in) long. The margins are usually rippled. On the undersides of mature fronds, rust coloured spore cases are arranged in a herringbone pattern. The are no flowers. It prefers gritty, alkaline soils (*see p.64*) and tolerates damp shade (*see p.238*). A fine architectural plant for a container (*see pp.448, 472*).

ALSO RECOMMENDED: *fronds of* Crispum Group *have very ruffled margins; those of* Cristatum Group *have curious crested margins;* A. trichomanes ♥ *(see p.78).*

☀ ◊◊ ❁❁❁　　　　**Perennial fern**

↕ 45–70cm (18–28in) ↔ 60cm (24in)

BERGENIA *'Sunningdale'*

An early-flowering perennial bearing clusters of rich pink flowers in spring. They are carried on upright stems above the clumps of broad, rounded, leathery, evergreen leaves; these turn coppery in winter. Good underplanting for shrubs, which give winter shelter from cold winds, and also as a ground-cover or pot plant (*see pp.326, 448*). Mulch in autumn. It tolerates chalky soils and damp sites (*see pp.64, 238*).

ALSO RECOMMENDED: *'Bressingham White'* ♀ *has white flowers; 'Morgenröte'* ♀ (see p.333); *'Silberlicht'* ♀ *has white flowers;* B. ciliata (see p.79).

☀ ◐ ◖◗ ✲ ✲ ✲   **Perennial**
↕ 30–45cm (12–18in) ↔ 45–60cm (18–24in)

BRUNNERA MACROPHYLLA *'Dawson's White'*

This clump-forming perennial with attractive foliage is ideal for ground cover in borders and among deciduous trees (*see p.326*). In mid- and late spring, open clusters of small, pale blue flowers appear above the heart-shaped leaves, which have irregular, creamy white margins. Choose a cool position in light, damp or dry shade (*see p.238*). It tolerates clay soils and exposed sites (*see p.12, 118*).

ALSO RECOMMENDED: B. macrophylla ♀ *has plain green leaves; those of 'Hadspen Cream'* ♀ *have irregular cream margins.*

☀ ◐ ◖◗ ✲ ✲ ✲   **Perennial**
↕ 45cm (18in) ↔ 60cm (24in)

CONVALLARIA MAJALIS
VAR. ROSEA

This pink-flowered lily-of-the-valley is a creeping perennial bearing small, very fragrant flowers, which hang from arching stems in late spring above a pair of narrowly oval leaves; they are good for cutting (*see p.524*). It makes excellent ground cover in damp or dry shade (*see pp.238, 326*), spreading rapidly under suitable conditions. Add a dressing of leaf mould in autumn. It tolerates sandy soils (*see p.38*).

ALSO RECOMMENDED: *C. majalis ♀ has white flowers; the leaves of 'Albostriata' are attractively cream-striped.*

☼ ◐ ◊◊ ❋❋❋ *f*　　　**Perennial**

‡ 20cm (8in) ↔ 30cm (12in)

CORYDALIS LUTEA

This low perennial forms a mound of delicately lobed, bright green foliage, which is decorated over a long season from spring to early autumn by unusually spurred, bold yellow flowers. It self-seeds freely and is suitable for a rock garden, or in crevices within dry stone walls or paving (*see p.348*).

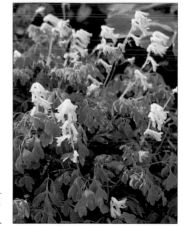

☼ ◐ ◊ ❋❋❋　　　**Perennial**

‡ 40cm (16in) ↔ 30cm (12in)

CYCLAMEN COUM
F. ALBISSIMUM

The rounded, green or silver-marked leaves of *C. coum* will carpet the ground beneath shrubs or trees. They appear in winter and spring with the flowers, which have upswept petals. This form has white flowers with carmine-red mouths. Grow in gritty, well-drained soil that dries out in summer. In cold areas, apply a deep, dry mulch annually as the leaves wither. Plant tubers in autumn.

ALSO RECOMMENDED: ALSO RECOMMENDED *C. coum* ♀ *has white to pink flowers; Pewter Group* ♀ *have silvered leaves.*

☀ ◊ ❀ ❀ ❀　　　　　**Perennial**
‡ 5–8cm (2–3in) ↔ 10cm (4in)

DESCHAMPSIA CESPITOSA
'Goldtau'

This evergreen grass forms tussocks of narrow, rigid leaves. Through summer, it bears clouds of glistening, red-brown flowers, which age to golden yellow; they are good for cutting (*see p.524*). Grow in a border or woodland garden with neutral to acid soil (*see p.92*). In dry soils, dig in compost before planting. Remove old flowerheads in early spring. Also sold as Golden Dew.

ALSO RECOMMENDED: *'Bronzeschleier' (syn. Bronze Veil) has bronze flowerheads; 'Goldschleier' (syn. Golden Veil) is taller with bright, silvery yellow flowerheads.*

☀ ◊ ❀ ❀ ❀　　　　　**Perennial**
‡↔ 75cm (30in)

DICENTRA CUCULLARIA

The feathery, blue-green leaves of Dutchman's breeches form low hummocks beneath the upright stems of small, heart-shaped white flowers. These appear in early spring, and the whole plant dies back after flowering. It needs gritty soil and should be kept almost dry when dormant in summer; dry spots beneath trees or shrubs make an ideal site. It is also suitable for shady niches in rock gardens and as ground cover (*see p.326*). Most other dicentras prefer moist soils. It tolerates chalky soils (*see p.64*).

☀ ◌ ❀❀❀   **Perennial**
‡ 20cm (8in) ↔ 25cm (10in)

DIGITALIS OBSCURA

Foxgloves are imposing plants when in flower, producing tall spires of flowers, which are attractive to bees (*see p.494*). This one has rusty, yellow or orange flowers from late spring to midsummer. It has a subshrubby appearance with lance-shaped, greyish green leaves, and it tolerates most soils, preferably in partial shade. Suitable for a border or woodland garden.

ALSO RECOMMENDED: D. purpurea *has purple flowers and is more tolerant of dry conditions.*

☀ ◐ ◌◌ ❀❀   **Perennial**
‡ 30–120cm (12–48in) ↔ 45cm (18in)

EUPHORBIA AMYGDALOIDES VAR. ROBBIAE ♀

Mrs Robb's bonnet, also known simply as *E. robbiae*, is a spreading, evergreen perennial bearing open heads of yellowish green flowers in spring. The long, dark green leaves are arranged in rosettes at the lower ends of the stems. Dig up invasive roots to control spread. The milky sap can irritate skin. Also useful for hot, dry sites (*see p.190*) and as ground cover (*see pp.304, 326*).

ALSO RECOMMENDED: *'Purpurea' has purple leaves and yellow flowers.*

☼ ◐ ◊◊ ❄ ❄ ❄   **Perennial**
↕ 60cm (24in) ↔ 30cm (12in)

EUPHORBIA DULCIS 'Chameleon'

This spreading plant has upright stems carrying narrow, rich purple leaves and, at their tips, open heads of purplish, yellow-green flowers in early summer. The leaves assume orange, red, and gold tints in autumn. Good for ground cover (*see pp.304, 326*) and for foliage contrasts in a shady border. It grows in any well-drained soil, including those on chalk and in hot, dry sites (*see pp.64, 190*). It self-seeds freely.

ALSO RECOMMENDED: *E. dulcis has dark or bronze-green leaves and yellow-green flowers.*

☼ ◐ ◊ ❄ ❄ ❄   **Perennial**
↕↔ 30cm (12in)

GALANTHUS NIVALIS
'Flore Pleno' ♥

This double-flowered form of common
snowdrop, *G. nivalis* ♥, bears drooping,
pear-shaped, pure white flowers from
late winter to early spring. There are
green markings on the tips of the inner
petals, and the narrow leaves are grey-
green. A reliable bulb for naturalising
in damp shade under deciduous trees
or shrubs in a wild garden (*see pp.238,
494*). Plant bulbs in autumn, and divide
clumps after flowering.

ALSO RECOMMENDED: G. elwesii ♥,
G. 'Magnet' ♥, and G. 'S Arnott' ♥
are twice as tall with single flowers.

☀ ◐ ◊◊ ❀❀❀   **Perennial bulb**
↕↔ 10cm (4in)

GERANIUM NODOSUM

With a creeping habit and dense
mounds of lobed, glossy leaves, this
hardy geranium makes great ground
cover (*see p.326*) in any dry, shady
spot. The purplish pink flowers with
darker veins are borne on red tinted
stems from spring to autumn. Very easy
to grow, it tolerates any but waterlogged
soil. Remove faded flowers and leaves
to encourage new growth. It can be
grown in a container (*see p.448*).

ALSO RECOMMENDED: G. macrorrhizum
'Czakor' (see p.339).

☀◐☀ ◊ ❀❀❀   **Perennial**
↕ 30–50cm (12–20in) ↔ 50cm (20in)

GERANIUM PHAEUM

Dusky cranesbill is a densely clump-forming perennial with deeply lobed, soft green leaves. In spring and early summer, tall, slender stems carry a profusion of dusky violet-blue, black-purple, or maroon flowers. Excellent in containers (*see p.448*) or for ground cover under shrubs or trees (*see p.326*); cutting back hard after flowering makes for denser cover and more flowers. Grow in any but waterlogged soil.

ALSO RECOMMENDED: *'Album' has white flowers;* G. endressii ♀ (see p.316).

☼☀ ◊�◊ ❈❈❈   **Perennial**
‡ 80cm (32in) ↔ 45cm (18in)

HELLEBORUS FOETIDUS ♀

The stinking hellebore is an upright, evergreen perennial forming clumps of dark green, deeply divided leaves, which smell unpleasant when crushed. In winter and early spring, pale clusters of nodding, cup-shaped flowers appear above the foliage; their green petals are often edged with red. An intriguing specimen for a winter border or for cut flowers (*see p.524*). Best on dry or damp, neutral to alkaline soils (*see pp.64, 238*) and planted among snowdrops.

ALSO RECOMMENDED: H. orientalis *subsp.* guttatus (see p.253).

☼☀ ◊◊ ❈❈❈   **Perennial**
‡ 80cm (32in) ↔ 45cm (18in)

IRIS FOETIDISSIMA
VAR. CITRINA

The stinking iris is not as unpleasant as
it sounds, although the evergreen, silvery
leaves do have a unpleasant scent if
crushed. This vigorous plant bears pale
yellow flowers in early summer, which
cut well for indoor display (*see p.524*),
followed by seed capsules; these split
in autumn to display decorative, scarlet,
yellow, or more rarely, white seeds. It
will grow as ground cover (*see p.326*)
and tolerates chalky soils (*see p.64*).

ALSO RECOMMENDED: I. foetidissima ♀
has purple flowers.

☀ ◑ ◊ ✿ ✿ ✿   **Perennial**

‡ 30–90cm (12–36in) ↔ indefinite

LIRIOPE MUSCARI ♀

The narrow, arching, dark green leaves
of this tuberous perennial spread slowly
to produce dense, ground-covering
swathes (*see p.326*). In autumn, purple-
green stems appear bearing crowded
spikes of long-lasting, bead-like, violet-
mauve flowers. Excellent in a woodland
garden or beneath shrubs in a border.
It also tolerates acid soils and hot,
dry sites (*see pp.92, 190*).

ALSO RECOMMENDED: *'Monroe White' has
white flowers; 'Variegata' has white-striped
leaves;* L. exiliflora *(syn.* L. muscari *'Majestic')
has tall spikes of rich lavender-blue flowers.*

☀ ◑ ◊ ✿ ✿ ✿   **Perennial**

‡ 30cm (12in) ↔ 45cm (18in)

LUNARIA REDIVIVA

This perennial honesty forms dense clumps of triangular, dark green leaves and bears heads of very fragrant, pale lilac flowers during spring and early summer; these attract butterflies and bees (*see p.494*). The silvery seed pods that follow are good for cutting and drying (*see p.524*). Excellent for a border or for naturalizing in woodland. Grow in any well-drained soil; it tolerates alkaline conditions (*see p.64*).

ALSO RECOMMENDED: L. annua *is a biennial with purplish flowers.*

:sun: :half-sun: ◊ ✼✼✼✼ *f*   **Perennial**
‡ 60–90cm (24–36in) ↔ 30cm (12in)

MECONOPSIS CAMBRICA

The Welsh poppy forms loose, basal tufts of divided, pale to bluish green leaves. From spring to autumn, on slender, leafy stems, it bears cup-shaped, lemon- to orange-yellow, delicate poppy flowers. A noted self-seeder, it is ideal for naturalizing in a wild or woodland gardens in sun or shade, tolerating chalky soils (*see p.64*). Remove dead flowers to prevent nuisance self-seeding.

ALSO RECOMMENDED: *var.* aurantiaca *has orange flowers;* 'Flore-Pleno' *has double yellow flowers.*

:sun: :half-sun: ◊◊ ✼✼✼   **Perennial**
‡ 45cm (18in) ↔ 25cm (10in)

PACHYSANDRA TERMINALIS ♥

This freely spreading, bushy plant is valued mainly for its glossy, dark green foliage. It is an excellent ground-cover plant for a dry or damp woodland garden or under trees and shrubs (*see pp.238, 326*). Small spikes of fragrant white flowers appear in early summer at the stem tips among a cluster of leaves. In very dry soils, dig in garden compost before planting. It tolerates acid soils (*see p.92*).

ALSO RECOMMENDED: *'Green Carpet' is more compact, 'Variegata'* ♥ *is less vigorous with white-margined leaves.*

☼◐ ◊ ❀❀❀ *f* **Perennial**
‡ 20cm (8in) ↔ indefinite

SYMPHYTUM TUBEROSUM

The tuberous comfrey is named for its creeping, rhizomatous roots, which may spread rapidly. They give rise to upright, hairy stems with long, dark green leaves. These are topped in early summer by heads of pale yellow, tubular flowers. Like other comfreys, it makes an excellent ground cover plant (*see pp.304, 326*).

ALSO RECOMMENDED: S. *'Goldsmith'* (see p.346); S. × uplandicum *'Variegatum'* ♥ *has blue flowers and variegated leaves.*

☼◐ ◊◊ ❀❀❀ **Perennial**
‡ 40–60cm (16–24in) ↔ 1m (3ft)

TELLIMA GRANDIFLORA

Fringe cups forms a ground-smothering mound of lobed, fresh green leaves. From late spring to midsummer, it produces slender spires of small, greenish white flowers with fringed petals. It makes excellent ground cover beneath trees or shrubs (see p.326) and good edging at the front of a border. Grow in any moderately fertile soil, including those heavy with clay (see p.12). It self-seeds freely.

ALSO RECOMMENDED: 'Purpurteppich' has purplish, red-tinted leaves and green-fringed red flowers; Rubra Group has purplish red leaves.

☀️ ◐ ◊◊ ❄❄❄   **Perennial**

‡ 80cm (32in) ↔ 30cm (12in)

TOLMIEA MENZIESII
'Taff's Gold' ♀

A spreading plant grown for its clumps of semi-evergreen, ivy-like, pale lime-green leaves, mottled with cream and pale yellow. An abundance of tiny, nodding, green and chocolate-brown flowers appear in slender, upright spikes during early summer. Plant in groups to cover the ground in a woodland garden or in a container (see pp.326, 448). Direct sun will scorch the leaves. It tolerates acid soils (see p.92).

ALSO RECOMMENDED: T. menziesii ♀, pick-a-back plant, has plain green leaves.

☀️ ◐ ◊◊ ❄❄❄   **Perennial**

‡ 30–60cm (12–24in) ↔ 1m (3ft)

VINCA MINOR

The lesser periwinkle is a trailing shrub with long, slender shoots. It gives a long season of violet-blue flowers, which are produced from spring to autumn amid the oval, dark green leaves. A useful plant for ground cover (*see pp.304, 326*), but it can be invasive if not cut back.

ALSO RECOMMENDED: *'Argenteovariegata'* ♥ has cream-margined leaves; V. major, greater periwinkle, is very vigorous; *'Variegata'* ♥ has cream-edged leaves.

☀️◐ ◊◊ ❄❄❄ **Perennial**
‡ 10–20cm (4–8in) ↔ indefinite

WALDSTENIA TERNATA

A vigorous woodland plant that spreads quickly to form a thick mat of strawberry-like, palmately lobed leaves. Loose clusters of golden yellow flowers illuminate the plant in late spring and early summer; they resemble small, single rose flowers. Good as ground cover for dry, shady banks or at the front of border (*see pp.304, 326*), but it may be invasive.

☀️◐ ◊◊ ❄❄❄ **Perennial**
‡ 10cm (4in) ↔ 60cm (24in)

PLANTS FOR DAMP SITES IN SHADE

A N OLD GARDENING adage states that if shade did not exist in a garden, it would be necessary to create some, for some of the most beautiful and desirable plants need at least a modicum of shade to show their best. The world's forests provide an abundance of bulbs, perennials, ferns, and shrubs, which thrive in damp shade. They illustrate the opportunities of colour and beauty through the seasons, from spring-flowering gems like *Anemonella thalictroides* (*see*

p.245) to the luscious berries of *Gaultheria × wisleyensis* 'Pink Pixie' (*see p.241*) in autumn. In the cool, humid environment that characterises damp shade, foliage plants, such as most ferns and the marbled-leaved trilliums (*see pp.117, 260*), grow lush and remain in better condition for longer than in more open sites. As a result, sophisticated tapestries of textured foliage can be created to clothe the ground. Flowering perennials, like *Digitalis × mertonensis* (*see p.250*), often perform for longer periods in shade and retain their colour better when not exposed to the bleaching effects of the sun, while those with pastel-coloured flowers, like *Aquilegia fragrans (see p.246)*, appear at their most luminous in shade.

IDEAL SHADY PLACES

Few modern gardens are large enough to accommodate a patch of woodland, which would be the natural choice of site for shade-loving plants. Instead, many have areas that are shaded by high walls, specimen trees, or borders of shrubs, and the most desirable form of shade is dappled or partial shade, since relatively few shade-lovers thrive in deep, permanently sunless shade. If the shade cast by trees is too dense, prune the lower branches from the trunk and thin the canopy to allow more light through. On large, mature trees, however, where the branches are large and heavy, this is most safely done by a professional tree surgeon. In shady courtyards, or where heavy shade is cast by tall walls,

you can increase ambient light levels by painting the walls in pale colours and by using pale-coloured gravel and paving at ground level. In a shrub border, especially if it is an otherwise open site, the shade beneath the shrubs is likely to be a patchwork of varying intensities, which changes through the days and seasons as the sun moves across the sky. Plants that need partial shade are likely to do best here, but they should be positioned so that they do, at least, receive shade at midday, otherwise their foliage is likely to scorch. Such a site is also ideal for shade-loving bulbs like snowdrops *(see p.231)* and anemones *(see pp.332, 528)*, which perform before the deciduous canopy closes over by late spring.

Since most of these plants are from woodland, they grow best in soils that are moist but well-drained and rich in leafy organic matter. Unless your soil is like this naturally, add well-rotted organic matter to the soil when planting and apply a mulch of the same annually in spring.

CAMELLIA JAPONICA
'Janet Waterhouse'

This elegant shrub for a shrub border or wooded area can also be grown as a free-standing specimen, either in the open ground, in a container, or against a shady wall (*see pp.262, 448*). The glossy dark, oval leaves heighten the brilliance of the semi-double white flowers in spring. These can be cut for indoor decoration (*see p.524*). Prune young plants to shape after flowering. Tolerant of acid soils (*see p.92*)

ALSO RECOMMENDED: *'Adolphe Audusson'* ♀ (*see p.450*); *'Lady Vansittart'* (*see p.99*); *'Tricolor'* ♀ *has flowers striped red and white.*

☼ ◐ ◊◊ ❀❀❀   **Evergreen shrub**
‡ 9m (28ft) ↔ 8m (25ft)

DAPHNE LAUREOLA

Although the spurge laurel is less showy than other daphnes, it does well in deep, damp or dry shade (*see p.216*). It is bushy with glossy dark green, leathery foliage, and clusters of small, night-scented, pale yellow-green flowers emerge from the leaf axils in late winter. Black berries follow. Grow in woodland or in a shrub border; it resents transplanting. All parts are toxic, and contact with the sap may irritate skin. Keep pruning to a minimum.

ALSO RECOMMENDED: *subsp.* philippi *is a spreading dwarf form, about 40cm (16in) tall, suitable for ground cover.*

☼ ◐ ◊◊ ❀❀❀ *f*   **Evergreen shrub**
‡ 1m (3ft) ↔ 1.5m (5ft)

FATSIA JAPONICA ♈

The Japanese aralia is a spreading
shrub grown for its large, palmately
lobed, glossy green leaves. Broad,
upright clusters of rounded, cream-
coloured flowerheads appear in
autumn. An excellent architectural plant
for a dry or damp, shady border, or
against a wall (*see pp.216, 262, 472*).
It tolerates urban pollution, thriving
in sheltered city gardens. Trim back
in late spring, if necessary.

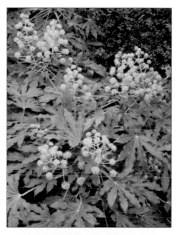

ALSO RECOMMENDED: *'Variegata'* ♈
has cream-edged leaves.

☼☀ ◊◊ ❋❋❋　　**Evergreen shrub**
↕↔ 1.5–4m (5–12ft)

GAULTHERIA × WISLEYENSIS
'Pink Pixie'

This compact shrub, spreading by
suckers, makes good ground cover in a
shaded border, rock garden, or wildlife
area (*see pp.326, 494*). It tolerates sun
if the soil remains reliably moist. Small,
pink-tinged white flowers appear in
late spring and early summer, followed
by purple-red fruits. Trim lightly after
flowering to keep compact. It associates
well with heathers, which also grow
in neutral to acid soil (*see p.92*).

ALSO RECOMMENDED: *G. × wisleyensis
is taller; 'Wisley Pearl' is also taller with
white flowers and dark red-purple fruits.*

☼☀ ◊◊ ❋❋❋　　**Evergreen shrub**
↕ 30cm (12in) ↔ 45cm (18in)

HYDRANGEA QUERCIFOLIA ♥

The oak-leaved hydrangea is a mound-forming shrub with large, lobed, oak-like leaves that turn rich bronze-purple in autumn. Showy, conical heads of white flowers that age to pink appear in midsummer and autumn. Excellent in a shrub border, as an architectural specimen, or in a shady container (*see p.448, 472*). Keep pruning to a minimum, in spring.

ALSO RECOMMENDED: *Snow Flake has arching heads of double flowers; Snow Queen, with large upright flowerheads, is free-flowering;* H. anomala *subsp.* petiolaris ♥ (see p.275).

☼ ☼ ◊◊ ❄❄❄   **Deciduous shrub**
↕ 2m (6ft) ↔ 2.5m (8ft)

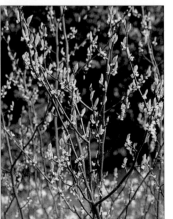

LINDERA BENZOIN

The spice bush is named and grown for its bright green leaves, which give a spicy odour when crushed and turn golden yellow in autumn. Small, flat-headed clusters of tiny, greenish yellow flowers appear in spring, succeeded by bright red berries if male and female plants are grown together. This rounded shrub suits acid soils and permanently moist ground (*see pp.92, 372*), growing naturally in damp woodland. Trim after flowering, if necessary.

ALSO RECOMMENDED: L. obtusiloba ♥ *reaches 6m (20ft) tall with yellow flowers.*

☼ ◊ ❄❄❄ *f*   **Deciduous shrub**
↕↔ 3m (10ft)

PAEONIA DELAVAYI ⚲

The nodding, bowl-shaped, glossy dark
red flowers of this shrubby tree peony
appear in early summer amid deeply
cut, dark green leaves; these are bluish
green beneath and turn yellow in
autumn. It is ideal as an architectural
specimen (*see p.472*), either alone, in
a shrub border, or in a wildlife garden
(*see p.494*). Grow in deep, fertile soil;
it tolerates clay and chalk (*see pp.12,
64*). Avoid regular hard pruning, but
occasionally cut out one or two old
stems at the base in autumn.

ALSO RECOMMENDED: *var.* lutea *has
yellow flowers; var.* ludlowii ⚲ (see p.505).

☼ ◐ ◊◊ ❋❋❋   **Deciduous shrub**
↕ 2m (6ft) ↔ 1.2m (4ft)

RHODODENDRON 'Polar Bear' ⚲

One of the last to flower, and among
the most fragrant, this sturdy, tree-like,
large-leaved rhododendron bears huge
trusses of waxy white flowers in late
summer. It is ideal for adding colour
to a shaded area, being spectacular
if grown in groves or avenues, and
it will also grow in a large container
(*see p.448*). Acid soils are essential
(*see p.92*). Little pruning is necessary.

ALSO RECOMMENDED: R. auriculatum *is
similar; Azor Group bear fragrant, pinkish
flowers in summer; Blue Diamond Group
(see p.160); 'Homebush' ⚲ (see p.454).*

☼ ◐ ◊ ❋❋❋ *f*   **Evergreen shrub**
↕ 5m (15ft) ↔ 4m (12ft)

SARCOCOCCA HOOKERIANA *VAR.* HUMILIS

A dense, suckering shrub with glossy dark green leaves that makes good ground cover, even in dry shade (*see pp.216, 326*). Clusters of pink-tinted white flowers appear in winter and are deliciously fragrant; they are followed by small, glossy blue-black fruits. It tolerates hard pruning and makes a fine low hedge (*see p.138*); trim in late spring. Tolerant of chalky soils and urban pollution (*see p.64*).

ALSO RECOMMENDED: S. ruscifolia *has creamy white flowers and red berries.*

☼ ☀ ◐◐ ❀❀❀ *f*   **Evergreen shrub**
↕ 60cm (24in) ↔ 1m (3ft)

VIBURNUM *'Pragense'* ♔

This evergreen viburnum makes a dark green, rounded bush. Its late spring flowers are pinkish then white, appearing in large, flat-headed clusters at the ends of the branches. The long and narrow leaves are deeply veined and wrinkled. Choose a site with shelter from cold, drying winds. Minimal pruning is required, although it can be clipped after flowering as an informal hedge (*see p.138*).

ALSO RECOMMENDED: V. davidii ♔ *is half the size;* V. rhytidophyllum (*see p.134*).

☼ ☀ ◐◐ ❀❀❀   **Evergreen shrub**
↕↔ 3m (10ft)

ACTAEA RUBRA ♥

The red baneberry is a clump-forming
plant with divided leaves. It bears
spikes of fluffy white flowers in mid-
spring and early summer; the glossy red
berries that follow are ornamental but
highly toxic. Grow in a woodland or
wild garden (*see p.494*), or in a shady
border. Water well in dry weather.

ALSO RECOMMENDED: *f. neglecta has
white berries*; A. pachypoda ♥ (*syn.
A. alba*) *has black-eyed white berries*;
A. spicata has black berries.

☀ ◐ ❀ ❀ ❀   **Perennial**

↕ 45cm (18in) ↔ 30cm (12in)

ANEMONELLA THALICTROIDES

Rue anemone is a spring-flowering
beauty of very delicate appearance. It
slowly forms a mound of blue-green,
finely divided foliage and bears fragile,
slender-stemmed, white or pink flowers.
Use beneath shrubs, or in a rock or
woodland garden. It must have moist
soil, but the tubers will rot in very
wet soils. Protect from slugs.

ALSO RECOMMENDED: *'Oscar Shoaf'
has double pink flowers.*

☀ ◐ ❀ ❀ ❀   **Perennial**

↕ 10cm (4in) ↔ 30cm (12in)

ANEMONOPSIS MACROPHYLLA

From mid- to late summer, this clump-forming perennial produces tall, dark stems of nodding, waxy textured flowers with lilac sepals and violet petals. They are held well above the mounds of divided, glossy dark green leaves. Provide shelter from cold, drying winds and choose a cool position in deep, fertile soil. Excellent for a shady border or woodland garden.

☀ ◊ ❄ ❄ ❄   **Perennial**
‡ 75cm (30in) ↔ 45cm (18in)

AQUILEGIA FRAGRANS

A graceful aquilegia that forms clumps of deeply lobed, blue-green leaves. In early summer, delicate clusters of fragrant, nodding, creamy white flowers with long, backward-pointing spurs rise above the foliage. It is ideal for naturalizing in a woodland garden or for the front of border, where its scent can be appreciated easily.

ALSO RECOMMENDED: A. flabellata ♀ has soft blue-purple flowers; A. 'Hensol Harebell' ♀ has soft blue flowers; A. vulgaris 'Nivea' ♀ (see p.511).

☀☀ ◊ ❄ ❄ ❄ f   **Perennial**
‡ 15–40cm (6–16in) ↔ 20cm (8in)

ARISAEMA CANDIDISSIMUM ♀

This plant is cultivated for its white-striped, light pink spathe, which is 8–15cm (3–6in) long and surrounds the greenish flower spike in summer. There is a sweet scent. A single leaf, palmately divided into three leaflets, emerges shortly afterwards from the underground tuber. It is best in partial shade, but it tolerates some sun. Plant tubers in winter or spring

ALSO RECOMMENDED. *A. amurense has a dark purple, white-striped spathe; A. flavum is hardier and has a smaller, green to yellow spathe.*

☼ ◐ ◊◊ ❀❀ *f*   **Perennial**
‡ 40cm (16in) ↔ 15cm (6in)

ARISARUM PROBOSCIDEUM

The mouse plant is named for its dark purple-brown spathes with long, curled tips, which look like the tails of mice. They enclose insignificant flower spikes in spring. The long-stalked, arrow-shaped, glossy green leaves form dense mats, making good ground cover (*see p.326*), but they often obscure the spathes. If successful, it will form a large colony in a woodland garden. Plant the rhizomes in autumn

☼ ◊ ❀❀❀   **Perennial**
‡ 15cm (6in) ↔ 25cm (10in) or more

ATHYRIUM FILIX-FEMINA *'Frizelliae'* ♀

Tatting fern is a diminutive form of the lady fern with bright green fronds, which resemble ribbons of hand-made lace; the frond segments are reduced to rounded lobes on either side of a midrib. Grow in a shady border or in a woodland garden, where it can be used as ground cover (*see p.326*). It needs fertile, neutral to acid soil (*see p.92*) and will also grow in a raised bed or shady container (*see p.448*).

ALSO RECOMMENDED: *'Minutissimum' is taller with dense, upright "shuttlecocks" of finely divided, lance-shaped fronds.*

☀ ◊◊ ❀❀❀   **Perennial fern**
‡ 20cm (8in) ↔ 30cm (12in)

BLECHNUM TABULARE ♀

This large, evergreen fern forms a spreading rosette of stiff, leathery fronds. It is similar to, and often confused with, *B. chilense* ♀. In a woodland garden, shady border, or rock garden, it would make a superb architectural plant (*see p.472*). It is easy to grow in rich, acid soils (*see p.92*).

ALSO RECOMMENDED: B. chilense ♀ *is larger with an indefinite spread;* B. penna-marina ♀ (see p.358); B. spicant ♀ *is smaller.*

☀☀ ◊ ❀❀❀   **Perennial fern**
‡ 1m (3ft) ↔ 60–120cm (24–48in)

CARDAMINE PENTAPHYLLA

An elegant addition to a shady border or woodland garden, this bittercress forms clumps of divided leaves with narrow, dark green leaflets. The loose clusters of four-petalled, white, pale purple, or lilac flowers appear among the foliage in late spring and early summer. Grow in damp, leafy soil.

ALSO RECOMMENDED: C. enneaphylla *has creamy white flowers in late spring;* C. pratensis *has longer heads of flowers, borne above the leaves.*

☼ ☀ ◐ ❄ ❄ ❄   **Perennial**
↕ 30–50cm (12–20in) ↔ 30cm (12in)

CIMICIFUGA SIMPLEX

At the beginning of autumn, this clump-forming perennial produces wand-like, often gracefully arching spires of tiny white flowers above mounds of divided, fresh green leaves. It is at home in a damp, shaded herbaceous border or woodland garden. Grow moist, leafy, fertile soil; it tolerates clay (*see p.12*). The flower stems may need unobtrusive support.

ALSO RECOMMENDED: *'Elstead'* ♀ *has purple-tinted flower buds;* 'White Pearl' *has greenish flower buds;* 'Brunette' *has maroon leaves and maroon-flushed flowers.*

☼ ◐ ❄ ❄ ❄   **Perennial**
↕ 1–1.2m (3–4ft) ↔ 60cm (24in)

DACTYLORHIZA FOLIOSA ♥

This hardy orchid has a sheaf of narrow, green, often brown- or purple-spotted leaves. From the middle of these arise sturdy stems bearing pink to bright purple flowers. They appear between late spring and early summer. A lovely addition to a rock or woodland garden, and it may also be naturalized in fine grass.

ALSO RECOMMENDED: D. elata ♥ *bears deep purple flowers in late spring;* D. fuchsii *bears white to pale pink or mauve flowers marked deep red or purple.*

☀ ◐ ❀ ❀ ❀   **Perennial**
‡ 60cm (24in) ↔ 15cm (6in)

DIGITALIS × MERTONENSIS ♥

The spires of dusky pink flowers make this foxglove a clear favourite for shady herbaceous borders and woodland gardens. They are good for cutting (*see p.524*) and arise in late spring and early summer above a basal rosette of glossy dark green leaves. It may self-sow, coming true from seed. Tolerant of dry shade (*see p.216*).

ALSO RECOMMENDED: D. ferruginea *has golden brown flowers with red-brown veins inside;* D. purpurea *f.* albiflora (see p.521).

☀ ◐◐ ❀ ❀ ❀   **Perennial**
‡ 90cm (36in) ↔ 30cm (12in)

ERANTHIS HYEMALIS ♥

Winter aconite is one of the earliest
spring-flowering bulbs, bearing
buttercup-like, bright yellow flowers.
These sit on a ruff of light green leaves,
covering the ground from late winter
until early spring (*see p.326*). It is
ideal for naturalizing in dappled shade
beneath deciduous trees and large
shrubs, especially in chalky soils (*see
p.64*). Plant bulbs in autumn and do
not allow the soil to dry out in summer.

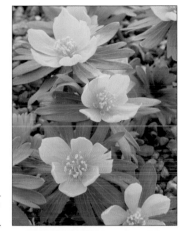

☼ ◊◊ ❋ ❋ ❋　　**Perennial bulb**
‡ 5–8cm (2–3in) ↔ 5cm (2in)

ERYTHRONIUM
CALIFORNICUM ♥

This clump-forming bulbous plant
looks good planted in the light shade
of deciduous trees and shrubs. Clusters
of off-white flowers with backward-
curving petals droop from the slender
stems in spring, above the oval, dark
green leaves. Plant bulbs in autumn.

ALSO RECOMMENDED. *'White Beauty'* ♥
is vigorous; E. dens-canis ♥*, the dog's
tooth violet, has white, pink, or lilac flowers;
E. 'Pagoda'* ♥ *is vigorous with yellow flowers.*

☼ ◊◊ ❋ ❋ ❋　　**Perennial bulb**
‡ 15–35cm (6–14in) ↔ 10cm (4in)

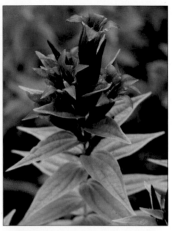

GENTIANA ASCLEPIADEA ♥

The willow gentian forms clumps of lance-shaped, fresh green leaves on upright or arching stems. In late summer and autumn, these leafy stems are surrounded by whorls of trumpet-shaped, dark blue flowers, often spotted or striped with purple on the insides. It is suitable for a shady border or large rock garden, and it associates well with grasses and ferns. Grow in neutral to acid, damp to permanently moist soils (*see pp.92, 372*).

ALSO RECOMMENDED: *var.* alba *has greenish white flowers.*

☀ ◐ ❀❀❀　　　　　　　**Perennial**
‡ 60–90cm (24–36in) ↔ 45cm (18in)

GLAUCIDIUM PALMATUM ♥

This slowly spreading perennial forms a low mound of crinkly, bright green, sharply lobed leaves. From late spring to early summer, it bears large, poppy-like, lilac-pink to mauve flowers, each with a small, central boss of golden stamens. Very effective in a shady border or woodland garden. Grow in moist, leafy, fertile soil with shelter from cold, drying winds.

ALSO RECOMMENDED: *var.* leucanthum *has white flowers.*

☀ ☀ ◐ ❀❀❀　　　　　　**Perennial**
‡↔ 45cm (18in)

HACQUETIA EPIPACTIS ♥

In late winter and early spring, this diminutive plant produces tiny yellow flowers, each cluster no more than 5cm (2in) tall, with a ruff of emerald-green bracts beneath. The glossy green leaves are divided into three wedge-shaped lobes and develop fully after flowering to form a low carpet. Grow in neutral to acid soil (*see p.92*). A very pretty plant for a woodland garden, a shady niche in a rock garden, or a peat bed.

☀ ◐ ✽✽✽   **Perennial**

‡ 15cm (6in) ↔ 15–30cm (6–12in)

HELLEBORUS ORIENTALIS *SUBSP.* GUTTATUS

Lenten roses are very variable and bear droopy flowers from midwinter to spring on upright stems above clumps of large and leathery, divided leaves. This one has creamy white flowers with dark red spots inside; they are good for cutting (*see p.524*). Tolerant of most sites, even dry shade (*see p.216*), but best in moist, neutral to alkaline soils (*see p.64*). Good for winter colour in a shady shrub border.

ALSO RECOMMENDED H. orientalis *is very variable with greenish white flowers, ageing to pink;* H. foetidus ♥ (see p.232); H. niger ♥ *flowers from early winter.*

☀ ◐◐ ✽✽✽   **Perennial**

‡↔ 45cm (18in)

HOSTA *'Wide Brim'* ♀

This hosta is prized for its clumps of broad and crumpled leaves with wide, creamy yellow margins, which pale with age. Light lavender-blue flowers appear on tall stems in summer. An architectural plant for bog gardens, pond margins, or containers (*see pp.372, 448, 472*). It tolerates clay soils and can be grown as ground cover (*see pp.12, 326*).

ALSO RECOMMENDED: *'Frances Williams'* ♀ (see p.381); *'Halcyon'* ♀ (see p.340); *'Shade Fanfare'* ♀ (see p.465); H. sieboldiana *var.* elegans ♀ (see p.490); H. ventricosa ♀ (see p.30).

☼ ◑ ◔◔ ✶✶✶   **Perennial**
‡ 45cm (18in) ↔ 1m (3ft)

JEFFERSONIA DUBIA

The delicate, two-lobed, blue-green leaves of this slender perennial are particularly beautiful as they unfold in spring; they are often tinted with purple when young. In late spring or early summer, it bears cup-shaped, clear lavender-blue flowers on dark stems. A lovely addition to a shady niche in a rock garden or peat bed, needing moist, humus-rich soil. Mulch annually with leaf mould in autumn.

ALSO RECOMMENDED: J. diphylla *is slightly taller with larger, kidney-shaped, deeply cleft, blue-grey leaves and white flowers.*

☼ ◑ ✶✶✶   **Perennial**
‡ 20cm (8in) ↔ 15cm (6in)

LEUCOJUM VERNUM
VAR. VAGNERI

The spring snowflake is a bulbous plant with stiffly upright, long and narrow, dark green leaves. Arising from between this thin clump of leaves, a tall stem emerges; when it is fully grown, in late winter and early spring, two bell-shaped white flowers hang from its tip. Plant bulbs in autumn in a damp border or at a pond margin (*see p.372*).

ALSO RECOMMENDED: L. vernum ♛ *is slightly taller, flowering in early spring,* L. aestivum *has white spring flowers.*

☀ ◐ ❄ ❄ ❄　　　　　**Perennial**

‡ 20cm (8in) ↔ 8cm (3in)

MITELLA BREWERI

This mitrewort is a good ground-cover perennial for the front of a damp, shady border or woodland garden (*see p.326*). It forms dense clumps of lobed leaves, and in spring and early summer, bears slender-stemmed spikes of many tiny, yellow-green flowers with fringed petals. Grow in moist and leafy, acid soil (*see p.92*); it self-seeds freely. Protect from slugs.

ALSO RECOMMENDED: M. stauropetala *is taller and more vigorous with purple-tinted leaves and white or purple flowers.*

☀ ◑ ◐ ❄ ❄ ❄　　　　**Perennial**

‡ 15cm (6in) ↔ 20cm (8in)

OMPHALODES CAPPADOCICA ♛

This perennial forms compact mounds of fresh green, heart-shaped leaves, which make good ground cover in a damp, shady border (*see p.326*), or in a rock or woodland garden. The loose clusters of white-eyed, azure-blue flowers, reminiscent of forget-me-nots, appear in early spring. Grow in humus-rich, moderately fertile soil. It is also good for paving crevices (*see p.348*).

ALSO RECOMMENDED: *'Cherry Ingram'* ♛ *is more compact with larger, deeper blue flowers; 'Starry Eyes' has larger flowers with a central white stripe on each petal.*

☼ ◑ ❀❀❀   **Perennial**
‡ 25cm (10in) ↔ 40cm (16in)

ONOCLEA SENSIBILIS ♛

The sensitive fern forms a beautifully textured mass of arching and divided, deciduous fronds. These are tinted pinkish bronze as they unfurl, later turning matt pale green. An ideal plant for ground cover in a damp, shady border, especially at the edge of water (*see pp.326, 372*); it thrives in acid soils and tolerates those rich in clay (*see pp.12, 92*). It must have a shady spot as the fronds scorch in excessive sun.

☼ ◑◑ ❀❀❀   **Perennial fern**
‡ 60cm (24in) ↔ indefinite

OSMUNDA REGALIS ♈

The royal fern is a stately plant forming clumps of bright green, finely divided fronds. There are no flowers. Distinctive, rust-coloured fronds are produced at the centre of each clump in summer. It is excellent in a damp border or at the margins of a pond or stream (*see p.372*), ideally in acid soil (*see p.92*). It tolerates clay soils (*see p.12*).

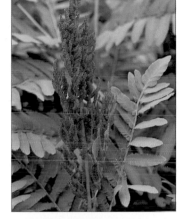

ALSO RECOMMENDED: *'Cristata'* ♈ *has attractively crested fronds; the fronds of 'Purpurascens' are purplish in spring.*

☼ ◑ ◖◖ ❀ ❀ ❀   **Perennial fern**
↕ 2m (6ft) ↔ 4m (12ft)

PERSICARIA MILLETII

This clump-forming and upright plant is densely clothed in narrowly lance-shaped, dark green leaves and makes good, long-flowering ground cover in a damp, shady border (*see p.326*). The slender-stemmed, wand-like clusters of many tiny, crimson-red flowers appear from early summer to late autumn. Grow in any permanently damp site including clay soils (*see p.12, 372*).

ALSO RECOMMENDED: *P. affinis 'Donald Lowndes'* ♈ (*see p.321*); *P. campanulata* (*see p.32*); *P. macrophylla is smaller with pink or red flowers.*

☼ ◑ ◖ ❀ ❀ ❀   **Perennial**
↕↔ 60cm (24in)

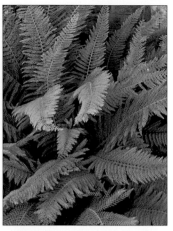

POLYSTICHUM SETIFERUM
Divisilobum Group

These soft shield ferns are tall and evergreen with finely divided, feathery, dark green fronds, which are soft to touch and form splayed clumps. They make fine architectural plants (*see p.472*) for shady borders or rock gardens with shelter from excessive winter wet. They are also good as ground cover or as pot plants (*see pp.326, 448*). Remove any dead or damaged fronds in spring. Tolerant of clay soils (*see p.12*).

ALSO RECOMMENDED: *The broad fronds of 'Herrenhausen' are more spreading;* P. munitum ♀ (see p.492).

☼☀ ◊◊ ❋❋❋   **Perennial fern**
‡↔ 50–70cm (20–28in)

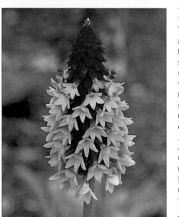

PRIMULA VIALII ♀

This deciduous border perennial has a basal rosette of narrow green leaves, from which emerges an upright flower stem in summer, topped by a dense spike of dark red buds. These open to violet-blue flowers. Choose a site with rich, neutral to acid soil (*see p.92*); full sun is tolerated if the soil remains moist (*see p.372*). It can also be grown as a container plant (*see p.448*).

ALSO RECOMMENDED: P. florindae ♀ (see p.389); P. japonica 'Postford White' ♀ (see p.389); P. polyanthus ♀ (see p.468); P. pulverulenta ♀ (see p.390); P. rosea ♀ (see p.390).

☼☀ ◊ ❋❋❋   **Perennial**
‡ 30–60cm (12–24in) ↔ 30cm (12in)

PRUNELLA GRANDIFLORA

Large self-heal is a vigorous plant with dark green leaves in clumps at ground level; it is good for ground cover in a damp, shady border and may be naturalized in fine turf (*see pp.304, 326*). The two-lipped purple flowers, borne in whorls on square stems in summer, attract a host of beneficial insects (*see p.494*). It grows in any soil, including clay (*see p.12*); give it space to expand so as not to swamp smaller plants.

ALSO RECOMMENDED: *'Pink Loveliness' has pink flowers; those of 'White Loveliness' are pure white.*

☼☀ ◐◊ ❄❄❄ **Perennial**
‡ 15cm (6in) ↔ 1m (3ft) or more

SCILLA PERUVIANA *'Alba'*

This bulbous plant bears a basal cluster of strap-like leaves, to 60cm (24in) long, throughout the year; there is no dormant period, and new leaves grow in autumn as the old ones die away. Dome-shaped clusters of many white flowers rise above the leaves in early summer. Plant bulbs under deciduous trees and shrubs or in grass in autumn. It also grows in sandy and chalky soils (*see pp.38, 61*), and coastal and hot, dry sites (*see pp.166, 190*).

ALSO RECOMMENDED: S. peruviana *has large heads of deep blue flowers.*

☼☀ ◐◊ ❄❄❄ **Perennial bulb**
‡ 15–30cm (6–12in) ↔ 10cm (4in)

THALICTRUM DELAVAYI *'Album'*

An upright, clump-forming perennial with finely divided, fresh green leaves producing its fluffy white flowers in branching heads from midsummer to autumn. This plant is an excellent textural foil for bold-leaved plants in a mixed or herbaceous border. Divide clumps every three years to maintain their vigour.

ALSO RECOMMENDED: T. delavayi ♀ *has purple-tinted stems and lilac or white flowers; 'Hewitt's Double' ♀ has rich mauve, double flowers and is very floriferous.*

☀ ◐ ◊◊ ❋❋❋ **Perennial**
‡ 1.2m (4ft) ↔ 60cm (24in)

TRILLIUM SESSILE

The wake robin is an upright, clump-forming plant valued for its stemless maroon flowers of late spring; they nestle atop whorls of oval, deep green, marbled leaves. Hostas make excellent companions to this plant in a damp border. Choose leafy, neutral to acid soil (*see p.92*), providing a mulch of leaf mould in autumn.

ALSO RECOMMENDED: T. chloropetalum *has fragrant, greenish white, yellow, or purple-brown flowers;* T. erectum ♀ (see p.117); T. luteum ♀ *has sweetly scented, golden or bronze-green flowers.*

☀ ☀ ◊◊ ❋❋❋ **Perennial**
‡ 30cm (12in) ↔ 20cm (8in)

TROLLIUS × CULTORUM *'Alabaster'*

This globeflower is a robust plant with pale yellow spring flowers. These are held above the clumps of mid-green leaves, which are deeply cut with five rounded lobes. Good for bright colour beside a pond or stream (*see p.372*) or in a damp border; the flowers can be cut for indoor decoration (*see p.524*). It grows well in heavy clay soils (*see p.12*).

ALSO RECOMMENDED: *'Earliest of All' has yellow flowers; 'Orange Princess'* ♥ *has golden orange flowers into summer.*

☼☼ ◐▲ ❄❄❄ **Perennial**
‡ 60cm (24in) ↔ 40cm (16in)

VIOLA RIVINIANA *Purpurea Group*

This group of small perennials derived from the common dog violet have oval and toothed, purple-tinged leaves with long stems, which all emerge from ground level. Pretty purple flowers with spurs appear in late spring. These violets grow well in damp or dry shade (*see p.216*); their invasive habit suits them to ground cover or as a colony in a wildlife garden (*see pp.326, 494*).

ALSO RECOMMENDED: V. riviniana *is less invasive with pale violet-blue flowers and mid-green leaves.*

☼☼ ◐◑ ❄❄❄ **Perennial**
‡ 10–20cm (4–8in) ↔ 20–40cm (8–16in)

PLANTS FOR NORTH- & EAST-FACING WALLS

Climbers and wall-trained shrubs establish a vertical element in a planting scheme, which is especially valuable in lending colour and variety to small gardens; no matter how extensive their vertical spread, climbers take up relatively little space at ground level. In the wild, many climbers, such as *Akebia quinata* (*see p.271*) and *Schisandra rubriflora* (*see p.278*), are to be found scrambling up and through trees, so they are well-adapted to shady conditions. Walls that face east receive more light, and may even be in direct sun for several hours in the morning. Plants that may be grown on east-facing walls, therefore, need not be shade-demanding plants. It is also the ideal site for plants like *Lonicera japonica* 'Halliana' (*see p.276*), which grow well in good light, but become stressed and more vulnerable to pests, such as aphids, if exposed to hot midday sun.

North- and east-facing walls can be dry places, since they often have a rain shadow at their base, especially if overhung by the house eaves, where rainfall is unable to penetrate. To avoid this problem, plant at least 45cm (18in) away from the foot of the wall.

There is one important feature of easterly walls to be borne in mind, especially during winter and early spring. Easterly walls receive the first morning light and its warmth can do considerable damage to the frozen leaves, buds, or flowers of otherwise hardy plants, particularly camellias (*see pp.99, 240, 264, 450*); frozen water in the plant cells causes them to rupture if thawing is rapid. The sun's warmth can also induce plants into early growth in spring, and the soft new growth is far more susceptible to cold damage. On a north wall, the temperature rises slowly, so it is much less likely to cause damage, and plants will not be tempted into early growth. Although a north wall may be relatively well-lit if it is in an open site, only plants that are tolerant of shade can be expected to thrive there.

TRAINING PLANTS

Climbers use different methods to attach themselves as they climb. Some, like *Hedera colchica* 'Sulphur Heart' (*see p.275*) and *Parthenocissus tricuspidata* (*see p.277*), attach themselves by aerial roots, which cling to any surface that offers purchase. They usually need a little initial guidance by means of canes, but once established, they become self-supporting. Twining or tendril climbers, like *Aconitum hemsleyanum* (*see p.271*) and *Clematis montana* (*see p.274*), must have some support that they can cling to, such as other shrubs or a framework of wires or trellis. Wall-trained shrubs that do not climb naturally, flowering quince for example (*see p.264*), need to be trained and tied in to their support. Fix wall supports before planting, attaching them to slats 10–15cm (4–6in) thick to allow space for air circulate, which helps reduce the incidence of diseases such as mildew. There will also be more room for plant stems to expand.

CAMELLIA × WILLIAMSII 'Golden Spangles'

This vigorous shrub is valued for its lustrous, dark green leaves, which have golden centres, and for its elegant and single, bright red-pink flowers from mid- to late spring. It is ideal for a north wall, but avoid east-facing sites, as the combination of morning sun after frost is damaging. It tolerates acid soils and damp shade (*see pp.92, 238*). Prune young plants to shape after flowering; the flowers cut well (*see p.524*).

ALSO RECOMMENDED: *'Bow Bells' has single pink flowers from winter; 'J.C. Williams'* ♀ *has pale pink, single flowers in spring.*

☼ ◐◊ ❀❀❀　　　**Evergreen shrub**
‡ 2–5m (6–15ft) ↔ 1–4m (3–12ft)

CHAENOMELES SPECIOSA 'Moerloosei' ♀

A fast-growing shrub that has tangled, spiny branches and glossy dark green leaves. It bears large, pink-flushed white flowers in early spring, followed by small, yellow-green fruits in autumn. It thrives on sunless walls; if wall-trained, shorten sideshoots to two or three leaves in late spring. It will also grow against sunnier walls, as a hedge, or as a free-standing shrub (*see pp.138, 280*). Tolerant of chalky soils (*see p.64*).

ALSO RECOMMENDED: *'Geisha Girl' has apricot-pink flowers; 'Nivalis' has pure white flowers.*

☼◑ ◊ ❀❀❀　　　**Deciduous shrub**
‡ 2.5m (8ft) ↔ 5m (15ft)

COTONEASTER HORIZONTALIS ♚

The herringbone branches of this spreading shrub are clothed in small, glossy dark green leaves. In summer, tiny pinkish white flowers attract bees; the profusion of bright red berries that follow persist well into winter unless consumed by birds (*see p.494*). It grows in most soils, including those on chalk, and tolerates dry shade (*see pp.64, 216*). Keep pruning to a minimum, in winter if necessary.

ALSO RECOMMENDED: C. integrifolius *is evergreen with dark pinkish red fruits*; C. simonsii ♚ *is deciduous with red fruits.*

☼ ◊ ✽ ✽ ✽   **Deciduous shrub**
‡ 1m (3ft) ↔ 1.5m (5ft)

CRINODENDRON HOOKERIANUM ♚

The lantern tree is an upright shrub with elegant, narrow, leathery, dark green foliage. In late spring and early summer, it bears hanging crimson flowers, which give rise to its common name. A most attractive specimen for a sheltered, north-facing or shady site (avoid east-facing positions) away from cold, drying winds. Grow in humus-rich, acid soil (*see p.92*). Keep pruning to a minimum.

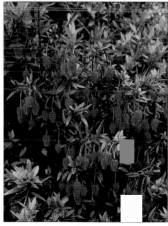

ALSO RECOMMENDED: C. patagua *bears fragrant white flowers late summer.*

☼ ◊◊ ✽ ✽   **Evergreen shrub**
‡ 6m (20ft) ↔ 5m (15ft)

DRIMYS WINTERI

Winter's bark is a superb and elegant specimen for a north wall. It forms a strongly upright shrub with elliptical, dark green leaves, and it bears large clusters of fragrant, ivory-white flowers from spring to early summer. Shelter from cold, drying winds and avoid east-facing walls. Keep pruning to a minimum. It tolerates clay soils and sunnier walls (*see pp.12, 280*).

ALSO RECOMMENDED: *var. andina is a dwarf, to 1m (3ft) tall; D. lanceolata is similar with dark red stems.*

☀ ◊ ❀❀   **Evergreen shrub**
↕ 15m (50ft) ↔ 10m (30ft)

EUCRYPHIA MILLIGANII

This slender, upright shrub with glossy dark green leaves is valued for its cup-shaped white flowers of midsummer, which have a central boss of golden stamens. Grow in fertile, neutral to acid soil (*see p.92*), and shelter from cold, drying winds. Keep pruning to a minimum.

ALSO RECOMMENDED: E. glutinosa ♀ *is taller and deciduous with double white flowers*; E. lucida, *also taller, has white flowers in early to midsummer.*

☀☀ ◊ ❀❀   **Evergreen shrub**
↕ 6m (20ft) ↔ 1.5m (5ft)

FORSYTHIA SUSPENSA ♔

An open shrub with strongly arching branches that is valued for its nodding, bright yellow flowers, which wreathe the bare branches in early to mid-spring. The leaves are oval and mid-green. It is also useful as a specimen shrub, in a border, or as an informal hedge (*see p.138*). It grows in most fertile, well-drained soils, including those on chalk (*see p.61*). Cut out some of the oldest stems on established plants each year after flowering. The flowers are good for cutting (*see p.524*).

ALSO RECOMMENDED: *f. atrocaulis and 'Nymans' have purplish young growth.*

☼ ☽ ◊ ✳ ✳ ✳   **Deciduous shrub**
↕ • 3m (10ft)

GARRYA × ISSAQUAHENSIS 'Pat Ballard'

This upright shrub, densely clothed in bright green leaves, is grown for its beautifully hanging, purple tinted, grey catkins, which festoon the branches in midwinter. It is especially effective when trained against a north-facing wall. It needs minimal pruning; if necessary, shorten outward-growing shoots after flowering.

ALSO RECOMMENDED: *'Glasnevin Wine' has purplish stems and green-red catkins;* G. elliptica (see p.219).

☼ ☽ ◊ ✳ ✳ ✳   **Evergreen shrub**
↕ 4m (12ft) ↔ 3m (10ft)

ILLICIUM ANISATUM

Chinese anise is a broadly conical shrub with glossy green leaves and clusters of fragrant, star-shaped, creamy white flowers in mid-spring. It does well on a north-facing wall, in a woodland garden, or in a shrub border. Grow in humus-rich, acid soil (*see p.92*) with shelter from cold, drying winds. It needs very little pruning.

ALSO RECOMMENDED: I. floridanum *has nodding, red-purple flowers.*

☼ ◐ ◯ ❀ ❀ ❀ *f*   **Evergreen shrub**
‡ 8m (25ft) ↔ 6m (20ft)

JASMINUM HUMILE

Yellow jasmine is a bushy plant with bright green leaves and fragrant, rich yellow flowers from late spring to early summer. It is suitable for a north-facing wall, although it flowers more freely in sun (*see p.280*); the flowers are good for cutting (*see p.524*). After flowering, shorten flowered shoots to a strong bud; when mature, remove one in five of the oldest, flowered stems. Also good in a sunny or shady border, or as ground cover in sun (*see p.304*). Tolerant of chalky soils (*see p.64*).

ALSO RECOMMENDED: *'Revolutum'* ♀ *has larger flowers*; J. nudiflorum ♀ (*see p.76*).

☼ ◐ ◯ ❀ ❀ ❀ *f*   **Evergreen shrub**
‡ 2.5m (8ft) ↔ 3m (10ft)

MAHONIA × MEDIA *'Charity'* ♥

A fast-growing shrub that bears dense, upright then spreading spikes of fragrant yellow flowers from late autumn to spring, suitable for a north-facing wall. It makes a fine architectural specimen for a damp, shady border or wildlife garden (*see pp.238, 472, 494*). The glossy dark green leaves are spiny, making it useful for vandal-proof barrier plantings. Prune any bare, leggy stems back hard after flowering. It tolerates chalky soils (*see p.64*).

ALSO RECOMMENDED: *Lionel Fortescue'* ♥ and *'Winter Sun'* ♥ are similar

☀ ◑ ❄ ❄ ❄   **Evergreen shrub**
‡ 5m (15ft) ↔ 4m (12ft)

PYRACANTHA *'Soleil d'Or'*

This spiny, upright shrub is good for training on walls of any aspect (*see p.280*). The clustered white flowers of early summer, offset against glossy dark green leaves, attract bees, and the bright golden yellow berries that follow and persist into winter are among the last to be taken by birds (*see p.494*). It can also be grown as a hedge or in exposed sites (*see pp.118, 138*). Cut back unwanted growth in mid-spring. It tolerates clay soils (*see p.12*).

ALSO RECOMMENDED: *'Golden Charmer'* (see p.159); *'Mohave'* (see p.19); *'Watereri'* ♥ (see p.505).

☀ ◑ ◊ ❄ ❄ ❄   **Evergreen shrub**
‡ 3m (10ft) ↔ 2.5m (8ft)

RIBES LAURIFOLIUM

This compact shrub with scalloped, leathery, dark green leaves is valued for its hanging clusters of pale green flowers in late winter and early spring. On female plants, flowers are followed by small, egg-shaped, red then black berries, if plants of both genders are grown together. It grows well on a north-facing wall. Trim after flowering, if necessary. It is also suitable for a damp, shady border (*see p.238*).

ALSO RECOMMENDED: R. alpinum (see p.222) *and* R. sanguineum *'Brocklebankii'* ♀ (see p.161) *both tolerate dry sites.*

☼ ☀ ◊◊ ❄ ❄ ❄   **Evergreen shrub**
‡ 1m (3ft) ↔ 1.5m (5ft)

ROSA *Danse du Feu*

The rounded, double, intense scarlet flowers of this stiff-stemmed, climbing rose are borne throughout summer and autumn against very glossy dark green foliage. It does well in shade, but flowers more profusely in sun (*see p.280*). Train the stems to cover the wall, then prune to keep it confined after flowering. It tolerates chalky soils and can be container-grown (*see pp.64, 412, 448*). The flowers cut well (*see p.524*).

ALSO RECOMMENDED: *'Albéric Barbier'* ♀ *has double white flowers;* *'New Dawn'* ♀ *has fragrant pink flowers;* *'Zéphirine Drouhin'* ♀ *has very fragrant, deep pink flowers.*

☼ ☀ ◊◊ ❄ ❄ ❄   **Deciduous shrub**
‡↔ 2.5m (8ft)

ACONITUM HEMSLEYANUM

This vigorous, twining perennial has lobed, fresh green leaves and produces curious, hooded, glossy violet flowers from midsummer to early autumn. Provide the support of a trellis if it is to grow on a wall, or allow it to scramble through earlier flowering shrubs to extend their period of interest. It is also suitable for a shady border. Cut flowered stems down in early spring.

☼ ◐ ◊◊ ❁❁❁   **Climber**

‡ 2–3m (6–10ft)

AKEBIA QUINATA

A woody stemmed, semi-evergreen, twining climber valued for its five-parted, dark green leaves, which flush purple in winter. Fragrant, brownish purple flowers in early spring give rise to sausage-like purple fruits if summers are long and hot. In areas with late frosts, avoid sites that receive morning sun to reduce the risk of flower damage. Grow on a wall or pergola, or train into a tree. Trim after flowering. It tolerates damp, shady sites (see p.210).

ALSO RECOMMENDED: A. trifoliata *has leaves that are bronzed when young, and purple flowers and fruits.*

☼ ◐ ◊◊ ❁❁❁ *f*   **Climber**

‡ 10m (30ft)

ASTERANTHERA OVATA

The bristly and rounded, bright green leaves of this evergreen climber are borne on white-hairy stems, offset by tubular, brilliant red-pink flowers in summer. It thrives in damp soils against sheltered, north-facing walls, but it may not survive severe winters. If not tied in to a support, it becomes creeping and stem-rooting, making good ground cover in damp shade (*see pp.238, 326*). Grow in humus-rich, acid soil (*see p.92*).

☀ ◐◊ ❋❋   **Climber**
↕ 4m (12ft) ↔ 2m (6ft)

BERBERIDOPSIS CORALLINA

The coral plant displays its hanging, spherical, dark red flowers against an evergreen backdrop of heart-shaped, dark green leaves from summer to early autumn. It is excellent on a north-facing wall, if supported on wires and sheltered from cold, drying winds. Grow in cool, humus-rich, neutral to acid soil (*see p.92*); protect the roots from frost with an autumn mulch. Pruning is best avoided, but a trim may be necessary in spring to keep the growth confined. It tolerates dry shade and can be grown as ground cover if allowed to trail without support (*see pp.216, 326*).

☀ ◐◊ ❋❋   **Climber**
↕↔ 5m (15ft)

CELASTRUS ORBICULATUS

The leaves of the oriental bittersweet turn yellow before falling in autumn. In summer, it bears clusters of tiny green flowers, which are followed by yellow fruits; these open to expose pink or red seeds. Both male and female plants must be grown in sun for reliable fruiting. Keep pruning to a minimum, removing damaged growth in early spring. It tolerates chalky soils and will grow in dry shade (*see pp.64, 216*).

ALSO RECOMMENDED: *Hermaphrodite Group* ♀ *bear both male and female flowers on the same plants.*

☀ ◊ ❀ ❀ ❀   **Climber**
↕ 14m (16ft)

CLEMATIS *'Nelly Moser'* ♀

This deciduous clematis produces large, mauve-pink flowers in early summer, and benefits from a shady root run. The flowers retain their best colour in shade, as do other pale-flowered clematis; although more flowers are produced in sun, they fade quickly. Remove dead or damaged growth in early spring, and cut healthy stems back to strong buds. It tolerates chalky soils and can be pot-grown (*see pp.64, 448*)

ALSO RECOMMENDED: *'Bee's Jubilee'* ♀ *has deep pink flowers; 'Bill Mackenzie'* ♀ *(see p.299); 'Hagley Hybrid' has pink flowers; 'Marie Boisselot'* ♀ *has large white flowers.*

☀☀ ◊ ❀ ❀ ❀   **Climber**
↕ 2–3m (6–10ft) ↔ 1m (3ft)

CLEMATIS MONTANA

This deciduous climber forms a tangled mass of stems and is almost obscured by a profusion of single white flowers in early summer. It thrives on walls of any aspect (*see p.280*) as well as in containers (*see p.448*). Prune after flowering, removing dead or damaged stems; shorten others as necessary. It tolerates chalky soils (*see p.64*).

ALSO RECOMMENDED: *f.* grandiflora ♥ *has larger flowers;* 'Tetrarose' ♥ *has pink flowers;* C. rehderiana ♥ (*see p.300*); C. tangutica (*see p.508*).

☼ ◐ ◊ ❋❋❋   **Climber**
‡ 5–14m (15–46ft) ↔ 2–3m (6–10ft)

CODONOPSIS CLEMATIDEA

The branching stems of this twining, herbaceous climber bear narrow and pointed, grey-green leaves. In late summer, nodding, bell-shaped, pale blue-grey flowers appear; their yellow, black and blue markings within are best seen from below. Train it against a wall, or allow it to scramble through shrubs in a shady border. Provide shelter from strong winds.

ALSO RECOMMENDED: C. convolvulacea ♥ *has violet-blue flowers and needs a very sheltered site;* C. tangshen *has yellow to olive-green flowers.*

☼ ◐ ◊◊ ❋❋❋   **Climber**
‡ 1.5m (5ft)

HEDERA COLCHICA
'Sulphur Heart' ♀

Persian ivy is a vigorous, self-clinging,
evergreen climber, which can also
be grown as ground cover or in a
container (*see pp.304, 326, 412, 448*).
The large, heart-shaped leaves are dark
green suffused with creamy yellow. It
tolerates dry shade and grows well in
alkaline soils (*see pp.64, 216*). Prune
at any time of year to restrict size.

ALSO RECOMMENDED: *'Dentata Variegata'* ♀
has light green leaves with cream margins;
H. helix *'Erecta'* ♀ (*see p.220*); *'Glacier'* ♀
(*see p.330*); *f. poetarum* (*see p.509*);
H. hibernica ♀ (*see p.331*).

☼◐ ◊◊ ❄❄❄   **Climber**
↕ 5m (15ft)

HYDRANGEA ANOMALA
SUBSP. PETIOLARIS ♀

This self-clinging climber forms a woody
framework that is attractive even after the
heart-shaped leaves have turned yellow
and fallen in autumn. Creamy white,
lacecap flowerheads cover the branches
for long periods in summer, illuminating
a shady wall to perfection. Keep pruning
to a minimum, trimming to size after
flowering, if necessary. It tolerates damp,
shady sites (*see p.238*) and will grow as
ground cover or in a pot (*see pp.326, 448*).

ALSO RECOMMENDED: H. seemannii
and H. serratifolia *give similar effects
but are evergreen and less frost hardy.*

☼◐ ◊◊ ❄❄❄   **Climber**
↕↔ 15m (50ft)

LAPAGERIA ROSEA ♔

The Chilean bell flower is a long-lived, twining climber with oval, evergreen leaves. From summer to late autumn, it produces large, narrowly bell-shaped, waxy, red to pink flowers. In cold areas, it needs the protection of a sheltered, shady wall; avoid east-facing sites and provide a deep winter mulch. Keep pruning to a minimum, removing damaged growth in spring. It tolerates sandy and acid soils, and dry sites in shade (*see pp.38, 216*).

☀ ◊ ❈❈   **Climber**
↕↔ 5m (15ft)

LONICERA JAPONICA *'Halliana'* ♔

This Japanese honeysuckle is a vigorous, evergreen, twining climber with very fragrant white flowers, which age to dark yellow. They appear from spring to late summer. Cut back shoots on established plants by up to a third in spring or after flowering. It can be grown as ground cover or in containers (*see pp.216, 448*) and tolerates chalky soils and dry shade (*see pp.64, 216*).

ALSO RECOMMENDED: *'Hall's Prolific' is more floriferous; var. repens* ♔ *has purple-flushed leaves and reddish white flowers; L. × americana is deciduous with yellow flowers.*

☀ ◐ ◊◊ ❈❈❈ *f*   **Climber**
↕ 10m (30ft)

PARTHENOCISSUS TRICUSPIDATA ♥

Boston ivy is a woody, deciduous, self-clinging climber with lobed, bright green leaves, which blaze up in intense shades of scarlet, crimson, and purple in autumn. Provide young plants with some support until established. Cut out unwanted growth in autumn. It tolerates chalky soils and can also be grown on a sunny wall (*see pp.64, 280*).

ALSO RECOMMENDED: *'Veitchii' has dark red-purple autumn foliage colour;* P. henryana ♥ (see p.77).

☼ ◑ ◊◊ ❄❄❄   **Climber**

↕ 20m (70ft)

PILEOSTEGIA VIBURNOIDES ♥

This woody, evergreen climber is slow-growing and self-clinging, and it is ideal for walls of any aspect, even deep, damp shade (*see pp.238, 280*). The glossy dark green leaves form an elegant backdrop to the clusters of small, star-shaped, creamy white flowers, which appear in late summer and autumn. Keep pruning to a minimum, but trim after flowering to keep it within bounds.

☼ ◑ ◊ ❄❄❄   **Climber**

↕↔ 6m (20ft)

SCHISANDRA RUBRIFLORA

A twining climber with lance-shaped, dark green leaves that turn yellow before falling in autumn. In spring and summer, it bears hanging, deep crimson flowers followed, on female plants, by pendent spikes of fleshy red fruit. Male and female plants are needed to obtain fruits. Train onto a wall or up into a tree; tie in young shoots until established. It tolerates coastal sites (*see p.166*).

ALSO RECOMMENDED: S. chinensis *and* S. grandiflora *have white or pale pink flowers in late spring and early summer.*

☼ ◐ ◊◊ ❊❊❊ **Climber**

‡ 10m (30ft)

SCHIZOPHRAGMA INTEGRIFOLIUM ♀

This deciduous climber forms an intricate branch pattern, which is attractive even when leafless in winter (*see p.472*). The dark green leaves complement the broad heads of creamy white flowers to perfection in midsummer. Tie to a support until it begins to cling by itself. Keep pruning to a minimum; trim to within its bounds in spring. It thrives on walls of any aspect and tolerates damp shade (*see pp.238, 280*).

ALSO RECOMMENDED: S. hydrangeoides *is similar; '*Roseum*' has flowers with pink bracts.*

☼ ◐ ◊ ❊❊❊ **Climber**

‡↔ 12m (40ft)

TROPAEOLUM SPECIOSUM ♀

The flame nasturtium is a slender,
herbaceous climber, producing long-
spurred, bright vermilion flowers
throughout summer and autumn. The
bright green leaves are attractively
divided into several leaflets. It is very
effective grown through dark-leaved
hedging, such as yew (*see p.144*), and
if given support and cool shade at
the roots, it will thrive on shady walls.
It will also grow as ground cover and
in containers (*see pp.304, 412, 448*).
Mulch over winter.

☼☀ ◔◑ ❄❄❄   **Climber**
↕↔ 3m (10ft) or more

VITIS AMURENSIS

Amur grape is a vigorous vine suitable
for training against a trellis or partially
shaded wall, or up into a large shrub
or tree. It is grown for its lobed and
toothed, deep green foliage, which
turns to beautiful shades of red and
purple before it falls in autumn. Small
bunches of inedible, white-bloomed
black grapes appear at the end of
summer. It has woody stems and climbs
using tendrils. Trim to size in midwinter.
It tolerates full sun (*see p.280*).

ALSO RECOMMENDED: *V. 'Brant'* ♀ *has
copper-bronze autumn leaf colour and
large bunches of edible, blue-black grapes.*

☼☀ ◔ ❄❄❄   **Climber**
↕↔ 12m (40ft)

PLANTS FOR SOUTH-
& WEST-FACING WALLS

M ANY PLANTS give their best
when allowed to bask in
the heat of a warm, sunny wall,
and they usually respond by
producing a greater profusion
of flowers. Since such walls
often bound the preferred site
for a patio or terrace – where
the gardener may also bask
during summer – they make the
perfect site for wall shrubs or
climbers with fragrant flowers,
such as *Magnolia grandiflora*
'Goliath' (*see p.283*) or *Rosa
banksiae* 'Lutea' (*see p.297*).
The warm, still air of such

sheltered sites quickly becomes
saturated with scent, especially
on warm summer evenings,
creating the most pleasing
ambience for outdoor dining,
entertaining, or simply relaxing
with a wine glass in hand.

EXTENDING THE RANGE
In cold districts, a warm wall
can really make a difference
to the survival of marginally
hardy plants, such as
Fremontodendron 'California
Glory' (*see p.293*) or *Coronilla
valentina* subsp. *glauca* (*see*

p.290). Even very hardy plants, like *Vitis vinifera* 'Purpurea' (*see p.303*) and *Cydonia oblonga* 'Vranja' (*see p.282*), fruit better given the extra warmth. A warm wall absorbs the heat of the sun and acts like a night-storage radiator, even in winter, conferring several degrees of frost protection to any plant growing against it. Wood that is well-ripened by sun and warmth in summer is harder and more resistant to winter cold, and it has energy in reserve to produce better quality flowers and fruit in greater abundance.

Since these sites do not receive the first light of morning, plants warm relatively slowly after frost, thus avoiding the damage that is often caused by the too-rapid thawing of frozen leaves and flower buds. For sun-loving plants that can't cope with scorching conditions, grow them against a south-west or west-facing wall; while these sites are still warm and sunny, they do not bear the full brunt of the midsummer sun at midday.

IMPROVING THE SITE

Unless a wall faces the direction of the prevailing wind, it is likely to be shadowed from rain at its base. This dryness is exacerbated when the wall faces the sun. On a south wall that receives the hottest midday sun, this is especially relevant. Plants not only have to contend with drought, but also with the increased likelihood of diseases, such as powdery mildew, which proliferate in hot, dry conditions and especially when the plants are stressed. To avoid this problem, plant at least 45cm (18in) away from the foot of the wall and set supporting wires or a trellis 10–15cm (4–6in) away from the wall to permit good air circulation. Improve the moisture-retaining capacities of the soil by incorporating plenty of well-rotted organic matter before planting and by mulching well in spring. You can use an organic mulch, or one of gravel or water-worn pebbles to help conserve moisture; the latter can be matched to blend with the materials used in the wall.

ACACIA PRAVISSIMA

Oven's wattle is a shrubby small tree with short branches clothed in grey-green foliage. The tiny and fluffy, bright yellow flowerheads that appear in late winter and spring are sweetly fragrant and are suitable for cutting (*see p.524*). Choose a sheltered wall in mild, almost frost-free climates; elsewhere it can be grown in a cool conservatory. Keep pruning to a minimum. It tolerates sandy soils and hot, dry sites (*see pp.38, 190*).

ALSO RECOMMENDED: *A. baileyana* ♀ *is similar, with feathery silver-grey leaves; A. dealbata* ♀ *is hardier and has silvery-blue foliage.*

☼ ◊ ❀ *f*   **Evergreen tree**
‡ 3–8m (10–25ft) ↔ 3–7m (10–22ft)

CYDONIA OBLONGA *'Vranja'* ♀

This quince is grown for its edible, golden yellow fruits, which are green before they ripen and follow the apple-blossom-like, white or pink flowers of spring. It forms a rounded crown of oval, dark green leaves and becomes increasingly picturesque with age. Ideal for fan-training on a south- or west-facing wall; in winter, cut back flowered shoots to within two to four buds of the framework; trim back inward- and outward-facing shoots.

ALSO RECOMMENDED: *Portugal (syn. 'Lusitanica') has grey-downy fruits.*

☼ ◊ ❀ ❀ ❀   **Deciduous tree**
‡↔ 5m (15ft)

MAGNOLIA GRANDIFLORA
'Goliath' ♥

The huge and fragrant creamy flowers of this dense, conical tree nestle among glossy dark green leaves. The flowers appear sporadically from summer to late autumn, and they are displayed to perfection if the plant is grown against a south or west wall. Best in acid soils, but it tolerates alkaline conditions (*see pp.64, 92*). Keep pruning to a minimum.

ALSO RECOMMENDED: *M. grandiflora* has smaller flowers; 'Exmouth' ♥ is hardier with smaller flowers; 'Little Gem' is smaller.

☼ ◐ ◊◊ ✽✽ *f* **Evergreen tree**
‡ 6–18m (20–60ft) ↔ 15m (50ft)

OLEA EUROPAEA ♥

The olive tree has a Mediterranean ambience and is characterised by its beautiful habit, rough grey bark and narrow, grey-green leaves. The summer flowers are insignificant, although they may be followed by green olives, which turn black when ripe. Where winters are mild, site against a sunny, sheltered wall; otherwise, grow in a cool greenhouse or conservatory. It can be container-grown (*see p.412*). Ensure the soil is sharply drained.

☼ ◊ ✽✽ **Evergreen tree**
‡↔ 10m (30ft)

ABELIA SCHUMANNII

A rounded shrub with arching branches and oval leaves that are bronze when young. Funnel-shaped, lilac-pink flowers appear from late summer to autumn. It thrives against a south- or west-facing wall, but it is also good in a sunny border or hot, dry site (*see p.190*). Prune back some of the oldest growth after flowering; remove dead or damaged growth in spring.

ALSO RECOMMENDED: A. × grandiflora ♀ *has fragrant, pinkish white flowers*; A. *'Edward Goucher'* ♀ *is smaller with deeper flowers.*

☼ ◊ ❊ ❊ ❊   **Deciduous shrub**
↕ 2m (6ft) ↔ 3m (10ft)

ABELIOPHYLLUM DISTICHUM

The white forsythia is an open, spreading shrub with matt dark green leaves, which turn purple before falling in autumn. The fragrant white flowers, borne in long clusters, appear between late winter and early spring. It flowers earlier and most profusely when grown against a warm, south- or west-facing wall. Prune after flowering; if wall-trained, cut flowered shoots back to within two to four buds of the base and shorten inward- or outward-growing shoots.

☼ ◊ ❊ ❊ ❊ *f*   **Deciduous shrub**
↕↔ 1.5m (5ft)

ABUTILON
'Souvenir de Bonn' ♥

This tree-like abutilon is suitable for
a sheltered, south- or west-facing wall
in mild, frost-free climates; elsewhere,
grow in a conservatory. It has lobed
green leaves with pale yellow margins,
and bears hanging, deep orange flowers
from spring to autumn. Remove or
shorten wayward shoots in early spring
In a large tub, it can be moved under
cover in winter (*see p.412*).

ALSO RECOMMENDED: *'Kentish Belle'* ♥
*has apricot-yellow flowers and dark green
leaves;* A. megapotamicum ♥ *has small
yellow flowers – both are hardier.*

☼ ◊ ❄   **Evergreen shrub**
↕ 3m (10ft) ↔ 2–3m (6–10ft)

ACCA SELLOWIANA

The pineapple guava makes quite a
large bush, and with its silvery grey-
green leaves, it has the appearance
of an olive tree. Instead, this plant
produces showy red flowers in
midsummer; they are very distinctive
with long stamens and white backs
to the petals. Edible, guava-like fruits
follow in warm areas. It tolerates
coastal and hot, dry conditions (*see
pp.166, 190*) and sandy soils (*see p.38*).
Prune back excessive or damaged
growth in spring.

☼ ◊ ❄ ❄   **Evergreen shrub**
↕ 2m (6ft) ↔ 2.5m (6ft)

ARTEMISIA ARBORESCENS

The finely cut, silvery white, aromatic foliage of this upright shrub is at its best when grown on a south- or west-facing wall. Small yellow flowerheads appear in summer and autumn. It provides fine textural contrasts in a sunny border. Cut back hard in spring for the best foliage effects. It tolerates sandy and chalky soils (*see pp.38, 64*), and coastal and hot, dry sites (*see pp.166, 190*).

ALSO RECOMMENDED: *A. abrotanum* ♀, *lad's love* or *southernwood, has aromatic, grey-green leaves; A. 'Powis Castle'* ♀ *is more compact with silver-grey leaves.*

☼ ◊ ❄ ❄ ❄ *f*   **Evergreen shrub**
‡ 1m (3ft) ↔ 1.5m (5ft)

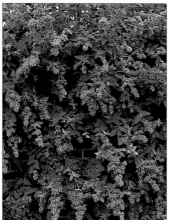

BUDDLEJA CRISPA

An excellent plant for attracting bees and butterflies (*see p.494*), this arching shrub has white-woolly shoots clothed in greyish green leaves. It bears masses of fragrant, lilac to purple flowers from summer to autumn, flowering most freely on a south- or west-facing wall. Cut back all stems close to the base each year as the buds begin to swell in spring.

ALSO RECOMMENDED: *B. lindleyana (see p.69); B. 'Lochinch'* ♀ *has long clusters of violet-blue flowers; B. × weyeriana 'Sungold'* ♀ *has dark orange-yellow flowers.*

☼ ◊ ❄ ❄ ❄ *f*   **Deciduous shrub**
‡↔ 3m (10ft)

CALLISTEMON CITRINUS *'Splendens'* ♀

The crimson bottlebrush is unmistakeable; its brilliant red, spring and summer flower spikes, which appear near the tips of the arching branches, radiate warmth and beauty. The narrow, leathery, grey green leaves have a lemony eucalyptus scent when crushed. It needs neutral or acid soils and tolerates coastal sites (*see pp.92, 166*). Pinch out tips to promote bushiness; hard prune in spring, if necessary.

ALSO RECOMMENDED: *C. citrinus is similar; C. salignus* ♀ *has green or white, sometimes pink flowers.*

☼ ◐ ○ ❀ ❀   **Evergreen shrub**
‡ 2–8m (6–25ft) ↔ 1.5–6m (5–20ft)

CARPENTERIA CALIFORNICA ♀

The tree anemone is a summer-flowering shrub bearing large, fragrant white flowers with showy yellow stamens. It has glossy dark green, narrow leaves. In cold areas, it positively benefits from the extra warmth and shelter given by a south- or west-facing wall; protect from cold, drying winds. In spring, remove branches that have become exhausted by flowering, cutting them back to their bases. Tolerant of chalky soils, and it is

☼ ○ ❀ ❀ *f*   **Evergreen shrub**
‡↔ 2m (6ft) or more

CEANOTHUS THYRSIFLORUS *'Skylark'*

This bushy shrub has glossy green leaves and bears a profusion of deep blue flowers in late spring and early summer. In cold areas, it benefits from the protection of a warm wall and flowers most freely there. Protect from cold, drying winds. Tip-prune in spring when young, and once established, prune only to shape after flowering.

ALSO RECOMMENDED: *C. 'Autumnal Blue'* ♥ (see p.69); *'Concha' has dark blue flowers that open from reddish buds; 'Puget Blue'* ♥ *is taller; 'Southmead'* ♥ *is more compact.*

☼ ◊ ❀ ❀　　　　**Evergreen shrub**
↕ 2m (6ft) ↔ 1.5m (5ft)

CESTRUM PARQUI ♥

Willow-leaved jessamine is valued for its broad clusters of night-scented yellow flowers, which are borne from summer to autumn; the berries that follow are violet-brown. It suits shrub borders against warm, south- or west-facing walls; if grown close to a window or patio area, its scent can be appreciated on summer evenings. Cut all stems back to the base in early spring. In cold areas, it may die back to the base in winter, but it usually recovers in spring.

ALSO RECOMMENDED: *C. 'Newellii'* ♥ *is evergreen with crimson flowers.*

☼ ◊ ❀ ❀ *f*　　　　**Deciduous shrub**
↕↔ 2m (6ft)

CHIMONANTHUS PRAECOX
'Grandiflorus' ♥

Wintersweet is a vigorous shrub grown for the fragrant flowers borne on its bare branches in winter; in this cultivar, they are large, cup-shaped and yellow, striped maroon within. It needs a sunny, sheltered site to flower well, so is ideal for a south or west-facing wall, especially near paths and doorways, where its scent can be appreciated. Cut back flowered stems of wall-trained plants in spring.

ALSO RECOMMENDED: *C. praecox has smaller flowers; var. luteus* ♥ *has clear yellow flowers.*

☼ ◊ ❀ ❀ ❀ *f*   **Deciduous shrub**
‡ 4m (12ft) ↔ 3m (10ft)

CHOISYA TERNATA ♥

Mexican orange blossom is fast growing with dark green leaves, each divided into three leaflets. Fragrant white flowers appear in spring, usually with a second flush late in the season. It does well in a wide range of sites, including chalky soils, city and coastal gardens, hot, dry sites, some dry shade, and cold walls (*see pp.64, 166, 190, 216, 262*). It needs minimal pruning and can be grown as a hedge (*see p.118*). Prone to frost damage in exposed sites.

ALSO RECOMMENDED: *Sundance* ♥ *has yellow-green foliage; C. 'Aztec Pearl'* ♥ *has pink-tinged flowers.*

☼ ◊ ❀ ❀ ❀ *f*   **Evergreen shrub**
‡↔ 2.5m (8ft)

CLIANTHUS PUNICEUS *'Albus'* ♈

Glory pea is a scrambling plant with dark green leaves, ideally suited to the warmth and shelter of south- and west-facing walls. It bears its drooping clusters of claw-like, greenish white flowers in profusion from spring to early summer. In cold areas, it may be cut back by frost, but it usually recovers in spring. Pinch-prune young plants to promote bushiness, otherwise keep pruning to a minimum. It tolerates sandy soils (*see p.38*).

ALSO RECOMMENDED: C. puniceus ♈ *has brilliant red flowers; 'Roseus' (syn. 'Flamingo') has pink flowers.*

☼ ◊ ❀ ❀　　　　**Evergreen shrub**
‡ 4m (12ft) ↔ 3m (10ft)

CORONILLA VALENTINA *SUBSP.* GLAUCA ♈

A compact shrub valued for its divided, blue-grey leaves and its clusters of scented, bright yellow, pea-like flowers. They are borne in late winter and early spring, and often again in late summer. It performs best against a south-facing wall, and it will also grow as a container plant (*see p.412*). It needs little pruning but can be cut back hard in spring to rejuvenate.

ALSO RECOMMENDED: C. valentina *is taller with bright green leaves; 'Citrina' ♈ has pale lemon-yellow flowers.*

☼ ◊ ❀ ❀ *f*　　　　**Evergreen shrub**
‡↔ 80cm (32in)

CYTISUS BATTANDIERI ♀

From early to midsummer, pineapple broom bears dense, upright clusters of pineapple-scented, bright yellow flowers above silky, greyish green leaves. It makes an attractive backdrop to herbaceous plantings; the loosely branched habit adapts well to training against a warm wall, where flowers are borne most freely. Good in sandy soils and hot, dry sites (*see pp.38, 190*). It needs little pruning; to rejuvenate, cut out the oldest wood after flowering.

ALSO RECOMMENDED: *'Yellow Tail'* ♀ *has larger flowers.*

☼ ◊ ❀ ❀ *f*   **Deciduous shrub**
↕↔ 5m (15ft)

DAPHNE ODORA *'Aureomarginata'*

A dense, rounded shrub that has glossy dark green leaves irregularly margined with yellow. It is valued for its intensely fragrant, red-purple flowers, which are much paler within. It benefits from the protection of a west-facing wall; provide an annual mulch of organic matter in early spring to keep the roots cool. Regular pruning is not necessary.

ALSO RECOMMENDED: D. odora *has plain green leaves;* f. alba *has cream flowers.*

☼ ◊ ❀ ❀ *f*   **Evergreen shrub**
↕↔ 1.5m (5ft)

ELSHOLTZIA STAUNTONII

This open, rounded shrub is valued for its narrow and toothed, mint-scented leaves, which turn red in autumn. The dense spikes of small, pink-purple flowers that appear in late summer and autumn are attractive to bees (*see p.494*). In all but the warmest areas, it grows best on a south- or west-facing wall, but it also suits a sheltered shrub or mixed border. Prune in early spring, as the buds swell, cutting back all shoots to a low framework.

☀ ◊ ❀ ❀ *f*   **Deciduous shrub**
↕↔ 1.5m (5ft)

FABIANA IMBRICATA
F. VIOLACEA ♥

A dense, mound-forming shrub with plume-like, horizontally held branches clothed in overlapping, dark green, needle-like leaves. Tubular, lavender-mauve flowers wreathe the branches in early summer. It is best with the shelter of a warm, south- or west-facing wall. It needs a neutral to acid soil, and tolerates coastal and hot, dry sites (*see pp.92, 166, 190*). Little or no pruning is required.

ALSO RECOMMENDED: F. imbricata *has white to pale mauve flowers;* 'Prostrata' *is low-growing with white flowers.*

☀ ◊ ❀ ❀   **Evergreen shrub**
↕↔ 2.5m (8ft)

FREMONTODENDRON *'California Glory'* ♥

This vigorous shrub has rounded, lobed, dark green leaves, which are the perfect foil for the cupped, golden yellow flowers; these appear from late spring to autumn. Wall-training suits its upright habit, and the warmth of a south- or west-facing wall induces profuse flowering. Shelter from cold winds. It is best with no pruning, although wall-trained plants can be trimmed in spring. Tolerant of chalky soils and hot, dry sites (*see pp.64, 190*).

ALSO RECOMMENDED: *F. californicum and F. 'Pacific Sunset' are similar.*

☼ ◊ ❋ ❋   **Evergreen shrub**
↕ 6m (20ft) ↔ 4m (12ft)

ITEA ILICIFOLIA ♥

Providing the soil is not too dry, this holly-like shrub flowers freely on a south or west wall against a mass of glossy, sharply toothed leaves. These tiny flowers are greenish white and borne in catkin-like clusters from midsummer to autumn. Shelter from cold winds and protect young plants with a winter mulch. It needs little pruning; trim wall-trained plants in spring. Tolerant of chalky soils (*see p.64*).

☼ ◊ ❋ ❋   **Evergreen shrub**
↕ 3–5m (10–15ft) ↔ 3m (10ft)

LEPTOSPERMUM SCOPARIUM 'Kiwi' ♥

New Zealand tea trees are compact shrubs with tiny, aromatic, dark green leaves. This dwarf form bears rose-like, dark pink or red flowers, which cover the plant in late spring. Suitable for a rock garden, but it may not survive cold winters. Trim new growth in spring for bushiness, but do not cut into old wood. It tolerates coastal gardens (*see p.166*).

ALSO RECOMMENDED: *'Red Damask'* ♥ *has double, dark red flowers and reaches 3m (10ft) tall and wide.*

☼ ◑ ◊ ✳ ✳ *f*   **Evergreen shrub**
‡↔ 1m (3ft)

MYRTUS COMMUNIS *SUBSP.* TARENTINA ♥

A compact, rounded shrub with glossy dark green leaves that bears fragrant, pink-tinted, creamy white flowers from spring to early autumn. It thrives with the shelter of a south or west wall, and in warm areas, it makes a good informal hedge (*see p.138*). It may also be grown in a container (*see p.412*). Trim in spring; it tolerates close clipping.

ALSO RECOMMENDED: *M. communis* ♥ *is taller; 'Variegata' has leaves margined with creamy white.*

☼ ◊ ✳ ✳ *f*   **Evergreen shrub**
‡↔ 1.5m (5ft)

OLEARIA PHLOGOPAPPA

Daisy bushes are typically dense shrubs with daisy-like, white and yellow flowers. This one displays its blooms in flat headed clusters during late spring amid the wavy-margined, dark green leaves. In cold areas, it is best against a warm, sheltered wall; in a mild, coastal climate, try it as a hedge (*see p.138, 166*). Remove any unwanted or frost-damaged growth in late spring. It is often sold as *O. stellulata*.

ALSO RECOMMENDED: *O.* × haastii *and O.* macrodonta ♥ *are hardier and flower in summer; O.* nummulariifolia (see p.176).

☼ ◊ ✿✿   **Evergreen shrub**
↕↔ 2m (6ft)

PHYGELIUS × RECTUS 'Salmon Leap' ♥

This upright shrub flowers most freely in the warmth of a south or west wall. Its tubular orange-red flowers are borne in large sprays above dark green foliage throughout summer. Remove dead flowerheads regularly; cut any frost-damaged growth back in spring. It is also ideal for a mixed or herbaceous border. Tolerant of chalky soils (*see p.64*).

ALSO RECOMMENDED: *'Devil's Tears'* ♥ *has red-pink flowers with yellow throats; 'Moonraker' has pale yellow flowers.*

☼ ◊◊ ✿✿✿   **Evergreen shrub**
↕ 1.2m (4ft) ↔ 1.5m (5ft)

PIPTANTHUS NEPALENSIS

This handsome shrub is valued for its yellow, pea-like flowers and glossy dark green, laburnum-like leaves, which are blue-white beneath. It is well-suited to a site against a west-facing wall, flowering in late spring and early summer; hanging green seed pods follow. After flowering, shorten inward- or outward-growing shoots on wall-trained plants. It may drop some of its leaves in cold winters.

☼ ☀ ◊ ❋ ❋   **Evergreen shrub**
‡ 2.5m (8ft) ↔ 2m (6ft)

ROBINIA HISPIDA ♥

The rose acacia is an upright and arching shrub with spiny shoots. Deep rose-pink, pea-like flowers appear in hanging spikes during late spring and early summer; these are followed by brown seed pods. The large, fresh green leaves are divided into many oval leaflets. Provide shelter from wind to avoid damage to the brittle branches. No pruning is necessary. It is also useful for shrub borders on poor, sandy soils in hot, dry sites (*see pp.38, 190*), but it tolerates all but waterlogged soils.

☼ ◊ ❋ ❋ ❋   **Deciduous shrub**
‡ 2.5m (8ft) ↔ 3m (10ft)

ROSA BANKSIAE *'Lutea'*

The rambling, yellow Banksian rose needs the shelter of a south-west or west wall to give of its best. The long, slender stems bear light green leaves, and in late spring, clusters of double, soft yellow flowers appear. They are good for cutting (*see p.524*), have a delicate scent of violets, and are borne in abundance in a warm site. Train against a support and prune only to remove old, unproductive wood. Tolerant of chalky soils (*see p.64*).

ALSO RECOMMENDED: R. *'Albertine'* ♀ (see p.77); *'American Pillar'* (see p.51); *'Maigold'* ♀ *has semi-double, bronze-yellow flowers.*

☀ ◊ ❀❀ *f*   **Deciduous shrub**
↕↔ 6m (20ft)

ROSA × ODORATA *'Mutabilis'* ♀

The cupped, single flowers of this rose, borne through summer, are yellow on opening, changing to copper and deep pink as they mature; they are good for cutting (*see p.524*). If given a site on a south-west or west wall, it will climb to 3m (10ft) and flower profusely; otherwise grow in a border. Prune lightly; shorten main stems and side-shoots by no more than one-third when dormant. It will grow in a large tub and tolerates chalky soils (*see pp.64, 112*).

ALSO RECOMMENDED: R. *Dublin Bay* ♀ *has double crimson flowers; 'Madame Grégoire Staechelin'* ♀ *has double pink flowers.*

☀◑ ◊ ❀❀❀   **Deciduous shrub**
↕ 1.2–3m (4–10ft) ↔ 1–2m (3–6ft)

SALVIA INVOLUCRATA 'Bethellii'

A bushy plant with upright stems that bear velvety, rich green leaves. Spikes of two-lipped, vivid crimson-purple flowers appear from late summer to autumn; they attract bees (*see p.494*). It is ideal for a border against a warm wall and is good in hot, dry sites (*see p.190*). It may not survive cold winters, so if it is grown in a large container, it can be overwintered under glass (*see p.412*). Tolerant of sandy soils (*see p.38*).

ALSO RECOMMENDED: S. involucrata ♀ *has less hairy leaves;* S. officinalis 'Tricolor' ♀ (see p.61).

☼ ◊ ❀ ❀   **Evergreen shrub**
‡ 1.5m (5ft) ↔ 1m (3ft)

VESTIA FOETIDA ♀

This upright shrub has glossy dark green leaves and bears hanging clusters of tubular, pale yellow flowers from spring to midsummer. In cold areas, it needs the protection of a south- or west-facing wall; if winters are severe, it may be sheltered in a cool conservatory. It needs little pruning; trim to shape and remove badly placed growth in mid-spring.

☼ ◊ ❀ ❀   **Evergreen shrub**
‡ 2m (6ft) ↔ 1.5m (5ft)

ACTINIDIA KOLOMIKTA ♥

A vigorous plant valued for its deep
green deciduous leaves, which are
purple-tinted when young, later
splashed with vivid pink and white.
Small, fragrant white flowers appear in
early summer, and they are followed
by egg shaped, yellow-green fruits, but
only if a male plant is grown nearby.
Tie in new shoots as they develop;
cut out badly placed shoots in summer.
It tolerates chalky soils (*see p.64*).

ALSO RECOMMENDED: A. deliciosa, *the
kiwi fruit, is less hardy to frost.*

☼ ◊ ❀ ❀ ❀ *f*   **Climber**
↕ 5m (15ft)

CLEMATIS *'Bill Mackenzie'* ♥

This vigorous, deciduous clematis
bears nodding yellow flowers with red
anthers from midsummer to autumn;
pretty, silky seedheads follow and
persist into winter. It flowers freely
on a warm wall but needs a cool root
run; shade the roots with a stone slab
or similar. Cut all the previous year's
stems back hard each year in spring.
Also tolerant of cold walls and chalky
soils (*see pp.64, 262*).

ALSO RECOMMENDED: C. montana (see
p.274); C. tangutica (see p.508); C. tibetana
'Orange Peel' has thick, orange-yellow petals.

☼☀ ◊ ❀ ❀ ❀   **Climber**
↕ 7m (22ft) ↔ 2–3m (6–10ft)

CLEMATIS REHDERIANA ♥

This rampant and unusual clematis is densely clothed with deciduous, glossy dark green leaves. Large clusters of small, bell-shaped, pale yellow flowers with a scent of cowslips cover the plant from midsummer to autumn. It is ideal for a warm wall, where it flowers profusely. Cut back hard each year in spring. Also tolerant of cold walls and chalky soils (*see pp.64, 262*). It will grow as ground cover (*see p.304*).

ALSO RECOMMENDED: *C. 'Paul Farges' bears star-shaped white flowers; 'The President'* ♥ *(see p.76); C. terniflora bears large clusters of star-shaped white flowers.*

☼ ◐ ◊ ❀❀❀ *f*   **Climber**
‡ 6–7m (20–22ft) ↔ 2–3m (6–10ft)

JASMINUM OFFICINALE *'Argenteovariegatum'* ♥

This variegated jasmine is a vigorous climber with cream-edged leaves made up of several pointed leaflets. Clusters of fragrant white flowers open from summer to autumn; they also do well in partial shade. If tied in initially, it will twine over a support, such as a trellis or an arch. It tolerates chalky soils and can be pot-grown (*see pp.64, 412*), but it may not survive in cold, exposed areas. Thin out after flowering.

ALSO RECOMMENDED: *J. officinale* ♥ *has plain foliage; 'Aureum' has yellow-marked leaves; f. affine has pink-tinged flowers.*

☼ ◐ ◊ ❀❀❀ *f*   **Climber**
‡ 12m (40ft)

LONICERA × TELLMANNIANA ☙

A twining, woody-stemmed climber that bears clusters of deep golden orange, tubular flowers from late spring to midsummer. The deep green foliage is deciduous. Train this honeysuckle onto a fence or wall, or up into a large shrub; it grows and flowers more reliably in a slightly shaded position. Trim shoots by one-third after flowering. It tolerates chalky soils (*see p.64*) and can be grown in a container (*see p.412*).

ALSO RECOMMENDED: L. fragrantissima (*see p.526*); L. sempervirens ☙ *and* L. tragophylla ☙ *both have later flowers.*

☼☀ ◊◊ ✳✳✳ **Climber**

↕ 5m (15ft)

PASSIFLORA CAERULEA *'Constance Elliot'* ☙

The blue passion flower is a vigorous, deciduous climber with lobed, rich green leaves. This white-flowered cultivar bears its intricate flowers from summer to autumn; they are followed by egg-shaped, unpalatable orange fruits, which will ripen on a warm, south- or west-facing wall. Shelter from cold winds. It tolerates chalky soils (*see p.64*). Remove crowded growth in spring; shorten flowered shoots at the end of the season.

ALSO RECOMMENDED: P. caerulea ☙ *has pale blue-purple flowers.*

☼ ◊ ✳✳ **Climber**

↕ 10m (30ft) or more

SOLANUM CRISPUM
'Glasnevin' ♥

The Chilean potato tree is a vigorous and shrubby climber, which benefits from the protection of a south or west wall. It bears deep purple-blue flowers from summer to autumn above narrow and deciduous, dark green leaves; small yellow berries follow. Tie in young shoots as growth proceeds; cut back weak or badly placed growth in spring. It tolerates chalky soils (*see p.64*).

ALSO RECOMMENDED: *S. laxum has bluish white flowers and black fruits; 'Album' ♥ has white flowers and more of a climbing habit.*

☼ ☀ ◊ ❄ ❄   **Climber**
‡ 6m (20ft)

TRACHELOSPERMUM JASMINOIDES ♥

Star jasmine has oval, glossy dark green leaves, and from mid- to late summer, it produces very fragrant, creamy white flowers with twisted petal lobes. In cold areas, it needs the protection of a sheltered, south- or west-facing wall and a deep winter mulch. Tie in young growth and trim in spring to confine to bounds. It is evergreen and tolerates chalky soils and some damp shade (*see p.64, 238*).

ALSO RECOMMENDED: *'Variegatum' ♥ has leaves splashed and margined with cream; T. asiaticum ♥ is hardier and more compact.*

☼ ☀ ◊ ❄ ❄ ❄ *f*   **Climber**
‡ 9m (28ft)

VITIS VINIFERA *'Purpurea'*

The lobed, rounded leaves of this vine are white-downy when young, turning to plum-purple, then assuming rich purple tints before they fall. The small purple grapes in autumn are inedible. An excellent plant for a sunny wall or pergola that needs slightly alkaline soil (*see p.64*) but tolerates clay and sandy sites (*see pp.12, 38*); autumn colour is best on poor soils. Prune back to an established framework each winter.

ALSO RECOMMENDED: V. amurensis (see p.279); V. *'Brant'* has copper-bronze autumn foliage and large bunches of edible, blue-black grapes.

☼ ◐ ◊ ❊ ❊ ❊   **Climber**
‡ 7m (22ft)

WISTERIA BRACHYBOTRYS *'Shiro-kapitan'*

This silky wisteria has twining stems and divided, softly hairy, deciduous leaves. In early summer, it bears short clusters of very fragrant white flowers, followed by silky green seed pods in warm climates. It is a beautiful specimen for a south or west wall. Prune back new growth in summer and in late winter to control spread. Also sold as W. sinensis 'Shiro-capital' and W. venusta.

ALSO RECOMMENDED: W. floribunda *and* W. sinensis ♥ *have long clusters of lilac or white flowers.*

☼ ◊ ❊ ❊ ❊ *f*   **Climber**
‡ 9m (28ft) or more

PLANTS FOR GROUND COVER IN SUN

THE ADVENT OF low-maintenance gardening has created a great deal of interest in the use of ground-cover plants to reduce weeding in the garden. At first, the term "ground cover" generally described low and dense, mat- or carpet-forming, evergreen plants. Many gardeners came to dislike the concept, however, because low, undulating mounds of planting – even when composed to form tapestries of different colours and textures – lacked the visual satisfaction of height and form.

In fact, any plant – spreading or upright – that forms a dense, light-excluding canopy will smother weeds, but it is essential that you choose plants that thrive in the growing conditions available. Unless they make dense growth quickly, they will not make effective cover, so carefully check the cultivation requirements of possible plants.

SUNNY SLOPES
The plants described in this chapter are known to perform well in full sun. Such ground

cover is an excellent way of furnishing sunny banks, where access can be difficult and turf would prove dangerous to mow, especially where a bank slopes steeply. Many of them root where they touch the ground, so they are very useful in stabilizing the soil on sloping sites.

WEED CONTROL

Even the most vigorous ground cover will only be fully effective if the soil is completely cleared of all perennial weeds and their roots before planting. This is especially true with thorny plants like the ground-cover roses, such as Surrey (*see p.309*), because removing docks and nettles from among the branches is painful as well as tedious.

On small areas, thorough cultivation and hand weeding is a satisfying way of removing weeds before planting. On larger areas, treating weeds when they are in active growth with a translocated weedkiller, such as one containing glyphosate, is the most practical method. This type of weedkiller is effective because it is transferred to the roots and destroys the whole plant. Tough weeds, like ground elder, brambles, and docks, will need more than one treatment. Organic gardeners often lay a light excluding layer of old carpet or black polythene on the soil for a season before planting to clear the weeds.

Until plants begin to grow well, weed seedlings will still take root in the bare soil, so regular weeding is essential. Alternatively, planting through woven landscaping fabric, or matting made of jute or hemp is ideal; unlike polythene sheeting, these materials allow plants to root into them. Hemp and jute are biodegradable, and the plants will have made good, dense cover by the time they decompose. Landscaping fabrics are not pretty, but they can be disguised with an appropriate mulch, like gravel or shale – materials that protect sun-lovers from winter wet. This fabric and mulch combination suppresses weeds very effectively.

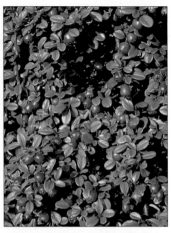

COTONEASTER CASHMIRIENSIS ♀

This compact shrub forms a dense, wide-spreading mat of small, glossy leaves. It is studded in summer with small white flowers, which are followed in autumn by shiny dark red berries. These attract birds (*see p.494*). It makes excellent ground cover for a sunny bank or at the front of a shrub border, and it tolerates clay and chalky soils (*see pp.12, 64*). Prune only to remove wayward shoots.

ALSO RECOMMENDED: C. dammeri ♀ *has larger leaves; those of* C. procumbens *are darker green.*

☼ ◊ ❉ ❉ ❉   **Evergreen shrub**
‡ 30cm (12in) ↔ 2m (6ft)

ERICA CARNEA *'Springwood White'* ♀

Early-flowering heathers are much appreciated when they bring a carpet of colour to the garden from late winter. This vigorous, trailing variety gives a profusion of white flowers above bright green foliage. It tolerates acid soils (*see p.92*) and can be pot-grown (*see p.412*). The flowers are good for cutting (*see p.524*). Trim after flowering.

ALSO RECOMMENDED: *'Foxhollow'* ♀ *has purplish flowers and bronze-yellow foliage;* *'Myretoun Ruby'* ♀ *has pink to red flowers;* E. cinerea (*see p.102*) *and* E. vagans (*see p.418*) *flower from summer to autumn.*

☼ ◊ ❉ ❉ ❉   **Evergreen shrub**
‡ 20–25cm (8–10in) ↔ 55cm (22in)

GENISTA HISPANICA

Spanish gorse forms a dense mound of spiny green stems, covered by a mass of golden yellow pea flowers in late spring and early summer. Narrow green leaves appear only on the flowering stems. Good in a rock garden or raised bed, or on a wall or sunny bank; it thrives in hot, dry sites (*see p.190*), coping with coastal conditions (*see p.166*) and flowering most freely in poor, sandy, well-drained soils (*see p.38*). Keep pruning to a minimum.

ALSO RECOMMENDED: *G. pilosa 'Vancouver Gold' is shorter, to 45cm (18in) tall.*

☼ ◊ ❉ ❉ ❉   **Deciduous shrub**
↕ 75cm (30in) ↔ 1.5m (5ft)

HEBE PINGUIFOLIA *'Pagei'* ♥

With arching, purple stems clothed in small, leathery, blue-green leaves, this shrub makes good ground cover for the front of a border, raised bed, or rock garden. Short spikes of tiny white flowers appear at the stem tips in late spring and early summer. It thrives in chalky soils, tolerates urban pollution and coastal sites, and looks good in pots (*see pp.64, 166, 412*). Trim in early spring.

ALSO RECOMMENDED: H. *'Autumn Glory'* (see p.175); *'County Park' has red-margined, grey-green leaves and violet flowers*; H. pimeleoides *'Quicksilver' ♥ has silver-grey leaves and lilac-blue flowers.*

☼ ◊ ❉ ❉ ❉   **Evergreen shrub**
↕ 30cm (12in) ↔ 90cm (36in)

JUNIPERUS SABINA *'Tamariscifolia'*

The sharply pointed, bright or bluish green leaves and spreading stems of this mounded, ground-covering shrub produce an attractively tiered habit of growth. It is ideal for a shrub border, sunny bank, or gravel garden, thriving in any well-drained position, including sandy or chalky soils (*see pp.38, 64*) and hot, dry sites (*see p.190*). Little, if any pruning is necessary.

ALSO RECOMMENDED: *'Blaue Donau' (syn. Blue Danube) has blue-grey leaves; J. horizontalis 'Wiltonii'* ♥ *is shorter, more spreading, and has bright blue leaves.*

☼ ◊ ❀ ❀ ❀   **Evergreen shrub**
‡ 1–2m (3–6ft) ↔ 2m (6ft)

MICROBIOTA DECUSSATA ♥

A low-growing, spreading, mound-forming conifer with scale-like, bright green foliage borne in flattened sprays. In cold weather, the foliage often assumes bronze tints. Its dense growth, which needs no pruning, makes excellent, low-maintenance ground cover at the front of a shrub border or on a bank; it can also be grown in a container (*see p.412*).

☼ ◊ ❀ ❀ ❀   **Evergreen shrub**
‡ 1m (3ft) ↔ indefinite

RHODANTHEMUM HOSMARIENSE ♀

A close ally of the chrysanthemum, this is a low and spreading subshrub valued for its profusion of daisy like flowers with white petals and yellow eyes. These are borne from spring to autumn, covering the silvery green, soft and hairy, finely divided leaves. Choose a very well-drained site at the base of a warm wall (*see p.280*) or in a rock garden; remove spent blooms to prolong flowering. It tolerates chalky soils (*see p.64*). Trim after flowering.

ALSO RECOMMENDED: *R. gayanum has pink and brown summer flowers.*

☼ ◊ ❋❋   **Evergreen shrub**
‡ 10–30cm (4–12in) ↔ 30cm (12in)

ROSA *Surrey* ♀

A splendid ground-cover rose with small, rich green foliage and a profusion of gentle pink blooms, borne over long periods in summer and into autumn Excellent for confined spaces, it may also be grown in containers (*see p.412*). Prune in winter, cutting back overlong shoots to an upward- or outward-facing bud. It tolerates chalky soils (*see p.64*).

ALSO RECOMMENDED: *Grouse, 'Nozomi'* ♀, *and Pink Bells have pale pink flowers; Robin Redbreast has red flowers; Snow Carpet* ♀ *is short with white flowers; Swany* ♀ *has white flowers; R. pimpinellifolia (see p.131).*

☼ ◊ ❋❋❋   **Deciduous shrub**
‡ 80cm (32in) ↔ 1.2m (4ft)

THYMUS PULEGIOIDES
'Bertram Anderson' ♚

This lemon-scented thyme is a low, wiry-stemmed subshrub with small, pleasantly aromatic leaves; these are often used to flavour meat. This cultivar has yellow-green foliage and heads of tiny, pale pink flowers in summer. It is an essential plant for a herb or wildlife garden with neutral to alkaline soil (*see pp.64, 494*). Also suitable for hot, dry sites and in paving (*see pp.190, 348*).

ALSO RECOMMENDED: *'Archer's Gold' has yellow-margined leaves; 'Aureus'* ♚ *has gold-dappled leaves; T. serpyllum 'Annie Hall'* (see p.352).

☼ ◊ ❀❀❀ *f*   **Evergreen shrub**
‡ 30cm (12in) ↔ 25cm (10in)

ACAENA SACCATICUPULA
'Blue Haze'

This vigorous, creeping evergreen forms a dense carpet of divided, grey-blue leaves, which will withstand a moderate amount of treading. It can be grown in a rock garden or raised bed, at the front of a border, or in paving crevices (*see p.348*). In summer, the spherical flowerheads are followed by decorative, dark red burrs. It is good for hot, dry sites (*see p.190*), sandy soils (*see p.38*), and sunny containers (*see p.412*).

ALSO RECOMMENDED: *A. microphylla 'Kupferteppich'* (syn. Copper Carpet) has bronzed leaves and bright red burrs.

☼ ◊ ❀❀❀   **Perennial**
‡ 10–15cm (4–6in) ↔ 1m (3ft)

ALCHEMILLA MOLLIS ♈

Lady's mantle is a drought-tolerant, clump-forming border plant, valued for its lobed, bright green leaves and its sprays of tiny, lime green flowers throughout summer. They are ideal for cutting and drying (*see p.524*); regular deadheading prevents nuisance self-seeding. It tolerates chalky soils (*see p.64*) and copes with exposed and coastal sites (*see pp.118, 166*).

ALSO RECOMMENDED: A. alpina (*see p.354*); A. conjuncta (*see p.181*); A. erythropoda ♈ *is smaller with blue green leaves;* A. xanthochlora *is taller with yellowish leaves.*

☼ ◊◊ ❀❀❀   **Perennial**
‡30cm (12in) ↔ 75cm (30in)

ARTEMISIA LUDOVICIANA 'Silver Queen' ♈

This western mugwort is a strongly spreading plant, forming bushy clumps of narrow, silvery white, softly felted leaves; they become green with age and are sometimes jaggedly toothed. Woolly white plumes of light brown flowers appear from midsummer to autumn. It grows well in sandy soils and in hot, dry sites (*see pp.38, 190*), indispensable in a silver-themed border. Cut back in spring for the best foliage effect.

ALSO RECOMMENDED: A. ludoviciana ♈ *is similar;* 'Valerie Finnis' ♈ *has more deeply cut leaves;* A. pontica ♈ (*see p.52*).

☼ ◊ ❀❀❀   **Perennial**
‡75cm (30in) ↔ 60cm (24in) or more

AUBRIETA *'Joy'*

The spreading mat of mid-green foliage that is formed by this aubrieta is often grown in a rock garden or in cracks within walls or paving (*see p.348*). Small, double-petalled mauve flowers appear in abundance in spring. It prefers neutral to alkaline soils (*see p.64*). Cut back after flowering to maintain a compact shape.

ALSO RECOMMENDED: *'Aureovariegata' has yellow-margined leaves and pink flowers; 'Doctor Mules'* ♀ *has bluish violet flowers.*

☀ ◊ ❄ ❄ ❄ **Perennial**
‡ 5cm (2in) ↔ 60cm (24in) or more

AURINIA SAXATILIS *'Dudley Nevill'*

This mound-forming evergreen bears clusters of pale orange-yellow flowers in late spring above dense clumps of oval, hairy, grey-green leaves. It is ideal for rock gardens or banks, for the front of a sunny border, or for cracks in walls and paving (*see p.348*). Trim after flowering to keep compact. It tolerates chalky soils and hot, dry sites (*see pp.64, 190*).

ALSO RECOMMENDED: *A. saxatilis* ♀, *gold dust, has bright yellow flowers; those of 'Citrina'* ♀ *are lemon-yellow; 'Variegata' has leaves margined with creamy white.*

☀ ◊ ❄ ❄ ❄ **Perennial**
‡ 20cm (8in) ↔ 30cm (12in)

CAMPANULA GLOMERATA 'Superba' ♀

This vigorous variety of the clustered bellflower spreads to form clumps of well-foliaged, stiffly upright stems. Throughout summer, they are topped by dense clusters of purple-violet flowers. Cut back after flowering to encourage another display. It tolerates chalky soils (*see p.64*).

ALSO RECOMMENDED: *C. 'Birch Hybrid'* ♀ (see p.358); *C. carpatica 'Bressingham White'* ♀ (see p.359); *C. cochleariifolia 'Elizabeth Oliver'* is short and spreading with pale blue flowers in summer .

☼ ◐ ◊◊ ❀❀❀ **Perennial**
‡ 60cm (24in) ↔ indefinite

CENTAUREA MONTANA

This knapweed is a creeping plant and forms soft, woolly mats or clumps of broad and pointed, mid-green leaves. The thistle-like, reddish purple-blue flowers have a spidery appearance and open from late spring to midsummer; they are attractive to butterflies and bees (*see p.494*). It is tolerant of exposed sites (*see p.118*), but stakes may be needed to support the stems.

ALSO RECOMMENDED: *'Alba'* has white flowers; those of *'Carnea'* are pink; *'Parham'* has large, dark blue flowers.

☼ ◐ ◊◊ ❀❀❀ **Perennial**
‡ 45cm (18in) ↔ 60cm (24in)

CERASTIUM TOMENTOSUM

The dense, white-woolly foliage of snow-in-summer makes a good weed suppressant. It forms a silvery carpet, which is covered by snow-white flowers in summer. It is ideal for poor, well-drained, dry and sandy soils, rock gardens, sunny banks, and crevices in dry walls and paving (*see pp.38, 348*); its enthusiastic growth may become invasive.

ALSO RECOMMENDED: *var.* columnae *is slightly taller, to 15cm (6in).*

☼ ◊ ✳ ✳ ✳   **Perennial**
‡5–8cm (2–3in) ↔ indefinite

DIANTHUS SUBACAULIS

This low-growing evergreen forms a dense carpet of narrow, dark grey-green leaves and is studded with a profusion of small, deep pink flowers during summer. It makes excellent ground cover for a rock garden or raised bed; it may also be grown in paving crevices (*see p.348*), as border edging, or in a container (*see p.412*). Choose sharply drained, sandy, neutral to alkaline soil (*see pp.38, 64*).

ALSO RECOMMENDED: D. alpinus ♀ *has pink to crimson flowers; the larger* D. gratianopolitanus ♀ *has fragrant flowers.*

☼ ◊ ✳ ✳ ✳   **Perennial**
‡5cm (2in) ↔ 10cm (4in)

DIASCIA *'Salmon Supreme'*

The trailing, wiry mats of this plant are clothed by small, heart-shaped leaves, which are outperformed for a long summer season by the dense clusters of pinkish apricot flowers. These have two downward-pointing spurs on the reverse, which give the plant its common name – twinspur. Grow at the front of a border or in a rock garden. Remove dead flowers, and pinch out shoot tips to encourage a bushy habit.

ALSO RECOMMENDED: *'Rupert Lambert'* ♥ *has pink flowers; those of* D. barbarae *'Blackthorn Apricot'* ♥ *and 'Ruby Field'* ♥ *are salmon;* D. vigilis ♥ *has pink blooms.*

☼ ◑ ❀ ❀   **Perennial**

‡ 15cm (6in) ↔ 50cm (20in)

DRYAS OCTOPETALA ♥

An easy plant for a rock garden, dry wall, or border edge, mountain avens forms a low, evergreen mat of small, lobed leaves, which resemble those of an oak tree. Aconite-like white flowers with yellow centres face the sky in late spring and early summer. It thrives in gritty soil and will grow in paving crevices (*see p.348*).

ALSO RECOMMENDED: *the foliage and flowers of 'Minor'* ♥ *are smaller.*

☼ ☼ ◊ ❀ ❀ ❀   **Perennial**

‡ 10cm (4in) ↔ 1m (3ft) or more

GERANIUM ENDRESSII ♀

This geranium is useful for infilling between larger plants in a mixed border. It forms clumps of deeply lobed, light green leaves and has a long season of light pink summer flowers with notched petals; they darken with age, and the display continues into autumn. It is tolerant of dry shade (*see pp.216, 326*) and most but waterlogged soils. Also good for containers (*see pp.412, 448*).

ALSO RECOMMENDED: G. *'Ann Folkard'* ♀ has *magenta flowers*; G. clarkei *'Kashmir White'* ♀ has *white flowers*; G. cinereum *'Ballerina'* ♀ (see p.333); G. dalmaticum ♀ (see p.363); G. renardii ♀ (see p.211).

☼ ◐ ◊◊ ❋❋❋   **Perennial**
‡ 45cm (18in) ↔ 60cm (24in)

GERANIUM × OXONIANUM

This hybrid of *G. endressii* (*above*) has similar uses in the garden, but it puts on taller, more enthusiastic growth with deeper pink, strongly veined flowers. Flowering from late spring to autumn, it is long-lived and requires minimal attention. Also suitable for containers (*see pp.412, 448*) and as ground cover in shade (*see p.326*).

ALSO RECOMMENDED: *'A.T. Johnson'* ♀ is *very free flowering*; *'Claridge Druce'* and *'Wargrave Pink'* ♀ are *very vigorous*; G. × riversleaianum *'Russell Prichard'* ♀ has *magenta flowers*; G. wallichianum *'Buxton's Variety'* ♀ has *lilac flowers*.

☼ ◐ ◊◊ ❋❋❋   **Perennial**
‡ 80cm (32in) ↔ 60cm (24in)

GYPSOPHILA REPENS
'Dorothy Teacher' ♥

This versatile, low-spreading plant
thrives in sandy or chalky soils in hot,
dry sites (*see pp.38, 64, 190*) as well as
in paving and wall crevices (*see p.348*).
It forms a dense mat of blue-green
leaves spangled with many tiny pink
flowers throughout summer, which are
good for cutting (*see p.524*). It needs
light, alkaline, sharply drained soil and
can also be container-grown (*see p.412*).

ALSO RECOMMENDED: *G. repens* ♥
has white, pink, or pink-purple flowers.
'Fratensis' has grey-green leaves and
pale pink flowers.

☼ ◊ ✽✽✽   **Perennial**
‡ 5cm (2in) ↔ 40cm (16in)

× HEUCHERELLA
TIARELLOIDES ♥

This spreading, clump-forming plant
forms good evergreen ground cover
at the front of a border with its mass
of rounded, lobed, light green leaves;
they are often brown-marked when
young. The slender-stemmed spikes
of tiny pink flowers arise in mid-spring
and early summer. Grow in light,
fertile, neutral to acid soil (*see p.92*).
It is also good for ground cover in
partial shade (*see p.326*).

ALSO RECOMMENDED: × *H. alba 'Bridget*
Bloom' has brown-veined, mid-green leaves
and white flowers.

☼◑ ◊◊ ✽✽✽   **Perennial**
‡↔ 45cm (18in)

HOSTA *'Birchwood Parky's Gold'*

This gold-leaved hosta has ribbed, heart-shaped leaves and bears spires of pale lavender-blue flowers in midsummer. The best foliage colour is produced in sun, but it needs a little midday shade and shelter from drying winds to avoid leaf scorch. Mulch every spring and protect from slugs. A good architectural plant for ground cover and containers (*see pp.304, 326, 412, 472*), tolerating clay and permanently damp soils (*see pp.12, 238, 372*).

ALSO RECOMMENDED: *'Fragrant Gold' and 'Golden Prayers' are similar.*

☼ ◐ ◊ ❀ ❀ ❀   **Perennial**
‡ 35–40cm (14–16in) ↔ indefinite

LYCHNIS CORONARIA

Although short-lived, rose campion will form dense, ground-covering colonies by self-seeding. Its vibrant magenta flowers appear in long succession from midsummer above basal clumps of lance-shaped, silver-grey leaves. It is best in light and sandy soils (*see p.38*) but also tolerates chalky ground (*see p.64*) and coastal and hot, dry sites (*see pp.166, 190*). Grow in a sunny, mixed or herbaceous border.

ALSO RECOMMENDED: *'Alba'* ♀ *bears white flowers; Atrosanguinea Group have crimson flowers; Oculata Group have pink-eyed white flowers.*

☼ ◊ ❀ ❀ ❀   **Perennial**
‡ 80cm (32in) ↔ 45cm (18in)

LYSIMACHIA PUNCTATA

This loosestrife is a robust border perennial with dense, basal clumps of dark green foliage. The plant spreads, sometimes invasively, by rhizomes. From midsummer, it bears tall spikes of bright yellow flowers. Tolerant of heavy clay and permanently moist soils (*see pp.12, 372*). Dig out excessive growth to control spread.

ALSO RECOMMENDED: L. vulgaris *is similar.*

☼ ◊◊ ❋ ❋ ❋   **Perennial**

‡ 1m (3ft) ↔ 60cm (24in)

MENTHA SUAVEOLENS *'Variegata'*

The aromatic pineapple mint forms dense, spreading clumps of hairy and wrinkled, grey-green leaves heavily splashed with creamy white. Spikes of two-lipped, very pale pink flowers appear in summer; they attract pollinating insects (*see p.494*). It is good for creating foliage contrasts in a herbaceous border and is best in poor, damp soils, being less invasive in dry sites. It tolerates clay soils (*see p.12*).

ALSO RECOMMENDED: M. × gracilis *'Variegata' is shorter and less invasive with gold-marked, aromatic leaves.*

☼ ◊ ❋ ❋ ❋ *f*   **Perennial**

‡ 1m (3ft) ↔ indefinite

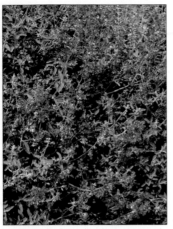

NEPETA × FAASSENII

Catmint is an excellent border plant, making a dense clump of arching stems clothed with aromatic, softly hairy, wrinkled, grey-green leaves. Through summer, it bears spikes of two-lipped, pale lavender-blue flowers, which attract a range of pollinating insects (*see p.494*). It tolerates sandy and chalky soils (*see pp.38, 64*) and performs well in hot, dry sites (*see p.190*). Cut back after flowering to encourage a fresh flush of foliage and flowers, and remove all old growth to the base in spring.

ALSO RECOMMENDED: *'Alba' has white flowers*; *N. 'Six Hills Giant' is much taller*.

☼ ◊ ❁ ❁ ❁ *f*   **Perennial**
↕↔ 45cm (18in)

ORIGANUM VULGARE

Oregano, or marjoram, is a spreading, bushy plant with tiny, dark green leaves, which are highly aromatic and are frequently used in cooking. Short spikes of tiny, pretty pink flowers are seen in summer. It is good for a well-drained bank or herb garden, growing well in sandy, alkaline soils (*see pp.38, 64*). Trim back after flowering to maintain a compact shape.

ALSO RECOMMENDED: *'Aureum' ♀ has gold leaves*; *'Gold Tip' has yellow-tipped leaves*

☼ ◊ ❁ ❁ ❁ *f*   **Perennial**
↕↔ 30–90cm (12–36in)

PERSICARIA AFFINIS
'Donald Lowndes' ♥

This vigorous evergreen produces
dense mats of lance-shaped, dark green
leaves, which take on attractive shades
of russet in autumn. From midsummer
to autumn, it bears long-lasting spikes
of pale pink flowers, and these mature
to a darker, dusky pink. Position at the
front of a border, in a gravel garden, or
in a container (*see pp.412, 448*). It thrives
in any moist but well-drained soil and
tolerates partial shade (*see p.326*).

ALSO RECOMMENDED: *'Darjeeling Red'* ♥
and 'Superba' ♥ *are similar.*

☼ ◐ ◊ ❁ ❁ ❁   **Perennial**
‡ 25cm (10in) ↔ 60cm (24in)

POTENTILLA MEGALANTHA ♥

This herbaceous cinquefoil is grown
for its profusion of small and rose-like,
rich yellow flowers in the second half
of summer. They are carried in upright
clusters above the dense clumps of
slightly hairy, mid-green leaves. It is
suitable for the front of a border,
where it can be used to fill patches
of bare earth between larger plants.
It will grow in sandy soils and hot,
dry sites (*see pp.38, 190*).

ALSO RECOMMENDED: *P.* × *tonguei* ♥ *is
spreading with a long summer display of
apricot-yellow flowers with red eyes.*

☼ ◊ ❁ ❁ ❁   **Perennial**
‡ 15–30cm (6–12in) ↔ 15cm (6in)

SAPONARIA OCYMOIDES ♛

Tumbling Ted is a sprawling plant, which forms a mat of bright green leaves. These are almost obscured in summer by tiny pink flowers. It is excellent for sunny banks or rock gardens; site carefully as it may swamp smaller plants. Cut back after flowering to keep it compact. Tolerant of sandy and alkaline soils (*see pp.38, 64*) and good in paving crevices and containers (*see pp.348, 412*).

ALSO RECOMMENDED: *'Alba' has white flowers and is less vigorous, 'Rubra Compacta'* ♛ *has dark red flowers and is more compact.*

☼ ◊ ❋ ❋ ❋　　　　　　**Perennial**
‡ 8cm (3in) ↔ 45cm (18in) or more

SCUTELLARIA ORIENTALIS

A spreading, stem-rooting perennial with divided, dark green leaves that bears a profusion of tubular, two-lipped, red-marked yellow flowers in summer. It is ideal for a rock or gravel garden, or at the front of a sunny border. The flowers are attractive to bees (*see p.494*). Grow in light and gritty soil; it thrives in chalky ground (*see p.64*).

ALSO RECOMMENDED: *S. baicalensis has pale and deep blue flowers; S. indica var. parvifolia has lilac-blue flowers.*

☼ ◊ ❋ ❋ ❋　　　　　　**Perennial**
‡ 25cm (10in) ↔ 30cm (12in)

SEDUM KAMTSCHATICUM *'Variegatum'* ♀

A carpeting perennial with fleshy, pink-tinted leaves margined with cream. In summer, starry yellow flowers, which age to crimson, nestle just above the foliage It looks good at the front of a border, in a rock garden, or in paving crevices (*see p.348*). Grow in gritty or sandy soil (*see p.38*). It tolerates partial shade and hot, dry sites (*see pp.190, 216, 326*).

ALSO RECOMMENDED: *var.* floriferum *'Weihenstephaner Gold' is trailing with yellow flowers ageing to orange;* S. acre (*see p.369*); S. spathulifolium *'Purpureum'* ♀ (*see p.370*).

☀ ◐ ◊ ❀ ❀ ❀   **Perennial**
‡ 10cm (4in) ↔ 25cm (10in)

SEMPERVIVUM TECTORUM ♀

The common houseleek is a vigorous, evergreen succulent forming mats of large, open rosettes of bristle-tipped, blue-green leaves; these are often suffused wine-red in summer when clusters of starry, red-purple flowers appear on upright stems. Good for rock gardens, troughs, or paving (*see pp.348, 412*); it grows attractively on old roof tiles or among terracotta fragments. Gritty, sharply drained, sandy soil is ideal (*see p.38*). It tolerates hot, dry sites (*see p.190*).

ALSO RECOMMENDED: S. arachnoideum ♀ (*see p.438*); S. ciliosum (*see p.370*).

☀ ◊ ❀ ❀ ❀   **Perennial**
‡ 15cm (6in) ↔ 50cm (20in)

SILENE SCHAFTA ♥

This clump-forming and spreading perennial has floppy stems bearing small, bright green leaves. From late summer to autumn, it bears profuse sprays of long-tubed, rich magenta flowers. Grow in a rock or gravel garden, raised bed, in paving crevices, at the front of a border, or in a container (*see pp.348, 412*). Provide light, neutral to alkaline soil (*see p.64*). It tolerates coastal sites (*see p.166*).

ALSO RECOMMENDED: *'Shell Pink' has pink flowers;* S. uniflora *'Robin Whitebreast' (syn. 'Flore Pleno') double white flowers.*

☼ ◐ ◊ ❁ ❁ ❁   **Perennial**

‡ 25cm (10in) ↔ 30cm (12in)

STACHYS BYZANTINA *'Silver Carpet'*

This evergreen plant does not flower, it simply forms a carpet of soft-textured, furry grey leaves; the common name is lambs' ears. Use it to create beautiful foliage contrasts at the front of a border. Good for alkaline soils, and coastal and hot, dry sites (*see pp.64, 166, 190*), although excessive winter wet may lead to poor or rotting growth. It may be container-grown (*see p.412*).

ALSO RECOMMENDED: S. byzantina *has pink-purple flowers in summer;* 'Big Ears' *also flowers and has large leaves;* 'Primrose Heron' *has yellowish grey leaves.*

☼ ◊ ❁ ❁ ❁   **Perennial**

‡ 45cm (18in) ↔ 60cm (24in)

TRIFOLIUM REPENS
'Purpurascens Quadrifolium'

This four-leaved clover spreads rapidly to form a mat of deep bronze-purple foliage; each leaflet has a narrow band of mid-green around its margin. Tiny heads of white pea flowers appear during summer. Suitable as part of a border or in a wildflower garden, as the flowers are a source of nectar for bees (*see p.494*). Some forms of this plant are aggressive weeds.

ALSO RECOMMENDED: T. pratense *'Susan Smith' has pink flowers, and yellow-marked leaves with three leaflets.*

☼ ◊◊ ❀❀❀   **Perennial**
↕ 10cm (4in) ↔ indefinite

VERONICA PROSTRATA
'Trehane'

This form of prostrate speedwell forms dense mats of golden foliage and, in early summer, produces upright spikes of intense, deep blue flowers. It is ideal in a rock garden, at the front of a border, or in paving crevices (*see p.348*), and it performs well on chalky soils (*see p.64*). Easily grown in any well-drained soil.

ALSO RECOMMENDED: V. prostrata ♀ *is more vigorous with bright green leaves and pale to deep blue flowers; 'Mrs Holt' has pink flowers.*

☼ ◊ ❀❀❀   **Perennial**
↕ 15cm (6in) ↔ 40cm (16in)

PLANTS FOR GROUND COVER IN SHADE

THERE ARE AREAS of shade in the garden beneath trees and shrubs, or at the base of walls and fences that may not receive any direct sunlight at all. Such areas are often thought of as problem sites. However, the world's woodlands and forests actually provide a wealth of plants that positively enjoy such cool, equable, and usually damp conditions, and the choice is actually quite extensive. Most of the plants described here occur naturally on the woodland floor where they have evolved to cope with the changing canopy of leaves and the competition of tree roots. Some plants flower early before the trees leaf out, others, like ferns, do not flower; to them, shade is a positive requirement if they are to produce luxuriant growth. These plants are shade-demanding rather than simply being shade-tolerant. Their lush growth is not only effective in covering the ground, but it also remains in good condition for much longer periods than it would in the face of bleaching sunlight. Shade provides legion opportunities for creating interesting tapestries of contrasting foliage textures.

CHOOSING PLANTS

When choosing ground cover for shady spots, it is vital to select plants that suit the conditions, because you need them to grow vigorously and well if they are to form the dense, light-excluding foliage canopy necessary to smother out the weeds. It is essential that the soil be cleared thoroughly of all weeds, especially perennial ones, before planting, because they compete vigorously with your chosen ground coverers for light, nutrients, and moisture

Weeds can be cleared either by using translocated weed killers (*see p.305*), by hand (if the area is small), or smothered by layers of old carpet or polythene sheeting for a season before planting. The establishment of ground cover is also helped enormously if the soil is improved; add well-rotted organic matter to improve fertility and moisture retention before planting, and then provide a thick mulch to the soil surface after planting. Even better than this is to use a permeable sheet mulch, such as hemp matting, in conjunction with a loose surface mulch, like granulated bark.

GROWTH RATES VARY

Even shade-tolerant plants may grow more slowly in deep shade than they would where light levels are higher in partial shade, and it will speed the completion of cover if smaller and more delicate plants, such as *Asarum europaeum* (*see p.333*), are planted more closely together than they would be otherwise. Rampant spreaders, like *Lamium galeobdolon* 'Hermann's Pride' (*see p.341*), or *Gaultheria shallon* (*see p.328*) need no such concessions. Quite the reverse is necessary, in fact, and it is essential to take their potential spread into account. If poorly sited, they will quickly swamp less robust plants.

GAULTHERIA SHALLON

Salal forms a spreading mound of leathery, dark green leaves, which is ideal ground cover for shady banks or beneath trees. In early summer, small, pink-tinted white flowers appear, followed by purple fruits. These attract birds (*see p.494*). Grow in moist, neutral to acid soil (*see p.92*); chop away spreading roots with a spade to restrict spread, as necessary. It tolerates urban pollution and dry shade (*see p.216*).

ALSO RECOMMENDED: G. procumbens ♀ *is low-growing with white or pale pink flowers and scarlet fruit.*

☼ ◐ ◊ ❈❈❈   **Evergreen shrub**
‡ 1.2m (4ft) ↔ 1.5m (5ft)

HYPERICUM CALYCINUM

The rose of Sharon spreads quickly by means of its creeping stems with dark green leaves, and it is an excellent ground-cover plant for most soil types. Showy, bright yellow flowers are displayed from midsummer to autumn. It tolerates dry shade as well as sun, where it may flower more profusely (*see pp.216, 304*). Cut to ground level in spring. The leaves are susceptible to rust.

ALSO RECOMMENDED: H. androsaemum *is deciduous and less spreading.*

☼ ◐ ◊◊ ❈❈❈   **Evergreen shrub**
‡ 60cm (24in) ↔ indefinite

LEUCOTHOE *Scarletta*

Switch ivy is an upright bush with arching stems grown for its luxuriant and very dark glossy green, pointed leaves. In this cultivar, also sold as 'Zeblid', the leaves are tinted red-purple when young and tinged with bronze in winter. Clusters of small, bell-shaped white flowers appear in spring, which hang amid the foliage. It prefers reliably damp, acid soils (*see pp.92, 238*). Trim after flowering, if necessary.

ALSO RECOMMENDED: L. walteri *'Rainbow' has cream- and pink-mottled leaves.*

☼ ◐ ◊ ❀ ❀ ❀   **Evergreen shrub**
↕ 1–2m (3–6ft) ↔ 3m (10ft)

MAHONIA REPENS *'Rotundifolia'*

An upright, suckering shrub with leathery, dark green leaves. Clusters of fragrant yellow flowers appear in mid to late spring, followed by spherical black berries. Best in fertile, moist but well-drained soil, but tolerant of dry, chalky, and clay soils (*see pp.12, 64, 216*). It can be used as an informal hedge (*see p.138*). Prune only to remove dead wood after flowering.

ALSO RECOMMENDED: M. repens *is shorter;* M. x wagneri *'Pinnacle'* ❧ *has more spiny leaves, which are bronzed when young, and larger flower clusters.*

☼ ◐ ◊◊ ❀ ❀ ❀ *f*   **Evergreen shrub**
↕ 1.5m (5ft) ↔ 2m (6ft)

VINCA DIFFORMIS

This low and shrubby periwinkle has narrow and pointed, glossy dark green leaves all over its wide-spreading shoots. These do not flower, but in late winter and early spring, upward-growing shoots appear and bear pale blue to white flowers. Choose a site sheltered from heavy frosts. It also copes with relatively dry soils in shade (*see p.216*). Cut back in spring.

ALSO RECOMMENDED: *V. major 'Variegata' ♀ has dark violet flowers and cream-margined leaves, tolerating deep shade, but it may be invasive; V. minor (see p.237).*

☼☀ ◊◊ ❄❄   **Evergreen shrub**
↕ 30cm (12in) ↔ indefinite

HEDERA HELIX *'Glacier'* ♀

Most ivies make excellent ground cover in sun and shade (*see p.304*). 'Glacier' is a versatile cultivar, which will also grow against a shady wall, in dry shade, in a container, or as an indoor plant (*see pp.216, 262, 412, 448*). Its climbing, self-clinging stems do not need support and are covered with small, evergreen, greyish leaves. These have triangular lobes and are variegated with grey and cream. It tolerates chalky soils (*see p.64*).

ALSO RECOMMENDED: *'Erecta' ♀ (see p.220); 'Ivalace' ♀ has dark green leaves with wavy margins; f. poetarum (see p.509).*

☼☀ ◊◊ ❄❄❄   **Climber**
↕ 2m (6ft) or more

HEDERA HIBERNICA ♀

Although Irish ivy is a climbing plant,
its fast-growing, clinging stems can
be allowed to spread as ground cover
in the dry shade of trees and shrubs
(*see p.216*). It is valued for its broadly
oval, dark green leaves, which have
five triangular lobes. Also useful for
exposed sites and shady walls (*see
pp.118, 262*). It prefers alkaline soils
(*see p.64*). Cut back at any time to
reduce spread.

ALSO RECOMMENDED: *H. colchica
'Sulphur Heart'* ♀ (*see p.275*); *H. helix
'Spetchley'* ♀ *has tiny, dark green leaves.*

☀ ☀ ◐◊ ❀ ❀ ❀   **Climber**
↕ 10m (30ft)

ADIANTUM ALEUTICUM ♀

Tough but of delicate appearance, the
Northern maidenhair fern forms a lacy
mat of pale green, finely divided fronds
on glossy black stalks; they are often
pink-tinted when young. Ideal for
shady borders and woodland gardens,
it is easily grown in leafy soil. Remove
old or damaged fronds in spring. It can
be container-grown (*see p.448*), and
it tolerates acid soils and damp shade
(*see pp 92, 238*).

ALSO RECOMMENDED: *A. pedatum* ♀ (*see
p.458*); *'Japonicum' has purple-pink new
fronds; A. venustum* ♀ *has fronds that
are bright bronze-pink on emergence.*

☀ ◐ ❀ ❀ ❀   **Perennial fern**
↕↔ 75cm (30in)

AEGOPODIUM PODAGRARIA *'Variegatum'*

Variegated ground elder is ideal for brightening a shady border or dark corner. It forms dense cover with its divided green leaves, which are broadly margined and splashed with creamy white. Although less aggressive than the green-leaved species – a pernicious weed – it may still swamp smaller, less robust species, so site it where it will not spread into other plants. Grow in any soil including poor, clay or chalky ones (*see pp.12, 64*). It may also be grown in a container (*see p.448*).

☼☀ ◊◊ ❄❄❄   **Perennial**

‡ 30–60cm (12–24in) ↔ indefinite

ANEMONE × LIPSIENSIS

The pale creamy yellow flowers of this carpet-forming anemone appear in spring, above toothed, divided dark green leaves. Perfect for a woodland garden, damp and shady border (*see p.238*), or for planting beneath shrubs. It tolerates chalky soils (*see p.64*).

ALSO RECOMMENDED: A. nemorosa ♥ *has white, often pink-flushed flowers;* A. sylvestris *is taller and has nodding white flowers with gold stamens.*

☼ ◊ ❄❄❄   **Perennial**

‡ 15cm (6in) ↔ 45cm (18in)

ASARUM EUROPAEUM

Asarabacca is a creeping plant that forms evergreen carpets of kidney-shaped, glossy dark green leaves. Hidden beneath them, in late spring, are small, narrowly bell shaped, greenish purple to brown flowers. Excellent in a moist woodland garden or damp, shady border (*see p.238*). Grow in neutral to acid soil (*see p.92*). Protect from slugs and snails.

ALSO RECOMMENDED: *A. hartwegii has bronze-green leaves with silver-marbled veins, A. shuttleworthii has dark green, often silver-marbled leaves.*

☼☼ ◑ ❀❀❀　　　　　**Perennial**
‡ 0cm (3in) ↔ 30cm (12in)

BERGENIA *'Morgenröte'* ♥

Also sold as Morning Red, this early-flowering, evergreen perennial forms clumps of rich green, fleshy and leathery, paddle-shaped leaves. Clusters of deep pink flowers on upright stems emerge in spring. Good underplanting for shrubs, which give necessary winter shelter, or grow in a pot (*see p.448*). Provide a mulch in autumn. It tolerates chalky soils and reasonably dry or damp shade (*see pp.64, 216, 238*).

ALSO RECOMMENDED: *'Abendglut' (syn. 'Evening Glow') has magenta-crimson flowers; 'Baby Doll' has pink flowers; 'Sunningdale' (see p.226); B. ciliata (see p.79).*

☼☼ ◐◑ ❀❀❀　　　　　**Perennial**
‡ 30cm (12in) ↔ 50cm (20in)

CARDAMINE TRIFOLIA

Trifoliate bittercress is a creeping plant with divided, dark green leaves, which are tinted red beneath. In late spring, it bears dense clusters of four-petalled, white, occasionally pink flowers. It is ideal for a permanently damp, shady border (*see pp.238, 372*) or for naturalizing in a woodland garden. Grow in moist, humus-rich soil.

ALSO RECOMMENDED: C. pratensis *'Flore Pleno'* ♥ *has double, lilac-pink flowers*; C. raphanifolia *has lilac, red-violet, or white flowers.*

☀ ◑ ◐ ❄ ❄ ❄   **Perennial**
‡ 15cm (6in) ↔ 30cm (12in)

CHELIDONIUM MAJUS *'Flore Pleno'*

This double-flowered form of the greater celandine is perfect for naturalizing in a woodland garden. Above a clump of lobed, deeply divided leaves, it bears a mass of deep yellow flowers in summer. It tolerates most soils and almost any situation, including dry shade (*see p.216*).

ALSO RECOMMENDED: C. majus *has single, bowl-shaped, poppy-like yellow flowers and self-seeds freely; var.* laciniatum *has deeply cut leaves and petals.*

☀ ◑ ◐◐ ❄ ❄ ❄   **Perennial**
‡ 60cm (24in) ↔ 20cm (8in)

CHRYSOGONUM VIRGINIANUM

Golden star produces a long succession of star-shaped yellow flowers from early spring to late summer. The heart-shaped leaves with toothed or scalloped margins are borne on red-green stalks; they form dense clumps and, in mild winters, often remain evergreen. Ideal ground cover for a shady border or woodland garden, and it may also be grown in sun where soils remain moist (*see p.304*).

☼ ◑ ◊ ❄ ❄ ❄   **Perennial**

‡ 25cm (10in) ↔ 60cm (24in)

CYCLAMEN HEDERIFOLIUM ♀

The Neapolitan cyclamen produces pale to deep pink flowers with backswept petals in autumn. These appear in advance of the ivy-like leaves, which are patterned with silvery grey. Excellent in dry shade beneath trees or shrubs (*see p.216*), or in containers (*see p.448*). Mulch each year as the leaves wither. It self-seeds freely, forming substantial colonies if protected from summer rainfall. Plant tubers in autumn. It tolerates chalky soils (*see p.64*).

ALSO RECOMMENDED: *f. albiflorum has white flowers; C. purpurascens ♀ bears red flowers with its leaves in late summer.*

☼ ◊ ❄ ❄ ❄   **Perennial**

‡ 10–13cm (4–5in) ↔ 15cm (6in)

DICENTRA *'Bacchanal'*

The clusters of dusky crimson spring flowers of this spreading perennial appear to glow amid the ferny, deeply cut, greyish green leaves. It forms very attractive ground cover for a woodland garden or damp, shady border (*see p.238*). It will grow in slightly alkaline soils (*see p.64*).

ALSO RECOMMENDED: *'Adrian Bloom' is similar; 'Langtrees'* ♀ *has silvery foliage and pinkish white flowers;* D. cucullaria (see p.229); D. spectabilis ♀ (see p.82).

☀ ◐◗ ❀❀❀   **Perennial**
‡ 35cm (14in) ↔ 45cm (18in)

DISPOROPSIS PERNYI

This rhizomatous perennial produces arching, mottled deep green stems clothed in lance-shaped, dark green leaves. In early summer, lemon-scented flowers hang from the stems like waxy white bells. A very elegant plant for a woodland garden or damp, shady border (*see p.238*). It associates beautifully with ferns. Grow in leafy, moist but well-drained soil.

☀ ◗ ❀❀❀ *f*   **Perennial**
‡ 40cm (16in) ↔ 30–40cm (12–16in)

DUCHESNEA INDICA

The Indian strawberry produces clumps of deeply veined, palmately divided, bright green leaves that are more or less evergreen; it spreads freely by means of rooting runners. Five-petalled yellow flowers appear in early and late summer followed by bright red, strawberry-like, unpalatable fruits. It is excellent as edging in a shady border and will also grow in a container (see *p.448*). Tolerant of most soils and sites.

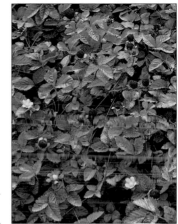

☼◐ ◊◊ ❀❀❀ **Perennial**

↕ 10cm (4in) ↔ 1.2m (4ft) or more

EPIMEDIUM × WARLEYENSE

This evergreen, clump-forming plant has fresh green leaves, which are tinted red in spring and autumn; it spreads freely by rhizomes. In mid- to late spring, slender stems carry nodding, cup-shaped yellow flowers with orange-red sepals. It is perfect for a mixed or herbaceous border, or for a woodland site. Clip back old leaves in late winter or early spring. It tolerates dry shade (see *p.216*).

ALSO RECOMMENDED: E. × perralchicum ♀ *has bright yellow flowers*; E. × versicolor *has pink and yellow flowers with reddish spurs.*

☼ ◊◊ ❀❀❀ **Perennial**

↕ 40cm (16in) ↔ 75cm (30in)

EUPHORBIA SIKKIMENSIS

A spreading plant with upright shoots that are bright pink when young; they are clothed in narrow green leaves, which become paler with red veins and margins as they age. Heads of yellow flowers appear from midsummer. It is ideal for a shady borders. Remove dead flowerheads after flowering; wear gloves, as the milky sap can irritate skin. Tolerant of chalky soils (*see p.64*).

ALSO RECOMMENDED: E. amaygdaloides *var.* robbiae ♀ (see p.230); E. dulcis (see p.230); E. griffithii *'Dixter'* ♀ *has coppery leaves and orange flowers;* E. schillingii ♀ *has bluish leaves and green-yellow flowers.*

☀ ◊ ❊ ❊ ❊   **Perennial**
‡ 1.2m (4ft) ↔ 45cm (18in)

GALAX URCEOLATA

The rounded and leathery, dark green leaves of this evergreen plant turn red-bronze in autumn. It is a robust and long-lived plant that is suitable for the front of a shady border, woodland garden, or large rock garden; it forms excellent ground cover beneath shrubs in both dry and damp shade (*see pp.216, 238*). Slender-stemmed spikes of many tiny white flowers appear late spring and early summer. Grow in acid soil (*see p.92*) and apply a lime-free mulch of pine needles or leafmould annually in spring.

☀ ◊ ❊ ❊ ❊   **Perennial**
‡ 30cm (12in) ↔ 1m (3ft)

GALIUM ODORATUM

Tolerant of almost any soil and site, sweet woodruff makes good ground cover, especially as its dense clusters of pure white, star-shaped summer flowers are very effective at brightening shady spots. It spreads rapidly, so site it away from less robust plants. The whorls of brilliant green leaves, which develop a strong scent of newly mown hay when dried, are lovely woven into garlands. It is best with shade from the hottest sun. Excessive growth can be pulled out easily by hand to limit its spread.

☼ ☽ ◊◊ ✤✤✤ *f* **Perennial**

↕ 45cm (18in) ↔ indefinite

GERANIUM MACRORRHIZUM

This geranium spreads to form a cover of light green, finely cut, sticky and strongly aromatic foliage, colouring well in autumn. Clusters of pink, purplish, or white flowers appear above the carpet of leaves in early summer. Tolerant of clay soils and dry shade (*see pp 12, 216*); it will also grow in a container (*see p.448*).

ALSO RECOMMENDED: *'Album'* ♥ has *white flowers*, *'Czakor'* has *magenta flowers*; *'Ingwersen's Variety'* ♥ has *pink flowers*; *G. endressii* ♥ (*see p.316*); *G. nodosum* (*see p.231*); *G. × oxonianum* (*see p.316*); *G. phaeum* (*see p.232*).

☼ ☽ ◊◊ ✤✤✤ *f* **Perennial**

↕ 30cm (12in) ↔ 60cm (24in)

HEUCHERA *'Green Ivory'*

This coral flower forms clumps of bright green, lobed and rounded foliage, which makes effective evergreen ground cover or edging if grouped together. Sprays of small, pale green flowers are lifted up into the air on upright stems in early summer; they are good for cutting and attract bees (*see pp.494, 524*). It tolerates full shade where the ground is reliably damp (*see p.238*). Also suitable for containers (*see p.448*).

ALSO RECOMMENDED: *'Chocolate Ruffles'* has brown, ruffled leaves; *'Rachel'* has pink flowers; H. micrantha *'Palace Purple'* ♀ (see p.464).

☀️◐ ◊◊ ❀❀❀   **Perennial**
‡↔ 75cm (30in)

HOSTA *'Halcyon'* ♀

Also sold as 'Holstein', the bright greyish blue foliage of this perennial make it a striking ground-cover or architectural plant (*see p.472*). The leaves are heart-shaped, about 20cm (8in) long, forming clumps from which emerge clusters of lavender flowers on upright stems in summer. Suits clay and damp or permanently moist soils (*see pp.12, 238, 372*) as well as containers (*see p.448*).

ALSO RECOMMENDED: *'Birchwood Parky's Gold'* (see p.318); *'Frances Williams'* ♀ (see p.381); *'Shade Fanfare'* ♀ (see p.465); *'Wide Brim'* ♀ (see p.254); H. sieboldiana (see p.490); H. ventricosa ♀ (see p.30).

☀️◐ ◊ ❀❀❀   **Perennial**
‡ 35–40cm (14–16in) ↔ 70cm (28in)

LAMIUM GALEOBDOLON
'Hermann's Pride'

This form of yellow archangel makes a dense carpet of silver-burnished green leaves, and it bears whorled spikes of yellow flowers in summer. It spreads vigorously, so site it well away from smaller plants. Growth is best on moist but well-drained soil; drier soils help reduce vigour. Tolerates both dry and damp shade (*see pp.216, 238*), and clay and chalky soils (*see pp.12, 64*).

ALSO RECOMMENDED: L. galeobdolon *is more vigorous;* 'Silver Angel' *is more trailing with silvery leaves.*

☀️ ◐ ◌◌ ❋ ❋ ❋   **Perennial**

↕ 60cm (24in) ↔ indefinite

LUZULA SYLVATICA *'Aurea'*

This bright-foliaged cultivar of the greater woodrush is a grass-like woodland plant and makes a useful, dense ground cover for dry or damp, shady places (*see pp.216, 238*); it copes with full sun if the soil is reliably moist. The clumps of evergreen, strap-shaped leaves are yellow-green, fading to yellow in winter. Airy clusters of light brown flowers appear from spring to early summer.

ALSO RECOMMENDED: 'Hohe Tatra' *is shorter;* 'Marginata' *has cream-margined, rich green leaves.*

☀️ ☀️ ◌◌ ❋ ❋ ❋   **Perennial**

↕ 70–80cm (28–32in) ↔ 45cm (18in)

MAIANTHEMUM BIFOLIUM

The false lily-of-the-valley is a vigorous, spreading plant with paired, broadly heart-shaped, dark green leaves. The slender-stemmed clusters of fluffy, star-shaped white flowers appear in early summer and are followed by red berries. Excellent ground cover for a wild or woodland garden, or on a cool, damp and shady bank (*see p.238*). It tolerates acid soils (*see p.92*) and can be invasive where conditions suit.

ALSO RECOMMENDED: M. canadense *is similar with narrower leaves.*

☼ ◑ ◊ ❄ ❄ ❄   **Perennial**
↕ 15cm (6in) ↔ indefinite

PACHYPHRAGMA MACROPHYLLUM

The rounded and scalloped, dark green leaves of this spreading perennial are semi-evergreen, persisting partially in basal clusters over winter. In early spring, dense heads of four-petalled, malodorous white flowers appear; the stems later elongate, so the heart-shaped fruits that follow are held well above the foliage. Good as ground cover beneath trees or shrubs, or at the front of a shady border. It tolerates dry shade (*see p.216*).

☼ ◊◊ ❄ ❄ ❄   **Perennial**
↕ 40cm (16in) ↔ 90cm (36in)

PHUOPSIS STYLOSA

The Caucasian crosswort is a creeping, mat-forming plant with whorls of narrow, pale green leaves. It is ideal for a bank, rock garden, or the front of a border. It bears rounded heads of many tiny pink flowers over long periods in summer. The plant forms good cover in both shade and sun (*see p.304*). Trim after flowering to keep it compact.

☼ ◔ ◊◐ ❋ ❋ ❋ **Perennial**

‡ 15cm (6in) ↔ 50cm (20in) or more

POLYPODIUM VULGARE

The common polypody is a robust fern with deeply divided, lance-shaped and leathery, dark green fronds. It makes good cover on shady banks or borders and can be established on fallen tree trunks. Tolerant of chalky and dry soils (*see pp.64, 216*). It grows well in humus-rich, gritty or stony, well-drained soils and can be container-grown (*see p.448*).

ALSO RECOMMENDED: *'Bifidomultifidum' has lacy, very finely divided fronds; 'Cornubiense Grandiceps' has finely divided fronds that are crested at the tips.*

☼ ◔ ◊ ❋ ❋ ❋ **Perennial fern**

‡ 30cm (12in) ↔ indefinite

PULMONARIA SACCHARATA *'Frühlingshimmel'*

This plant forms an evergreen mat of silver-spotted leaves. From late winter to late spring, pink buds open to sky blue flowers with darker eyes. Also good for a damp, shady border, wildlife garden, or container (*see pp.238, 448, 494*). Remove old leaves after flowering to induce new growth and reduce risk of powdery mildew. It tolerates clay soils and exposed sites (*see pp.12, 118*).

ALSO RECOMMENDED: *Argentea Group* ♀ *has very silvery leaves and red flowers, which age to deep violet; 'Mrs Moon' has pink buds that open to bluish lilac flowers.*

☼☀ ◔ ❀❀❀   **Perennial**

‡ 25cm (10in) ↔ 60cm (24in)

RANUNCULUS ACONITIFOLIUS *'Flore Pleno'* ♀

White bachelor's buttons is a double-flowered form of the buttercup. Its late spring, pure white flowers are almost spherical in shape and are borne above the clumps of large and luxuriant, deeply lobed and toothed, dark green leaves. It tolerates clay soils (*see p.12*) and makes good ground cover for a woodland or shady garden.

ALSO RECOMMENDED: *R. aconitifolius is similar with single flowers.*

☼☀ ◐ ❀❀❀   **Perennial**

‡ 60cm (24in) ↔ 45cm (18in)

SANGUINARIA CANADENSIS

Bloodroot forms a low mat of kidney-shaped, blue-grey leaves and makes excellent cover in a wild or woodland garden, or in a shady niche in a rock garden. The lovely, crystalline-textured, white, or pink-tinged flowers emerge from between vertically folded leaves as they unfurl in spring. It will also grow in containers (*see p.448*) and tolerates clay soils and damp sites in shade (*see pp.12, 238*).

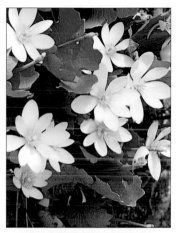

ALSO RECOMMENDED: *'Plena'* ♥ *has longer-lasting, double white flowers.*

☀ ◊ ❄❄❄   **Perennial**

↕ 15cm (6in) ↔ 30cm (12in)

SAXIFRAGA *'Tricolor'* ♥

A woodland saxifrage grown for its colourful rosettes of rounded to deeply cut, red, white, and green leaves, which die back over winter. Gentle clusters of tiny white flowers with uneven petals rise above the foliage in summer on slender stems. It also tolerates chalky soils and dry shade (*see pp.64, 216*). Grow in a border, rock garden, or container (*see p.448*) with shelter from heavy frosts.

ALSO RECOMMENDED: S. fortunei ♥ *is similar;* S. cuneifolia *and* S. × urbium ♥ *both form spreading mats.*

☀☀ ◊◊ ❄❄   **Perennial**

↕↔ 30cm (12in)

SYMPHYTUM *'Goldsmith'*

This plant, less rampant than variants with plain green leaves, spreads vigorously to form dense cover with its wrinkled, gold- and cream-variegated, dark green leaves. From mid-spring, a mass of tubular, pale blue, pink, or cream flowers rise just above the foliage. Grow in a woodland garden or in a dry or damp, shady border (*see pp.216, 238*).

ALSO RECOMMENDED: *'Hidcote Blue' has plain, dark green leaves and pale blue flowers; 'Hidcote Pink' has pale pink and white flowers; S. tuberosum (see p.235).*

☼ ☀ ◊ ❀ ❀ ❀   **Perennial**

↕↔30cm (12in)

TIARELLA CORDIFOLIA ♀

Foam flower is named for its clouds of starry, creamy white flowers, which appear in summer. It makes a weed-smothering, evergreen mat of lobed, pale green leaves. Excellent in a woodland garden or at the front of a damp, shady border (*see p.238*); the foliage flushes bronze-red in autumn. It copes with a wide range of soils.

ALSO RECOMMENDED: *T. wherryi ♀ is less vigorous, with maroon-tinted foliage and white or pink flowers; 'Bronze Beauty' has red-bronze foliage.*

☼ ☀ ◊ ❀ ❀ ❀   **Perennial**

↕ 10–30cm (4–12in) ↔ 30cm (12in)

TRADESCANTIA *Andersoniana Group 'Osprey'* ♥

This perennial is admired for its bright white, summer to autumn flowers, which are illuminated by the arching, deep purplish green leaves. The blooms have three triangular petals and appear at the tips of the stems. A long-flowering plant for filling gaps in a border, or for a container (*see p.448*).

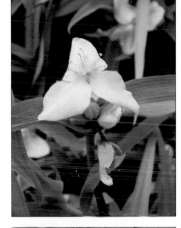

ALSO RECOMMENDED: *'Isis' ♥ makes a fine, dark-blue flowered companion; 'Purple Dome' has rich purple flowers.*

☼-◐ ◊ ❀ ❀ ❀   **Perennial**
‡ 60cm (24in) ↔ 45cm (18in)

VANCOUVERIA HEXANDRA

Tough but of delicate appearance, this spreading perennial is ideal for a large, shady rock garden or under trees or shrubs. The lobed leaves are smooth-textured and bright green, and loose clusters of small, nodding white flowers appear on wiry stems in late spring and summer. It is best with shelter from cold, drying winds and tolerates damp shade (*see p.238*).

ALSO RECOMMENDED: V. chrysantha *is wider spreading with leathery, evergreen leaves and yellow flowers.*

☼ ◊ ❀ ❀ ❀   **Perennial**
‡↔ 40cm (16in)

PLANTS FOR WALLS & PAVING

Fᴵʀꜱᴛ ᴀɴᴅ ꜰᴏʀᴇᴍᴏꜱᴛ, walls, paths, and patios are practical features. Paths allow people to use the garden without getting their feet dirty, patios provide an area for dining and outdoor entertaining, and walls serve to divide the garden into separate areas. Although these surfaces may seem to be mundane, there is no reason why they cannot form yet another planting niche for the gardener to exploit.

Walls and paving can appear hard, monotonous, and bland without plants to soften their severe lines. When paths are studded with aromatic herbs, such as *Mentha requienii* (*see p.365*) or thyme (*see pp.310, 352, 507*), that release their fragance when gently trodden by passing feet, and walls are softened by flowers and handsome foliage, these areas become features of real beauty.

Many plants that do well in wall and paving crevices do best with hot, dry conditions at their heads (*see p.190*), good drainage at their necks, and roots in the cool, damp conditions that they find beneath the slabs or stones. The stonework also insulates the roots, keeping temperatures more even in summer and protecting them from frost in the winter months.

IDEAL PLANTS FOR PAVING

In paving, plants need to be small enough not to impede progress and low-growing so that they do not cause the unwary to trip. Larger mound-formers, like lavenders (*see pp.155, 200*), *Euryops acraeus* (*see p.350*), or *Artemisia schmidtiana* 'Nana' (*see p.357*), have a role to play in softening the hard lines at the margins; place them carefully away from lines of pedestrian access across the paving. Bear in mind that few plants will withstand constant treading or having garden furniture placed on top of them.

CULTIVATION TIPS

Instead of mortaring all wall and paving crevices, fill them or some of them with a gritty or sandy compost mix to provide a good, well-drained growing medium. Plants can be introduced either by sowing seed directly into the crevices or by planting them when still small – before the root system becomes too large to introduce without damaging it. You will need to weed around young plants and seedlings and keep them well watered until they are established. Once they get going, they will help to prevent further invasion by weeds. Some plants, like *Alchemilla alpina* (*see p.354*) or *Geranium dalmaticum* (*see p.363*), will even find their own way into crevices by self-seeding; the only aid they need is to thin the seedlings to give them sufficient space to grow. If you are building a new patio or wall, consider omitting some slabs or bricks to form planting pockets to accommodate a few taller or larger species – you could even create a chequer-board effect in paving by missing out alternate slabs. Top-dress the soil surface with grit or gravel, which acts as a weed-suppressing mulch.

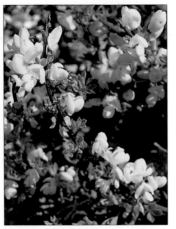

CYTISUS ARDOINOI ♥

This ground-hugging broom forms a hummock of arching stems and small, deep green leaves, which are palmately divided into three narrow leaflets. Bright yellow pea flowers are borne in the axils of these leaves from late spring to summer. It grows well on poor, sandy or acid soils (*see pp.38, 92*), where it likes to remain undisturbed. Minimal pruning is necessary. Also suitable for rock gardens.

☼ ◊ ❀❀❀   **Deciduous shrub**
‡↔ 20–60cm (8–24in)

EURYOPS ACRAEUS ♥

This silver-grey-leaved shrub forms a tight dome of foliage, which is studded in late spring and early summer by a mass of bright yellow, daisy-like flowerheads. Both foliage and flowers are offset beautifully by mellow stone or brick pavers. Excellent in hot, dry sites and in containers (*see pp.190, 412*), but it is also suitable for a rock garden, raised bed, or at the front of a sunny border. Trim lightly after flowering to keep compact.

☼ ◊ ❀❀❀   **Evergreen shrub**
‡↔ 30cm (12in)

HELIANTHEMUM LUNULATUM

The spreading stems of this low shrub are clothed in grey-green leaves. In late spring and early summer, a profusion of small, saucer-shaped yellow flowers cover the plant. It thrives on sandy and chalky soils, and hot, dry sites (*see pp.38, 64, 190*), and it also makes good ground cover (*see p.304*). Trim after flowering to keep compact. It is suitable for a sunny container (*see p.412*).

ALSO RECOMMENDED: H. *'Ben Hope' has pale grey-green leaves and carmine-red flowers*; H. oelandicum *subsp.* alpestre *has grey-green leaves and yellow flowers.*

☼ ◊ ❀ ❀ ❀　　　**Evergreen shrub**
‡ 15cm (6in) ↔ 25cm (10in)

LINUM ARBOREUM ♀

The tree flax is actually a dwarf shrub with spatula-shaped, thick and dark blue-green leaves crowded along its shoots. It is grown for its lengthy season of bright yellow, funnel-shaped flowers, which appear for many weeks from late spring to summer. Also suitable for a rock garden and chalky soils (*see p.64*), but shelter it from excessive winter wet.

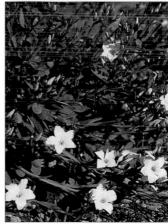

ALSO RECOMMENDED: L. *'Gemmel's Hybrid' ♀ is smaller.*

☼ ◊ ❀ ❀ ❀　　　**Evergreen shrub**
‡↔ 30cm (12in)

TEUCRIUM POLIUM

This rounded shrub has aromatic, wrinkled, white-woolly, grey-green leaves, and dense heads of purple or yellow, two-lipped flowers, which appear in summer; they are attractive to bees (*see p.494*). It also suits rock gardens and raised beds. In paving, grow it in pockets of gritty, well-drained, neutral to alkaline soil (*see p.64*). Trim in early spring to keep it compact. It may also be clipped as a low hedge (*see p.138*).

ALSO RECOMMENDED: *T. aroanium is more compact with silver-hairy leaves and purple flowers; T. subspinosum is spiny with grey-green leaves and pink flowers.*

☼ ◊ ❄❄❄ *f*   **Deciduous shrub**
‡↔ 30cm (12in)

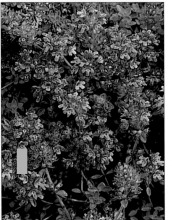

THYMUS SERPYLLUM
'Annie Hall'

A creeping, mound-forming plant with tiny, aromatic green leaves and tight heads of two-lipped purple-pink flowers in summer; they attract bees (*see p.494*). In paving, the foliage releases a lovely fragrance when stepped on. Thyme thrives in chalky soils and hot, dry sites (*see pp.64, 190*), and it makes good ground cover (*see p.304*). Trim after flowering to keep the growth compact.

ALSO RECOMMENDED: *'Coccineus'* ♀ *has crimson-pink flowers; 'Pink Chintz'* ♀ *has grey-green leaves and flesh pink flowers; 'Snowdrift' has white flowers.*

☼ ◊ ❄❄❄ *f*   **Evergreen shrub**
‡ 25cm (10in) ↔ 45cm (18in)

ACANTHOLIMON GLUMACEUM

This compact evergreen forms a mat of stiff and needle-like, dark green leaves. In summer, it is covered by dense, short-stemmed spikes of rose-pink flowers. Grow in pockets of sharply drained, gritty soil. It tolerates chalky soils and hot, dry sites (*see pp.64, 190*), and it also suits raised or scree beds. Susceptible to rotting in areas with wet winters, but planting in wall crevices helps protect the vulnerable plant neck. Leave undisturbed once established.

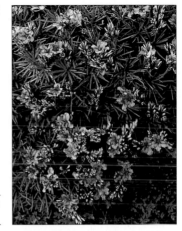

☼ ◊ ❀❀❀   **Perennial**

↕ 5–8cm (2–3in) ↔ 30cm (12in)

AETHIONEMA GRANDIFLORUM ♥

This pretty stonecress is a woody-based, evergreen perennial, and it bears masses of pale to deep pink, cross-shaped flowers in late spring and early summer above its neat and narrow, blue-green leaves. It is best in light, sandy or chalky soils (*see pp.38, 64*), but tolerates acid conditions (*see p.92*). Good for coastal and hot, dry sites (*see pp.166, 190*). It is often short-lived.

ALSO RECOMMENDED: *A. armenum is more compact with pale pink flowers;* *A. 'Warley Rose' ♥ has blue-grey leaves and rich pink flowers.*

☼ ◊ ❀❀❀   **Perennial**

↕↔ 20–30cm (8–12in)

AJUGA REPTANS
'Catlin's Giant' ♀

An excellent evergreen perennial for
both paving and ground cover (*see
pp.304, 326*). It bears whorls of dark
blue flowers along the upright stems
in early summer. The glossy, deep
bronze-purple leaves can be up to
15cm (6in) long. Also useful as border
edging, coping with both dry and
damp shade (*see pp.216, 238*). It
is tolerant of clay soils (*see p.12*).

ALSO RECOMMENDED: *'Multicolor'* (see
p.225); *'Variegata' is denser with cream-
splashed leaves.*

☼ ☀ ◑ ◊◊ ❄❄❄   **Perennial**
‡ 20cm (8in) ↔ 1m (3ft)

ALCHEMILLA ALPINA

Alpine lady's mantle has a creeping
rootstock and forms low mats of lobed,
dark green leaves, which are densely
silver-hairy beneath. Loose clusters of
yellow-green flowers appear throughout
summer. It is ideal for paving crevices,
where it may spread by self-seeding,
and it is also good for a rock garden or
as ground cover (*see p.304*). It tolerates
coastal conditions (*see p.166*).

ALSO RECOMMENDED: *A. conjuncta* (see
p.181); *A. ellenbeckii has pale green leaves
on wiry red stems.*

☼ ◑ ❄❄❄   **Perennial**
‡ 8–12cm (3–5in) ↔ 50cm (20in)

ANAGALLIS TENELLA 'Studland' ♀

This mat-forming plant has bright green leaves, which are almost obscured in late spring and early summer by a profusion of small, fragrant pink flowers. Also good for ground cover at the front of a sunny border (*see p.304*) or in a rock garden. It may be short-lived.

ALSO RECOMMENDED: A. monellii ♀ *is taller and has blue flowers.*

☼ ◊ ❀ ❀ ❀ *f*   **Perennial**
‡ 5–10cm (2–4in) ↔ 40cm (18in)

ANDROSACE CARNEA SUBSP. LAGGERI ♀

This evergreen, cushion-forming plant has rosettes of narrow, fleshy leaves and produces yellow-eyed, deep pink flowers in late spring. Grow in pockets of gritty, moist but sharply drained soil and top dress with grit or gravel to keep the stem and leaves dry. Also good for a rock garden, trough, or raised bed. It tolerates chalky soils (*see p.304*).

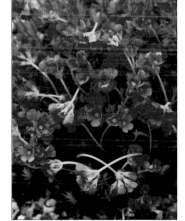

ALSO RECOMMENDED: A. lanuginosa ♀ *has greyish leaves and pink flowers;* A. semper- vivoides ♀ *has fragrant pink flowers.*

☼ ◊ ❀ ❀ ❀   **Perennial**
‡ 5cm (2in) ↔ 8–15cm (3–6in)

ARABIS BLEPHAROPHYLLA
'Frühlingszauber' ♀

A mat-forming evergreen with dark green leaves that bears compact clusters of fragrant, deep pink flowers in late spring and early summer. As well as for paving, it is suitable for rock gardens and raised beds, and tolerates hot, dry sites (*see p.190*). It may be short-lived. Protect from excessive winter wet. Also sold as Spring Charm.

ALSO RECOMMENDED: *A. alpina 'Flore Pleno'* ♀ *has double white flowers; A.* × *arendsii 'Rosabella' has rose-pink flowers.*

☼ ◊ ❋❋❋ *f*   **Perennial**
‡ 10cm (4in) ↔ 20cm (8in)

ARENARIA PURPURASCENS

This sandwort is a low-growing and spreading perennial, freely bearing an abundance of starry pink flowers in midsummer. They are highlighted by the background of small and narrow, sharply pointed, greyish green leaves on wiry, mat-forming stems. It is easily grown in both wall and paving crevices, or in a rock garden. It tolerates sandy soils (*see p.38*).

ALSO RECOMMENDED: A. montana ♀ *has white flowers in early summer.*

☼ ◊ ❋❋❋   **Perennial**
‡ 2–5cm (¾–2in) ↔ 20cm (8in)

ARTEMISIA SCHMIDTIANA
'Nana' ♛

A compact, evergreen plant with very
finely divided, silvery grey foliage and
heads of tiny yellow flowers in summer.
The pale foliage is beautifully offset
by stone or brick pavers; plant it in
pockets of gritty soil. It is also good
for a rock garden or raised bed.
Tolerant of sandy and chalky soils (*see
pp.38, 64*), and hot, dry sites (*see p.190*).

ALSO RECOMMENDED: A. stelleriana
*'Boughton Silver' has deeply toothed
or lobed, silver-white leaves.*

☼ ◊ ❀❀❀   **Perennial**
‡ 8cm (3in) ↔ 30cm (12in)

ASARINA PROCUMBENS

The trailing stems of this evergreen
plant are for good for paving in partial
shade. They display pretty pale yellow,
snapdragon-type flowers through
summer amid pairs of heart-shaped,
hairy green leaves. It prefers sandy soils
(*see p.38*) and copes with dry shade
(*see p.216*). The stems can also be
allowed to cascade over the sides
of walls, rocks, raised beds, or dry
banks. It can be grown as ground
cover (*see p.326*).

☼ ◊ ❀❀   **Perennial**
‡ 5cm (2in) ↔ 60cm (24in)

BLECHNUM PENNA-MARINA ♚

The attractive, dark green, narrow fishbone foliage of this evergreen fern is useful in any damp and shady site (*see p.238*). As well as wall and paving crevices, it also grows well as ground cover in rock gardens, herbaceous borders, or woodland, where it forms sizeable mats. The leaves may be reddish when young, and there are no flowers. It thrives in acid soils (*see p.92*).

ALSO RECOMMENDED: B. spicant ♚ *is taller and less spreading.*

☼ ◐ ◊ ✽✽✽   **Perennial fern**
‡ 10–20cm (4–8in) ↔ indefinite

CAMPANULA *'Birch Hybrid'* ♚

An attractive, ground-hugging bellflower with small, evergreen, heart-shaped, bright green leaves. Plentiful clusters of deep mauve-blue flowers appear in summer. It can also be used as ground cover (*see p.304*), or in a rock garden or container (*see p.412*). Chalky soils are tolerated (*see p.64*).

ALSO RECOMMENDED: C. cochleariifolia ♚ *has white to blue flowers;* C. latiloba *'Hidcote Amethyst'* ♚ *(see p.26);* C. portenschlagiana ♚ *and* C. poscharskyana *are similar.*

☼ ◐ ◊◊ ✽✽✽   **Perennial**
‡ 10cm (4in) ↔ 50cm (20in) or more

CAMPANULA CARPATICA
'Bressingham White'

Forming low clumps of heart-shaped leaves, this plant bears its pure white, upward-facing bellflowers over a long summer season. It grows well on dry stone walls, in paving crevices or rock gardens, in containers, or as ground cover (*see pp.304, 412*). It tolerates chalky soils (*see p.64*).

ALSO RECOMMENDED: *'Blaue Clips'* (syn. Blue Clips) has blue flowers. *'Weisse Clips'* (syn. White Clips) is white-flowered.

☀ ◐◔ ✿✿✿ **Perennial**
‡ 15cm (6in) ↔ 30–60cm (12–24in)

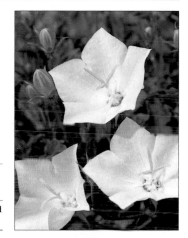

CHIASTOPHYLLUM
OPPOSITIFOLIUM ♥

A fleshy plant that is naturally found in shady rock crevices, so it is ideal for a dry stone wall or rock garden. Its spreading, evergreen growth forms dense mats of rounded, fleshy, pale green leaves. Long, arching stems of yellow flowers decorate the plant in early summer. Prone to slug and snail damage.

ALSO RECOMMENDED: *'Jim's Pride'* is low and spreading with cream-margined leaves.

☀ ◐◔ ✿✿✿ **Perennial**
‡ 15–20cm (6–8in) ↔ 15cm (6in)

COLCHICUM AGRIPPINUM ✓

This perennial bears its narrow, funnel-shaped, purplish pink flowers, marked with darker veins, in autumn. They precede the narrow leaves. It is also good at the foot of a sunny bank, in a rock garden, or at the front of a border. To grow in paving crevices, plant corms in early summer, in pockets of fertile, moist but well-drained soil. It tolerates chalky soils and hot, dry sites (*see pp.64, 190*).

ALSO RECOMMENDED: C. autumnale (see p.80); C. speciosum ✓ *has pale to deep pinkish purple flowers.*

☼ ◊ ❀ ❀ ❀   **Perennial corm**
‡ 8–10cm (3–4in) ↔ 8cm (3in)

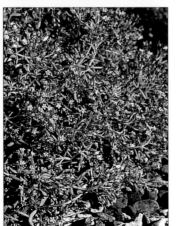

CRASSULA SARCOCAULIS

This compact and bushy succulent has fleshy stems, which carry narrow green leaves. These are tinted red and are relatively small, as are the unpleasantly scented, star-shaped, pinkish white summer flowers. Choose a hot, dry site (*see p.190*) with sharply drained, sandy soil (*see p.38*), where it may grow with other succulents.

☼ ◊ ❀ ❀   **Perennial**
‡↔ 30cm (12in)

CROCUS CORSICUS ♥

This dwarf perennial brings vase-shaped violet flowers to the garden in spring. They emerge from an underground bulb at about the same time as the narrow, dark green leaves. It tolerates sandy and chalky soils (*see pp.38, 64*) as well as coastal and hot, dry sites (*see pp.166, 190*). Also effective in drifts at the front of a border or rock garden, or in a raised bed or container (*see p.412*). Plant corms in autumn; keep it completely dry over summer.

ALSO RECOMMENDED. *C. angustifolius* ♥ *has orange-yellow flowers.*

☼ ◊ ❀ ❀ ❀ *f* **Perennial corm**
‡ 8–10cm (3–4in) ↔ 4cm (1½in)

DIANTHUS *'La Bourboule'* ♥

This charming, evergreen pink bears a mass of clove-scented, clear pink flowers with fringed petals. They are borne in summer above a neat mound of narrow, grey-green leaves. It is also good for a rock garden, raised bed, trough, or container (*see p.412*). In paving, grow in pockets of sharply drained, gritty soil. It thrives in shallow ground over chalk (*see p.64*) as well as in sandy soils (*see p.38*).

ALSO RECOMMENDED: D. *'Annabelle' has double, cherry-pink flowers;* D. deltoides *'Leuchtfunk' has dark green leaves and cherry flowers;* D. subacaulis *(see p.314).*

☼ ◊ ❀ ❀ ❀ *f* **Perennial**
‡ 8–10cm (3–4in) ↔ 20cm (8in)

EDRAIANTHUS PUMILIO ♥

This diminutive plant produces dense tufts of grass-like foliage and upturned, bell-shaped flowers of pale to deep violet in early summer. It thrives in light, sharply drained, chalky soils (*see p.64*), but it tends to be short-lived. Good in a dry wall or rock garden.

ALSO RECOMMENDED: *E. graminifolius* ♥ *is taller with spherical heads of bell-shaped, deep purple flowers; E. serpyllifolius is mat-forming with deep violet flowers.*

☼ ◊ ❋ ❋ ❋   **Perennial**
‡ 2.5cm (1in) ↔ 15cm (6in)

ERIGERON KARVINSKIANUS ♥

This evergreen perennial, sometimes sold as *E. mucronatus* or 'Profusion', forms a carpet of grey-green foliage, which is covered by yellow-centred, daisy-like flowerheads in summer. The outer petals are white, ageing to pink or purple. It can also be grown as a trailing container plant (*see p.412*). Tolerant of coastal conditions (*see p.166*), but it may not survive very frosty winters.

☼ ◊ ❋ ❋   **Perennial**
‡ 15–30cm (6–12in) ↔ 1m (3ft) or more

GERANIUM DALMATICUM ♥

This low-growing, usually evergreen
plant forms mounds of glossy light
green leaves and bears profuse clusters
of pale to bright pink flowers in
summer. An undemanding plant that is
also good for ground cover (*see p.304*),
containers (*see p.412*), rock gardens,
and the fronts of sunny borders. It
tolerates a range of soils and sites.

ALSO RECOMMENDED: G. cinereum *subsp.*
subcaulescens *has black-eyed, brilliant
magenta flowers,* G. 'Kate' *has bronzed
leaves and pale pink flowers.*

☼ ◊ ❁ ❁ ❁   **Perennial**

‡ 15cm (6in) ↔ 50cm (20in)

HELICHRYSUM *'Schwefellicht'*

Fluffy heads of sulphur-yellow flowers
appear on this clump-forming plant in
late summer above a mound of woolly,
silver-grey leaves. It works well at the
front of a sunny, mixed or herbaceous
border and tolerates hot, dry sites (*see
p.190*). Also sold as Sulphur Light.

ALSO RECOMMENDED: H. sibthorpii *is more
compact with white-woolly leaves and gold
flowerheads;* H. thianschanicum 'Goldkind'
has papery, golden yellow flowerheads.

☼ ◊ ❁ ❁ ❁   **Perennial**

‡ 40cm (16in) ↔ 30cm (12in)

LEONTOPODIUM ALPINUM

With its mounds of grey-green leaves and densely white-woolly, yellowish white flowerheads, which appear in spring or early summer, edelweiss is a charming addition to a planting pocket in paving. It also thrives on top of dry stone walls and in rock gardens. Grow in sharply drained, neutral to alkaline soil (*see p.64*). It may be short-lived.

ALSO RECOMMENDED: *'Mignon' is compact with white flowerheads; subsp. nivale has densely white woolly leaves and pure white flowerheads;*

☼ ◊ ❁ ❁ ❁   **Perennial**
‡ 20cm (8in) ↔ 10cm (4in)

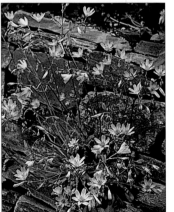

LEWISIA *'George Henley'*

This evergreen plant has rosettes of fleshy, dark green leaves and bears open sprays of funnel-shaped flowers from late spring to late summer; they are purplish pink with magenta veining. Excellent planted on its side in a dry stone wall. In planting pockets, provide sharply drained, neutral to acid soil (*see p.92*). Choose a site where plants will be protected from excessive winter wet.

ALSO RECOMMENDED: *L. cotyledon hybrids have bright pink, magenta, orange, or yellow flowers; L. tweedyi ♀ has white to peach-pink flowers.*

☼ ◊ ❁ ❁ ❁   **Perennial**
‡↔ 10cm (4in)

MENTHA REQUIENII

Corsican mint is a mat-forming plant with creeping, rooting stems. The glossy bright green leaves are tiny but have a strong peppermint scent; this is released if brushed by passing feet, although it will not withstand heavy treading. Short spikes of tiny, tubular lilac flowers appear in summer, and they attract bees (*see p.494*).

ALSO RECOMMENDED: M. pulegium *has sharply scented leaves.*

☀ ◑ ✿ ✿ ✿ *f*   **Perennial**
‡ 1cm (½in) ↔ indefinite

MYOSOTIS SYLVATICA *'Music'*

Although most often used as short-lived bedding plants, compact cultivars of the forget-me-not are ideal for crevices in damp, lightly shaded areas of paving. This cultivar has very large, bright blue flowers from spring to early summer. It will self-seed, but its offspring may not retain the same characteristics. Tolerant of clay soils (*see p.12*).

ALSO RECOMMENDED: *'Blue Ball' is more compact with azure flowers; 'Pompadour' has deep rose-pink flowers; 'Ultramarine'* ♀ *has indigo-blue flowers.*

☀ ◐ ◑◑ ✿ ✿ ✿   **Perennial**
‡ 25cm (10in) ↔ 15cm (6in)

OXALIS ENNEAPHYLLA 'Rosea'

This spreading, rhizomatous plant produces umbrella-like tufts of pleated, blue-grey leaves and bears widely funnel-shaped, pale purple-pink flowers in early summer. Excellent for paving, it may also be used as ground cover in sun (*see p.304*). It tolerates coastal and hot, dry sites (*see pp.166, 190*).

ALSO RECOMMENDED: O. enneaphylla ♀ *has fragrant, white to deep pink flowers; 'Minutifolia' is more compact with white flowers; O. 'Ione Hecker' ♀ has blue-violet flowers with darker veins.*

:☼: ◊ ❋❋❋   **Perennial**
‡ 8cm (3in) ↔ 15cm (6in)

PRATIA PEDUNCULATA

Paving crevices make an ideal home for this creeping, ground-hugging plant, which forms a carpet of rounded leaves. Above these, a scattering of starry, pale blue flowers appear over long periods in summer. Also good as ground cover in damp, shady spots (*see pp.238, 326*). It can be invasive, but not rampant, even in dry shade (*see p.216*).

ALSO RECOMMENDED: *'County Park' is similar;* P. angulata *'Treadwellii' is larger and more invasive with white flowers.*

:☼::☼: ◊◊ ❋❋❋   **Perennial**
‡ 1.5cm (½in) ↔ indefinite

PUSCHKINIA SCILLOIDES

This small bulb, with grass-like foliage,
produces densely packed spikes of
open-bell-shaped, pale blue spring
flowers, each petal with a darker blue
stripe. It looks charming in paving
crevices and is equally suitable for
a rock garden. It can also be grown
in containers (see p.412) or beneath
shrubs. Plant bulbs in early autumn
in any well drained soil.

ALSO RECOMMENDED: *var.* libanotica
has smaller white flowers.

☼ ◐ ◊ ❀ ❀ ❀   **Perennial bulb**
‡ 20cm (8in) ↔ 5cm (2in)

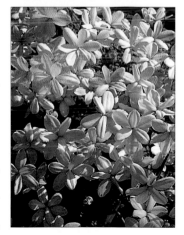

RHODOHYPOXIS
'Margaret Rose'

This alpine plant forms a compact
clump of grass-like, greyish green,
hairy foliage. Clear pink flowers
blossom all over the plant through
summer, bringing life to the dull foliage.
As well as in paving and wall crevices,
it can be grown in a trough, rock
garden, or alpine house. It must
have well-drained soil with shelter
from excessive winter wet.

ALSO RECOMMENDED: R. baurii ♀ *has
pale to deep reddish pink flowers.*

☼ ◊ ❀ ❀ ❀   **Perennial**
‡↔ 10cm (4in)

SAPONARIA × OLIVANA ♥

Ideal for sunny areas of paving, this cushion-forming plant forms a tight mound of narrow leaves, which are almost obscured by pale pink flowers in summer. It may also be grown in a rock garden or scree bed, or in a container (*see p.412*). Provide gritty, sharply drained, preferably alkaline soil (*see p.64*) and top-dress with gravel.

ALSO RECOMMENDED: *S. 'Bressingham'* ♥ *is mat-forming with deep pink flowers; S. caespitosa has pink to purple flowers.*

☼ ◐ ◌ ❁ ❁ ❁   **Perennial**
‡ 5cm (2in) ↔ 15cm (6in)

SAXIFRAGA *'Gregor Mendel'* ♥

The tiny rosettes of this saxifrage are densely packed to form a deep green mat of foliage, which sprouts flower stems in early spring; these form a swathe of pale yellow flowers above the leaves. Good for a rock garden as well as wall and paving crevices. Grow in neutral to alkaline soil (*see p.64*), in a site protected from hot sun to prevent leaf scorch. It can be pot-grown (*see p.412*). Sometimes sold as *S. × apiculata*.

ALSO RECOMMENDED: *'Cranbourne'* ♥ *has deep pink flowers; 'Faldonside'* ♥ *grows vigorously with bright yellow flowers.*

☼ ◐ ◌ ❁ ❁ ❁   **Perennial**
‡ 10cm (4in) ↔ 30cm (12in)

SAXIFRAGA *'Cloth of Gold'*

This moss-textured saxifrage forms a golden cushion of tightly packed leaf rosettes. Flat-topped clusters of small and starry, creamy yellow flowers rise above this mat of foliage from late spring to early autumn. It is best in partial shade to keep the sharply drained soil reliably moist. It prefers neutral to alkaline soils and can be container-grown (*see pp.64, 440*).

ALSO RECOMMENDED: *'Jenkinsiae' has pale pink flowers with dark centres in spring, 'Southside Seedling'* ♥ *has red-spotted white flowers in early summer.*

☼ ◊ ❀ ❀ ❀   **Perennial**
‡ 10cm (4in) ↔ 30cm (12in)

SEDUM ACRE

Common stonecrop forms an evergreen mat of small and rounded, fleshy, pale green leaves. This is topped by starry, yellow-green flowers over long periods in summer. Any small piece will root easily if pushed carefully into a paving crevice. It grows well in hot, dry sites, suits shallow containers, and can be grown as ground cover (*see pp.190, 304, 412*). Tolerant of sandy and alkaline soils (*see pp.38, 64*)

ALSO RECOMMENDED: *'Aureum' has bright yellow leaves;* S. lydium *has tight rosettes of red-tipped leaves and white flowers.*

☼ ◊ ❀ ❀ ❀   **Perennial**
‡ 5cm (2in) ↔ 60cm (24in) or more

SEDUM SPATHULIFOLIUM *'Purpureum'* ♡

This fast-growing, summer-flowering succulent forms tight, evergreen mats of fleshy purple leaves; young foliage is covered with a silvery bloom. Flat clusters of small, star-shaped, bright yellow flowers appear through summer. It also suits rock gardens and the fronts of well-drained borders, and it will grow as ground cover in sun (*see p.304*). Tolerant of sandy soils and hot, dry sites (*see pp.38, 190*). Trim occasionally to prevent encroachment on other plants.

ALSO RECOMMENDED: *'Cape Blanco'* ♡ *has silvery green leaves.*

☼ ◐ ◊ ❋ ❋ ❋   **Perennial**
‡ 10cm (4in) ↔ 60cm (24in)

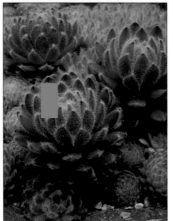

SEMPERVIVUM CILIOSUM

This evergreen succulent makes dense and hairy rosettes of grey-green leaves, which will form a spreading mat. Heads of star-shaped, yellow-green flowers rise above the foliage through summer; the rosettes that flower die afterwards, but they are rapidly replaced. Grow in gritty, sharply drained soil; it survives drought but dislikes winter wet or humidity. Tolerant of sandy soils and hot, dry sites (*see pp.38, 190*), and it will grow as ground cover in sun (*see p.304*).

ALSO RECOMMENDED: S. arachnoideum ♡ (see p.438); S. tectorum ♡ (see p.323).

☼ ◊ ❋ ❋ ❋   **Perennial**
‡ 8cm (3in) ↔ 30cm (12in)

SOLEIROLIA SOLEIROLII

This mat-forming perennial forms a very fine-textured carpet of tiny, rounded, emerald-green leaves. It is evergreen in frost-free zones, but is deciduous and often damaged by frost in cooler climates; it recovers quickly in spring. Any soil is suitable, in sun or shade. Although it is invasive and difficult to eradicate, it is useful as ground cover in difficult sites (*see pp.304, 326*). An ideal solution to containment is to plant it in paving crevices, where it spreads to form an exceptionally pretty, neat green outline to pavers.

☼ ☼ ◊◊ ✳✳✳　　　　**Perennial**

↕ 5cm (2in) ↔ indefinite

TANACETUM ARGENTEUM

Valued for its filigree carpet of silver-grey leaves, this mat-forming, usually evergreen perennial bears white, daisy-like flowerheads in summer. It tolerates most soils, as long as they are neither heavy nor wet; it grows best on sandy, well-drained soil (*see p.38*). In addition to paving crevices, it is suitable in a rock garden or as ground cover at the front of a sunny border (*see p.304*).

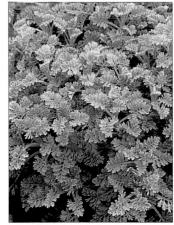

ALSO RECOMMENDED: T. densum *subsp.* amani *and* T. haradjanii *are similar with yellow flowerheads.*

☼ ◊ ✳✳✳　　　　**Perennial**

↕ 20cm (8in) ↔ 30cm (12in)

PLANTS FOR RELIABLY MOIST SOILS

AN AREA OF permanently moist soil in the garden, perhaps in a low-lying hollow, can be a cause for rejoicing rather than a perennial problem if you select the right plants – and there are many to choose from. Nearly all of the plants that thrive in such conditions occur naturally in damp meadows, bogs, and by watersides, whether a stream, river, or lake. There is also a great number of other plants that are normally grown in shade, but will thrive in full sun where the soil stays constantly moist (*see p.238*). Collectively, these plants are known as moisture-lovers, but they are sometimes offered for sale as bog plants. This can be misleading, as many moisture-loving plants will not tolerate totally water-logged soils. Boggy soil saturated with water is usually better for shallow-water, or marginal, aquatic plants (*see p.394*).

PLANTING PLACES

An area of permanently moist soil is the perfect opportunity to create a luxuriant moisture garden, populated by beautiful, ground-covering foliage plants and stately heads of flowers. These plants can also be used to surround ponds or pools to bridge the gap between water and land. Here, they will mask the water's edge in a most attractive way, and if the pool is still and clear, plants like *Salix alba* 'Britzensis' (*see p.375*) or *Lysichiton camtschatcensis* (*see p.385*) give more than double the value when their form is reflected in its mirror-like surface. Moisture-lovers thrive in the muddy margins of ponds or streams, where their roots are kept just above water level. These plants provide cover for the wildlife that lives in or around water, or for those that visit to drink and bathe.

MAINTAINING MOISTURE

When constructing a new pond, it is always worth the effort to provide planting pockets or shallow ledges of moist soil to accommodate moisture-loving plants. Barring accidents, the soil will never dry out in these situations. In other sites, you may need to take a few steps to ensure that the soil does remain moist. Few plants, particularly moisture-lovers, can withstand being almost inundated with water at one moment, and then left high and dry the next. This is often the case with damp hollows that lie over impermeable clay, which are wet as long as the moisture is replenished by rain, but they are often baked as hard as brick come summer. It may be sufficient to improve drainage by breaking up the soil, adding grit and generous amounts of organic matter before planting, with an annual autumn or spring mulch. Alternatively, you may wish to go the whole hog and create a proper permanently moist garden by excavating the top 25cm (10in) or so of soil, and lining the hollow with plastic liner. Before backfilling with the excavated soil (improved with copious quantities of organic matter), stab the plastic with a garden fork to allow water to drain slowly and prevent waterlogging.

ALNUS CORDATA ♔

The Italian alder is a large and fast-growing, conical tree with shiny dark green leaves. The bark is smooth and grey, and yellow-brown catkins emerge on the bare branches in late winter. Small brown cones follow, persisting into the next season. It grows well in most soils, including dry ones, but it is at its best next to water. Useful as a windbreak or hedge (*see pp.118, 138*). Prune in winter, if necessary.

ALSO RECOMMENDED: A. glutinosa *'Imperialis'* ♔ (*see p.121*); A. incana (*see p.140*); A. rubra *is similar.*

☼ ◊◊ ❀❀❀   **Deciduous tree**
‡ 25m (80ft) ↔ 6m (20ft)

METASEQUOIA GLYPTOSTROBOIDES ♔

This elegant conifer with a neat, narrowly conical outline has soft, fern-like leaves, which are emerald-green on emergence; they contrast beautifully with the shaggy, cinnamon-brown bark. In autumn, the leaves assume warm, russety gold tones before falling. An ideal architectural waterside specimen (*see p.472*). It tolerates clay and chalky soils (*see pp.12, 64*), and atmospheric pollution. Pruning is seldom required.

☼☀ ◊ ❀❀❀   **Deciduous tree**
‡ 20–40m (70–130ft) ↔ 5m (15ft)

SALIX ALBA *'Britzensis'* ♛

The white willow has narrow green leaves and bears yellow catkins as the leaves emerge in spring. This form is valued for its orange-red winter stems and makes a large tree if left unpruned. For the best stem effects, cut all shoots to the base or to a short trunk, each or every other year in late winter. It is excellent for waterside plantings, and can be grown as a hedge (*see p.138*). It tolerates coastal sites (*see p.166*).

ALSO RECOMMENDED: *subsp.* vitellina ♛ *has rich yellow to orange stems;* S. exigua (see p.50); S. purpurea (see p.162).

☼◐ ◊ ❄❄❄   **Deciduous tree**
↕ 25m (80ft) ↔ 10m (30ft)

ARONIA ARBUTIFOLIA

Red chokeberry is an ideal specimen or border shrub of manageable size. It is grown for its yellow or orangey red autumn leaves, its flat-headed clusters of white flowers in late spring, and for the profusion of bright red berries that follow, which are favoured by birds (*see p.494*). It tolerates clay soils (*see p.12*).

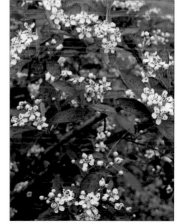

ALSO RECOMMENDED: A. melanocarpa, *black chokeberry, has black berries.*

☼◐ ◊ ❄❄❄   **Deciduous shrub**
↕ 3m (10ft) ↔ 1.5m (5ft)

CORNUS ALBA
'Elegantissima' ♥

This variegated form of the red-barked dogwood has greyish green, white-margined leaves as well as bright red young stems. For the best stem and foliage display, cut all shoots on established plants back hard each spring, and feed the soil. Particularly effective in a prominent site close to water. It tolerates clay soils and exposed sites (*see pp.12, 118*).

ALSO RECOMMENDED: *'Kesselringii'* (see p.128); *'Spaethii'* ♥ *has yellow-margined leaves.*

☼ ◑ ◌◌ ❄❄❄   **Deciduous shrub**
↕↔ 3m (10ft)

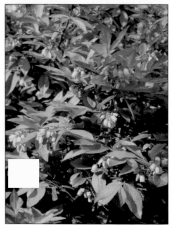

VACCINIUM CORYMBOSUM ♥

The highbush blueberry is a dense, arching shrub with oval leaves, which turn yellow or red in autumn. In late spring and early summer, it bears hanging clusters of small, white or pink flowers, followed by edible, blue-black berries. Grow in a shrub border or woodland garden, in acid, humus-rich soil (*see p.92*). Prune in winter to remove dead, badly placed, or old, unproductive wood. Birds will feed on the berries (*see p.494*).

ALSO RECOMMENDED: *'Bluecrop' has brilliant red autumn colour*; V. floribundum *is evergreen with pink flowers and red fruits.*

☼☀ ◑ ◌◌ ❄❄❄   **Deciduous shrub**
↕↔ 1.5m (5ft)

ASTILBE × CRISPA *'Perkeo'* ♥

This clump-forming plant is shorter
than many other astilbes and produces
upright plumes of tiny, star-shaped,
rich pink flowers in summer, which
are useful for indoor arrangements
(*see p.524*). It makes a dense mound
of finely cut, crinkled dark green leaves
and is good as ground cover in damp,
shady spots (*see pp.230, 326*). Tolerant
of clay soils (*see p.12*).

ALSO RECOMMENDED: A. *'Bronce Elegans'*
♥ *has dark green leaves and pink-red
flowers; 'Deutschland'* (*see p.25*); *'Willie
Buchanan'* (*see p.530*).

☀ ◖ ❀ ❀ ❀   **Perennial**
‡ 15–20cm (6–8in) ↔ 15cm (6in)

ASTILBOIDES TABULARIS

This clump forming perennial forms
a dense mound of enormous, rounded
and lobed, pale green leaves, up to
90cm (36in) long. Tall plumes of many
small, creamy white flowers rise well
above the foliage in early summer.
It forms an architectural specimen
(*see p.472*), ideal for woodland and
streamside plantings. It is also excellent
as ground cover in shade (*see p.326*),
and it tolerates clay soils (*see p.12*).
Protect from slugs, which may eat
resting winter buds. It is sometimes
sold as *Rodgersia tabularis*.

☀ ◖ ❀ ❀ ❀   **Perennial**
‡ 1.5m (5ft) ↔ 1.2m (4ft)

CAREX ELATA *'Aurea'* ♀

Bowles' golden sedge is a colourful and tussock-forming, deciduous perennial for a moist border, bog garden, or the margins of a pond or stream. The bright leaves are narrow and golden yellow. In spring and early summer, small spikes of relatively inconspicuous, dark brown flowers are carried above the leaves. Often sold as Bowles' Golden.

ALSO RECOMMENDED: *C. grayi has rich green foliage and spiky flowerheads; C. siderosticha 'Variegata' is shorter with white-striped leaves.*

☼ ◐ ◊◊ ❄❄❄   **Perennial**

‡ 70cm (28in) ↔ 45cm (18in)

CAREX PENDULA

Weeping sedge is named for its catkin-like, dark brown flower spikes in late spring and early summer, which are upright at first then droop with age. They are carried on tall, arching flower stems above the evergreen clumps of shiny green leaf blades. It self-seeds where conditions suit. Also suitable for a wildlife garden (*see p.494*).

ALSO RECOMMENDED: *C. muskingumensis is half the size with bright green leaves and upright flower spikes.*

☼ ◐ ◊◊ ❄❄❄   **Perennial**

‡ 1.4m (4½ft) ↔ 1.5m (5ft)

CIMICIFUGA RACEMOSA ♛

Black snakeroot is a clump-forming plant that produces long spikes of unpleasantly scented, tiny white flowers in midsummer, above a mound of divided, dark green leaves. It is suitable for a damp, shady border or woodland garden (*see p.238*), preferably away from paths or seating areas.

ALSO RECOMMENDED: *C. simplex 'Brunette' has maroon leaves and maroon-flushed flowers; 'White Pearl' has white flowers.*

☀ ◐ ❄ ❄ ❄   **Perennial**

‡ 1.2–2.2m (4–7ft) ↔ 60cm (24in)

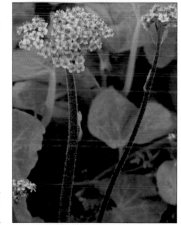

DARMERA PELTATA ♛

The sturdy stems of this spreading plant arise from the bare earth in late spring, terminating in a broad, flat cluster of many tiny, white to bright pink, star-shaped flowers. The enormous, rounded and deeply lobed leaves that follow form a handsome and imposing, umbrella-like clump (*see p.472*). It forms excellent ground cover in shady or sunny, damp sites (*see pp.238, 304, 326*). Tolerant of clay soils (*see p.12*).

☀ ◐ ◐ ❄ ❄ ❄   **Perennial**

‡ 2m (6ft) ↔ 1m (3ft)

EUPHORBIA PALUSTRIS ♥

For bright colour in a damp border
or alongside water in sun, this clump-
forming perennial is ideal. Its sturdy,
pale green stems bear narrow, bright
green leaves, which turn orange
and yellow in autumn. Large yellow
flowerheads appear in spring. It
will grow in any reliably moist soil.

☼ ◊ ❋ ❋ ❋   **Perennial**
‡↔ 90cm (36in)

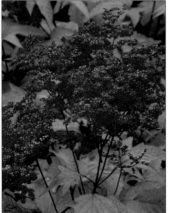

FILIPENDULA RUBRA
'*Venusta*' ♥

A vigorous, upright perennial that bears
feathery plumes of tiny, fragrant, deep
rose-pink flowers on tall branching stems
in midsummer. The dark green leaves
that underpin the flower display are
large and jagged. This plant is excellent
for waterside plantings and damp sites
in shade (*see p.238*).

ALSO RECOMMENDED: *F. camtschatica
is taller with fragrant, white or pale pink
flowers; F. purpurea* ♥ *(see p.28); F. rubra
has deep peach-pink flowers on red stems.*

☼ ◊◊ ❋ ❋ ❋ *f*   **Perennial**
‡ 2–2.5m (6–8ft) ↔ 1.2m (4ft)

GUNNERA MANICATA ♔

A massive, clump-forming perennial that produces the largest leaves of any hardy plant, to 2m (6ft) long. These are rounded, lobed, sharply toothed, and dull green, with stout, prickly stalks. Tall spires of tiny, greenish red flowers appear in summer. An imposing, architectural plant by water or in a bog garden (*see p.472*), needing protection to survive winter in cold climates; fold the dead leaves over the dormant crown before winter. It tolerates clay soils (*see p.12*).

ALSO RECOMMENDED: G. tinctoria (syn. G. chilensis) is shorter and denser.

☼◐ ◊◊ ❀❀ **Perennial**

‡ 2.5m (8ft) ↔ 3–4m (10–12ft) or more

HOSTA '*Frances Williams*' ♔

This blue-green plantain lily forms a clump of heart-shaped, very crinkled leaves with paler margins; white flowers emerge in early summer. A fine architectural plant for a damp, shady border (*see pp.238, 472*), which can be grown as ground cover or confined to a container (*see pp.326, 448*). It is also sold as 'Eldorado' and 'Golden Circles'. It tolerates clay soils (*see p.12*).

ALSO RECOMMENDED: '*Birchwood Parky's Gold*' (see p.318); '*Halcyon*' ♔ (see p.340); '*Shade Fanfare*' ♔ (see p.465); '*Wide Brim*' ♔ (see p.254); H. sieboldiana var. elegans ♔ (see p.490); H. ventricosa ♔ (see p.30).

☼◐ ◊ ❀❀❀ **Perennial**

‡ 60cm (24in) ↔ 1m (3ft)

IRIS FORRESTII ♥

The scented, pale yellow blooms of this early-summer-flowering iris possess a subtle elegance that looks good by water or in a border. The clumps of narrow leaves, which are green above and grey-green beneath, are also attractive. Grow in reliably moist but well-drained soil with plenty of space to allow it to spread. The flowers can be cut for indoor display (*see p.524*).

ALSO RECOMMENDED: I. chrysographes ♥ (see p.536); I. laevigata *'Variegata'* ♥ (see p.401).

☀️◐ ◊◊ ❀❀❀ *f*   **Perennial**
‡ 35–40cm (14–16in) ↔ indefinite

IRIS VERSICOLOR *'Kermesina'*

This red-purple-flowered form of the blue flag (*I. versicolor*) is a pretty water iris with upright, long and narrow leaves. It flowers in the first half of summer, each stem bearing up to five flowers at once. The downward-pointing fall petals are marked with white. Particularly effective at the margin of a pond or stream in lime-free soils (*see p.92*).

ALSO RECOMMENDED: I. ensata ♥ (see p.400); I. pseudacorus ♥ (see p.401).

☀️◐ ◊◊ ❀❀❀   **Perennial**
‡ 60cm (24in) ↔ 1m (3ft)

LIGULARIA 'Gregynog Gold' ♀

This large and vigorous perennial forms clumps of luxuriant, toothed leaves. From late summer to early autumn, tall stems rise above the foliage, bearing pyramidal spikes of daisy-like golden flowers. This is an excellent plant with a strong architectural form (*see p.472*) for reliably moist soil close to water, where it may naturalize freely. Shelter from strong winds. It tolerates clay soils (*see p.12*).

ALSO RECOMMENDED: *'The Rocket'* ♀ *has yellow flowers on very dark green stems from early summer.*

☼ ◐ ◗ ❄ ❄ ❄   **Perennial**
↕ 2m (6ft) ↔ 1m (3ft)

LIGULARIA PRZEWALSKII

An imposing waterside plant with a similar habit to *L. 'Gregynog Gold'* (*above*) that is valued for its tall pillars of sunny yellow flowers on purplish stems in the later half of summer. The irregularly lobed and toothed, deeply cut leaves heighten its architectural stature (*see p.472*). It tolerates clay soils (*see p.12*).

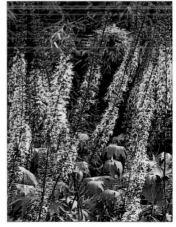

ALSO RECOMMENDED: L. dentata *'Desdemona'* ♀ *and 'Othello' are shorter and have orange flowers in flattened, rather than spire-like, flowerheads.*

☼ ◐ ◗ ❄ ❄ ❄   **Perennial**
↕ 2m (6ft) ↔ 1m (3ft)

LOBELIA CARDINALIS ♛

The cardinal flower forms clumps of
bronze-tinged green leaves, and in late
summer and early autumn, produces
spires of two-lipped, luminous scarlet
flowers. It is very effective at the edge
of water or in a border. It is often short-
lived; divide the clumps in spring.

ALSO RECOMMENDED: *L. 'Bees' Flame' has
red-purple leaves and crimson flowers;
'Queen Victoria'* ♛ *has vivid red flowers
and deep purple-red leaves.*

☼ ◊ ❀❀❀ **Perennial**
‡ 90cm (36in) ↔ 30cm (12in)

LOBELIA SIPHILITICA

The blue cardinal flower bears spires
of two-lipped, rich bright blue flowers
on leafy stems from late summer to
mid-autumn. Its basal clumps of softly
hairy, lance-shaped leaves are light
green. An excellent plant for a damp,
mixed or herbaceous border, or beside
a pool or stream.

ALSO RECOMMENDED: *'Alba' has white
flowers; L. × gerardii 'Vedrariensis' (syn.
L. vedrariensis) bears spires of deep violet-
purple flowers throughout summer.*

☼ ◊ ❀❀❀ **Perennial**
‡ 60–120cm (24–48in) ↔ 30cm (12in)

LYSICHITON AMERICANUS ♛

The yellow skunk cabbage is a strikingly architectural plant when it flowers in early spring (*see p.472*). The bright yellow spathes, which enclose a spike of tiny green flowers, look fabulous it reflected in still water; they appear before the foliage has expanded fully. Grow at the water's edge, or in shallow water up to 8cm (3in) deep (*see p.394*), allowing plenty of room for the huge leaves to develop. It tolerates clay soils and provides shelter for aquatic animals (*see pp.12, 494*). The whole plant has a musky scent.

☼☀ ◑◑ ❋❋❋ **Perennial**

↕ 1m (3ft) ↔ 1.2m (4ft)

LYSICHITON CAMTSCHATCENSIS ♛

With similar ornamental virtues to the yellow-flowered species (*above*), the white skunk cabbage has an elegant combination of creamy white spathes and green flower spikes. As with the yellow skunk cabbage, it is an architectural plant good in clay soils and for sheltering aquatic animals (*see pp.12, 472, 494*). It grows well in shallow water to 8cm (3in) deep (*see p.394*).

☼☀ ◑◑ ❋❋❋ **Perennial**

↕ 1m (3ft) ↔ 1.2m (4ft)

LYSIMACHIA CLETHROIDES ♚

This spreading, clump-forming plant is grown for its tapering spires of tiny, star-shaped white flowers. The spires droop sinuously when in bud, straightening as the flowers open in the later half of summer. The narrow, bright green leaves turn red in autumn. An excellent plant for a woodland or bog garden. Protect from slugs and snails.

ALSO RECOMMENDED: L. barystachys *is shorter*; L. ephemerum *is slightly less hardy*; L. nummularia *'Aurea'* ♚ (see p.136); L. punctata (see p.319).

☼ ◐ ◊ ❉ ❉ ❉   **Perennial**
‡ 1m (3ft) ↔ 60cm (24in)

LYTHRUM SALICARIA *'Feuerkerze'* ♚

Purple loosestrife is a clump-forming plant with narrow, mid-green leaves. Its upright shape is defined by the tall, slender flower spikes, which are an intense deep pink in this cultivar and rise above the foliage from midsummer to early autumn. Firecandle is a common alternative name. It tolerates clay soils (*see p.12*).

ALSO RECOMMENDED: L. salicaria *is taller with purple-pink flowers;* 'Blush' *is similar.*

☼ ◊ ❉ ❉ ❉   **Perennial**
‡ 1m (3ft) ↔ 45cm (18in)

MATTEUCCIA STRUTHIOPTERIS ♔

The shuttlecock fern forms architectural clumps of upright or gently arching, pale green fronds (*see p.472*). From the centre of each clump in summer, smaller, dark brown fronds appear, which persist through winter, long after the green fronds have withered away. It is excellent for a damp, shady border or container (*see pp.238, 448*) in a woodland garden or beside water. It tolerates clay and acid soils (*see pp.12, 92*).

☼ ◊◊ ✳ ✳ ✳   **Perennial fern**

‡ 1–1.5m (3–5ft) ↔ 75cm (30in)

OENANTHE JAVANICA *'Flamingo'*

This spreading, moisture-loving plant has celery-like leaves variegated with pink, cream, and white; they are divided into many toothed leaflets. Flat-headed clusters of tiny, star-shaped white flowers appear in late summer. A fine foliage perennial for a bog garden. Protect from slugs and snails.

☼☼ ◊◊ ✳ ✳   **Perennial**

‡ 60cm (24in) ↔ 1m (3ft)

PARNASSIA PALUSTRIS

This grass of Parnassus is a low-growing, rosette-forming plant with heart-shaped, pale green leaves and star-shaped, green-veined white flowers, which appear in late spring and early summer. It makes a very pretty addition to a bog garden and may be naturalized in marshy grass. Grow in humus-rich, limey soil (*see p.64*).

☼ ◖◗ ❄❄❄   **Perennial**
‡ 20cm (8in) ↔ 10cm (4in)

PONTEDERIA CORDATA ♈

Pickerel weed is an elegant, architectural plant (*see p.472*) with smooth, fresh green, lance-shaped leaves and dense spikes of tubular blue flowers, which appear in late summer. As well as beside a pond or stream, or in a reliably damp border, it can also be grown in up to 12cm (5in) of water (*see p.394*). It may even be accommodated in large, water-filled tubs on a sunny, sheltered patio. Tolerant of clay soils (*see p.12*).

☼ ◗ ❄❄❄   **Perennial**
‡ 1.2m (4ft) ↔ 60–75cm (24–30in)

PRIMULA FLORINDAE ♈

The giant cowslip produces tall stems topped by clusters of scented, nodding, funnel-shaped, sulphur-yellow flowers in early summer. The fresh green leaves are deciduous. It is ideal for bog garden and waterside plantings, and it makes excellent ground cover in damp, shady places (*see pp.238, 326*). It tolerates clay and acid soils (*see pp.12, 92*), self-seeding if conditions suit.

ALSO RECOMMENDED. P. prolifera ♈ *is evergreen with candelabra like tiers of pale to golden yellow flowers.* P. sikkimensis *has yellow or cream flowers.*

☼ ◑ ◐ ✻ ✻ ✻ *f*   **Perennial**

‡ 1.2m (4ft) ↔ 90cm (36in)

PRIMULA JAPONICA 'Postford White'

The Japanese primrose is a vigorous, deciduous perennial for damp, shady places (*see p.238*). At ground level, it forms a rosette of spoon-shaped and scalloped, pale green leaves, from which emerges a tall and sturdy flower stem in late spring; in this cultivar, it is topped with white, red-eyed flowers. It tolerates clay soils (*see p.12*).

ALSO RECOMMENDED: P. japonica ♈ *has red-purple flowers;* 'Miller's Crimson' *has crimson flowers;* P. viallii ♈ (*see p.258*).

☼ ◑ ◐ ✻ ✻ ✻   **Perennial**

‡ ↔ 45cm (18in)

PRIMULA PULVERULENTA ♛

This deciduous candelabra primula has rosettes of lance-shaped leaves and produces tiered spires of tubular, dark red or red-purple flowers in late spring and early summer. It is lovely when grown *en masse* in a bog garden or waterside planting, or in a damp, shady border (*see p.238*). It tolerates acid soils (*see p.92*).

ALSO RECOMMENDED: *'Bartley Pink' has red-eyed, shell-pink flowers*; P. beesiana *has yellow-eyed, rich red-pink flowers.*

☀ ◗ ❄ ❄ ❄   **Perennial**
↕ 1m (3ft) ↔ 60cm (24in)

PRIMULA ROSEA ♛

This deciduous primula has rounded clusters of glowing pink, long-throated flowers on sturdy, upright stems in spring. The oval, toothed, mid-green leaves, which are tinted red-bronze when young, emerge fully after flowering. It is good for a bog garden or waterside planting, or in a damp, shady border (*see p.238*). It tolerates acid soils and full sun if the soil remains moist (*see pp.92*).

ALSO RECOMMENDED: *'Grandiflora' is more vigorous with larger flowers*; P. sieboldii ♛ *is taller with rose-violet to lilac-purple, or deep crimson flowers.*

☀ ◗ ❄ ❄ ❄   **Perennial**
↕↔ 20cm (8in)

RHEUM PALMATUM *'Atrosanguineum'*

Chinese rhubarb is a big architectural perennial (*see p.472*) with palmately lobed and toothed, dark green leaves to 90cm (36in) long. In this cultivar, the foliage has a purplish tint when young, and tall and feathery, cherry-pink flowerheads rise above it in early summer. It will grow as ground cover (*see p.304*); provide a mulch each spring. It tolerates clay soils (*see p.12*).

ALSO RECOMMENDED: *R. 'Ace of Hearts' is half the size with white flowers; R. palmatum ♀ and var tanguticum have cream to red flowers.*

☼ ◑ ◊◊ ❋❋❋   **Perennial**
‡ 2.5m (8ft) ↔ 2m (6ft)

RODGERSIA PINNATA *'Superba'* ♀

A clump-forming, architectural plant (*see p.472*) that bears upright clusters of starry, bright pink flowers above bold, heavily veined, deep green leaves; these are purplish bronze when young. It is ideal for a bog garden or waterside planting and can be grown as ground cover in damp shade (*see pp.238, 326*). Shelter from cold, drying winds.

ALSO RECOMMENDED: *R. aesculifolia ♀ (see p.34); R. pinnata has white, pink, or red flowers.*

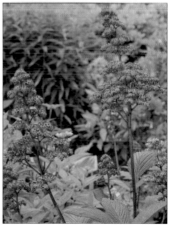

☼ ◑ ◊ ❋❋❋   **Perennial**
‡ 1.2m (4ft) ↔ 75cm (30in)

RODGERSIA PODOPHYLLA ♚

A robust, architectural perennial that forms mounds of deeply lobed, glossy dark green leaves, suitable for a damp border or waterside planting. The leaves are bronzed when young and bronze-red in autumn. In mid- to late summer, it bears sprays of creamy green flowers. Shelter from cold, drying winds. It tolerates clay soils and can be grown as ground cover in partial shade (*see pp.12, 326*).

ALSO RECOMMENDED: *R. sambucifolia has white or pink flowers from early summer.*

☼ ◐ ◊ ❄ ❄ ❄   **Perennial**
‡ 1.5m (5ft) ↔ 1.8m (6ft)

SAGITTARIA LATIFOLIA

The duck potato is named for its walnut-sized tubers, which attract ducks and other water birds (*see p.494*). As well as moist ground, it also grows in water no deeper than 30cm (12in), so it is ideal for a pond margin (*see p.394*). White flowers appear on tall flower stems in summer, above the arrow-shaped leaves; these are large and distinctive. Trim back spreading growth in late summer.

☼ ◊◊ ❄ ❄ ❄   **Perennial**
‡ 45–90cm (18–36in) ↔ 90cm (36in)

VERATRUM ALBUM

White hellebore is an imposing plant, which forms an elegant mound of deeply pleated, bright green foliage. In early to midsummer, stout stems rise to bear many starry white flowers. It is invaluable as a feature plant in a mixed or herbaceous border, or in a woodland setting (*see p.472*). It also forms good ground cover in sun or shade (*see pp.304, 326*).

ALSO RECOMMENDED: *V. nigrum* ♥ *has dusky red-brown to almost black flowers; V. viride has green flowers and tolerates the wettest soils.*

☼ ◐ ◊◊ ❄❄❄   **Perennial**

‡ 2m (6ft) ↔ 60cm (24in)

ZANTEDESCHIA AETHIOPICA ♥

The arum lily is well known for its large, pure white spathes in the first half of summer, which enclose finger-like flower spikes; they are proudly held up above the arrow-like leaves. It is a strong, architectural plant (*see p.472*), evergreen in mild climates, which can be grown in shallow water or in a sunny container (*see pp.394, 412*). It tolerates coastal sites (*see p.166*) but must be sheltered from heavy frosts; mulch deeply over winter. The flowers cut well (*see p.524*).

ALSO RECOMMENDED: *'Crowborough' ♥ has smaller spathes; 'Green Goddess' ♥ has green spathes with white centres.*

☼ ◐ ◊�● ❄❄   **Perennial**

‡ 90cm (36in) ↔ 60cm (24in)

PLANTS FOR WATER GARDENS

PONDS AND POOLS not only make superb focal points in the garden, but they are also the most effective way of bringing wildlife into the garden, even if they are not designed for that purpose. Water gardens provide a web of interdependent mini-habitats, with niches that suit a variety of plants, as well as a range of aquatic and amphibious creatures and visiting birds and mammals.

A healthy pond requires plantings at several levels. Within the water itself, there should be floating or bottom-rooting plants, such as curled pondweed (*see p.408*), hornwort (*see p.398*), and curly water thyme (*see p.402*). These plants perform the vital function of oxygenating the water; without dissolved oxygen in the water, fish and amphibians would not be able to survive. Submerged plants also help to remove excess nutrients from the water, which would otherwise fuel the rapid growth of algae and turn the water green. Introduce these plants to the pond simply by casting them in as weighted bundles of stems.

ORNAMENTAL PLANTS

Floating water plants, such as water fringe (*see p.407*), that root at the bottom of the pond, cover the surface of the water with their floating leaves. As well as being pretty, the leaves offer shade and shelter to fish, and reduce algal growth by excluding light. To grow them, they can either be allowed to root in the muddy bottom of the pond, but more usually, they are grown in aquatic planting baskets lined with hessian and filled with a heavy, loamy soil mix. The soil mix surface is then topped with a layer of grit or gravel to prevent the soil muddying the water. Planting baskets are ideal in smaller ponds, because they help to contain the spread of vigorous plants.

For the poolside, select marginal plants. These will root in the mud or moist soil that surrounds the pond, and they tolerate shallow to relatively deep water, depending on the species. They can also be very vigorous, although their spread will be limited by their depth tolerance. Popular marginal plants include the bog bean (*see p.403*), which spreads its leathery leaves over the surface of the water, and more upright plants like the variegated club rush (*see p.402*). Marginal plants look good around the edge of a pool, softening the transition from water to land, and more upright species with reedy or grass-like stems, such as the flowering rush (*see p.397*) form a perfect egg laying perch for creatures like dragonflies and damselflies. Marginals can also be planted in aquatic baskets, as for the floating-leaved plants, but it is easier to create naturalistic clumps if they are allowed to root directly into wet soil confined in special planting bays. They are planted exactly as for dry-land plants, but should not be given fertilizer, since this will leach into the water, causing the proliferation of algae. Fertilizers are also directly detrimental to fish and other pond life.

APONOGETON DISTACHYOS

Water hawthorn is valued for its handsomely shaped, bright green, floating foliage, which is accompanied from spring until autumn by V-shaped white flowerheads. These are held above the water's surface, then they fold over and fade to green. It is easy to grow in water 30–90cm (12–36in) deep, preferably in full sun, but do not let the water freeze over. It tends to smother water lilies (*see pp.405–406*), so keep these plants apart. Also suitable for a water-filled tub.

☼ ◑ ❄ ❄   **Perennial**
↔ 1.2m (4ft)

AZOLLA FILICULOIDES

Fairy moss lives and grows on the surface of water, and its fractal-like, floating leaves make an attractive, fast-growing cover with a soft appearance. This will help to keep the pond water clear by suppressing the growth of algae; thin out invasive growth as necessary. The plants may die after frost in winter; scatter small bunches of new stock on the pool surface in early summer, when the danger of frost has passed. It will grow in a water-filled tub. Sometimes sold as *A. caroliniana*.

☼ ◑ ❄   **Perennial**
↔ indefinite

BUTOMUS UMBELLATUS ♟

The flowering rush is a robust marginal
plant of delicate appearance. In spring,
bronzed shoots develop into long and
twisted, rush like leaves, bronze-purple
at first then dark olive-green. Tall
cylindrical stems emerge in late
summer, bearing open sprays of
fragrant, cup-shaped pink flowers.
Grow in fertile mud at the water's edge
in water 5–40cm (2–16in) deep. It will
also grow in planting baskets, but they
must be lifted and divided frequently
to maintain free-flowering. Tolerant
of clay soils (*see p.12*).

☼ ✳ ✳ ✳ *f*　　　　　　**Perennial**

‡ 75cm (30in) ↔ 45cm (18in)

CALLA PALUSTRIS

The bog arum has heart-shaped, glossy
dark green leaves, which form an
attractive feature in themselves at
the margin of a pool or slow-moving
stream. It also bears shapely, cowl-like
white bracts in midsummer; these
surround a spike of insignificant
flowers, later giving rise to dull red
berries in autumn. Grow in mud, or
in planting baskets in water no deeper
than 25cm (10in); it must have lime-
free conditions

☼ ✳ ✳ ✳　　　　　　**Perennial**

‡ 1.5m (5ft) ↔ 1.2m (4ft)

CALTHA PALUSTRIS ♀

The marsh marigold is a clump-forming plant with kidney-shaped, glossy dark green leaves. In spring, it bears wax-textured, buttercup-like, glossy bright yellow flowers. It does well in water no more than 23cm (9in) deep as well as in fertile, permanently moist sites (*see p.372*). Tolerant of clay soils (*see p.12*).

ALSO RECOMMENDED: *var.* alba *has white flowers;* 'Flore Pleno' ♀ *has double yellow flowers.*

☼ ◐ ❋ ❋ ❋   **Perennial**
‡ 10–40cm (4–16in) ↔ 45cm (18in)

CERATOPHYLLUM DEMERSUM

Hornwort is a deciduous perennial with slender stems and forked leaves. It grows underwater and is valued for its ability to oxygenate pond water, and as it tolerates shade, it grows in deeper water than most other oxygenators. Young plantlets break away from the main plant, and they may sink to the pond bottom and overwinter as dormant buds. Grow in water up to 60cm (24in) deep.

☼ ◑   ❋ ❋ ❋   **Perennial**
↔ indefinite

FONTINALIS ANTIPYRETICA

This evergreen perennial moss with submerged stems has olive-green, scale-like leaves. It is grown for its ability to oxygenate water and is best in cold streams, as it is much less vigorous in still water; plant in water up to 45cm (18in) deep by weighting the plant between boulders on which the roots will cling and spread. Thin the growth if it begins to dominate.

☼◑ ❋ ❋ ❋   **Perennial**
↕ 8cm (3in) ↔ indefinite

HOTTONIA PALUSTRIS

The water violet is a deciduous, underwater perennial with masses of spreading, light green and deeply divided foliage both on and under the surface of the water. Pale lilac flower spikes emerge above the water on upright stems in spring. It is a useful plant to keep a pond clear and well-oxygenated. Thin periodically.

☼ ❋ ❋ ❋   **Perennial**
↕ 30–90cm (12–36in) ↔ indefinite

HYDROCHARIS MORSUS-RANAE

Frogbit is a free-floating water plant with rosettes of kidney-shaped, shiny green leaves. They are accompanied throughout summer by paper white flowers with yellow centres. It provides useful shelter for pond creatures, but it is vulnerable to snail damage. New plantlets form on the runners. Grow in water up to 30cm (12in) deep; it prefers still and shallow conditions.

☼ ❁❁❁   **Perennial**
↔ indefinite

IRIS ENSATA ♀

This Japanese iris will grow either in a pond or in permanently moist ground (*see p.372*). In a pond, grow it in a planting basket, as it needs to be removed from saturated soil in winter. Dense tufts of bold, sword-shaped leaves rise up from ground level, and large purple flowers open in midsummer, which are good for cutting (*see p.524*). It needs lime-free soil (*see p.92*).

ALSO RECOMMENDED: *'Moonlight Waves' bears white flowers with lime-green centres; 'Rose Queen'* ♀ *has pink flowers; 'Variegata'* ♀ *has variegated leaves.*

☼ ◖◖ ❁❁❁   **Perennial**
‡ 60–90cm (24–36in) ↔ indefinite

IRIS LAEVIGATA *'Variegata'* ♥

This deciduous iris forms clumps of sword-shaped, white- and green-striped leaves. Its sparsely branched flower stems produce up to four purple-blue, broad-petalled flowers in early and midsummer. It thrives in pond margins and other reliably moist places (*see p.372*), and tolerates clay soils (*see p.12*). The flowers can be cut for indoor display (*see p.524*).

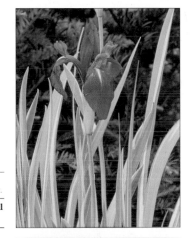

ALSO RECOMMENDED: I. laevigata ♥ *has plain green leaves; 'Alba' has white flowers.*

☼ ◑◆ ❄❄❄ **Perennial**
‡ 80cm (32in) ↔ indefinite

IRIS PSEUDACORUS ♥

The yellow flag is a very vigorous, rhizomatous iris, which will spread widely at the edge of water. It has ribbed, sword-shaped, grey-green leaves and, from early to late summer, bears golden yellow flowers marked with brown or violet on the lower petals; they can be cut for indoor decoration (*see p.524*). Plant in water up to 30cm (12in) deep or in permanently moist soil (*see p.372*). It tolerates chalky soils (*see p.12*).

ALSO RECOMMENDED: I. pseudacorus *var.* bastardii *has sulphur-yellow flowers;* 'Variegata' ♥ *has cream-variegated leaves.*

☼◑ ◆ ❄❄❄ **Perennial**
‡ 1–1.5m (3–5ft) ↔ indefinite

LAGAROSIPHON MAJOR

Also sold as *Elodea crispa*, curly water thyme is an underwater plant, which is used to keep pond water oxygenated. It forms a dense mass of dark green, snaking, fragile stems, which are covered by incurved, scale-like leaves. Insignificant, tiny pink flowers appear in summer. Grow in a submerged planting basket in water up to 1m (3ft) deep, and thin growth in summer as necessary, cutting back in autumn; remove dead stems to prevent them from decomposing in the water.

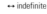

☼ ❄❄❄   **Perennial**
↔ indefinite

MARSILEA QUADRIFOLIA

Water clover is actually a fern and is grown for its shamrock-like leaves, which are downy when young and form a floating canopy on the water's surface. In muddy shallows, the leaves may rise above the water. Grow at the margins of a pool, either in open soil or in lattice baskets, at a depth of up to 60cm (24in).

☼ ❄❄❄   **Perennial**
↕ 15cm (6in) ↔ indefinite

MENYANTHES TRIFOLIATA

The dark stems of the bog bean rise above the water, keeping the leathery green leaves clear of the surface. In summer, it produces upright clusters of star shaped white flowers with attractively fringed and bearded petals. Grow in shallow, still or slow-moving water, planting in the muddy margins of a pool or in water no deeper than 23cm (9in). It is excellent for disguising hard edges in formal water features. Confine its spread by planting in a basket.

☼ ✻✻✻   **Perennial**
↕ 20–30cm (8 12in) ↔ indefinite

MIMULUS LUTEUS

Yellow musk is a spreading plant, bearing a profusion of yellow, snapdragon like flowers, often with dark red spots, from midsummer to autumn. It self-seeds freely and is well-suited to shallow, still or fairly fast-moving water at streamsides or pool margins, and in permanently moist ground (*see p.372*).

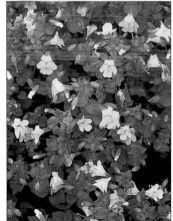

ALSO RECOMMENDED: M. guttatus *has yellow flowers with red-spotted throats;* M. ringens *is taller with violet, violet-blue, white, or pink flowers.*

☼ ◖◖ ✻✻✻   **Perennial**
↕ 30cm (12in) ↔ 60cm (24in)

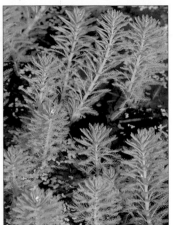

MYRIOPHYLLUM AQUATICUM

Parrot feather is a submerged oxygenating plant with spreading stems covered by whorls of delicate, bright green leaves. It is ideal for shallow water, where the stems may extend above the surface, but it will grow to a depth of 1m (3ft) or more. Inconspicuous flowers appear in summer. The top growth may be damaged by frost, but it should re-emerge in spring, and young shoots may be eaten by fish. Algae or detritus in the water chokes the leaves, which provide a valuable refuge for fish fry.

ALSO RECOMMENDED: M. verticillatum *is hardier to frost.*

☀ ❄❄❄ **Perennial**
↔ indefinite

NUPHAR LUTEA

The yellow pond lily is a deciduous perennial with large, heart-shaped, floating leaves. While the plant is valued for its round yellow flowers, which are held just above the water's surface in summer, its deep green foliage provides valuable shelter for pond creatures and shades out the growth of algae. It grows in still or slowly moving water to a depth of 30cm (12in), preferably in lime-free water and with a free root run. It is suitable for a wildlife pond.

☼☀ ❄❄❄ **Perennial**
↔ 2m (6ft)

NYMPHAEA *'Froebelii'*

A good water lily for barrels or small
ponds as it likes shallow water up to
30cm (12in) deep. Its bronzed young
leaves mature to small, round or heart-
shaped, pale green lily pads, useful
for reducing algae growth. Deep red
flowers, 10–13cm (4–5in) across, force
their heads up between the foliage in
summer; they are cup-shaped at first,
then star-shaped. Grow in still water.

ALSO RECOMMENDED: *'Aurora' has
mottled leaves and yellow flowers that
age to orange with red flecks.*

☼ ✳✳✳   **Perennial**
↔ 1m (3ft)

NYMPHAEA *'Gonnère'* ♥

This magnificent, white-flowered water
lily is ideal for any size of pond. Its
slightly bronzed young leaves mature to
round, pea-green lily pads, up to 22cm
(9in) across; they help keep the pond
cool and shade out algal growth. The
fully double, globe-shaped, fragrant
white flowers stay open until late in the
afternoon, closing at night. Grow in still
water at a depth of 30–45cm (12–18in).

ALSO RECOMMENDED: *N. alba, the white
water lily, is more spreading with larger
leaves and fragrant white flowers.*

☼ ✳✳✳ *f*   **Perennial**
↔ 1–1.2m (3–4ft)

NYMPHAEA 'Lucida'

This free-flowering water lily suits any size of pond with still water 30–45cm (12–18in) deep. Its large, dark green lily pads keep the pond cool and shaded, and they are heavily marked with dark purple. Star-shaped flowers, 12–15cm (5–6in) wide, emerge from below in summer; they have red inner petals and outer petals of pale pink with deeper pink veins.

ALSO RECOMMENDED: *'James Brydon'* ♥ *has vivid rose-red flowers.*

☼ ❄❄❄ **Perennial**
↔ 1.2–1.5m (4–5ft)

NYMPHAEA 'Marliacea Chromatella' ♥

Also sold as 'Tuberosa Flavescens', this is one of the most reliable yellow water lilies, bearing its large, primrose-coloured, semi-double summer flowers in abundance. It will grow in any size of pond at a depth of 30–45cm (12–18in) in calm water. Its coppery, purple-streaked young leaves mature to an attractive purple-mottled green.

ALSO RECOMMENDED: *'Marliacea Albida' has white flowers with yellow stamens; 'Marliacea Carnea' has light pink flowers with yellow stamens.*

☼ ❄❄❄ **Perennial**
↔ 1.2–1.5m (4–5ft)

NYMPHOIDES PELTATA

The water fringe has floating, glossy green, heart-shaped leaves, which look rather like those of a miniature water lily. The small, funnel-shaped flowers are bright yellow with fringed petals; they appear just above the water's surface through summer. Grow in water to a depth of 45cm (18in) deep; in small pools, confine the spreading rhizomes by planting in a basket.

☼ ❀❀❀   **Perennial**
↔ indefinite

ORONTIUM AQUATICUM

Golden club is a deciduous perennial, and it will grow in water up to 45cm (18in) deep. The blue-green leaves with silvery undersides float on the surface of the water, and from late spring to summer, poker-like, yellow-tipped flowerheads rise well above the foliage. Remove them when they fade. It is ideal at the margin of a pool among water irises.

☼ ❀❀❀   **Perennial**
‡ 30–45cm (12–18in) ↔ 60–75cm (24–30in)

PERSICARIA AMPHIBIA

The amphibious bistort roots itself in soil up to 45cm (18in) underwater, sending out floating, narrow, willow-like leaves on long stalks. In mid-summer, light pink flowers in dense heads are held above the water on upright stems. It will also grow in boggy pond margins. Thin back growth as necessary

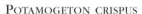

☼ ❋❋❋   **Perennial**
↔ indefinite

POTAMOGETON CRISPUS

Curled pondweed is a seaweed-like aquatic with submerged, translucent green leaves. Insignificant crimson and creamy white flowers are carried just above the water in summer. It spreads rapidly in mud-bottomed pools and tolerates cloudy or shady water better than any other oxygenating plant. Grow in water up to 1m (3ft) deep, thinning back frequently to keep it in check.

☼◐ ❋❋❋   **Perennial**
↔ indefinite

RANUNCULUS AQUATILIS

Water crowfoot is a submerged,
evergreen perennial, holding its yellow-
centred white buttercup flowers and
some of its rounded leaves just above
water. It flowers in midsummer and is
best in large wildlife ponds or streams
at a depth of 15–60cm (6–24in), where
it will spread and root in muddy bottoms.

ALSO RECOMMENDED: *R. lingua has
bright yellow flowers and prefers still
or slow-moving water at pond margins.*

☀ ❊❊❊   **Perennial**
↔ indefinite

SCHOENOPLECTUS LACUSTRIS
'Zebrinus'

This variegated club rush has almost
leafless, grey-green stems banded with
creamy white. In early to late summer,
it bears branched clusters of brown
flower spikelets. Grow in water up
to 30cm (12in) deep or in permanently
moist soil at the water's edge (*see
p.372*). In small pools, restrict growth
by cutting back rhizomes annually.
Trim non-variegated stems back to
the base, as necessary.

ALSO RECOMMENDED: *'Albescens' has
white stems with vertical green stripes.*

☀ ◗ ❊❊❊   **Perennial**
↕ 1m (3ft) ↔ 60cm (24in) or more

STRATIOTES ALOIDES

Water soldier is a free-floating, semi-evergreen perennial, which will grow as an attractive foliage plant in still or slow-moving water up to 1m (3ft) deep. "Pineapple-top" rosettes of deep green, spiky leaves rise above the surface of the water in midsummer, when the plant bears cup-shaped, white or pink-tinged flowers. It must be thinned regularly to control its spread.

☼ ❋❋❋ **Perennial**
‡ 40cm (16in) ↔ indefinite

TYPHA LATIFOLIA

The bulrush is a deciduous perennial forming a dense stand in shallow water, to 25cm (10in) deep; it is only suitable for the margin of a large wildlife pool, where deep water limits its spread. The characteristic, dark brown, cylindrical flower spikes, useful for dried flower arrangements (*see p.524*), are carried on top of tall, grass-like stems in summer. Flexible pond liners may be punctured by the thick, spreading rhizomes.

ALSO RECOMMENDED: *'Variegata' is much less vigorous with cream-striped leaves;* T. minima *is suitable for a small pond, reaching 75cm (30in) tall.*

☼☀ ❋❋❋ **Perennial**
‡ 2m (6ft) or more ↔ indefinite

URTICULARIA VULGARIS

Great bladderwort is a deciduous, submerged perennial with pouched, bright yellow, crimson-streaked flowers held well above the water in summer. An amazing feature of this oxygenating plant is its feathery, bronze-green leaves, which bear bladder-like structures. These trap insects, and the plant thrives in still or stagnant water that attracts insect larvae. Grow in lime-free water to 1m (3ft) deep.

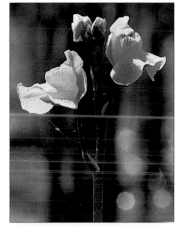

☼ ❄❄❄ **Perennial**
↔ 60–90cm (24–36in)

VERONICA BECCABUNGA

Brooklime is an excellent scrambling plant for a pond's edge, either in water up to 12cm (5in) deep or in permanently moist soil (*see p.372*). Its succulent, creeping stems are covered by fleshy, semi-evergreen leaves, and from late spring until the end of summer, clusters of light blue flowers appear in the leaf axils. Replace plants when the growth becomes straggly.

☼ ◗ ❄❄❄ **Perennial**
↕ 10cm (4in) ↔ indefinite

PLANTS FOR CONTAINERS IN SUN

Growing plants in containers is an extremely versatile way of decorating sunny patios. They can also be used to mark an entrance or to create a focal point, and window boxes and hanging baskets are a great way of introducing living colour to even the smallest of spaces. Container and bedding plants are also very useful for creating quick displays in new gardens.

You can use containers, too, for permanent plantings of frost-tender plants, like lemon verbena (*see p.415*) or lemon trees (*see p.414*), which will lend a Mediterranean air to a sunny patio. They can be moved to a cool greenhouse or conservatory for winter, before the first frosts. Another idea is to plant pots or tubs with seasonal bulbs to ring the changes through winter, spring, and summer.

CHOOSING CONTAINERS

Provided a container has drainage holes in the bottom, almost any receptacle can be used. Materials should be frost-resistant if they are to be left outdoors in winter, and choose containers that are in balance with the plants to ensure that plants are not top-heavy in the face of wind.

TIPS ON CULTIVATION

Container-grown plants rely heavily on the gardener for food and water, so site them within easy reach of a water source. They dry out more rapidly than in the open border and, in sunny sites, are likely to need watering at least daily in hot, dry weather. A compost mixed with water-retaining granules helps. Loam-based composts (such as John Innes No.2, or 3 for permanent plants) are ideal for containers, because they are heavy and lend stability; they also contain fertilizers and retain moisture well. Loamless composts are excellent for hanging baskets or window boxes, where weight is a disadvantage, but they are more prone to drying out and can be difficult to re-wet. Use a deep layer of broken crocks at the bottom of the pot for drainage and ballast, and leave about 2–2.5cm (¾–1in) between the compost surface and the rim of the pot to allow for watering. A top-dressing of gravel helps retain water and keep the roots cool. Give container plants a balanced liquid feed every two weeks or use a slow-release granular fertilizer. Deadhead regularly to ensure continuous and abundant flowering.

Plants in containers seldom achieve the height and spread that they would in open ground, so for mixed displays of summer bedding, pack plants closely in pots and hanging baskets. For permanent plants, remove the top 5–8cm (2–3in) of compost and replace with fresh compost each spring. When the roots fill the pot, pot on to a slightly larger container in spring, or prune the roots and refresh the compost. Since plants in pots are especially vulnerable to damage in cold weather, some kind of protection is often needed if they are to remain outside during winter, such as insulating with bubble-wrap plastic or straw (*see p.449*).

CITRUS LIMON

This small tree is an ideal specimen for a large tub on a sunny patio. Its glossy dark green leaves form the perfect backcloth for its fragrant, waxy white flowers, which appear from spring to summer. The lemons that follow take a year to ripen. Water freely when in growth; apply a balanced fertilizer every 2–3 weeks when in growth. Keep just moist in winter. Minimum temperature 3°C (37°F). Prune to shape in early spring.

ALSO RECOMMENDED: *C. × meyeri 'Meyer' is more compact with fragrant flowers and small, almost spherical fruits.*

☼ ◊ *f*   **Evergreen tree**
‡ 2–7m (6–22ft) ↔ 1.5–3m (5–10ft)

CORDYLINE AUSTRALIS 'Variegata'

The New Zealand cabbage palm is a palm-like, architectural tree with spiky leaves (*see p.472*). 'Variegata' has matt green leaves with cream stripes. It is unlikely to grow very tall in cold areas, and it is best brought under cover during winter. Remove dead leaves and faded flower stems as necessary. It tolerates coastal sites (*see p.166*).

ALSO RECOMMENDED: *C. australis ♀ has plain light green leaves; 'Torbay Dazzler' has boldly cream-striped leaves.*

☼ �○ ❄ ❄   **Evergreen tree**
‡ 3m (10ft) ↔ 1m (3ft)

SALIX CAPREA *'Kilmarnock'* ♀

The Kilmarnock willow is a small and weeping tree, ideal for a pot. It forms a dense, umbrella-like crown of yellow-brown shoots studded with silvery catkins in spring, before the arrival of the new foliage. These broad, toothed leaves are dark green on top and grey-green beneath. Prune annually in late winter to prevent the crown becoming congested, and remove shoots that arise on the clear trunk. Also sold as var. *pendula*. Plant in loam-based compost.

☀ ◊◊ ❋ ❋ ❋   **Deciduous tree**
‡ 1.5–2m (5–6ft) ↔ 2m (6ft)

ALOYSIA TRIPHYLLA ♀

Lemon verbena is grown mainly for its strongly lemon-scented, bright green foliage, used in both cookery and pot-pourri. Slender spikes of pale lilac or white flowers appear in late summer. It is ideal in a container; in very cold areas, move it onto a patio during summer and overwinter under glass. Water freely when in growth and apply a balanced liquid fertilizer monthly; keep the soil just moist in winter. Trim to shape in spring. In the garden, grow it against a warm, sheltered wall (*see p.280*). It is also sold as *A. citriodora*.

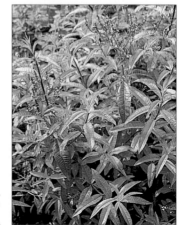

☀ ◊ ❋ ❋ ❋ *f*   **Deciduous shrub**
‡↔ 2m (6ft)

ARGYRANTHEMUM
'Vancouver' ♔

This compact, summer-flowering subshrub is valued for its double, daisy-like pink flowerheads with rose-pink centres and fern-like, grey-green leaves. In frost-prone areas, grow as summer bedding or in a container that can be sheltered in frost-free conditions over winter. It tolerates coastal conditions (*see p.166*). Pinch out growing tips to encourage bushiness. Minimum temperature 2°C (35°F).

ALSO RECOMMENDED: *'Jamaica Primrose'* ♔ *has light yellow flowerheads.*

☼ ◊ **Evergreen shrub**
↕ 90cm (36in) ↔ 80cm (32in)

BRUGMANSIA × CANDIDA
'Grand Marnier' ♔

Festooned with hanging, trumpet-shaped flowers, this frost-tender shrub is an impressive plant. The apricot-coloured, night-scented flowers appear from summer to autumn. Water freely and apply a balanced liquid fertilizer monthly in growth; keep just moist in winter. Prune to a woody framework in spring, and move under glass in winter. Minimum temperature 7°C (45°F). Also known as datura.

ALSO RECOMMENDED: *B. × candida has white, or soft yellow flowers;* *'Knightii'* ♔ *has double flowers.*

☼ ◊ *f* **Evergreen shrub**
↕ 3–5m (10–15ft) ↔ 2.5m (8ft)

CESTRUM AURANTIACUM

A vigorous shrub with arching branches that bear matt mid-green leaves and clusters of tubular orange flowers in spring and early summer. It is ideal for decorating a sunny patio in summer; move under glass for the winter in cold climates. Water freely and apply a balanced liquid feed monthly; keep just moist in winter. Trim to shape in spring. Minimum temperature 5°C (41°F).

ALSO RECOMMENDED: *C. elegans* ♥ *has crimson to purple-red or pink flowers from late summer to autumn; crimson-flowered C. 'Newellii'* ♥ *can withstand light frosts.*

☼ ◊   **Evergreen shrub**
↕↔ 3m (10ft)

× CITROFORTUNELLA MICROCARPA ♥

The Panama orange is a large shrub with leathery, bright glossy green leaves, occasionally with a few spines on the stems. White flowers appear from spring to summer, followed by small, orange-like, inedible fruits. Move under cover in frost-prone climates, or grow as a greenhouse or indoor plant all year round. Prune to size and shape in late winter. It is also sold as × *C. mitis*.

ALSO RECOMMENDED: *Tiger' (syn. 'Variegata') has leaves streaked and margined with white.*

☼ ◊ ❄   **Evergreen shrub**
↕ 3–6cm (10–20ft) ↔ 2–3m (6–10ft)

ERICA VAGANS *'Birch Glow'* ♥

This summer-flowering heather is a low and spreading shrub, looking good on its own in a pot of bark-based ericaceous compost. Its deep pink flowers continue well into autumn. Trim in early spring. In the garden, grow in acid soil, although it tolerates chalk (*see pp.64, 92*). It can be grown as ground cover (*see p.304*), and is suitable for coastal gardens (*see p.166*).

ALSO RECOMMENDED: *'Lyonesse'* ♥ *has white flowers; 'Mrs D.F. Maxwell'* ♥ *has deep pink flowers; 'Valerie Proudley'* ♥ *has yellow foliage and white flowers.*

☼ ◊ ❀❀❀   **Evergreen shrub**
‡ 30cm (12in) ↔ 50cm (20in)

FELICIA AMELLOIDES *'Read's White'*

This white-flowered form of the blue daisy has narrow, deep green foliage, and flowers from late spring to autumn. It is excellent in hanging baskets and mixed container displays. Treat it as an annual in frost-prone climates, pinching out the tips to promote bushiness and deadheading to prolong flowering. Take cuttings in autumn for plants next year. Minimum temperature 3°C (37°F). It tolerates coastal sites (*see p.166*).

ALSO RECOMMENDED: *'Read's Blue' is compact with blue flowerheads; 'Santa Anita'* ♥ *bears large, rich blue flowerheads.*

☼ ◊   **Evergreen shrub**
‡↔ 30–60cm (12–24in)

FUCHSIA *'Thalia'* ♀

This small and vigorous bush performs well in sun. It makes a superb patio or bedding plant, but it needs winter cover at a minimum temperature of 5°C (41°F). Masses of long-tubed, rich orange-scarlet flowers appear continuously from summer to autumn amid the dark green leaves. Pinch-prune when young to encourage bushiness; or train as a standard to lend height to displays.

ALSO RECOMMENDED: *'Billy Green'* ♀ *has salmon pink flowers; those of 'Coralle'* ♀ *are orange-red; 'Mary'* ♀ *has brilliant crimson flowers.*

☼ ◐ ◊◊　　　　**Evergreen shrub**
↕ ↔ 45　90cm (18　36in)

HELICHRYSUM PETIOLARE ♀

A silvery, mound-forming, shrubby evergreen with trailing stems which cascade beautifully over the sides of hanging baskets and other containers. Its small leaves are densely felted and silver-grey and combine well with flowering plants in mixed displays. Often grown as an annual in frost-prone areas, although it can be overwintered under glass at a minimum temperature of 2°C (35°F). Pinch-prune young stems to encourage bushiness.

ALSO RECOMMENDED: *'Variegatum'* ♀ *has cream-variegated foliage.*

☼ ◊　　　　**Evergreen shrub**
↕ 50cm (20in) ↔ 2m (6ft) or more

IBERIS SEMPERVIRENS ♀

This subshrubby candytuft bears dense, rounded heads of tiny white flowers in late spring and early summer, sometimes in such profusion as to obscure the dark green foliage. It is often grown in a rock garden, but it is also suitable for troughs and other containers. Trim lightly after flowering to keep the growth compact. It tolerates coastal conditions (*see pp.166, 304*).

ALSO RECOMMENDED: *'Schneeflocke'* ♀ (Snowflake) *is mound-forming with snow-white flowers;* *'Weisser Zwerg'* *is more compact.*

☼ ◊ ❋ ❋ ❋　　　**Evergreen shrub**
‡ 30cm (12in) ↔ 40cm (16in)

LANTANA *'Radiation'*

This prickly stemmed shrub with wrinkled, dark green leaves is usually grown as annual bedding in cold areas, but it is ideal for containers in warm, sunny sites. Its vibrant heads of brilliantly coloured, fiery red and orange flowers from late spring to late autumn are incredibly eyecatching. Water freely and apply a balanced liquid feed once a month in summer. Minimum temperature 10°C (50°F).

ALSO RECOMMENDED: L. camara *has flowers in shades of white, yellow, pink, or purple.*

☼ ◊　　　**Evergreen shrub**
‡ 45–60cm (18–24in) ↔ 25cm (10in)

LOTUS BERTHELOTII ♛

Known as parrot's beak for its hooked
flowers, this trailing subshrub is used in
hanging baskets and containers for its
narrowly cut, silvery leaves on long
trailing stems. The striking orange-red
to scarlet flowers may appear in
summer. It must be brought under glass
for winter and kept at a minimum
temperature of 2°C (35°F). Cut out
some older stems after flowering to
encourage new growth.

ALSO RECOMMENDED: *L. maculatus* ♛
is similar with red-tipped yellow flowers.

☼ ◊   **Evergreen shrub**
‡ 20cm (8in) ↔ indefinite

MELIANTHUS MAJOR ♛

The honey bush is an excellent
architectural foliage shrub (*see p.472*)
with grey-green to bright blue-green
divided leaves. Spikes of blood-red
flowers may appear in summer but it
is grown in pots for its outstanding
foliage. In the garden, treat this plant
as herbaceous in cold areas, cutting
right back in spring; in milder climates,
particularly against a warm wall (*see
p.280*), it can be allowed to develop
fully. It tolerates coastal sites (*see
p.166*), needing protection from cold,
drying winds and winter wet.

☼ ◊ ❀❀   **Evergreen shrub**
‡ 2–3m (6–10ft) ↔ 1–3m (3–10ft)

NERIUM OLEANDER

Oleander is an upright shrub with narrow, dark grey-green leaves. The flowers, usually pink, red, or white, appear throughout summer. It looks good on a patio in summer, where it tolerates coastal and hot, dry conditions (*see pp.166, 190*); move it to a greenhouse or conservatory in winter, kept at a minimum temperature of 2°C (36°F). Cut back in late winter, if necessary. All parts of this plant are toxic.

☼ ◊ **Evergreen shrub**
‡ 2m (6ft) ↔ 3m (10ft)

OSTEOSPERMUM *'Whirligig'* ♥

Like other osteospermum hybrids, 'Whirlygig' is grown for its daisy-like, bright and cheerful flowers, borne from spring to autumn. It is ideal for a sunny summer border or container; treat as an annual in frost-prone areas, or take autumn cuttings to overwinter. Plants can also be overwintered under glass. Tolerant of coastal and hot, dry sites (*see pp.166, 190*). Good in mixed displays with other tender perennials. Also sold as 'Tauranga'.

ALSO RECOMMENDED: *'Buttermilk'* ♥ *has primrose yellow flowerheads; O. jucundum* ♥ *(see p.188).*

☼ ◊ ❄ **Perennial**
‡↔ 60cm (24in)

PARAHEBE CATARRACTAE ♈

A small shrub bearing loose clusters of red-eyed, purple-veined white flowers throughout summer. It is very effective when tumbling over the edges of large containers or hanging baskets. It may not survive outdoors in cold climates, but it can be overwintered in a cool greenhouse or conservatory. It tolerates coastal conditions (*see p.166*). In the garden, shelter from cold, drying winds.

ALSO RECOMMENDED: *'Delight'* ♈ has blue flowers; *'Miss Willmott'* has rose-lilac flowers with mauve veins.

☼ ◊ ❀ ❀ **Evergreen shrub**
‡ 60–75cm (24–30in) ↔ 45cm (18in)

PICEA MARIANA *'Nana'* ♈

This diminutive variant of the black spruce forms a short, dense mound of soft, blue-grey needles, and is ideal in containers – a pair flanking a path or entrance can be very effective. Keep it well-watered in hot weather and shelter from cold, drying winds. Every spring replace the top 5cm (2in) with fresh compost. In the garden, it is useful as an architectural plant in a rock garden. It tolerates acid soils (*see p.166*).

ALSO RECOMMENDED: P. abies *'Ohlendorffii'* (see p.106); P. glauca *'Conica'* ♈ is taller, very slow-growing, and pyramidal with short, blue-green needles.

☼ ☼ ◊ ◊ ❀ ❀ ❀ **Evergreen shrub**
‡↔ 50cm (20in)

PROSTANTHERA ROTUNDIFOLIA ♔

The round-leaved mint bush is a spreading shrub with very aromatic, small and rounded, deep green leaves. Short clusters of bell-shaped, purple to lilac flowers appear in late spring and early summer. In frost-prone areas, overwinter container plants under glass. Trim after flowering. It tolerates partial shade (*see p.448*).

ALSO RECOMMENDED: *'Rosea'* (syn. *'Chelsea Girl'*) has greyish leaves and rich pink flowers.

☼ ◑ ◊◊ ❄ *f*   **Evergreen shrub**
‡ 2–4m (6–12ft) ↔ 1–3m (3–10ft)

RICINUS COMMUNIS *'Impala'*

The castor oil plant is an upright shrub, often grown as an annual for its shapely, palmately lobed foliage, which is reddish purple in this variety. Less significant are the yellowish green male flowers and red female flowers in summer. In the garden, it makes a good feature plant in a sunny border, where it may need to be staked.

ALSO RECOMMENDED: *'Zanzibarensis'* is taller, with large, white-veined, mid-green leaves.

☼ ◊ ❄   **Evergreen shrub**
‡ 1.2m (4ft) ↔ 1m (3ft)

ROSA *'The Fairy'* ♥

This dwarf rose forms a dense cushion of glossy green leaves. It is topped from late summer to autumn by a mass of small, double, soft pink flowers. Feed regularly throughout summer. Trim main stems and side-shoots by up to one-third in late winter. In the garden, it tolerates chalky soils (*see p.12*) and is effective planted among pinks or violas.

ALSO RECOMMENDED: *Angela Rippon has rose- to salmon-pink flowers; Queen Mother* ♥ *has pink flowers; Surrey has double pink flowers; 'White Pet' has double white flowers.*

☼ ◊ ✳ ✳ ✳   **Deciduous shrub**

↕↔ 60–90cm (24–36in)

SENECIO CINERARIA *'Silver Dust'* ♥

This mound-forming shrub is usually grown as an annual for its attractive, lacy leaves, which are velvety, deeply cut, and almost white. Plants kept into the second year bear loose heads of mustard-yellow flowers in midsummer; most gardeners prefer to remove them. It is ideal for massed foliage effects in bedding schemes, and for mixed plantings in containers. In the garden, it tolerates sandy soils, and coastal, and hot, dry sites (*see pp.38, 166, 190*).

ALSO RECOMMENDED: *'White Diamond'* ♥ *has oak-like, grey-white leaves*

☼ ◊ ✳ ✳   **Evergreen shrub**

↕↔ 30cm (12in)

BOUGAINVILLEA
'San Diego Red'

This vigorous climber needs the protection of a frost-free greenhouse or conservatory if it is to grow in a cold climate, but it is worthwhile for its incredibly vibrant, bright scarlet flower bracts from summer to autumn. The oval, mid-green leaves may fall in winter. Also sold as Scarlett O'Hara or 'Hawaiian Scarlet'. Bring outside during summer onto sheltered sunny patios. Feed regularly in summer. Keep on the dry side in winter.

☼ ◊ ❀   **Climber**
‡ 8–12m (25–40ft)

PASSIFLORA *'Amethyst'* ♀

This is a strong-growing passion flower with slender, climbing stems and three-fingered leaves. It is valued for its large, purple-blue flowers, to 11cm (4½in) across, in late summer and autumn. Orange fruits follow. Grow in a large tub in a greenhouse or conservatory with a minimum winter temperature of 5°C (41°F). Water freely in summer; sparingly in winter. Shade from the midday sun in hot weather. Prune back after flowering to keep within bounds.

ALSO RECOMMENDED: P. antioquiensis ♀, *the red banana passion flower, has bright rose-red, pendulous flowers.*

☼ ☼ ◊◊   **Climber**
‡ 4m (12ft) or more

PLUMBAGO AURICULATA ♔

Cape leadwort is a scrambling, semi-evergreen plant, which can be tied to a support and trained as a climber. It bears dense trusses of long-throated, sky blue flowers from summer to late autumn amid the oval leaves. In cold climates, plants overwintered under glass can be moved outside in summer. Pinch out the tips of young plants to promote bushiness, and cut back to a permanent framework in early spring. Also sold as *P. capensis*.

ALSO RECOMMENDED: *var.* alba *has white flowers.*

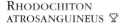 ❄ ❅ **Climber**

‡3–6m (10–20ft) ↔ 1–3m (3–10ft)

RHODOCHITON ATROSANGUINEUS ♔

This slender, evergreen climber has heart-shaped, rich green leaves and hanging flowers from summer to autumn. These have a dark purple-black tube beneath a flaring, dusty red-purple "skirt". It is very effective grown in a container with a pyramidal trellis support, or allowed to spill from a hanging basket, especially in association with plants with deep blue flowers. Minimum temperature 3°C (37°F). In the garden, it can be grown as an annual in cold climates. It is best with the roots in shade.

☼ ◊◊ **Climber**

‡3m (10ft)

THUNBERGIA ALATA

Black-eyed Susan is an evergreen climber named for its brilliant, orangey yellow, flat-faced flowers with distinctive black centres. The twining stems need support unless the plant is grown in a hanging basket. To keep over winter, take into a warm greenhouse or conservatory with a minimum temperature of 7°C (45°F). In the garden, it is often grown outdoors as an annual trained against a warm wall (*see p.280*) or other support.

ALSO RECOMMENDED: T. grandiflora ♀, *the blue trumpet vine, has light violet-blue flowers.*

☼ ◊◐   **Climber**
‡ 1.5–2.5m (5–8ft)

AEONIUM *'Zwartkop'* ♀

This upright and shrubby, succulent perennial is sparsely branched, but bears neat rosettes of leathery, deep black-purple leaves at the tip of each stem. In a container, grow in gritty, free-draining compost such as cactus compost, and water regularly. Overwinter in a conservatory or greenhouse, with a minimum temperature of 10°C (50°F); keep plants dry in winter. In very hot summers, shade from midday sun.

ALSO RECOMMENDED: A. arboreum *'Atropurpureum'* ♀ *is similar.*

☼ ☀ ◐ ◊   **Perennial**
‡↔ 2m (6ft)

AGAPANTHUS PRAECOX
SUBSP. ORIENTALIS

Useful in a large container as a late-flowering perennial, this African blue lily bears its large and showy, spherical clusters of rich blue, trumpet flowers in late summer and early autumn. Below are the evergreen clumps of strap-like, dark green leaves. Tolerant of coastal conditions (*see p.280*), but it needs the protection of a greenhouse in areas with cold winters.

ALSO RECOMMENDED. *var.* albiflorus *has white flowers;* A. *'Blue Giant'* (see p.181) *and* 'Bressingham Blue' *are hardy.*

☼ ◑ ❄   **Perennial**
‡ 60–90cm (24–36in) ↔ 60cm (24in)

AGAVE AMERICANA
'Variegata' ♥

This barbed succulent is grown for its spiny-margined and spine-tipped, fleshy leaves with bold yellow stripes. They eventually form a large, evergreen rosette, which makes an excellent architectural feature plant for a large container (*see p.472*). It will need to be moved under glass during cold winters. Grow in a gritty, free draining compost such as cactus compost.

ALSO RECOMMENDED: A. americana ♥ *has plain green leaves.*

☼ ◊ ❄   **Perennial**
‡↔ 1.5m (5ft)

BIDENS FERULIFOLIA ♀

This clump-forming plant, often grown as an annual, is a spreading, short-lived perennial with finely divided, fresh green leaves. During summer it bears a profusion of yellow, daisy-like flowerheads. It is very popular in hanging baskets or other containers, where its sprawling flowering stems will spill over the sides.

☼ ◊ ❀❀   **Perennial**
‡ 30cm (12in) ↔ indefinite

CAMPANULA ISOPHYLLA ♀

The Italian bellflower is also known as falling stars for its plentiful, pale blue, bell-shaped flowers on trailing stems in midsummer. It is ideal for cascading over the side of a large container or hanging basket. The small, heart-shaped leaves are light green. Cut back dead stems in winter.

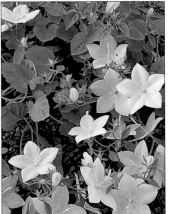

ALSO RECOMMENDED: *'Alba' has white flowers;* C. *'Birch Hybrid'* ♀ (see p.358); C. carpatica *'Bressingham White'* (see p.359).

☼☼ ◊◊ ❀   **Perennial**
‡ 15–20cm (6–8in) ↔ 30cm (12in)

CANNA *'Assaut'*

Indian shot plants are popular summer bedding plants grown as much for their upright stature (*see p.472*) as for their bright, gladiolus-like flower spikes. 'Assaut' bears broad, rounded, purple-brown leaves and orangey red flowers from midsummer to autumn. Move plants to a cool greenhouse or conservatory in winter. Hundreds of colourful varieties exist.

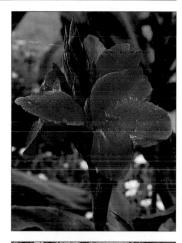

ALSO RECOMMENDED: *'Black Knight' has dark red flowers; 'King Midas' (see p.486); 'Striata' has orange flowers and variegated leaves.*

☼ ◊ ❄ **Perennial**

‡ 2m (6ft) ↔ 50cm (20in)

CHRYSANTHEMUM *'Mary Stoker'*

This bushy chrysanthemum bears sprays of apricot flowerheads in late summer and early autumn. The green centres turn to yellow as the flowers open. It is excellent on a sunny patio and is also suitable for cutting (*see p.524*). Use a loam-based potting compost. Water freely when in growth, and apply a balanced liquid fertilizer weekly from midsummer until the end of the season.

ALSO RECOMMENDED: *'Bronze Elegance' has pompon-like bronze flowerheads; 'Emperor of China' has silvery pink flowerheads with quilled petals.*

☼ ◊ ❄❄❄ **Perennial**

‡ 1.2m (4ft) ↔ 75cm (30in)

CONVOLVULUS SABATIUS ♡

A compact, trailing perennial bearing trumpet-shaped, vibrant blue-purple flowers from summer into early autumn. The slender stems are clothed with small, oval leaves. It is ideal for trailing over the sides of a container, but it may not survive in cold areas unless sheltered under glass during winter. Sometimes sold as *C. mauritanicus*. It prefers gritty or sandy soil.

ALSO RECOMMENDED: C. cneorum ♡ (see p.44).

☼ ◊ ❄ ❄ ❄   **Perennial**

‡ 15cm (6in) ↔ 50cm (20in)

GAZANIA *Mini-star Series*

These useful, vigorous and spreading summer bedding plants are usually grown as annuals. They are valued for their long summer display of large and fiery, daisy-like flowers, quite similar to sunflowers, although they close in cool or dull weather. Colours range from orange to golden yellow, beige, bronze, or bright pink, some zoned with contrasting colours. The leaves are dark green. They grow well in containers and are tolerant of coastal conditions (*see p.166*).

ALSO RECOMMENDED: *Daybreak Series also have flowers in a spectrum of colours.*

☼ ◊ ❄   **Perennial**

‡ 20cm (8in) ↔ 25cm (10in)

HYACINTHUS ORIENTALIS *'Ostara'* ♥

This violet-flowered hyacinth is a bulbous perennial grown as spring bedding for its dense, upright spikes of bell-shaped, fragrant blooms. Bright green leaves emerge from the base of the plant. Prepared bulbs can be grown indoors from autumn for winter flowers. Outdoors, plant bulbs in autumn and shelter form excessive winter wet. Tolerant of coastal conditions (*see p.166*).

ALSO RECOMMENDED: *'Anna Marie'* ♥ *has pale pink flowers; 'Delft Blue'* ♥ *has soft blue flowers; those of 'Gipsy Queen'* ♥ *are salmon-orange.*

☼ ☀ ◊ ❀ ❀ ❀ *f*   **Perennial bulb**
‡ 20–30cm (8–12in) ↔ 8cm (3in)

LILIUM REGALE ♥

Regal lilies bear fragrant, trumpet-shaped white flowers in midsummer; each stem carries up to 25 blooms, which can be cut for indoor display (*see p.524*). It makes an elegant, architectural plant for containers (*see p.472*), but needs staking. Ideal for patios where the scent can be appreciated easily. Plant bulbs in autumn. It tolerates most soils, and sunny sites (*see pp.38, 64, 190*).

ALSO RECOMMENDED: *'Fire King', orange; 'Journey's End' (see p.538); L. longifolium, white, scented; 'Star Gazer', dark pink.*

☼ ☀ ◊ ❀ ❀ ❀ *f*   **Perennial bulb**
‡ 0.6–2m (2–6ft)

MATTHIOLA INCANA
Cinderella Series

Stocks are short-lived perennials, often grown as annuals, valued for their dense spikes of sweet-scented, double flowers. This selection comes in a range of colours from white through pink to dark blue and purple. Single colours are also available. They make an attractive addition to a summer border; the flowers are good for cutting (*see p.524*). Sow seeds in spring in a heated propagator. Plant out in a sheltered site after the danger of frost has passed. Tolerant of coastal conditions (*see p.166*).

☼ ◊ ❀ ❀ *f*   **Perennial**
‡ 20–25cm (8–10in) ↔ 25cm (10in)

MIMULUS *'Andean Nymph'* ♛

This spreading monkey flower can be allowed to sprawl over the sides of containers and hanging baskets, showing its patchy pale pink, trumpet-shaped flowers for a long summer season amid the pale green leaves. Keep the soil moist at all times. Also suitable for containers in shade.

ALSO RECOMMENDED: *Seed selections Magic Series and Mystic Series.*

☼ ☀ ◊ ❀ ❀   **Perennial**
‡ 20cm (8in) ↔ 30cm (12in)

MUSCARI ARMENIACUM ♀

A strong-growing, bulbous plant that
bears dense spikes of tubular, rich blue
flowers in early spring. The mid-green
leaves are strap-like and begin to
emerge from underground in autumn.
Plant bulbs in autumn, either in
containers in layers to prolong the
flowering display, massed together in
borders, or in grass, where they may
naturalize, although their spread can be
invasive. Tolerant of sandy soils and
hot, dry sites (*see pp.38, 190*).

ALSO RECOMMENDED: M. *azureum* ♀ *is
half as tall, suitable for a rock garden.*

☼ ◊ ❋ ❋ ❋   **Perennial bulb**
↕ 20cm (8in) ↔ 5cm (2in)

NARCISSUS 'Tête à Tête' ♀

This miniature daffodil is famous for its
twin- or triplet-headed, golden yellow
spring flowers above strap-shaped
leaves. It suits both indoor and outdoor
displays, effective when planted *en
masse*. Plant bulbs in late summer. In
pots, plant in staggered layers to
prolong the display. Feed with a high
potash fertilizer at flowering time and
after flowering. Tolerant of chalky soils
and coastal conditions (*see pp.64, 166*).

ALSO RECOMMENDED: *'February Gold' ♀
taller with solitary flowers; 'Hawera' ♀ has
up to five flowers per bulb; 'Jack Snipe' ♀
has white and yellow flowers.*

☼ ◊ ❋ ❋ ❋   **Perennial bulb**
↕ 15cm (6in) ↔ 5–8cm (2–3in)

PELARGONIUM
'Happy Thought' ♀

Flowering pelargoniums are mostly bushy, evergreen perennials with bold flowers from spring to summer, making them popular bedding plants. In containers, they can be grown indoors or outside in summer. 'Happy Thought' bears clusters of bright red flowers above leaves with greenish yellow centres. Minimum temperature 2°C (35°F). Keep fairly dry during winter.

ALSO RECOMMENDED: *Trailing ivy-leaved 'Barbe Bleu' with dark purple flowers is good for hanging baskets; 'The Boar' ♀ has pink flowers and also trails.*

☼ ☀ ◊   **Perennial**

↕ 40–45cm (16–18in) ↔ 20–25cm (8–10in)

PELARGONIUM
'Lady Plymouth' ♀

This evergreen perennial is grown specifically for its prettily lobed and silver-margined, eucalyptus-scented foliage. The bluish pink flowers are less showy and more delicate than those bred purely for their flowers. It will perfume a greenhouse or conservatory and can be used as summer edging along a path or in pots on a patio, the leaves releasing their scent when brushed against. Minimum temperature 2°C (35°F).

ALSO RECOMMENDED: *'Attar of Roses' ♀, 'Chocolate Peppermint' ♀, and 'Prince of Orange' also have scented leaves.*

☼ ◊ *f*   **Perennial**

↕ 30–40cm (12–16in) ↔ 15–30cm (6–12in)

PETUNIA *'Purple Wave'*

Petunias are grown as annuals. This one is ideal for hanging baskets, containers or summer bedding, where it may cover an area up to 1m (3ft) across. The trumpet-shaped flowers open over a long period from late spring to autumn. Plant out in spring only when danger of frost has passed, preferably in a sheltered site. It grows well in poor soils. The Wave Series come in a range of colours other than purple

ALSO RECOMMENDED: *Surfinia Series are very vigorous and trailing with abundant flowers; Ultra Series have a profusion of large flowers. Both stand up to bad weather.*

☼ ◊ ❋❋ **Perennial**

↕ 45cm (18in) ↔ 30–90cm (12–36in)

PTEROCEPHALUS PERENNIS

This low-growing, scabious-like perennial forms an evergreen mat of fiddle-shaped, grey-green leaves. It bears flat, clustered heads of pale pinkish purple flowers in summer; papery seedheads follow. Grow in any well-drained soil. It is effective both in a container or at the front of a sunny border.

☼ ◊ ❋❋❋ **Perennial**

↕ 8cm (3in) ↔ 20cm (8in)

SALVIA SPLENDENS
'Scarlet King' ♥

The scarlet sage is a compact and bushy perennial with dense spikes of tubular flowers, which are an invaluable, long-lasting addition to any bedding or container display. It is commonly grown as an annual in cool climates. 'Scarlet King' is one of several cultivars that have brilliant scarlet flowers from summer to autumn above dark green, toothed leaves.

☼ ◊ ❀ ❀   **Perennial**
‡ 25cm (10in) ↔ 23–35cm (9–14in)

SEMPERVIVUM
ARACHNOIDEUM ♥

The cobweb houseleek is a mat-forming, evergreen succulent with rosettes of reddish green leaves webbed with silvery white hair. Flat clusters of star-shaped, red-pink flowers appear on leafy stems in summer. Grow in gritty, sharply drained soil; it is good for scree beds, troughs, or in dry stone wall crevices (*see p.348*). It makes a fine feature in a disused chimney pot. Tolerant of sandy soils and coastal and hot, dry sites (*see pp.38, 166, 190*).

ALSO RECOMMENDED: S. tectorum (see p.323).

☼ ◊ ❀ ❀ ❀   **Perennial**
‡ 8cm (3in) ↔ 30cm (12in)

TULIPA *'Keizerskroon'* ♥

Whether massed in spring bedding, in groups in a border, or filling a container on the patio, this tulip brings welcome colour to the spring garden. Plant bulbs in autumn. After flowering, the bulbs can be lifted, heeled in until the foliage dies down, then stored in a cool greenhouse or shed. It tolerates chalky soils, and coastal and hot, dry sites (*see pp.64, 166, 190*). The flowers can be cut for indoor display (*see p.524*).

ALSO RECOMMENDED: *'Apricot Beauty'* ♥ *has soft salmon-pink flowers; 'Red Riding Hood'.*

☼ ◊ ❀ ❀ ❀   **Perennial bulb**

‡ 30cm (12in) ↔ 8–13cm (3–5in)

VERBENA *'Sissinghurst'* ♥

This pretty, sprawling verbena has deeply cut, dark green leaves and bears heads of magenta-pink flowers from late spring to autumn. It is best used in mixed plantings in containers, including hanging baskets. Take cuttings in late summer or pot up and overwinter in a cool greenhouse.

ALSO RECOMMENDED: *'Peaches and Cream'* (see p.215); *Tapien Series, trailing and comes in a range of colours.*

☼ ◊ ❀ ❀   **Perennial**

‡ 20cm (8in) ↔ 1m (3ft)

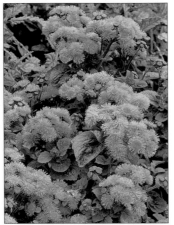

AGERATUM HOUSTONIANUM *'Adriatic'*

Floss flowers are popular little plants for edging in summer beds and containers. Their compact flowerheads form a frothy or fluffy mass of colour just above the deep green leaves from midsummer until the first frosts. 'Adriatic' is one of several blue-flowered ageratums. Water freely and deadhead to encourage an extended display. Also suitable for the cracks between paving and chalky soils (*see pp.64, 348*).

ALSO RECOMMENDED: *'Summer Snow'* ♀ *has white flowerheads; 'Swing Pink' has pink flowerheads.*

☼ ◊◊ ❀ **Annual**
↕ 15–20cm (6–8in) ↔ 15–30cm (6–12in)

BASSIA SCOPARIA *F.* TRICHOPHYLLA ♀

The burning bush is named for its bushy, cone-shaped habit and the feathery, close-set, light green leaves, which, in autumn, turn to bright red and purple. The flowers are inconspicuous. Sow in late spring in the growing position, or raise in modules and plant in pots. In the garden, plant in small groups in a bedding scheme or in a line to make a temporary low screen. Trim untidy plants in summer. It tolerates coastal conditions (*see p.166*).

☼ ◊ ❀ **Annual**
↕ 30–150cm (12–60in) ↔ 30–45cm (12–18in)

BRACHYSCOME IBERIDIFOLIA

The Swan River daisy is a faithful bedding plant grown for its profusion of daisy flowerheads. These are borne in summer and early autumn and are normally mauve-blue in colour, although they are sometimes white, purple, or pink. The weak-stemmed, trailing growth makes it useful for containers and hanging baskets.

ALSO RECOMMENDED: *Splendour Series have black-eyed, white, lilac-pink, or purple flowerheads.*

☼ ◊ ❄ **Annual**

‡ 45cm (18in) ↔ 35cm (14in)

BRACTEANTHA BRACTEATA *'Dargan Hill Monarch'*

This strawflower is an upright annual with papery, daisy-like, rich yellow flowerheads from late spring to autumn. The leaves are grey-green. Sow in pots and use to fill gaps in a border; the flowers are long lasting and cut and dry well (*see p.524*). It tolerates sandy soils (*see p.38*). Also listed under *Helichrysum*.

ALSO RECOMMENDED: *Bright Bikinis Series* ♥ *are low-growing, suitable for border edging or a window box; 'Skynet' has pinky cream flowerheads.*

☼ ◊ ❄ ❄ **Annual**

‡ 1–1.5m (3–5ft) ↔ 30cm (12in)

DAHLIA 'Yellow Hammer' ♀

Dwarf bedding dahlias are raised from seed and treated as annuals. Sow in spring under heat. Pinch out growing tip when young to encourage bushiness. Deadhead regularly. Useful for containers or to fill gaps in a border display. 'Yellow Hammer' has showy yellow flowers above bronze-tinged, divided leaves. The flowers are ideal for cutting (*see p.524*) and perform from midsummer to autumn when many other plants are past their best.

ALSO RECOMMENDED: *'Fascination'* ♀ *has dark pink flowers; 'Sunny Yellow'* ♀ *has semi-double, bright yellow flowers.*

☼ ◊ ❀❀ **Annual**
‡ 60cm (24in) ↔ 45cm (18in)

ESCHSCHOLZIA CAESPITOSA ♀

Californian poppies are known for their colourful, poppy-like flowers that close in dull weather. This short, upright species is ideal for containers and has finely divided, bluish leaves and many bright yellow, scented flowers in summer. It is a hardy annual that should be sown where it is to grow in spring or early autumn. It prefers sandy soils (*see p.38*) and tolerates coastal and hot, dry sites (*see pp.166, 190*).

ALSO RECOMMENDED: *'Sundew' has paler yellow flowers.*

☼ ◊ ❀❀❀ **Annual**
‡↔ 15cm (6in)

LIMNANTHES DOUGLASII

The poached egg plant forms a carpet of glossy bright yellow-green leaves and produces a profusion of shining yellow, white-edged, buttercup-like flowers from summer to autumn. It is excellent for troughs, path edging, and paving crevices (*see p.348*). Sow where it is to grow; it self-seeds freely and can become an almost permanent fixture once introduced. The flowers attract hoverflies, which help control aphids. In containers, it makes a cheerful addition to a patio. It tolerates sandy soils and coastal sites (*see pp.38, 166*).

☼ ◊ ✱ ✱ ✱   **Annual**
‡↔ 15cm (6in) or more

NEMESIA STRUMOSA '*KLM*'

A fast-growing and colourful annual with a bushy habit that is useful in containers or bedding displays, where it produces blue and white, lipped flowers with yellow throats during the second half of summer. Sow seed indoors in spring, and plant out seedlings only after the danger of frost has passed. Pinch out growing tip for bushy plants.

ALSO RECOMMENDED: '*Blue Gem*' has *bright blue flowers; 'Danish Flag' has red and white flowers; those of 'Prince of Orange' are orange.*

☼ ◊◊ ✱   **Annual**
‡ 18–30cm (7–12in) ↔ 10–15cm (4–6in)

NEMOPHILA MACULATA

Five-spot is a fleshy-stemmed annual with divided, bright green leaves. It bears saucer-shaped white flowers, each petal with a small, blue-violet spot at its tip. Often grown as border edging, it is also suitable for containers and hanging baskets. Keep it well-watered in hot weather to ensure a succession of flowers throughout summer.

ALSO RECOMMENDED: N. menziesii *has bright blue flowers, paler at the centre and with darker spots; 'Oculata' has pale blue, purple-centred flowers.*

☼ ◐ ◊ ❀ ❀ ❀   **Annual**
↕↔ 15–30cm (6–9in)

PAPAVER RHOEAS
Shirley Mixed

A colourful selection derived from the common field poppy (*P. rhoeas*); like it, they are upright annuals with solitary, nodding flower buds borne on slender stalks in summer. These open to bowl-shaped, crepe-paper-like flowers, which are single, semi-double, or double in yellow, pink, orange, and sometimes red. They tolerate sandy soils (*see p.38*). Sow seeds where they are to grow.

ALSO RECOMMENDED: P. rhoeas, *the field poppy, has bright red flowers with black marks on the petal bases.*

☼ ◊ ❀ ❀ ❀   **Annual**
↕ 60cm (24in) ↔ 30cm (12in)

SALPIGLOSSIS SINUATA
Casino Series ♀

These upright and compact, weather-resistant annuals, ideal for summer bedding, freely produce a contrasting display of funnel-shaped flowers through summer and autumn. Colours range from blue and purple to red, yellow, or orange, heavily veined in deeper tints. The lance-shaped, mid-green leaves have wavy margins. Plant out after the risk of frost has passed; staking is usually necessary. Remove dead flowers regularly.

ALSO RECOMMENDED: *Bolero Hybrids are similar; 'Kew Blue' has deep blue flowers.*

☼ ◊ ❀ ❀ **Annual**
‡ 60cm (24in) ↔ 30cm (12in)

SANVITALIA PROCUMBENS

Creeping zinnia forms a low mat of mid-green foliage, which is covered throughout summer and into autumn by single, bright yellow daisy flowers with black centres. It is ideal for border edging and containers, including tubs, troughs, pots, and hanging baskets. Sow seed where it is to grow in autumn or spring.

ALSO RECOMMENDED: *'Gold Braid' has golden flowerheads; 'Mandarin Orange' has semi-double, rich orange flowerheads – both are more compact, to 10cm (4in) tall.*

☼ ◊ ❀ ❀ **Annual**
‡ 20cm (8in) ↔ 45cm (18in)

SCHIZANTHUS *'Hit Parade'*

The poor man's orchid is known for its dense clusters of very pretty, orchid-like, lipped flowers, which come in shades of white, yellow, pink, purple, or red. 'Hit Parade' has deep pink flowers with yellow throats, almost covering the light green, fern-like leaves for a long season from spring to autumn. Pinch back young growth to encourage bushiness. It tolerates sandy soils (*see p.38*). Minimum temperature 5°C (41°F).

☼ ◊◊ **Annual**

‡ 20–50cm (8–20in) ↔ 23–30cm (9–12in)

TAGETES *Boy Series*

French marigolds are compact plants with extremely colourful, bright yellow, orange, or red-brown, velvety, pompon-like flowers in late spring and early summer. They are suitable for containers or as edging in mixed summer borders and tolerate sandy or chalky soils (*see pp.38, 64*) and coastal sites (*see p.166*). The finely divided, rich green foliage gives a feathery or fern-like effect.

☼ ◊ ❊ **Annual**

‡ 15cm (6in) ↔ 30cm (12in)

THYMOPHYLLA TENUILOBA

Golden fleece has pungently scented, feathery leaves and produces an abundance of daisy-like, bright yellow flowers from spring to summer. It is excellent for hanging baskets and other containers, as well as for summer bedding. Sow seed under glass in mid-spring and set out when danger of frost has passed; alternatively sow seed where it is to grow in late spring.

☼ ◊ ❄❄ *f*   **Annual**
↕↔ 30cm (12in)

TROPAEOLUM MAJUS *'Alaska'* ♔

A fast-growing, scrambling annual that has very bright and eye-catching spurred flowers in shades of yellow, orange, mahogany, or cream in summer and autumn. It is ideal for a hanging basket or as ground cover (*see p.304*) in a summer border. The light green, rounded leaves are attractively speckled white. It tolerates coastal sites (*see p.166*) and flowers best in poor soils.

ALSO RECOMMENDED: *'Hermine Grashoff'* ♔ *has double red flowers;* T. peregrinum, *the canary creeper, is an annual climber with small yellow flowers and prettily lobed leaves*

☼ ◊◊ ❄   **Annual**
↕ 30cm (12in) ↔ 45cm (18in)

PLANTS FOR CONTAINERS IN SHADE

MANY GARDENS have shady areas, such as courtyards enclosed by high walls, or beds overshadowed by trees and shrubs. In paved or concreted areas, containers provide the obvious solution to brightening the gloom. The plants themselves often benefit from the protection of walls and fences, making permanent plantings of shrubs or herbaceous perennials particularly suitable. Since they are under less stress than when sited in full sun, plants grow well. Shade narrows the choice of bedding plants, but those that do enjoy shade, such as lobelia (*see p.466*), go on flowering for longer than when growing in sun.

An enormous range of shade-loving plants are amenable to container cultivation. Even relatively large shrubs can be grown, such as the architectural × *Fatshedera lizei* (*see p.450*), which often respond to "captivity" by growing more slowly and becoming more compact. Many shade-loving plants, like the Japanese painted fern (*see p.459*), are grown mainly for their graceful foliage and can be used in containers. Introduce vibrant colour with jewel-bright Polyanthus primulas in spring (*see p.468*), or *Lobelia erinus* and begonias in summer (*see pp.466, 459, 460*), and add fragrance with flowering tobacco plants (*see p.471*)

TIPS ON CULTIVATION

Container plants in shade are planted and fertilized as for those in sun (*see p.412*) but do not need such meticulous attention to watering, since they usually dry out less rapidly than those in hot, sunny sites. Avoid standing containers in spots where walls or fences may have created a wind tunnel as plants are unlikely to thrive.

Since surfaces in shady spots are often damp, the drainage from the bottom of the pot can become critical, especially during the cooler months. Pots in direct contact with damp surfaces may not drain freely, and compost can easily become waterlogged. Then, not only does the root system suffer, but the pots themselves become more susceptible to cracking and flaking when subjected to the freeze-thaw cycle in winter. Choose frost-resistant pots for permanent plants and use special pot feet, or old bricks, to assist drainage by creating a gap between the floor and pot.

If containers are to be left outdoors during the colder winter weather, group pots together and take steps to insulate them and the plant roots by wrapping a layer of bubble-plastic or straw around the outside of the pot. Make sure that the wrapping does not interfere with drainage.

While many insects pests, such as aphids, proliferate more freely in sunny sites, a few, notably slugs and snails, thrive in damp shade, so be vigilant. Check beneath pot rims in the evening, which are a favourite lurking place for snails. Either remove slugs and snails by hand, or place pellets in the containers, perhaps under a small, upturned pot, so that they are not accessible to children, pets or other animals.

Camellia japonica *'Adolphe Audusson'* ♥

This compact camellia is fine both in the open garden and in a container. Choose a site sheltered from early morning sun, cold winds, and late-season frosts, and it will repay with healthy, glossy dark green leaves and large, semi-double red flowers in spring. Trim young plants to shape and size, and maintain a mulch of chipped bark. Grow in ericaceous (lime-free) compost. In the garden, it tolerates damp shade and north-facing walls (*see pp. 238, 262*).

ALSO RECOMMENDED: *'Hagoromo'* ♥, *pink semi-double; 'Lady Vansittart'* (see p.99).

☼ ◐◊ ❄❄❄ **Evergreen shrub**
‡ 2m (6ft) ↔ 1.5m (5ft)

× Fatshedera lizei ♥

The tree ivy is a spreading shrub with very glossy, ivy-like leaves. Pinch out young shoots to promote bushiness. In autumn, it produces clusters of greenish white flowers. An elegant container plant for a shady terrace or courtyard. In the garden, it will grow against a shady wall (*see p.262*).

ALSO RECOMMENDED: *'Annamieke'* ♥ *(syn. 'Lemon and Lime', 'Maculata')* has *yellow-variegated leaves; 'Variegata'* ♥ *has green leaves narrowly cream-margined.*

☼ ◊ ❄❄❄ **Evergreen shrub**
‡ 1.2–2m (4–6ft) ↔ 3m (10ft)

FUCHSIA *'Annabel'* ♀

An especially floriferous and versatile
fuchsia that is suitable for both pots
and hanging baskets. It can also be
trained with a clear stem as a tree-like
standard. 'Annabel' has pendulous,
pinkish white flowers through summer
and into autumn. Shelter from cold,
drying winds and move to a frost-
free environment in winter. Pinch out
growing tips to promote bushiness.

ALSO RECOMMENDED: *'Checkerboard'* ♀
*has red and white flowers; 'Alice Hoffman',
with pink and white flowers, and
'Display'* ♀*, with red and pink flowers, are
suitable for training as standards.*

☼ ☀ ◐ ◊◊ ❄   **Evergreen shrub**
‡↔ 30–60cm (12–24in)

FUCHSIA *'Lady Thumb'* ♀

'Lady Thumb' is a small fuchsia in
all respects, which makes it a superb
choice for a window box. Its low
growth is made up of small mid-green
leaves and little, red and white, hanging
flowers. Shelter from cold, drying
winds, and keep it free from frost
in winter. Pinch out growing tips of
young plants to promote bushiness.

ALSO RECOMMENDED: *'Dark Eyes'* ♀ *has
red and violet flowers; 'Son of Thumb'* ♀
and 'Tom Thumb' ♀ *are both compact.*

☼ ☀ ◐ ◊◊ ❄❄   **Evergreen shrub**
‡ 15–30cm (6–12in) ↔ 30–45cm (12–18in)

FUCHSIA PROCUMBENS

A fascinatingly unusual fuchsia with small, upward-looking flowers that are like miniature golden goblets with green sepals and blue pollen – colours very rarely found in fuchsias. Plum-like fruits follow. The long, creeping stems with rounded leaves suit this plant to a hanging basket. It is easy to grow.

ALSO RECOMMENDED: *More traditional trailing fuchsias include: 'Autumnale' with reddish young leaves and scarlet flowers; 'Jack Shahan'* ♀ *with pink flowers; 'La Campanella'* ♀ *with white and purple flowers; 'Marinka'* ♀ *with dark red flowers.*

☼ ◐ ◊◐ ❀❀   **Evergreen shrub**
‡ 10–15cm (4–6in) ↔ 1–1.2m (3–4ft)

ILEX CRENATA *'Convexa'* ♀

This form of the box-leaved holly has a dense, broadly rounded habit and bears very glossy leaves on dark purple stems. The small white flowers of spring and early summer give rise to a profusion of shiny black berries, which are a food source for birds (*see p.494*). It makes an elegant specimen for a shady courtyard, especially in formal designs. Clip to shape in summer.

ALSO RECOMMENDED: *'Convexa' makes a dense bush with small leaves; 'Golden Gem'* ♀ *is compact with golden leaves; 'Mariesii' has tiny leaves and grows slowly.*

☼ ◐ ◊ ❀❀❀   **Evergreen shrub**
‡ 2.5m (8ft) ↔ 2m (6ft)

NANDINA DOMESTICA ♥

Heavenly bamboo is not actually a bamboo, but an upright shrub with fine spring and autumn colour. The divided leaves are red when young, maturing to green, then flushing red again in late autumn. Conical clusters of small white flowers with yellow centres appear in midsummer, followed, in warm climates, by long-lasting, bright red fruits. Move to a sheltered site in cold winters, and prune in spring to keep the plant shapely and tidy.

ALSO RECOMMENDED: *'Firepower' is dwarf and compact, to 45cm (18in) tall.*

☼ ◐ ◊ ✿ ✿   **Evergreen shrub**
‡ 2m (6ft) ↔ 1.5m (5ft)

PIERIS JAPONICA *'Little Heath'* ♥

A dwarf form of *P. japonica* suitable for container cultivation. It has a rounded shape and bears small, pink-flushed white flowers in late winter and early spring. These are carried in drooping clusters amid glossy dark green leaves with silver margins; the young foliage is bronze-tinted. A good early-flowering shrub, although it needs ericaceous (lime-free) compost. In the garden, it succeeds in damp, shady places (*see p.238*).

ALSO RECOMMENDED: P. formosa *'Wakehurst'* ♥ (see p.107) *is larger.*

☼ ◐ ◊◊ ✿ ✿ ✿   **Evergreen shrub**
‡ 4m (12ft) ↔ 3m (10ft)

PITTOSPORUM EUGENIOIDES *'Variegatum'* ♀

This pretty foliage shrub tolerates clipping. It has glossy leaves with wavy, creamy-yellow-splashed margins. The leaves release a lemon scent when crushed, giving the plant its common name – lemonwood. Clusters of tiny flowers appear in spring and summer. It must be given a sheltered site and moved under glass in frosty winters. If necessary, prune in winter to keep an open balanced shape.

ALSO RECOMMENDED: *'Garnettii'* ♀ *is similar but with smaller leaves.*

☼ ◐ ◊◊ ❀ *f* **Evergreen shrub**
‡ 5–12m (15–40ft) ↔ 2–5m (6–15ft)

RHODODENDRON *'Homebush'* ♀

A compact rhododendron with a bushy habit that is suitable for a large tub. Its dense clusters of neat, bright pink, trumpet-shaped flowers make a fine, late-spring display. It needs an ericaceous (lime-free) compost. In the garden, it is happy in damp, shady sites (*see p.238*). Deadhead carefully, otherwise little pruning is needed.

ALSO RECOMMENDED: *'Carmen'* ♀ *has dark red flowers; 'Shamrock' has pale yellow flowers; 'Vuyk's Scarlet'* ♀ *has crimson flowers.*

☼ ◐ ◊◊ ❀❀❀ **Evergreen shrub**
‡↔ 1.5m (5ft)

SASA VEITCHII

What appears to be a variegated bamboo is actually a plain-leaved species with glossy dark green leaves that wither attractively at the edges from late autumn. It has slender, branching, usually purple canes. Plant in a large container to contain its spreading habit; pots can be sunk into the ground over winter.

ALSO RECOMMENDED: *S. palmata* ♀ *and J. nebulosa are similar with paler leaves.*

☼ ☀ ◒◊ ✳✳✳   **Evergreen bamboo**
↕ 1–1.2m (3–4ft) ↔ indefinite

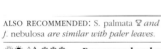

SKIMMIA × CONFUSA *'Kew Green'* ♀

This compact, dome-shaped, male shrub bears conical spikes of creamy white flowers in spring. It is an excellent pollinator for berry-bearing, female skimmias. In a container, it is ideal for a courtyard. Little or no pruning is required. In the garden, it is ideal for a dry, shady bed or border (*see p.216*). It tolerates clay and acid soils (*see pp.12, 92*).

ALSO RECOMMENDED: *S. japonica (see p.223); 'Rubella'* ♀ *(see p.108); 'Veitchii' is female with red berries.*

☼ ☀ ◊ ✳✳✳ ◆   **Evergreen shrub**
↕ 0.5–3m (1½–10ft) ↔ 1.5m (5ft)

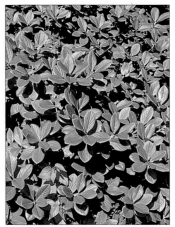

VACCINIUM GLAUCOALBUM ♔

This blueberry forms a mound of dense, dark green, oval leaves with bright whitish blue undersides. Hanging clusters of small, pinkish white flowers appear from the leaf axils in early summer, and these are followed by the edible, blue-black berries. Plant in ericaceous compost; in cold winters, it may need to be brought under cover. It suits a woodland garden, but it must have an acid soil (*see p.92*).

ALSO RECOMMENDED: *V. corymbosum* ♔ *is the highbush blueberry, grown specifically for its edible fruits; V. floribundum has red fruits.*

☼ ☀ ◑◊ ❄❄   **Evergreen shrub**
‡ 50–120cm (20–48in) ↔ 1m (3ft)

VIBURNUM TINUS *'Variegatum'*

A compact bush that has dense, dark green foliage with creamy yellow margins. Flattened heads of pink buds open to tiny star-shaped white flowers from late winter to spring; small, dark blue-black fruits follow. Trim to shape after flowering. In the garden, it can be grown as an informal hedge (*see p.138*) in a sheltered site. Tolerant of chalky soils, coastal sites, and dry shade or sun (*see pp.64, 166, 216, 412*).

ALSO RECOMMENDED: *'Eve Price'* ♔ *has pink flower buds; 'Gwenllian'* ♔ *has pink-flushed flowers and red buds.*

☼ ☀ ◑◊ ❄❄❄   **Evergreen shrub**
‡↔ 3m (10ft)

CISSUS ANTARCTICA ♥

The kangaroo vine is usually grown as
a house or conservatory plant in cold
areas, but it may be moved outdoors
for the frost-free summer months. Train
up a support or allow to trail. Ideal for
hanging baskets, it is valued for its
glossy dark green leaves; the flowers
are small and insignificant. Apply a
balanced fertilizer monthly when in
growth. Keep just moist in winter.
Minimum temperature 5°C (41°F).

ALSO RECOMMENDED: *C. rhombifolia* ♥
*has diamond-shaped leaves with rusty-
hairy undersides; 'Ellen Danica' ♥ is
bushier with lobed leaves.*

☀ ◊   **Climber**
‡ 5m (15ft)

FICUS PUMILA ♥

The creeping fig is an evergreen
perennial, clinging by means of aerial
roots. On climbing stems, the leathery,
dark green leaves are asymmetrically
oval, and on non-climbing ones, the
leaves are narrower and very glossy.
It is ideal as a house or conservatory
plant; provide support or grow in a
hanging basket. When in growth, water
moderately and apply a high-nitrogen
fertilizer once a month; keep the soil
just moist in winter. Minimum
temperature 5°C (41°F).

☀☀ ◊   **Climber**
‡ 3–5m (10–15ft)

ADIANTUM PEDATUM ♥

A maidenhair fern that bears long, mid-green fronds up to 35cm (14in) tall which die down in winter. These have glossy dark brown or black stalks that emerge from creeping rhizomes. There are no flowers. Remove dead fronds in spring. In the garden, it is also suitable for light woodland or a damp, shady border (*see p.238*), where it can be planted as ground cover (*see p.326*).

ALSO RECOMMENDED: A. aleuticum ♥ (*see p.331*); A. venustum ♥ *is short, to 15cm (6in) tall.*

☀️◐ ◊ ❄❄❄ **Perennial fern**
‡↔ 30–40cm (12–16in)

ASPIDISTRA ELATIOR 'Variegata' ♥

Although commonly grown indoors, the cast-iron plant is a useful, very shade-tolerant foliage perennial for pots. Small cream flowers appear in early summer. It will even overwinter outside in the garden in mild climates, where it can be planted as ground cover in shade (*see p.326*). This variegated variety has large, dark green, cream-striped leaves, to 70cm (28in) long. Choose a sheltered site.

ALSO RECOMMENDED: A. elatior ♥ *has shorter, plain dark green leaves.*

☀️◐ ◊◊ ❄❄ **Evergreen perennial**
‡↔ 60cm (24in)

ATHYRIUM NIPONICUM

The Japanese painted fern has finely divided grey-green deciduous fronds with purplish midribs and makes an elegant container plant for a shady courtyard or a cool conservatory. Use ericaceous (lime-free) or bark-based compost mixed with equal parts grit and leafmould. In the garden, it is excellent as ground cover in damp, partially shaded sites (*see pp. 238, 326*); it spreads by red-brown rhizomes.

ALSO RECOMMENDED: *var.* pictum ♀ *has silvery fronds;* A. filix-femina *'Frizelliae'* ♀ (see p.248).

☼ ◐ ◊ ❀ ❀ ❀   **Perennial fern**

↕ 20–30cm (0–12in) ↔ indefinite

BEGONIA *Non Stop Series* ♀

Often grown outdoors as bedding, these tuberous begonias have bold, double blooms throughout summer in white, red, orange, apricot, pink, or yellow. They are excellent in containers and hanging baskets. Apply a balanced fertilizer at alternate waterings when in full growth. Minimum temperature 10°C (50°F); to overwinter in cold climates, lift tubers before first frosts in autumn and store dry at 5–7°C (41–45°F).

ALSO RECOMMENDED: *'Can can' has yellow flowers with red edges; Illumination Series begonias are pendulous with pink or orange flowers, ideal for hanging baskets.*

☼ ◊   **Perennial**

↕↔ 30cm (12in)

BEGONIA SUTHERLANDII ♛

Pendulous or trailing begonias like this orange-flowered species are ideal for hanging baskets and other containers. It has long and slender stems clothed with large, oval, bright green leaves with red veins. The relatively small flowers are freely borne in hanging clusters during summer. Fertilize when in growth and move under glass in winter.

ALSO RECOMMENDED: *B. grandis subsp. evansiana is upright, better for summer bedding, with pink or white flowers.*

☼☀ ◊ ❄   **Perennial**

‡ 75cm (30in) ↔ 45cm (18in)

BROWALLIA SPECIOSA *'White Troll'*

The sapphire flower is usually grown as an annual in cold winter climates and is ideal for summer bedding and containers. This cultivar bears a profusion of white flowers through summer above a mound of sticky, matt green leaves. Water freely and apply a balanced liquid feed monthly when in full growth. Pinch out growing tips to promote bushiness. Minimum temperature 13°C (55°F).

ALSO RECOMMENDED: *'Blue Bells' is compact with violet-blue flowers; 'Silver Bells' has white flowers.*

☼☀ ◊   **Perennial**

‡ 60cm (24in) ↔ 25cm (10in)

CHLOROPHYTUM COMOSUM *'Vitiatum'* ♉

Spider plants are famous for their clumps of ribbon-like, fresh green leaves, which have an off-white central stripe in this cultivar. Long, slender flower stems freely arch over the foliage, tipped by small, starry white flowers and miniature plantlets; in a hanging basket, the plantlets can cascade over the edge. Ideal for year-round display in a conservatory, they can be moved outside in summer. Minimum temperature 7°C (45°F).

ALSO RECOMMENDED: *'Variegatum'* ♉ is similar, with white-margined leaves.

☼ ◐ ◊◊ **Perennial**
‡ 15–20cm (6–8in) ↔ 15–30cm (6–12in)

CYCLAMEN PERSICUM

A tender cyclamen available in white and many shades of pink and purple. It is ideal for a cool greenhouse or conservatory in light shade, or on a windowsill, and bears its flowers from early winter to early spring above deep green, often silver-marbled leaves. Avoid draughts and hot, dry air, and water moderately when in leaf; cease watering when the foliage begins to wither after flowering. Minimum temperature 10°C (50°F). Lovely in winter window boxes in sheltered urban sites.

☼ ◐ ◊ ◊ **Perennial**
‡↔ 15cm (6in) or more

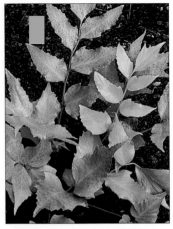

CYRTOMIUM FALCATUM ♥

The Japanese holly fern has evergreen, glossy dark green fronds with holly-like leaflets; these make a strong contrast among other ferns with more delicate, lacy foliage. There are no flowers. In cold areas, move the plant indoors in winter, where it will make a handsome foliage plant, or cover the crown with straw. Pot up in equal parts bark-based compost, grit and leafmould. In the garden, its spreading habit is also suited to dry areas in quite deep shade (*see p.216*). Choose a sheltered site.

ALSO RECOMMENDED: C. fortunei ♥ *is hardier and less spreading.*

☀️◐ ◊◊ ❆❆ **Perennial fern**
‡ 60cm (24in) ↔ 1.1m (3½ft)

DRYOPTERIS WALLICHIANA ♥

Wallich's wood fern is a handsome plant for a large container. The long, upright fronds form an elegant, dark green shuttlecock. They are golden green when young, and the midribs are clothed in shaggy dark brown scales, which make attractive colour contrasts. They die down in winter. Choose a site sheltered from wind. Pot up into equal parts bark-based compost and leafmould.

ALSO RECOMMENDED: D. cycadina ♥ *is compact with bright green fronds;* D. erythrosora ♥ *has dark green fronds, which are copper-red when young.*

☀️◐ ◊ ❆❆❆ **Perennial fern**
‡ 90cm (36in) ↔ 75cm (30in)

EPIMEDIUM GRANDIFLORUM 'Lilafee'

Also sold as 'Lilac Fairy', this small, deciduous plant produces spikes of delicate, violet-purple flowers above the light green foliage in mid- and late spring. The leaves are tinged bronze when young. Evergreen, but clip back the old leaves in late winter for the best display. In the garden, this is useful in the dry shade of trees and shrub (see p.216).

ALSO RECOMMENDED: *'Rose Queen'* ♥ *has rose-pink flowers;* E. × perralchicum ♥ *has bright yellow flowers;* E. × rubrum ♥ *has crimson and pale yellow flowers.*

☀ ◐◐ ✸✸✸　　　**Perennial**
‡ 20–30cm (8–12in) ↔ 30cm (12in)

FRAGARIA VESCA 'Multiplex'

Ornamental strawberries make pretty pot plants with trailing stems. Typical characteristics include leaves split into three, toothed leaflets, rose-like flowers, and fleshy, edible red fruits. This cultivar has bright green foliage and relatively large white flowers in spring and summer followed by small strawberries. In the garden it grows well in chalky soils and can be used as ground cover (see pp.64, 326).

ALSO RECOMMENDED: F. *Pink Panda has rich pink flowers, but rarely bears fruits. Dessert fruiting strawberries are also suitable for growing in containers.*

☀☀ ◐◐ ✸✸✸　　　**Perennial**
‡ ↔ 30cm (12in)

HAKONECHLOA MACRA
'Aureola' ♔

This colourful, deciduous grass forms a clump of narrow, arching, bright yellow leaves with cream and green stripes. They flush red in autumn and persist well into winter. Reddish brown flower spikes appear in late summer. It tolerates full sun, but the leaf colour is best in partial shade. It is a versatile plant, which can also be used in a border or rock garden.

ALSO RECOMMENDED: 'Alboaurea' has gold-striped leaves.

 Perennial

‡ 35cm (14in) ↔ 40cm (16in)

HEUCHERA MICRANTHA
'Palace Purple' ♔

A clump-forming perennial valued for its dark purple-red, almost metallic foliage. It is topped by airy sprays of white flowers in summer. The leaves have five pointed lobes. It tolerates deep shade if the compost is kept moist. In the garden, plant in groups as ground cover for a damp, shady site (see pp.238, 326), but it can be slow to spread.

ALSO RECOMMENDED: H. 'Green Ivory' (see p.340) is less upright; 'Pewter Moon' has large, pale pink flowers.

Perennial

‡↔ 45–60cm (18–24in)

HOSTA *'Shade Fanfare'* ♀

A variegated-leaved hosta that is also
suitable for ground cover in damp,
shady places (*see pp.238, 326*). It forms
clumps of bright green, boldly cream-
margined leaves; their broad, heart
shape gives an architectural quality (*see
p.472*). Lavender blue flowers appear
in summer. Growing in pots reduces
slug damage.

ALSO RECOMMENDED: *'Frances
Williams'* ♀ (*see p.381*); *'Halcyon'* ♀ (*see
p.340*); H. sieboldiana *var* elegans ♀ (*see
p.490*); H. ventricosa ♀ (*see p.30*); *'Wide
Brim'* ♀ (*see p.254*).

☀◐ ◊ ❉ ❉ ❉   **Perennial**

↕ 45cm (18in) ↔ 60cm (24in)

IPHEION UNIFLORUM *'Wisley Blue'* ♀

The vigorous bulb produces clumps of
narrow, strap-shaped, bluish green
leaves in autumn, and bears scented,
star-shaped, lilac-blue flowers in spring.
Ideal for a container in a lightly or
partially shaded courtyard; it tolerates
sun. Plant bulbs in autumn. In the
garden, it enjoys sandy soils (*see p.38*)
and sun, but it may not survive very
harsh winters.

ALSO RECOMMENDED: *'Album'* has pure
white flowers; *'Froyle Mill'* ♀ has dusky
violet flowers.

☀◐ ◊ ◊ ❉ ❉ ❉ *f*   **Perennial bulb**

↕↔ 15–20cm (6–8in)

LOBELIA ERINUS
'Lilac Fountain'

This trailing perennial, often grown as an annual bedding plant, is ideal for mixed container plantings, including hanging baskets. It bears a profusion of two-lipped, lilac-pink flowers throughout summer into autumn. The tiny leaves are dark green and bronzed. Plant out after the risk of frost has passed in spring. Many colourful trailing and non-trailing varieties exist.

ALSO RECOMMENDED: *Cascade Series have red, violet-blue, blue, pink, or white flowers.*

☼ ◐ ◊ ❄   **Perennial**
‡ 15cm (6in) ↔ 10–15cm (4–6in)

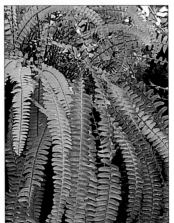

NEPHROLEPSIS CORDIFOLIA

The sword fern has long and arching, fishbone-like, bright green fronds, which will hang over the side of a pot or hanging basket. It makes an easy indoor, greenhouse, or conservatory plant, and it can be stood outdoors in summer. The fronds are evergreen and there are no flowers. Water sparingly in the cooler months. It needs an open compost, bark based or with added grit and leafmould.

ALSO RECOMMENDED: *N. exaltata* ♥ *is very similar.*

☼ ◐◊ ❄   **Perennial fern**
‡ 80cm (32in) ↔ 1.5m (5ft) or less

OPHIOPOGON JABURAN 'Vittatus'

White lilyturf is a grass-like plant with clumps of arching foliage. This variety has cream and yellow-striped leaves. Spikes of small white flowers appear in late summer and are followed by round blue-black fruits. Grow in an ericaceous or bark-based compost. In the garden, it can be used to edge a summer border; in mild areas it might survive winter. Grow in acid soil; it tolerates dry shade (*see pp.92, 261*).

ALSO RECOMMENDED. *O. planiscapus 'Nigrescens'* ♥ *is hardier with unusual black foliage.*

☼ ◑ ◊◊ ❈❈   **Perennial**

‡ 60cm (24in) ↔ 30cm (12in)

PAROCHETUS AFRICANUS ♥

The shamrock pea is an ideal winter-flowering trailing plant for a hanging basket in a frost-free greenhouse or conservatory. It is named for its pretty, trifoliate, clover-like leaves. The flowers are small and bright blue, borne from late autumn until late spring. Use a gritty compost.

☼ ◊◊ ❈   **Perennial**

‡ 10cm (4in) ↔ 60–100cm (24–39in)

PRIMULA *Polyanthus Group*

Polyanthus primulas are rosette-forming evergreens with colourful clusters of flat-faced flowers from late winter to early spring; they are available in an array of pastel and primary colours. These plants are splendid for containers, as well as in mixed plantings or on their own. Plant out in autumn. In the garden, they tolerate damp sites in shade (*see p.238*).

ALSO RECOMMENDED: *Cowichan Series have bronzed leaves and red, yellow, blue, or purple flowers; Crescendo Series have large flowers available in single colours.*

☼ ◐ ◊◊ ❀❀❀   **Perennial**
‡ 15cm (6in) ↔ 30cm (12in)

STRELITZIA REGINAE ♥

The crane flower is a clump-forming evergreen with long, paddle-shaped leaves. The exotic orange and purple flowers appear from winter to spring. Grow in a greenhouse or conservatory in sun or light shade (*see p.412*); in hot weather, provide plenty of ventilation and extra shade. Water freely and fertilize every month when in growth, and water sparingly in winter. Minimum temperature 10°C (50°F). Use a loam-based potting compost for preference.

ALSO RECOMMENDED: *'Humilis' is a dwarf form, reaching 80cm (32in) tall.*

☼ ◐ ◊   **Perennial**
‡ 2m (6ft) ↔ 1m (3ft)

VIOLA × WITTROCKIANA

Pansies are bushy, short-lived
perennials with bold and colourful
flowers. They make reliable, free-
flowering container or window box
plants if deadheaded regularly. Many
different selections exist, among them
offering a wide range of flower colours.
They also include pansies that have
been bred to flower in winter and early
spring; these are popular plants for
winter colour. In the garden, they are
tolerant of clay soils (*see p.12*).

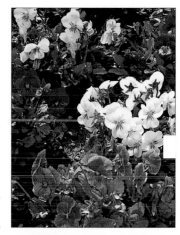

☼ ☼ ◐◊ ❋ ❋ ❋   **Perennial**

↕ 15–23cm (6–9in) ↔ 23–30cm (9–12in)

WOODWARDIA RADICANS ♈

The European chain fern is a tall,
architectural plant (*see p.472*) with
large and arching, dark green, feathery
fronds. It is evergreen. Best potted in a
bark-based compost with added grit
and leafmould. An impressive plant for
a large container. In the garden, site in
a damp, shady place near water. It
should survive outdoors over winter in
mild areas, otherwise mulch deeply
with straw and bracken. Tolerant of
clay soils (*see p.12*).

☼ ◊ ❋ ❋   **Perennial fern**

↕ 2m (6ft) ↔ 3m (10ft)

CALCEOLARIA
'Bright Bikinis'

Grown in containers, these calceolarias offer summer-long colour with their dense heads of slipper-like flowers in hot shades of yellow, orange and red. Provide shelter from wind, and water freely and apply a balanced fertilizer every month when in full growth. Raise from seeds sown late in late summer or early spring, preferably in a heated propagator. These plants can be used in mixed displays. Plant out once fear of frost has passed.

ALSO RECOMMENDED: *Anytime Series are early- and free-flowering and compact.*

☼ ◐ ◊ ❀ ❀　　　　　　**Biennial**
↕↔ 20cm (8in)

LUNARIA ANNUA

Honesty bears spires of red-purple flowers in late spring and summer, which later give rise to flat, oval, silvery seedheads. Raise plants from seeds sown early in summer and pot up in autumn. In the garden it also suits mixed borders and cottage gardens; the self-seeding habit makes it ideal for naturalizing in a woodland garden. The seedheads are popular for indoor arrangements, either fresh or dried (*see p.524*). It tolerates chalky soils (*see p.64*).

ALSO RECOMMENDED: *var.* albiflora ♀ *has white flowers;* 'Variegata' *has red-purple or purple flowers and white-variegated leaves.*

☼ ◐ ◊ ❀ ❀ ❀　　　　　　**Biennial**
↕ 90cm (36in) ↔ 30cm (12in)

IMPATIENS WALLERIANA
Swirl Series

These busy Lizzies are excellent annual bedding or container plants bearing long-lasting summer flowers. These are pink and orange with red petal margins. The oval leaves are light green. Many other types of busy Lizzies exist, in a wide range of pastel colours from white to orange, red, pink, and violet; there are also bicoloured forms. Plant out after the last frost, and give shelter from wind. They tolerate coastal sites (*see p.166*). Minimum temperature 10°C (50°F). Use alone or in mixed displays. Suitable for hanging baskets.

☀ ◖ **Annual**

‡ 15–20cm (6–8in) ↔ 60cm (24in)

NICOTIANA × SANDARAE
Domino Series

The abundant, flat-faced, fragrant flowers of these tobacco plants come in many shades, including white, yellow, lime green, pink, red, and purple. They are borne throughout summer and are excellent for containers or bedding in either sun or shade (*see p.412*). Plant out in spring only after the danger of frost has passed.

ALSO RECOMMENDED: *Havana Series are compact in pink and lime-green shades; Starship Series have pink, white, lime-green, or lilac flowers.*

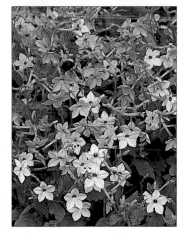

☀ ◑ ◖ ❄ *f* **Annual**

‡ 30–45cm (12–18in) ↔ 30cm (12in)

PLANTS FOR SHAPE & STRUCTURE

BY VIRTUE OF THEIR SIZE, and distinctive bold outlines, "architectural" plants are ranked among the star performers of the garden. In many cases, their sculptural beauty is not necessarily reliant on flowers, so they can often be guaranteed to provide an exceptionally long season of interest.

The elegant, tiered branching habit of *Cornus alternifolia* 'Argentea' (*see p.476*), for example, is exquisite when in full leaf, but it is almost equally beautiful when forming a

leafless tracery of branches against a winter sky. *Rhus tyhina* also forms a starkly elegant outline in winter, when it holds its stagshorn branches like an organic candelabra. The South American bamboo, *Chusquea couleou* (*see p.481*), forms an arching, fountain-like clump of glossy canes fringed with whiskery tufts of narrow leaves, which are as good to look at in the depths of winter as at the height of summer. Some architectural plants have other virtues, too: the cardoon (*see p.487*) has huge jagged, arching, silver-grey leaves and towering heads of thistle-like flowers, and *Eupatorium purpureum* (*see p.488*) has massive, flattened heads of tiny purple flowers – both deserve a place in any self-respecting wildlife garden. Their nectar-rich flowerheads are an invaluable, late-summer food source for butterflies and bees (*see p.494*).

DESIGN IDEAS

Many architectural plants really do deserve a spot in centre stage, and they are best used as stand-alone specimens. Examples include *Liriodendron tulipifera* 'Aureomarginata' (*see p.477*) on a clear sweep of fine turf, or *Magnolia campbellii* (*see p.478*) in an open glade in a woodland garden, distantly framed by other lower, less spectacular plants.

Spiky plants like cordyline (*see p.414*) and yucca (*see pp.215, 483*) can look fabulous set in a container on a sea of gravel; a flat surface of muted colour sets off a sharp outline to perfection. You can use such plants as a living exclamation mark to draw the gaze from several viewpoints. Yet others, such as the billowing *Macleaya microcarpa* 'Kelway's Coral Plume' (*see p.491*) or tall hollyhocks like *Alcea rosea* 'Nigra' (*see p.493*), with slender, long-lived spires of almost black flowers, can be used as focal points in beds and borders. Their height and strong vertical outline stand out from lower, more horizontally spreading plants and draw the eye into and along the design.

CARE AND CULTIVATION

If architectural plants are to give of their best, they do need to be grown well. Before choosing, check each plant's individual cultivation requirements and then adhere to them closely. These plants will probably perform poorly in less-than-ideal sites. Apart from that, all they require is a little imagination in seeking a site that will display their ornamental virtues to their full potential.

ARAUCARIA ARAUCANA

The monkey puzzle is an unmistakeable, umbrella-shaped tree, forming a perfectly dome-shaped shrub when young. As it grows, it gradually loses its lower branches, which are in whorls around the dark grey-brown trunk. The sharply pointed leaves are very tough and scale-like, bright at first, then deepening to dark green; they persist for up to ten years. It is slow to reach maturity. No pruning is necessary.

☼ ◑◑ ❀❀❀   **Evergreen tree**
‡ 15–20m (50–70ft) ↔ 7–10m (22–30ft)

BETULA PENDULA *'Tristis'* ♀

This silver birch is an elegant tree for a reasonably small garden. It has a narrow shape with drooping branchlets and attractive white bark on the trunk. Yellow-brown male catkins appear in early spring before the triangular green leaves, which turn golden yellow in autumn. It tolerates sandy, chalky, and acid soils (*see pp.38, 64, 92*). Prune in late winter, if necessary.

ALSO RECOMMENDED: *The trunk base of B. pendula ♀ becomes fissured with age; 'Laciniata' ♀ has deeply cut leaves and strongly pendent branchlets; 'Youngii' ♀ is much shorter, dome-shaped, and weeping.*

☼ ◐ ❀❀❀   **Deciduous tree**
‡ 25m (80ft) ↔ 10m (30ft)

CATALPA BIGNONIOIDES ♥

The Indian bean tree forms a fine, spreading canopy of large and handsome, heart-shaped, mid-green leaves. Upright clusters of white flowers appear in summer, followed by long and slender, bean-like pods, which persist through winter. It tolerates clay and chalky soils (*see pp.12, 64*). Choose a sheltered site and protect young plants from frost. Branches can be pruned back heavily when dormant, to create a compact shape.

ALSO RECOMMENDED: *'Aurea'* ♥ *has bright yellow foliage and is less vigorous.*

☼ ◐◑ ✳ ✳ ✳   **Deciduous tree**
‡↔ 15m (50ft)

CEDRUS DEODARA *'Aurea'* ♥

This slow-growing, dwarf form of the deodar cedar is a conical conifer with spreading branches covered in golden yellow needles, which become greener with age. The drooping shoot tips give the tree a shaggy appearance. The bark is very dark brown, and upright cones appear on the branches. Tolerant of exposure and hot, dry sites (*see pp.118, 190*). Little pruning is necessary.

ALSO RECOMMENDED: C. deodara ♥ *and* C. libani ♥, *the cedar of Lebanon, are for large gardens only.*

☼ ◊ ✳ ✳ ✳   **Evergreen tree**
‡↔ 5m (15ft)

CORNUS ALTERNIFOLIA
'Argentea' ♀

With spreading, tiered branches clothed in elliptical, white-margined green leaves, this dogwood makes an irresistibly elegant specimen in woodland or other sheltered sites. The leaves turn red and purple in autumn. Its light canopy allows for an underplanting of spring-flowering bulbs. Keep pruning to a minimum.

ALSO RECOMMENDED: *C. alternifolia has plain dark green leaves*; C. controversa *'Variegata' ♀ has white-margined leaves.*

☼ ◐ ◊ ❄ ❄ ❄   **Deciduous tree**
↕↔ 6m (20ft)

CORYLUS AVELLANA
'Contorta' ♀

The corkscrew hazel has strongly twisted shoots, which are striking in winter. Later in this season, the display is enhanced with the appearance of pale yellow catkins. The mid-green leaves are almost circular and jaggedly toothed. Thin out congested branches in late winter; these can be displayed indoors (*see p.524*). The autumn nuts attract wildlife (*see p.494*).

ALSO RECOMMENDED: *'Aurea' has straight shoots and bright yellow then yellow-green foliage*; C. maxima *'Purpurea' ♀ (see p.141).*

☼ ◐ ◊ ❄ ❄ ❄   **Deciduous tree**
↕↔ 5m (15ft)

LARIX DECIDUA ♀

Unlike most conifers, the European
larch sheds its soft, pale green needles
in winter, fading to straw yellow
beforehand. It has a conical shape with
a spreading crown and smooth, scaly
grey bark. Small, rounded cones appear
in spring, and they usually persist on
the branches. A useful, easily grown
specimen tree that tolerates a wide
range of conditions.

ALSO RECOMMENDED: L. kaempferi ♀,
the Japanese larch, is very similar.

☼ ◊ ✱ ✱ ✱   **Deciduous tree**
↕ 30m (100ft) ↔ 4–6m (12–20ft)

LIRIODENDRON TULIPIFERA
'Aureomarginata' ♀

This tulip tree makes a stately and
elegant specimen. The columnar crown
of distinctive, saddle-shaped leaves with
broad, golden yellow margins turns
yellow in autumn. Cupped, orange-
banded, pale green flowers may appear
in midsummer. Plant young saplings
and allow them to grow undisturbed.
Keep pruning to a minimum.

ALSO RECOMMENDED: L. tulipifera ♀ *is
taller with plain green leaves;* 'Fastigiatum' ♀
is narrowly conical with upright branches.

☼ ☼ ◊◊ ✱ ✱ ✱   **Deciduous tree**
↕ 20m (70ft) ↔ 10m (30ft)

MAGNOLIA CAMPBELLII

This vigorous tree magnolia becomes increasingly picturesque as it spreads with age. It has long, narrow leaves, and after 25 years or so bears its waxy, "cup-and-saucer-shaped", white, rose-pink, or crimson flowers on its bare branches in late winter and early spring. Mulch with leafmould in spring and shelter the early flowers from frost and strong winds. Keep pruning to a minimum.

ALSO RECOMMENDED: *For specimens that flower on younger plants, grow* M. × loebneri *'Leonard Messel'* ♀, *a small tree with pale pink flowers, or* M. × soulangeana (*see p.15*).

☀ ◐ ◊◊ ❀❀❀ **Deciduous tree**
‡ 15m (50ft) ↔ 10m (30ft)

PAULOWNIA TOMENTOSA ♀

The foxglove tree is named for its fragrant, trumpet-shaped, pinkish lilac flowers, which may appear in late spring. The large, heart-shaped, bright green leaves make this an excellent shade tree. It is fast-growing, and if pruned back hard each winter, it will give especially big leaves on smaller, shrubby plants. It tolerates urban pollution and chalky soils (*see p.64*), but choose a site sheltered from cold, drying winds. It flowers best in areas with long, hot summers; light brown seed capsules follow.

☀ ◊ ❀❀ *f* **Deciduous tree**
‡ 12m (40ft) ↔ 10m (30ft)

PICEA OMORIKA ♀

The Serbian spruce is a narrow, spire-like tree, popular as a landscape tree in large gardens. Its branches hang downwards, curving back up at the tips, and are clothed with dense, dark blue-green needles and the occasional hanging, red-brown cone. It copes with a range of soils, from chalk to acid (*see pp.64, 92*).

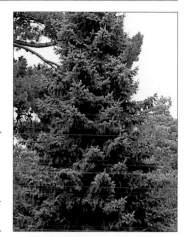

ALSO RECOMMENDED: P. abies *'Ohlendorffii' (see p.106); P. glauca 'Conica' ♀ is a compact, conical shrub; P. mariana 'Nana' ♀ (see p.423); P. pungens 'Koster' ♀ is a silvery blue tree with horizontal branches.*

☼ ◊ ❀❀❀   **Evergreen tree**
‡ 20m (70ft) ↔ 2–3m (6–10ft)

PRUNUS 'Kiku-shidare-zakura' ♀

Also sold as 'Cheal's Weeping', this small cherry tree is grown for its weeping branches and clear pink spring blossom. This appears with or before the mid-green leaves, which are flushed bronze when young. Ideal for a small garden. Prune after flowering, if necessary, and remove any shoots growing from the bare trunk as they appear. It tolerates chalky soils (*see p.64*).

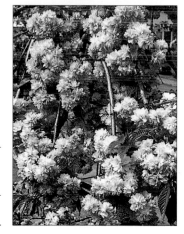

ALSO RECOMMENDED: *'Spire' ♀ is taller, to 10m (30ft), and cone- to vase-shaped; P. serrula ♀ has glossy, mahogany-red bark and white spring blossom.*

☼ ◊◊ ❀❀❀   **Deciduous tree**
‡↔ 3m (10ft)

TRACHYCARPUS FORTUNEI ♡

The chusan palm is one of the hardiest palm trees. It has a single, upright stem with a head of fan-shaped, dark green leaves with many pointed lobes. Small yellow flowers may appear in large, hanging clusters in early summer, followed by small, round black berries on female plants. Ideal for a small space in a warm, sheltered spot, but may not survive in cold areas. It will grow in a large container (*see p.412*).

☼ ◊ ❀ ❀   **Evergreen palm**
‡ 20m (70ft) ↔ 2.5m (8ft)

ZELKOVA SERRATA ♡

The Japanese zelkova is an imposing, elm-like tree for larger gardens only. It has a spreading habit with smooth grey, peeling bark. The narrow, toothed, dark green foliage gives good autumn colour when it turns to yellow, orange, or red. Choose a site sheltered from cold, drying winds.

ALSO RECOMMENDED: *'Goblin' is a dwarf, bushy shrub, to 1m (3ft) tall and wide.*

☼ ☀ ◊◊ ❀ ❀ ❀   **Deciduous tree**
‡ 30m (100ft) ↔ 25m (80ft)

CHUSQUEA CULEOU ♀

This is among the most graceful of bamboos, forming an elegant, fountain-like clump of whiskered, glossy olive-green canes with papery white leaf sheaths. The narrow leaves are subtly chequered and mid-green. It is a perfect specimen for a woodland garden, but provide ample space, so its graceful habit can develop fully. Alternatively, confine the roots with slates or metal plates sunk into the soil. Shelter from strong and cold winds.

☼ ☀ ◊ ✽ ✽ ✽　　**Evergreen bamboo**

↕ 6m (20ft) ↔ 2.5m (8ft) or more

ERIOBOTRYA JAPONICA ♀

The loquat is a vigorous, easily grown shrub with stout shoots and large and leathery, downward-curving leaves. They are glossy dark green and deeply veined. In cold areas, it needs the protection of a sheltered, sunny wall (*see p.280*) or cool conservatory. Open clusters of fragrant white flowers appear from autumn to winter, followed by rounded, orange-yellow, ornamental fruits in spring. Keep it compact by pruning once the fruiting display is over.

☼ ◊ ✽ ✽ *f*　　**Evergreen shrub**

↕↔ 8m (25ft)

EUPHORBIA CHARACIAS

A dramatic, blue-green bush that bears large, rounded heads of dark-eyed, pale yellow-green flowers at the tips of the upright stems in spring and early summer. It is ideal for long-lasting colour in a spacious, Mediterranean-style garden. Shelter from cold winds and heavy frosts. Cut back to the base in autumn; wear gloves as the milky sap can irritate skin. It suits sandy soils (*see p.38*), and coastal and hot, dry sites (*see pp.166, 190*).

ALSO RECOMMENDED: *subsp.* wulfenii ♀ *and its cultivars* 'John Tomlinson' ♀ *and* 'Lambrook Gold' ♀ *are similar.*

☀ ◊ ❄❄　　　　　　**Evergreen shrub**
↕↔ 1.2m (4ft)

RHUS GLABRA

The scarlet sumach is a suckering shrub with large, divided, shining blue-green leaves, which blaze rich red in autumn; colour is best in full sun. In summer, it produces large clusters of yellow-green flowers; these give rise to flame-shaped, winter-persistent clusters of red fruits on female plants only. It is an ideal specimen for a shrub or mixed border. Keep pruning to a minimum.

ALSO RECOMMENDED: R. typhina ♀ *is reliable and even more elegant with orange-red autumn colour;* 'Dissecta' ♀ *has finely cut leaves.*

☀ ◊ ❄❄❄　　　　　**Deciduous shrub**
↕↔ 2.5m (8ft)

TROCHODENDRON ARALIOIDES

This large, bushy plant is sometimes known as the wheel tree for its spirally arranged, handsome foliage. Clusters of unusual, vivid green flowers appear in late spring and early summer at the shoot tips. The dark green leaves have a leathery texture, and the bark is aromatic. It is suitable for a woodland garden or among other shrubs and trees, in a site sheltered from cold, drying winds. It tolerates acid soils (*see p.92*) and may suffer in heavy frosts. Remove badly placed growth in spring.

☀️◐ ◊◊ ❄❄   **Evergreen shrub**
‡ 10m (30ft) ↔ 8m (25ft)

YUCCA FILAMENTOSA *'Bright Edge'* ♀

An almost stemless plant with basal rosettes of rigid, lance-shaped, dark green leaves, to 75cm (30in) long, with broad yellow margins. Nodding, bell-shaped white flowers, on spires to 2m (6ft) or more tall, are borne in the second half of summer; remove old flower stems at the end of the season. It is good in a border or courtyard, and suits coastal and hot, dry sites (*see pp.166, 190*), and sandy soils (*see p.38*). Provide a winter mulch in frosty areas.

ALSO RECOMMENDED: *'Variegata'* ♀ has white margins; Y. whipplei (see p.215).

☀️ ◊ ❄❄   **Evergreen shrub**
‡ 75cm (30in) ↔ 1.5m (5ft)

ACANTHUS MOLLIS

Bear's breeches is a striking border plant, forming mounds of arching, deeply lobed, glossy dark green leaves. In summer, spires of two-lipped white flowers with purple-shaded bracts rise well above the foliage, persisting as equally attractive seedheads. It is good as ground cover in sun or dry, partial shade (*see pp.216, 304, 326*).

ALSO RECOMMENDED: *Latifolius Group have broader, conspicuously veined leaves;* A. spinosus ♥ *has spiny, deeply cut leaves.*

☼ ◑ ◊ ❀ ❀ ❀   **Perennial**
‡ 1.5m (5ft) ↔ 90cm (36in)

ACIPHYLLA AUREA

This clump-forming plant bears its majestic spikes of tiny, golden brown flowers with spiny bracts from early to late summer, but it must have a mild, sunny climate to do so. The narrow, greyish leaves with bold yellow edges and midribs have sharp, terminal spines, so site with care. A superb specimen for a gravel garden. It resents root disturbance, so set out plants when they are young and small.

ALSO RECOMMENDED: *A. pinnatifida has bronzed, dark green leaves.*

☼ ◊ ❀ ❀ ❀   **Perennial**
‡↔ 1m (3ft)

ANGELICA ARCHANGELICA

This short-lived perennial forms clumps of large and divided, glossy green, very aromatic leaves. In its second summer, it produces huge, rounded heads of greenish yellow flowers on sturdy, ridged stems. Grow in a mixed or herbaceous border. It will self-seed if conditions suit; thin out seedlings as necessary, or transplant when small.

ALSO RECOMMENDED: A. gigas *has dark purple flowers on dark red stems;* A. sylvestris *has white or pale pink flowers and is suitable for a wild garden.*

☼ ☼ ◑ ◊ ❄ ❄ ❄ *f*   **Perennial**
↕ 2m (6ft) ↔ 1.2m (4ft)

BESCHORNERIA YUCCOIDES ♛

This fleshy plant forms an impressive rosette of strap-shaped, grey-green leaves at ground level, and a tall, red, yellow, or orange flower spike emerges from the centre of the rosette in summer. It is a good plant for a Mediterranean-style or gravel garden, or against a sunny, sheltered wall; in frost-prone climates, it grows better in a large container (*see p.412*), as it can be moved into a cool conservatory or greenhouse in winter. It must have sharply drained soil.

☼ ◊ ❄   **Perennial**
↕ 1.5m (5ft) ↔ 1m (3ft) or more

CANNA *'King Midas'*

This Indian shot plant is an upright perennial with a single, cane-like stem clothed with large, oval, dark green leaves. It is topped by golden yellow flowers from midsummer to early autumn. Its colour and stature make it popular in summer bedding (*see p.412*). Where winters are frosty, lift plants in late autumn and store over winter in a cool, frost-free place in barely moist compost. Replant in late spring. Hundreds of colourful varieties exist.

ALSO RECOMMENDED: *'Assaut'* (see p.431); *'Endeavour' has red flowers;* C. indica *has bright red or soft orange flowers.*

☼ ◊ ❄   **Perennial**
↕ 1.5m (5ft) ↔ 50cm (20in)

CIRSIUM RIVULARE *'Atropurpureum'*

The thistle-like, deep crimson flowerheads of this clump-forming plant arise on pale, branched stems in the first half of summer. They are held well above the prickly, divided, dark green foliage. It is excellent in a mixed or herbaceous border, or in a meadow garden. Remove dead flowerheads to prevent nuisance self-seeding; the flowers can be cut for indoor arrangements (*see p.524*).

ALSO RECOMMENDED: C. japonicum *'Rose Beauty' has carmine-red flowerheads; those of 'Pink Beauty' are rose-pink.*

☼ ◊ ❄ ❄ ❄   **Perennial**
↕ 1.2m (4ft) ↔ 60cm (24in)

CORTADERIA SELLOANA
'Sunningdale Silver' ♛

This evergreen pampas grass forms
huge, weather-resistant clumps of
arching, sharp-edged leaf blades, and
silvery flower plumes in late summer.
Cut out any dead foliage with the
previous year's flower plumes in late
winter – wear gloves to protect your
hands. It tolerates sandy and chalky soils
(*see pp.38, 64*), and exposed, coastal,
and hot, dry sites (*see pp.118, 166, 190*).

ALSO RECOMMENDED. *Aureolineata' ♛
(syn. 'Gold Band') is shorter with yellow-
margined leaves; 'Pumila' ♛ is shorter still
with silvery yellow plumes.*

☼ ◐ ❄❄   **Perennial**

‡ 3m (10ft) or more ↔ 2.5m (8ft)

CYNARA CARDUNCULUS ♛

The cardoon forms a sculptural mound
of arching, deeply divided, silvery
grey leaves. It is topped, in mid- to
late summer, by stout, grey, woolly-
stemmed, thistle-like purple flowerheads;
these attract bees and butterflies and
are useful in dried flower arrangements
(*see pp.494, 524*). It makes a fine focal
point in a mixed or herbaceous border
with shelter from strong winds. The
leaf stalks are edible when blanched.
Prepare them like asparagus.

ALSO RECOMMENDED: *The flowerheads
of Scolymus Group, the globe artichoke,
are edible in bud.*

☼ ◐ ❄❄❄   **Perennial**

‡ 1.5m (5ft) ↔ 1.2m (4ft)

DICKSONIA ANTARCTICA 🏆

This tree fern has a very fibrous, upright trunk topped by an umbrella of very large, feathery, bright green fronds. Each one can measure up to 3m (10ft) long, and as they age, they turn to dark green. A fine specimen for a sheltered, damp and shady spot (*see p.238*), but it will survive winters in mild climates only; elsewhere, grow it in a large container in a cool, north-facing greenhouse or conservatory (*see p.448*). Grow in acid soil (*see p.92*) and hose the trunk down in hot weather. There are no flowers, and it is very slow-growing.

☼ ◐ ◊ ❋ ❋   **Perennial fern**
↕ 3m (10ft) ↔ 4m (12ft)

EUPATORIUM PURPUREUM

Joe Pye weed is a versatile plant, at home in clay, chalky, or permanently moist soils (*see pp.12, 64, 372*), in a border or woodland garden. Stiff, upright stems clothed in purple-tinged leaves are topped with domed, fluffy heads of tiny pink, purple, or white flowers in summer and autumn; they are very attractive to bees and butterflies (*see p.494*).

ALSO RECOMMENDED: E. cannabinum *has flat-topped heads of pink, purple, or white flowers*

☼ ◐ ◊◊ ❋ ❋ ❋   **Perennial**
↕ 2.2m (7ft) ↔ 1m (3ft)

FERULA COMMUNIS

The giant fennel is a fine foliage plant. It grows strongly to produce a mass of finely divided, light green foliage. After several years, the plant may finally flower in the first half of summer when many globular clusters of tiny yellow flowers are borne on a tall, stout stem. The plant sometimes dies after seeding. Grow it in a warm, sheltered site at the back of a border or as a specimen plant; provide a dry, bracken mulch during winter. This is not the culinary fennel (*Foeniculum*).

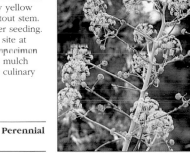

☼ ◊ ❄ ❄ *f*　　　　　　　**Perennial**

↕ 2–3m (6–10ft) ↔ 60cm (24in)

GLADIOLUS COMMUNIS *SUSBP.* BYZANTINUS ♈

In late spring, this elegant, upright plant gives a blaze of magenta flowers. These are arranged in spikes above fans of narrow leaves. It is ideal for a border, and the flowers are good for cutting (*see p.524*). Plant corms in spring on a bed of sharp sand to improve drainage. In frosty climates, they will not need lifting over winter as long as a deep mulch is applied in autumn. It tolerates clay and chalky soils (*see pp.12, 64*), and hot, dry sites (*see p.190*).

ALSO RECOMMENDED: G. papilio ♈ *is less hardy, with yellowish flowers.*

☼ ◊ ❄ ❄ ❄　　　　　　**Perennial corm**

↕ 1m (3ft) ↔ 8cm (3in)

HOSTA SIEBOLDIANA VAR. ELEGANS ♥

Also sold as 'Elegans' or 'Robusta', this hosta forms grey-blue clumps of broad, heart-shaped, puckered foliage, giving an architectural quality. It is suitable as ground cover in damp, shady places (*see pp.238, 326*) and tolerates clay and moist soils (*see pp.12, 372*). Pale lilac-grey flowers appear in early summer. It will also grow in a container (*see p.448*).

ALSO RECOMMENDED: *'Birchwood Parky's Gold'* (see p.318); *'Frances Williams'* ♥ (see p.381); *'Halcyon'* ♥ (see p.340); *'Shade Fanfare'* ♥ (see p.465); *'Wide Brim'* ♥ (see p.254); H. ventricosa ♥ (see p.30).

☀◐ ◊ ❀❀❀   **Perennial**
↕ 1m (3ft) ↔ 1.2m (4ft)

LILIUM CANDIDUM ♥

The Madonna lily has upright stems, each bearing up to 20 highly fragrant, trumpet-shaped, pure white flowers in midsummer. They are good for cutting (*see p.524*). The leaves are lance-shaped and glossy. Grow in neutral to alkaline soils (*see p.64*) in full sun with the base in shade. It is also suitable for hot, dry sites (*see p.190*). Plant bulbs just below the soil surface in winter, unlike other lilies, which are planted deeper.

ALSO RECOMMENDED: L. martagon *has rich pink, turkscap flowers*; L. regale ♥ (see p.433); L. superbum ♥ (see p.113).

☀ ◊ ❀❀❀❀ *f*   **Perennial bulb**
↕ 1–2m (3–6ft)

MACLEAYA MICROCARPA *'Kelway's Coral Plume'* ♥

This clump-forming perennial is grown
for its foliage and graceful plumes of
tiny, coral pink to buff flowers. These
open from pink buds in early and
midsummer, above large, olive-green
leaves. Grow in a mixed or herbaceous
border with shelter from strong
winds, confine to bounds by chopping
away excess roots from the margins, as
necessary. It tolerates clay soils (*see p.12*).

ALSO RECOMMENDED: *M. cordata* ♥
*has buff-white flowers, 'Flamingo' has
pink buds and buff-pink flowers.*

☼☀ ◊◊ ❄❄❄ **Perennial**
‡ 2.2m (7ft) ↔ 1m (3ft) or more

MUSA BASJOO

The Japanese banana is hardier than
most and produces several slender,
arching green leaves over 2m (6ft) long.
A large brown flower spike may appear
in summer from the centre of the plant.
Greenish bananas may develop, which
are small and inedible. This exotic plant
must have a sheltered site as strong
winds will shred the leaves. Grow as
a specimen or as part of a summer
border; in autumn, provide a thick
mulch in mild areas or pot it up
and overwinter under glass.

☼ ◊◊ ❄❄ **Perennial**
‡ 5m (15ft) ↔ 4m (12ft)

PLEIOBLASTUS AURICOMUS ♥

This upright bamboo forms an evergreen screen of brilliant green, yellow-striped foliage. The bristly edged, lance-shaped leaves are carried on purple-green canes. Plant in an open glade in a woodland garden, or against a backdrop of trees or tall shrubs. Provide shelter from cold, drying winds, and thin overcrowded clumps in late spring. To confine its invasive spread, bury a barrier around the roots.

ALSO RECOMMENDED: *P. variegatus* ♥ *is shorter, to 75cm (30in) tall, with cream- and green-striped leaves.*

☼ ◊◊ ❀❀❀   **Perennial bamboo**
↕↔ 1.5m (5ft)

POLYSTICHUM MUNITUM ♥

The sword fern, with its evergreen shuttlecocks of leathery, dark green fronds is an attractive specimen plant for a damp or dry, shady border (*see pp.216, 238*). The spiny-toothed leaf segments add to its spiky, hard-edged appearance. Remove old fronds as new ones unfurl in spring. It can be pot-grown (*see p.412*).

ALSO RECOMMENDED: *P. aculeatum* ♥ *is similar, with prickly, dark green fronds;* P. setiferum *Divisilobum Group (see p.258).*

☼☀ ◊ ❀❀❀   **Perennial fern**
↕ 90cm (36in) ↔ 1.2m (4ft)

ALCEA ROSEA *'Nigra'*

This is the darkest-flowered of all the hollyhocks, bearing impressive spires of funnel-shaped, chocolate-maroon flowers in early and midsummer. These rise above a mound of crinkled, lobed, light green leaves. Indispensable in a cottage garden, it looks good at the back of a herbaceous border. Hollyhocks can be raised from seed and come in white, pink, purple, yellow, and red shades, with double or single flowers. Those with single flowers are most attractive to bees and butterflies (*see p.494*).

☼ ◊ ❀ ❀ ❀   **Biennial**

‡ 1.5–2.5m (5–8ft) ↔ 60cm (24in)

AMARANTHUS TRICOLOR *'Illumination'*

Chinese spinach is a fast-growing, upright and bushy bedding plant grown for its brightly coloured foliage. The upper leaves are brilliant rose red topped with gold, and the lower leaves are copper-brown. The flowers are insignificant. Choose a sheltered site. It can also be container-grown (*see p.412*).

ALSO RECOMMENDED: *'Flaming Fountains' has narrow, red and bronze leaves; 'Joseph's Coat' has red, green, yellow, and brown lower leaves.*

☼ ◊ ❀   **Annual**

‡ 45cm (18in) ↔ 30–45cm (12–18in)

PLANTS FOR WILDLIFE GARDENS

PLANTING FOR WILDLIFE conjures a picture of chaotic, jungle-like plantings, which only the most committed of enthusiasts could tolerate. Wild creatures, however, don't pass judgement on style – their primary concerns are food, water, and shelter – so even those who garden in a more formal, tidy manner can provide a valuable haven for birds, mammals, and insects.

To attract wildlife into your garden, grow a diversity of native species; these include several so-called weeds, but remember that many of these are essential food for emerging caterpillars of butterflies and moths. You will be able to observe wild creatures at close quarters, and enjoy the feel-good factor that derives from playing a small part in their conservation. A healthy wildlife population also helps with pest control; blue-tits pick off aphids, while many birds winkle out soil pests from upturned earth. Hedgehogs, toads, and frogs consume large quantities of slugs, while lacewings, ladybirds, and hoverflies have young that eat aphids and other sap-sucking pests. Wildlife gardeners seldom use chemical pest controls because of the risks it carries to wild creatures, but once a wildlife garden is established, chemical controls are seldom needed. Infestations of pests hardly ever reach damaging levels when controlled by predatory insects and birds.

ATTRACTING WILDLIFE

Bring beneficial insects into the garden by planting plenty of colourful, nectar-rich flowers, like *Melissa officinalis* 'Aurea' (*see p.516*) or *Buddleja davidii* 'Empire Blue' (*see p.500*). Other inviting flowers include nearly all daisy-like blooms and those with two-lipped flowers, such as *Hyssopus officinalis* (*see p.504*). Aim to provide a nectar supply from early spring onwards; bees particularly need access to a source of nectar and pollen when they emerge from hibernation. To help, plant spring flowers like snowdrops (*see p.231*) and pulmonarias (*see pp.34, 344*).

A shrub border provides good shelter for nesting and can lend cover for birds that come to feed at the bird table. Choose autumn-fruiting shrubs that bear fruits in autumn to ensure that birds are well fed in winter. Red fruits, like those of *Sorbus commixta* (*see p.499*) and *Rosa rugosa* (*see p.178*), are almost always the birds' first choice, so choose some of other colours too. Birds take yellow, white, or purple berries sooner or later, especially in hard winters, but you will at least get some pleasure from them before they are consumed. Grow thistle-like plants and grasses, like *Stipa tenuissima* (*see p.521*), for seed-eating birds; they also like the seedheads of perennials, so delay tidying the border until early spring.

A garden pond is the single most important feature for attracting wildlife (*see p.394*). Make the sides slope gently so that animals can get down easily to drink and bathe, and they can escape if they fall in. Also provide log piles nearby in out-of-the-way places as a home for hibernating toads and hedgehogs.

ABIES KOREANA

The Korean fir is a dense, conical tree with shiny dark green leaves, which are silver beneath. It bears very ornamental, violet-blue cones, even on very young trees. A superb architectural specimen tree (*see p.472*) that lends good cover for birds; owls often use the uppermost branches as a viewpoint when hunting and finches may extract seeds from the cones. Grow in neutral to slightly acid soil; it tolerates clay (*see pp.12, 92*). Shelter from cold, drying winds. Little pruning is necessary.

ALSO RECOMMENDED: *'Silberlocke'* ♀ *has twisted leaves with pale silvery undersides.*

☼ ◊ ❀❀❀ **Evergreen tree**
‡ 10m (30ft) ↔ 6m (20ft)

ACER CAMPESTRE ♀

The field maple is a small tree with lobed leaves, which are red when young, then dark green, turning yellow and red in autumn. The green flowers give rise to winged fruits, and these are a food source for small animals. It makes excellent hedging (*see p.138*), providing a good nesting site for birds; trim hedges in winter. Tolerant of chalky soils (*see p.64*).

ALSO RECOMMENDED: *'Postelense' has red-stalked, golden yellow leaves.*

☼ ◊ ❀❀❀ **Deciduous tree**
‡ 8m (25ft) ↔ 4m (12ft)

ILEX × ALTACLERENSIS *'Golden King'* ♔

A shrubby holly that has glossy dark green leaves edged with gold; their margins may be smooth or toothed. Red berries develop in autumn if a male plant is nearby; these are a food source for birds. It tolerates urban pollution and coastal sites, making a good windbreak or impenetrable hedge where winters are not too severe (*see pp.118, 130, 166*). Trim or prune in spring, as necessary.

ALSO RECOMMENDED: *'Camelliifolia'* ♔ *has plain, dark green leaves*; *Lawsoniana* ♔ *has gold splashed leaves*; I. aquifolium *'Golden van Tol'* (*see p.154*).

☼ ◐ ◊ ❈ ❈ ❈   **Evergreen tree**

↕ 6m (20ft) ↔ 4m (12ft)

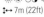

MALUS *'Professor Sprenger'*

This round-headed tree is very attractive to wildlife. In spring, its pink buds hum with bees as they open to fragrant white flowers, and the amber crab apples that follow will be consumed by birds, especially in hard winters. The leaves turn gold in late autumn. It will grow in any but waterlogged soil, including those rich in clay and chalk (*see pp.12, 64*). Remove crossing branches in winter when young to form an open crown; older trees need little pruning.

ALSO RECOMMENDED: *'Evereste'* ♔ *has red-orange fruits*; *'John Downie'* ♔ (*see p.16*); *'Red Sentinel'* ♔ *has glossy dark red fruits.*

☼ ◐ ◊◊ ❈ ❈ ❈   **Deciduous tree**

↕↔ 7m (22ft)

PHOTINIA DAVIDIANA

This upright tree has lance-shaped, dark green leaves; the old ones turn red before they fall – at any time of year – especially in autumn. In midsummer, it bears clusters of small, rather ill-scented white flowers, which attract beneficial insects. Matt bright red fruits follow. Grow in a shrub border or on its own as a specimen.

ALSO RECOMMENDED: P. *'Redstart'* ♥ *is smaller, with bronze-red young leaves and orange-red fruits; P. serratifolia has red young leaves and scarlet fruits.*

☼ ☀ ◊◊ ❀❀❀   **Evergreen tree**
↕ 8m (25ft) ↔ 6m (20ft)

PRUNUS PADUS

The bird cherry is a spreading, often multi-stemmed tree with dark green leaves, which turn red or yellow in autumn. In late spring, it bears hanging clusters of small, fragrant white flowers, attractive to pollinating insects. The small, pea-like black cherries that follow are readily consumed by birds. Keep pruning to a minimum, in midsummer if necessary.

ALSO RECOMMENDED: *'Albertii' is free-flowering; 'Colorata'* ♥ *has red-purple young foliage and pink flowers; P. laurocerasus* ♥ *is a dense, evergreen shrub.*

☼ ☀ ◊ ❀❀❀   **Deciduous tree**
↕ 15m (50ft) ↔ 10m (30ft)

SORBUS ARIA *'Lutescens'* ♈

This compact whitebeam forms a beautiful specimen tree, tolerating a range of conditions, including clay and chalky soils (*see pp.12, 64*). The broad and toothed leaves are silvery grey and turn russet and gold in autumn. Clusters of white spring flowers are followed by dark red berries, which are a food source for birds. It also suits exposed, city, or coastal gardens (*see pp.118, 166*). Remove any dead wood in summer.

ALSO RECOMMENDED: *'Magnifica' has larger, glossier leaves; 'Majestica'* ♈ *is taller with larger leaves.*

☼ ☀ ◊◔ ❀ ❀ ❀   **Deciduous tree**
‡ 10m (30ft) ↔ 8m (25ft)

SORBUS COMMIXTA

The Japanese rowan is a small, conical tree with finely divided, dark green leaves, which flush yellow, red, and purple in autumn. In late spring, it produces broad clusters of white flowers followed by an abundance of orange-red or red berries. These are eaten by birds, especially mistle thrushes and blackbirds. Keep pruning to a minimum. It tolerates exposed sites (*see p.118*).

ALSO RECOMMENDED: S. aucuparia (see p.126); S. sargentiana ♈ *bears bright red berries in profusion.*

☼ ☀ ◊◔ ❀ ❀ ❀   **Deciduous tree**
‡ 10m (30ft) ↔ 7m (22ft)

BERBERIS DICTYOPHYLLA ♀

This upright shrub has white-bloomed shoots clothed in spiny leaves, which turn red in autumn. The pale yellow flowers of late spring form a valuable nectar source for bees; they later give rise to red fruits favoured by birds. It tolerates chalk and clay soils, and coastal and urban sites (*see pp.12, 64, 166*). Thin out dense growth in winter.

ALSO RECOMMENDED: B. julianae (*see p.146*); B. × stenophylla *'Corallina Compacta'* ♀ (*see p.127*); B. thunbergii *'Dart's Red Lady'* (*see p.147*).

☼ ◊◔ ❋ ❋ ❋　　　　**Deciduous shrub**

↕ 2m (6ft) ↔ 1.5m (5ft)

BUDDLEJA DAVIDII *'Empire Blue'* ♀

The arching flower spikes of all *B. davidii* cultivars attract a profusion of butterflies and other pollinating insects in summer and autumn. This one has violet-blue flowers. All are fast-growing, arching shrubs with greyish green leaves. Prune back hard to a woody framework in spring for the best foliage and flowers. It tolerates chalky soils and exposed sites (*see pp.64, 118*).

ALSO RECOMMENDED: *'Black Knight'* ♀ *has dark purple-blue flowers; 'Royal Red'* ♀ *has red-purple flowers; 'White Profusion'* ♀ *has white flowers.*

☼ ◊ ❋ ❋ ❋ *f*　　　　**Deciduous shrub**

↕ 3m (10ft) ↔ 5m (15ft)

CARYOPTERIS ✕ CLANDONENSIS *'Kew Blue'*

This upright shrub has dark grey-green leaves and, in late summer and early autumn, dense clusters of dark blue flowers. As well as lending late colour to the border, they provide a useful nectar source for pollinating insects. Cut all stems back to low buds in late spring. It tolerates chalky soils and hot, dry sites (*see pp.64, 190*).

ALSO RECOMMENDED: *'Heavenly Blue'* ♥ is similar; *'Worcester Gold'* has yellow leaves and lavender-blue flowers.

☼ ◊ ❀ ❀ ❀   **Deciduous shrub**
‡ 1m (3ft) ↔ 1.5m (5ft)

CLERODENDRUM TRICHOTOMUM

This upright shrub with dark green leaves is valued for its large, sweetly fragrant clusters of white flowers, which appear in the leaf axils from late summer to autumn. Each flower is surrounded by a ring of pinkish red sepals. Like the shiny blue berries that follow, the flowers make quite a display. Good in a border where it will attract beneficial insects. Prune in early spring, if necessary.

ALSO RECOMMENDED: *var.* fargesii ♥ has bronze young leaves and flowers with green sepals.

☼ ◊◊ ❀ ❀ ❀ *f*   **Deciduous shrub**
‡↔ 5–6m (15–20ft)

DAPHNE MEZEREUM

Mezereon has pale to soft grey-green leaves, and in late winter and early spring, its upright stems are wreathed to the tips in very fragrant, deep purple-pink flowers. The fleshy red fruits that follow, though highly poisonous to humans, are enjoyed by birds. Pruning should be avoided.

ALSO RECOMMENDED: *f. alba has creamy white flowers and yellow fruits; 'Bowles' Variety' is vigorous with pure white flowers and yellow fruits.*

☀ ◑ ◊ ❄ ❄ ❄ *f*   **Deciduous shrub**
↕ 1.2m (4ft) ↔ 1m (3ft)

DECAISNEA FARGESII

This distinctive, upright shrub with long, divided, dark green leaves bears hanging clusters of bell-shaped, yellow-green flowers in early summer. They are followed, in autumn, by fat, sausage-shaped, deep blue pods, which contain energy-rich seeds and jelly, enjoyed by birds. A good architectural plant for a shrub border (*see p.472*); shelter from strong winds. It needs very little pruning.

☀ ◑ ◊ ❄ ❄ ❄   **Deciduous shrub**
↕↔ 6m (20ft)

HEBE *'Great Orme'* ♀

A rounded shrub that carries slender spikes of small, deep pink flowers from midsummer to autumn, which fade to white and attract beneficial insects. The leaves are lance-shaped and glossy dark green. It is ideal for a mixed or shrub border; shelter from wind at the base of a warm wall in cold climates (*see p.280*). Pruning is unnecessary, but leggy plants can be cut back in spring. It can be pot-grown and tolerates chalky soils (*see pp.64, 412*).

ALSO RECOMMENDED: *H. × franciscana 'Variegata' ♀ has cream-margined leaves and purple flowers.*

☀ ◐ ◊◊ ❄❄   **Evergreen shrub**
↕↔ 1.2m (4ft)

HELIOTROPIUM ARBORESCENS

Cherry pie is a compact shrub, often grown as an annual for summer bedding or as a conservatory pot plant in cold climates (*see p.412*). It is prized for its sweetly fragrant heads of deep violet-blue summer flowers, which attract butterflies and appear above the wrinkled leaves. It will not survive outdoors in areas with cold winters.

ALSO RECOMMENDED: *'Chatsworth' ♀ has strongly scented, deep purple flowers.*

☀ ◊◊ ❄ *f*   **Evergreen shrub**
↕ 45–120cm (18–48in) ↔ 30–45cm (12–18in)

HYSSOPUS OFFICINALIS

Hyssop is an upright, aromatic shrub with narrow, dark green leaves. The dense spikes of nectar-rich, two-lipped, deep blue flowers that appear from midsummer to early autumn are attractive to bees and butterflies. Grow at the front of a mixed border or in a herb garden, where it is effective as low edging (*see p.138*). It thrives on chalky soils and in hot, dry sites (*see pp.64, 190*).

ALSO RECOMMENDED: *f. albus has white flowers; 'Roseus' has pink flowers.*

☼ ◊ ❀ ❀ ❀ *f*   **Evergreen shrub**
↕ 60cm (24in) ↔ 1m (3ft)

LEYCESTERIA FORMOSA

Himalayan honeysuckle is an attractive flowering shrub with bamboo-like, dark green young stems. Chains of white flowers with wine-red bracts dangle from the branches in summer and early autumn; these are followed by maroon to purple-black fruits, which are a food source for birds. Trim or cut back hard in spring. It is suitable as an informal hedge (*see p.138*).

ALSO RECOMMENDED: L. crocothyrsos *has arching shoots, golden yellow flowers from late spring, and small green berries.*

☼ ☀ ◊ ❀ ❀ ❀   **Deciduous shrub**
↕ 6m (20ft)

PAEONIA DELAVAYI
VAR. LUDLOWII ♛

This vigorous tree peony has an open,
upright form, which is displayed to
best effect standing on its own as
an architectural shrub (*see p.472*) or
in a shrub border. In late spring, the
nodding, glossy bright yellow flowers
open among deeply cut, bright green
leaves. The flowers are attractive to
bees. Cut back old, leggy stems to the
base occasionally in autumn. It tolerates
clay and chalky soils, and damp, shady
sites (*see pp.12, 64, 238*).

ALSO RECOMMENDED: P. delavayi ♛
(see p.243).

☼ ◗ ○◗ ❋ ❋ ❋   **Deciduous shrub**
↕↔ 2.5m (8ft)

PYRACANTHA *'Watereri'* ♛

A vigorous, upright and spiny shrub
that forms a dense screen of dark green
foliage, ornamented by an abundance
of white spring flowers and bright red
berries in autumn. It makes an attractive
nesting place for birds and has many
uses in the garden: as a barrier hedge,
border plant, or as a wall-trained shrub
(*see pp.138, 262, 280*). It tolerates clay
soils and exposed sites (*see pp.12, 118*).
Cut back unwanted growth in mid-
spring, if necessary.

ALSO RECOMMENDED: *'Golden Charmer'*
(see p.159); *'Mohave'* (see p.19);
'Soleil d'Or' (see p.269).

☼ ◗ ○ ❋ ❋ ❋   **Evergreen shrub**
↕↔ 2.5m (8ft)

RIBES ODORATUM

The buffalo currant is valued for its
spice-scented foliage, which gives
good autumn colour, and for its fragrant
yellow flowers in spring; these are
followed by small black berries – a
food source for birds. It has an upright
habit with broad, three-lobed, bright
green leaves, turning red and purple
before they fall. Selectively remove
wayward shoots after flowering.

:☼: ◊ ❀❀❀ *f*　　　　　**Deciduous shrub**
↕↔ 2m (6ft)

ROSA *'Geranium'* ♥

This shrub rose forms a clump of
thorny, arching stems clothed in dark
green leaves. In summer, it is covered
in single, sealing-wax-red flowers and
a humming mass of pollinating bees.
The large, brilliant red hips of autumn
are eaten by birds and small mammals.
Cut out old, spent stems at the base
after flowering. Grow in a border, as
an informal hedge, or as a pot plant
(*see pp.138, 412*); it tolerates chalky
soils (*see p.64*).

ALSO RECOMMENDED: *'Eddie's Jewel' is
repeat-flowering with fire-red flowers and
thorns;* R. pimpinellifolia (*see p.131*).

:☼: ◊ ❀❀❀　　　　　**Deciduous shrub**
↕ 2.5m (8ft) ↔ 1.5m (5ft)

RUBUS SPECTABILIS
'Olympic Double'

Salmonberry is a suckering shrub that
forms thickets of raspberry-like canes;
the leaves are lobed and bright green.
In late spring and early summer, it
bears double, bright magenta flowers,
which are attractive to bees; there are
no fruits. Cut spent stems back to the
base after flowering. Good as part of
a barrier planting.

ALSO RECOMMENDED: R. odoratus
has purple pink flowers and red fruits,
R. spectabilis *has single flowers and
bears red or yellow fruits.*

☼☀ ◊ ✿✿✿   **Deciduous shrub**
↕↔ 2m (6ft)

THYMUS VULGARIS
'Silver Posie'

This thyme forms a rounded, wiry-
stemmed subshrub clothed with tiny,
white-margined, greyish leaves. Masses
of bright purple flowerheads are borne
in summer. Good in a herb garden –
the aromatic foliage is useful in cooking
– and as ground cover or in paving
crevices (*see pp.304, 348*). It tolerates
chalky soils and hot, dry sites (*see pp.64,
190*). Attractive to beneficial insects.

ALSO RECOMMENDED: T. pulegioides
'Bertram Anderson' ♚ (see p.310);
T. serpyllum *'Annie Hall'* (see p.352);
T. vulgaris *has plain leaves.*

☼ ◊ ✿✿✿✿ *f*   **Evergreen shrub**
↕ 15–30cm (6–12in) ↔ 40cm (16in)

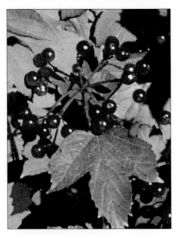

VIBURNUM OPULUS *'Compactum'* ♥

This slow-growing, compact and very dense form of the guelder rose bears maple-like leaves, which turn red in autumn. Flat heads of showy white flowers are borne in early summer, followed by large bunches of bright red berries – a food source for birds. Prune after flowering, if necessary. It tolerates clay and permanently moist soils, and exposed sites (*see pp.12, 118, 372*).

ALSO RECOMMENDED: *'Roseum'* ♥ *(syn. 'Sterile')* has pinkish flowers and purple autumn leaves; *'Xanthocarpum'* ♥ has yellow berries – both plants to 4m (12ft) tall.

☼ ◐ ◊◊ ❄❄❄ *f*   **Deciduous shrub**
↔ 1.5m (5ft)

CLEMATIS TANGUTICA

This vigorous, deciduous, late-flowering clematis bears its hanging, bell-shaped flowers from midsummer to autumn, followed by silky-hairy seedheads that last well into winter. As with many yellow flowers, they attract beneficial insects. Grow against a wall or support with the roots in shade and the top-growth in sun or partial shade (*see pp.262, 280*). Cut back hard before growth begins in early spring. It enjoys chalky soils (*see p.64*).

ALSO RECOMMENDED: *C. 'Aureolin'* ♥ *is similar with lemon-yellow bells.*

☼ ◐ ◊ ❄❄❄   **Climber**
↕ 5–6m (15–20ft) ↔ 2–3m (6–10ft)

HEDERA HELIX F. POETARUM

This and the common ivy, *H. helix*, are both wonderful wildlife plants, giving cover and food to birds, insects, and small mammals. This form is known as poet's ivy. The round heads of yellowish flowers in autumn are a valuable source of nectar, and the small, orange-yellow fruits that follow are winter sustenance for wildlife. A versatile, evergreen plant, tolerant of chalky soils and dry shade (*see pp.64, 216*), and will grow on most walls, or as ground cover, or in a pot (*see pp.262, 280, 304, 326, 412, 448*).

ALSO RECOMMENDED: *H. helix, common ivy, has smaller leaves and black fruits.*

☼ ◑ ◊◊ ❄❄❄   **Climber**
‡ 3m (10ft)

LONICERA PERICLYMENUM 'Serotina' ♥

The late Dutch honeysuckle is a fast-growing, twining climber for training onto a support, or up into a large shrub (*see p.280*). It has deciduous, oval leaves and very fragrant, rich red-purple, tubular flowers from mid-summer; red berries may follow. Prune by up to one-third after flowering to keep it in bounds. Keep the base in shade. It tolerates chalky soils (*see p.64*).

ALSO RECOMMENDED: *'Graham Thomas' ♥ has white to yellow flowers; L. tatarica (see p.129); L. japonica 'Halliana' ♥ (see p.276).*

☼ ◑ ◊◊ ❄❄❄ *f*   **Climber**
‡ 7m (22ft)

ACHILLEA MILLEFOLIUM
'Cerise Queen'

This yarrow is fast-growing, forming a mat of finely divided, dark green foliage. In summer, long-lasting flat heads of many tiny, deep pink flowers hover above the foliage on upright stems. They attract pollinating insects and the flowerheads dry well (*see p.524*). Grow at the front of a sunny border. It tolerates sandy soils (*see p.38*).

ALSO RECOMMENDED: A. filipendulina *'Gold Plate'* ♀ (see p.52); A. ptarmica, *sneezewort, has off-white flowers;* A. *'Summerwine'* (see p.527).

☼ ◊ ❈ ❈ ❈   **Perennial**
‡↔ 60cm (24in)

ALLIUM SCHOENOPRASUM

Chives are grown mainly for their grass-like, edible leaves and round heads of pale purple flowers. This is a very versatile herb and may be grown as edging in the herb or vegetable garden, or at the front of a herbaceous border. The flowers attract pollinating insects. It tolerates sandy and chalky soils, and hot, dry sites (*see pp.38, 64, 190*). Clip off the flowers once faded for a fresh flush of foliage.

ALSO RECOMMENDED: *'Forescate' is tall and vigorous with deep purple-pink flowers;* A. cernuum (see p.203).

☼ ◊ ❈ ❈ ❈   **Perennial bulb**
‡ 30–60cm (12–24in) ↔ 5cm (2in)

AQUILEGIA VULGARIS *'Nivea'* ♀

An upright, vigorous, clump-forming plant, sometimes sold as Munstead White, bearing leafy clusters of nodding, short-spurred, pure white flowers in late spring and early summer. Each greyish green leaf is deeply lobed. An attractive, luminous perennial for light woodland or herbaceous borders. It tolerates clay soils (*see p.12*).

ALSO RECOMMENDED: *A. vulgaris, granny's bonnet, has purple, pink, blue, or white flowers with short spurs; Vervaeneana Group has variegated leaves with white, pink, and purple flowers.*

☼ ◐ ◊ ❀ ❀ ❀ **Perennial**

‡ 90cm (36in) ↔ 45cm (18in)

ASTER × FRIKARTII *'Wunder von Stäfa'* ♀

This upright, bushy plant bears a long succession of daisy-like, orange-centred blue flowerheads from late summer to autumn. As well as lending useful late colour to the herbaceous border, it provides a rich source of nectar for bees and butterflies. Tolerant of clay and chalky soils (*see pp.12, 64*). Mulch annually after cutting back in late autumn. The flowers are good for indoor display (*see p.524*). Also sold as Wonder of Stafa.

ALSO RECOMMENDED: *'Flora's Delight' has lilac flowers; 'Mönch' ♀ has lavender flowers.*

☼ ◊ ❀ ❀ ❀ **Perennial**

‡ 70cm (28in) ↔ 35–40cm (14–16in)

CAREX FLAGELLIFERA

This sedge is a densely tufted evergreen, forming an arching mound of tough, narrow, grass-like, red-brown leaves. The flowering stems, which appear in mid- to late summer, bear brown inflorescences, followed by red-brown seeds, which attract birds. Grow in any soil that is not dry or waterlogged. It is suitable for mixed and wildflower borders, and it will grow in a container (*see p.412*).

ALSO RECOMMENDED: C. pendula (see p.378); C. testacea *is taller with pale olive-green to orange-brown leaves.*

☼ ◑ ○◑ ❄ ❄ ❄   **Perennial**
‡ 1.1m (3½ft) ↔ 90cm (36in)

CENTAUREA DEALBATA 'Steenbergii'

All knapweeds attract bees and butter-flies with their thistle-like flowerheads and are ideal for herbaceous borders. This is a clump-forming plant with divided, light green leaves, bearing rich pink flowerheads over long periods in summer. It is easily grown and does well on chalky ground (*see p.64*). Remove dead flowerheads to encourage a second flush of flowers.

ALSO RECOMMENDED: C. dealbata *has white-centred flowerheads;* those of C. hypoleuca 'John Coutts' *are deep pink;* C. macrocephala (see p.27); C. montana (see p.313).

☼ ○ ❄ ❄ ❄   **Perennial**
‡↔ 60cm (24in)

CENTRANTHUS RUBER

Red valerian is a clumping perennial with slightly fleshy, cloudy green stems and oval leaves. It has a long flowering season, from late spring to early summer, when it bears very colourful, rounded flowerheads of small, rose-pink flowers. It self-seeds freely. Grow in chalky soil; it also tolerates sandy sites (*see pp.38, 64*). Good for coastal gardens and for naturalizing in dry stone walls (*see pp.166, 348*).

ALSO RECOMMENDED: *'Albus' is a white-flowered cultivar.*

☼ ◌ ❀ ❀ ❀   **Perennial**
↕↔ 1m (3ft)

CEPHALARIA GIGANTEA

The giant scabious is an imposing plant for the back of a wildflower or herbaceous border. It forms a mound of rather coarse, divided, dark grey-green leaves and bears pincushion flowers of soft primrose yellow on tall, branched stems in summer. They are attractive to bees, butterflies, and other pollinating insects. Tolerant of chalky soils (*see p.64*).

ALSO RECOMMENDED: C. alpina *is slightly shorter;* C. flava *is about 90cm (36in) tall, so more suited to smaller borders*

☼ ◌ ❀ ❀ ❀   **Perennial**
↕ 2.5m (8ft) ↔ 60cm (24in)

ECHINACEA PURPUREA *'Robert Bloom'*

This upright coneflower is grown for its large, daisy-like flowerheads, up to 12cm (5in) across, from midsummer to autumn. They have cone-shaped, dark orange-brown centres and mauve-crimson, slightly downward-facing petals. The oval leaves are rough and hairy. Cut back as the flowers fade to encourage another display; they are useful for indoor arrangements (*see p.524*). Good for coastal gardens (*see p.166*).

ALSO RECOMMENDED: *'Magnus' has orange and purple flowerheads; 'White Swan' has orange and white flowerheads.*

☼ ☀ ◊ ❀ ❀ ❀   **Perennial**

‡ 1.5m (5ft) ↔ 45cm (18in)

ECHIUM VULGARE

Viper's bugloss is a bushy, short-lived perennial with bristly hairy leaves, stems, and flowers. It is grown for its early summer flowers, which are borne in short spikes amid the narrow leaves. The flowers are purple in bud, opening to broadly bell-shaped, violet-blue, sometimes pink or white flowers. Suitable for coastal gardens (*see p.166*).

☼ ◊ ❀ ❀ ❀   **Perennial**

‡ 60–90cm (24–36in) ↔ 30cm (12in)

EPILOBIUM ANGUSTIFOLIUM *VAR.* ALBUM

This form of rosebay willow herb, less invasive than the pink-flowered species, attracts a range of beneficial insects into the garden. It is a tall, clump-forming perennial, bearing spires of saucer-shaped white flowers from midsummer to early autumn. Grow in a wild garden or herbaceous border; it self-seeds freely unless the dead flowerheads are removed.

ALSO RECOMMENDED: E. dodonaei *is shorter, with deep pink-purple flowers;* E. glabellum *is even shorter (see p.185).*

☼☀ ◊ ❋❋❋   **Perennial**
‡ 1.5m (5ft) ↔ 1m (3ft) or more

INULA HOOKERI

This daisy-like, clump-forming perennial is ideal for late colour in a wild garden. It has golden yellow flowerheads with fine, narrow petals from late summer to mid-autumn; they attract pollinating insects. The hairy green leaves are borne on willowy stems. It tolerates clay soils *(see p.12).*

ALSO RECOMMENDED: I. magnifica *is taller, to 2m (6ft), with flowers from midsummer;* I. racemosa *is even taller, to 2.5m (8ft) – both may need support.*

☼ ◊◊ ❋❋❋   **Perennial**
‡ 60–75cm (24–30in) ↔ 60cm (24in) or more

IRIS *'Shelford Giant'* ♈

This vigorous iris forms upright clumps of sword-shaped leaves. In early summer, it produces large, very pale lemon-yellow flowers with a yellow patch on each of the drooping fall petals. A beautiful plant for a mixed or herbaceous border. The marks on the lower petals act as "guides" for insect pollinators. It tolerates chalky soils and the flower can be cut for indoor arrangements (*see pp.64, 524*).

ALSO RECOMMENDED: *'Imperial Bronze' has brown-veined, deep yellow flowers.*

☼ ◊ ✳ ✳ ✳　　　　　**Perennial**

‡ 1.8m (6ft) or more

MELISSA OFFICINALIS *'Aurea'*

Lemon balm is a bushy perennial named for its spikes of small white summer flowers, which attract bees and other insects. This cultivar has dark green leaves heavily splashed gold at the margins; they smell strongly of lemons when bruised and may be used in pot-pourri or herbal tea. A decorative, drought-tolerant plant useful for sandy soils (*see p.38*). Cut back in early summer and protect from excessive winter wet.

ALSO RECOMMENDED: *M. officinalis has plain green leaves; 'All Gold' has golden yellow leaves and lilac-tinted white flowers.*

☼ ◊ ✳ ✳ ✳ ✳ *f*　　　　　**Perennial**

‡ 60–120cm (24–48in) ↔ 30–45cm (12–18in)

MELITTIS MELISSOPHYLLUM

This clump-forming perennial is very attractive to bees. It has oval, honey-scented leaves and its whorls of lipped flowers are rich in nectar; they are white, pink, purple, or creamy white with pink and purple lips and spots – these markings direct the bees to the nectar-secreting glands. The flowers appear in late spring and early summer. It is good in a shady, mixed or herbaceous border.

☀ ◐ ◊ ❀ ❀ ❀ *f*   **Perennial**

‡ 20–70cm (8–28in) ↔ 50cm (20in)

MONARDA *'Croftway Pink'* ♛

A clump-forming bergamot or bee balm that bears shaggy heads of tubular pink flowers above small and aromatic, light green leaves from midsummer to early autumn. It suits mixed or herbaceous borders, and the flowers are attractive to bees. Choose a site sheltered from excessive winter wet. It tolerates clay soils (*see p.12*).

ALSO RECOMMENDED: *'Mahogany'* (see p.32); M. didyma, *bee balm, has red or pink flowers*; M. fistulosa, *wild bergamot, is taller with pinkish purple flowers.*

☀ ◐ ◊ ❀ ❀ ❀   **Perennial**

‡ 1m (3ft) ↔ 45cm (18in)

NEPETA SIBIRICA

This catmint is an upright, leafy perennial with branching stems clothed by aromatic, dark green foliage. Its long, whorled clusters of lavender-blue flowers appear in the second half of summer; they attract bees. Good in sandy soils and hot, dry sites (*see pp.38, 190*).

ALSO RECOMMENDED: N. × faassenii (see p.320); N. *'Six Hills Giant' forms large clumps.*

☼ ◊ ❀ ❀ ❀ *f*   **Perennial**
‡ 90cm (36in) ↔ 45cm (18in)

PENSTEMON *'Sour Grapes'*

Penstemons are elegant perennials valued for their spires of tubular, foxglove-like flowers, which are rich pink-purple in this cultivar. They appear from midsummer to autumn and attract beneficial insects. Suitable for a border or container (*see p.412*), but it must have the protection of a dry winter mulch in areas susceptible to heavy frosts. It may be short-lived.

ALSO RECOMMENDED: *'Andenken an Friedrich Hahn'* ♀ (syn. *'Garnet'*) has deep red flowers; *'Schoenholzeri'* ♀ (syn. *'Firebird'*) has scarlet flowers – both are hardier.

☼ ☼ ◊ ❀ ❀   **Perennial**
‡ 60cm (24in) ↔ 45cm (18in)

PRUNELLA VULGARIS

Self-heal is a low, vigorously creeping
plant with pointed, oval leaves. Its
spikes of lipped violet flowers, which
are occasionally white or pink, appear
from early summer to autumn. They are
much-visited by bees and other nectar-
feeding insects. It is suitable for a
wildflower border and makes good
ground cover in either sun or shade
(see pp.304, 326). It grows in all but
waterlogged soil.

ALSO RECOMMENDED: *P. grandiflora*
(see p.259).

☼ ◑ ◊◑ ❄ ❄ ❄   **Perennial**
↕ 15cm (6in) ↔ 1m (3ft) or more

SAPONARIA OFFICINALIS

Soapwort spreads rapidly by runners
and forms a ground covering carpet
of tough, oval leaves in sunny spots
(see p.304). From summer to autumn,
it produces profuse clusters of pink,
white, or red flowers, which attract
a range of nectar-feeding, beneficial
insects. It is good in a wildflower
border but can be invasive. Tolerant
of clay soils (see p.12).

ALSO RECOMMENDED: *'Dazzler' is less
vigorous with variegated foliage.*

☼ ◊ ❄ ❄ ❄   **Perennial**
↕ 60cm (24in) ↔ 50cm (20in)

SCABIOSA CAUCASICA

The beautiful pincushion flower is named for its solitary, pale to lavender-blue flowerheads, which are ideally suited to a cottage garden. They are borne above the clumps of grey-green leaves during the later half of summer and are good for indoor arrangements (*see p.524*). Remove dead flowerheads to prolong flowering. It tolerates chalky soils (*see p.64*).

ALSO RECOMMENDED: S. atropurpurea *is taller and has scented lilac flowers.*

☼ ◊ ❀ ❀ ❀ **Perennial**
‡↔ 60cm (24in)

SEDUM *'Herbstfreude'* ♥

Also named Autumn Joy, this fleshy perennial forms a clump of unbranched stems clothed in succulent, dark grey-green leaves. In early autumn, flat heads of many tiny, star-shaped, deep pink flowers appear and age to pink-bronze and copper-red. Bees and butterflies find them irresistible. Grow in a mixed or herbaceous border; it tolerates sandy soils and hot, dry sites (*see pp.38, 190*).

ALSO RECOMMENDED: *'Ruby Glow'* ♥ *is shorter with red flowers;* S. spectabile ♥ *has grey-green leaves and pink flowers.*

☼ ◊ ❀ ❀ ❀ **Perennial**
‡↔ 60cm (24in)

STIPA TENUISSIMA

This fluffy grass forms a dense tuft of mid-green leaves. Throughout summer, a profusion of greenish white, feathery flowerheads top the display. The whole plant billows in the slightest breeze. The seedheads provide a winter food source for finches and other seed eating birds. It tolerates exposed sites (*see p.118*).

ALSO RECOMMENDED: S. arundinacea *is taller with purplish green flower spikes;* S. calamagrostis *has blue-green leaves and silvery, purple to buff spikelets.*

☼ ◊ ❀ ❀ ❀   **Perennial**
‡ 60cm (24in) ↔ 30cm (12in)

DIGITALIS PURPUREA
F. ALBIFLORA

This ghostly foxglove bears tall, stately spires of tubular, pure white flowers during summer. They attract bees and open above a rosette of coarse, bright green leaves. A fine addition to a woodland garden or mixed border, tolerating damp or dry sites in sun or partial shade (*see pp.216, 238*). Sow the seed where it is to grow; the emergent plants will not flower until their second year. Sometimes sold as 'Alba'

ALSO RECOMMENDED: D. purpurea *has pink-purple flowers and self-seeds freely;* D. obscura (*see p.229*)

☼ ☼ ◊◊ ❀ ❀ ❀   **Biennial**
‡ 1–2m (3–6ft) ↔ 60cm (24in)

SILYBUM MARIANUM

Blessed Mary's thistle is an excellent plant for attracting bees and butterflies. It bears purple-pink flowerheads from summer to autumn the year after sowing; they are followed by fluffy seedheads. The clump of basal leaves are glossy dark green with white veins and marbling. Grow as an architectural plant in free-draining, sandy soil (*see pp.38, 472*), or in a hot, dry site mulched with gravel (*see p.190*). Sow the seed where it is to flower in late spring or early summer. It tolerates chalky soils (*see p.64*).

☼ ◊ ❀ ❀ ❀   **Biennial**
↕ 1.5m (5ft) ↔ 60–90cm (24–36in)

CONVOLVULUS TRICOLOR *'Royal Ensign'*

The beautiful royal blue, funnel-shaped, white- and yellow-eyed flowers of this bushy bindweed attract a number of beneficial and pollinating insects, such as as hoverflies. It is well-suited to a sunny hanging basket (*see p.412*). Each flower lasts just one day, but they are soon replaced by new ones throughout summer.

ALSO RECOMMENDED: *C. tricolor (syn. C. minor) has slightly smaller flowers.*

☼ ◊ ❀ ❀ ❀   **Annual**
↕ 30–40cm (12–16in) ↔ 23–30cm (9–12in)

HELIANTHUS ANNUUS

The sunflower is a well-known summer-flowering plant, grown for its large, golden yellow flowerheads on top of tall, stout stems. Leave them to stand over winter so the birds can pick the seeds. The large, heart-shaped leaves are coarsely textured and mid-green. A good architectural plant for a sheltered, sunny border (see p.472). Tolerant of clay soils (see p.12). It may need support.

ALSO RECOMMENDED: *'Autumn Beauty' has flowerheads with zones of red, brown, and gold; 'Music Box' is a much shorter form with pale yellow to dark red flowerheads.*

☀ ◊ ❉ ❉ ❉   **Annual**
‡ 2m (6ft) or more ↔ 60cm (24in)

NIGELLA DAMASCENA
'Persian Jewels'

These love-in-a-mist cultivars are tall and slender annuals bearing pretty summer flowers in a range of colours from sky blue to violet, deep pink, and white; each flower is surrounded by a feathery ruff of bright green foliage. Attractive, inflated seed pods follow. The flowers last well when cut, and the seed pods can be dried for indoor flower arrangements (see p.524). It self-seeds freely.

ALSO RECOMMENDED: *Miss Jekyll' ♀ has sky-blue flowers; 'Mulberry Rose' has pale pink flowers, deepening with age.*

☀ ◊ ❉ ❉ ❉   **Annual**
‡ 40cm (16in) ↔ 23cm (9in)

PLANTS FOR CUTTING & DRYING

THE PERFECT SITUATION for most gardeners would be to have enough space to devote a border entirely to cut flowers and foliage. The dilemma of whether or not to leave plants looking beautiful in the garden, or to cut them in their prime for the house, would therefore be solved. Since most modern gardens have too little room for a cutting border, however, a compromise is necessary. Perhaps the best approach is to show restraint when pillaging the border, with the aim of getting as good value as possible from the flowers that are cut.

The best time for cutting is in the cool of early morning when plants are firm and full of water, and before the blooms are fully open. If flowers are cut when they are in bud, make sure that the buds show good colour, otherwise they may not open indoors. Choose healthy material with sound stems and foliage, avoiding any diseased or old material, because it rots rapidly and fouls the water.

CUTTING FLOWERS

For maximum vase life, speed is of the essence, especially for hollow-stemmed flowers like delphiniums (*see pp.81, 534*), if plants wilt, they may recover, but seldom last as long. The counsel of perfection is to carry a bucket of cold water with you on your cutting forays and to plunge stems into it immediately they are cut. Failing that, place stems as soon as possible after cutting in cool, deep water up to their necks for a few hours. Cut the stems again, at an angle across their base – while they are still under water – before arranging. It's a good idea to use a proprietary cut-flower food in the water and to refresh water frequently, as this also helps to prolong the vase life.

PROFESSIONAL IDEAS

Before arranging, professional florists often scald the stems to lengthen the life of an arrangement. Plunge the bottom inch or so of the stems into boiling water and transfer them immediately to deep cold water up to the neck. This helps to expel air bubbles from the stem, so water can be drawn up the stem unimpeded. It is especially effective with heavy-headed stems, like roses (*see pp.270, 297, 506, 527*), chrysanthemums (*see p.533*), dahlias (*see pp.442, 547*), and tulips (*see pp.439, 544*); if they are plunged into the cold water through wire mesh so that their heads are held in position, they remain upright when they are arranged, instead of flopping as they usually do. Use a scrunch or wire, wire mesh, or florists' foam to help keep the stems upright or at the desired angle.

DRYING FLOWERS

In some plants, like statice and teasels (*see pp.538, 545*), and many grasses, such as *Panicum virgatum* 'Heavy Metal' (*see p.541*), the flowerheads are excellent for dried indoor arrangements. Cut them before they are fully ripe, and hang them upside down in small bundles in a cool, dry and airy place out of direct sunlight, which will bleach the colours.

LONICERA FRAGRANTISSIMA

This bushy honeysuckle has dark green leaves with blue-green undersides and very fragrant, creamy white flowers in winter and early spring. Together, the flowers and foliage make pretty, if short-lived, winter posies. After flowering, prune flowered shoots back to strong buds; on mature plants, prune out one in five of the oldest shoots. It tolerates chalky soils (*see p.64*).

ALSO RECOMMENDED: L. × purpusii *'Winter Beauty'* ♀ *has white flowers with yellow anthers;* L. standishii *has intensely fragrant, creamy white flowers.*

☼ ◐ ◊ ✽✽✽ *f*   **Deciduous shrub**
‡ 2m (6ft) ↔ 3m (10ft)

PITTOSPORUM TENUIFOLIUM *'Tom Thumb'* ♀

A compact and rounded shrub grown for its bronze-purple foliage, useful in flower arrangements. It would suit a sheltered border designed for year-round interest. It can also be pot-grown (*see p.412*). Tiny, honey–scented purple flowers are borne in early summer. Provide a warm, sheltered site in cold climates. Trim to shape in spring, if necessary. It tolerates coastal sites (*see p.166*).

ALSO RECOMMENDED: P. tenuifolium ♀ *(see p.157);* 'Warnham Gold' ♀ *has golden leaves – both are larger, to 10m (30ft) tall.*

☼ ◐ ◊◊ ✽✽ *f*   **Evergreen shrub**
‡ 1m (3ft) ↔ 60cm (24in)

ROSA *'Remember Me'* ♀

This large-flowered bush rose has lovely deep copper-orange, double flowers borne singly or in small clusters from early summer; repeat displays continue until autumn. The abundant foliage is glossy dark green on a vigorous, spreading plant, which suits a summer border. It tolerates chalky soils (*see p.64*).

ALSO RECOMMENDED: *Blessings* ♀ *has pink flowers; Just Joey* ♀ *has apricot flowers; those of 'Madame Isaac Pereire'* ♀ *are purple-pink, Royal William* ♀ *has red flowers; Tequila Sunrise* ♀ *has yellow flowers with red-rimmed petals.*

☀ ◑◐ ❄❄❄ **Deciduous shrub**
‡ 1m (3ft) ↔ 60cm (24in)

ACHILLEA *'Summerwine'*

This upright, evergreen yarrow is grown for its flat, dark red flowerheads and feathery, deep green foliage. The mid- to late summer flowers can be displayed when fresh or allowed to dry; take care when handling as the leaves may aggravate skin allergies. Suitable for a mixed or herbaceous border, or in a rock or wildlife garden (*see p.494*). It tolerates sandy soils (*see p.38*).

ALSO RECOMMENDED. *'Taygetea' has creamy yellow flowers; A. filipendulina 'Gold Plate'* ♀ *(see p.52); A. millefolium 'Cerise Queen' (see p.510).*

☀ ◑◐ ❄❄❄ **Perennial**
‡ 60cm (24in) ↔ 45cm (18in)

ALSTROEMERIA LIGTU
Hybrids ♀

These summer-flowering, tuberous perennials bear heads of widely flared flowers, which are considerably varied in colour, from white to shades of pink, yellow, and orange – often spotted or streaked with contrasting colours. They are ideal for sunny borders in moist but well-drained soil. Mulch thickly in areas with very cold winters. Leave undisturbed to form clumps.

ALSO RECOMMENDED: *A. aurea (syn. A. aurantiaca) has bright orange or yellow flowers; A. psittacina (syn. A. pulchella) has greenish red flowers.*

☀ ◊◊ ❀❀❀   **Perennial**

‡ 50cm (20in) ↔ 75cm (30in)

ANEMONE HUPEHENSIS
'Bressingham Glow'

This lovely Japanese anemone bears its wiry-stemmed, silky-hairy, deep pink flowers over long periods from mid- to late summer, and they are excellent for cutting. The lobed, dark green leaves are less significant, held below the upright flower stems. Grow in a mixed or herbaceous border; it tolerates clay and chalky soils (*see pp.12, 64*), and damp sites in shade (*see p.238*).

ALSO RECOMMENDED: *'Prinz Heinrich' ♀ (syn. Prince Henry) is similar but more vigorous; A. × hybrida 'September Charm' ♀ has pale pink flowers.*

☀ ◊◊ ❀❀❀   **Perennial**

‡ 60–120cm (24–48in) ↔ indefinite

AQUILEGIA *McKana Group*

These vigorous, often short-lived
aquilegias are indispensable in a
cottage garden and well-suited to
a mixed or herbaceous border. The
spurred flowers, which last well in
water, come in single and bicoloured
shades of blue, yellow, and red.
They rise well above the clumps of
divided, mid green leaves from late
spring to midsummer.

ALSO RECOMMENDED: A. vulgaris 'Nivea' ♀
(see p.511); 'Nora Barlow' ♀ has double,
pink, white, and green flowers.

☼ ◊ ✳ ✳ ✳   **Perennial**
↕ 75cm (30in) ↔ 60cm (24in)

ASTER PRINGLEI
'Monte Cassino' ♀

This dainty Michaelmas daisy has
slender stems with dark green leaves.
From late summer to late autumn, it
bears open sprays of small, daisy-like
flowers with white petals and golden
centres. It makes a beautiful border
perennial, and its cut flowers are
especially useful for providing an
airy backcloth to flower displays
of more substantial weight.

ALSO RECOMMENDED: A. ericoides 'Blue
Star' ♀ has sprays of small blue flowerheads;
'Esther' has sprays of pink flowerheads; A. ×
frikartii 'Wunder von Stäfa' ♀ (see p.511).

☼ ◐ ◊◊ ✳ ✳ ✳   **Perennial**
↕ 1m (3ft) ↔ 30cm (12in)

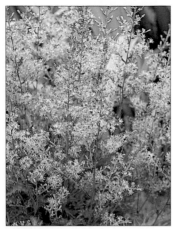

ASTILBE *'Willie Buchanan'*

A leafy, clump-forming dwarf perennial that suits damp, shady borders and waterside plantings (*see pp.238, 372*). It bears feathery, tapering plumes of tiny, star-shaped, creamy pink flowers in summer, which arch elegantly over a mass of broad, red-tinted leaves composed of many narrow leaflets. It tolerates clay and chalky soils (*see pp.12, 64*).

ALSO RECOMMENDED: *'Deutschland'* (see p.25); *'Sprite'* ♥ is larger with shell-pink plumes; A. × crispa *'Perkeo'* ♥ (see p.377).

☼ ◐ ◊ ❋ ❋ ❋   **Perennial**
‡ 23–30cm (9–12in) ↔ 20cm (8in)

BAPTISIA AUSTRALIS ♥

Blue false indigo is a spreading perennial with a long season of interest. It has bright blue-green leaves on grey stems and bears spires of lupin-like, soft indigo-blue flowers in early summer. They last well in water. The dark grey seed pods that follow can also be cut and dried for winter arrangements. Grow in a mixed or herbaceous border; it tolerates sandy soils and hot, dry sites (*see pp.38, 190*).

ALSO RECOMMENDED: B. lactea *(syn. B. leucantha) has creamy white flowers with purple marks.*

☼ ◊ ❋ ❋ ❋   **Perennial**
‡ 1.5m (5ft) ↔ 60cm (24in)

CALAMAGROSTIS ×
ACUTIFLORA *'Overdam'*

This feather reed grass forms a clump of flat, narrow green leaves, which are striped and margined with pale yellow. In mid- to late summer, airy, stiff-stemmed, glistening, purple-tinted inflorescences appear and age to greyish pink; they can be used in fresh or dried arrangements. For drying, cut before the flower spikes open fully.

ALSO RECOMMENDED: *'Karl Foerster'* has *pink-bronze flowerheads that age to buff.*

☼ ◐ ◊ ❀ ❀ ❀   **Perennial**
↕ 1.2m (4ft) ↔ 60cm (24in)

CAMASSIA LEICHTLINII
SUBSP. SUKSDORFII

This bulbous border perennial with long, linear leaves is grown for its spires of relatively large, creamy white flowers in late spring. As each flower ages, its segments twist together. Plant bulbs in autumn; in areas with prolonged frosts, provide a thick winter mulch. It tolerates damp shade (*see p.372*), but do not allow the soil to become waterlogged.

ALSO RECOMMENDED: *'Semiplena'* has *semi-double flowers; C. quamash has bright blue flowers.*

☼ ◐ ◊◊ ❀ ❀   **Perennial bulb**
↕ 60–130cm (24–52in) ↔ 10cm (4in)

CAMPANULA LACTIFLORA
'Prichard's Variety' ♥

An upright plant that produces sprays of large and nodding, bell-shaped, deep purple flowers from midsummer above mid-green leaves. It is an excellent border perennial, but it may need staking in an exposed site. Trim after flowering to encourage a second, although less profuse flush of flowers. It tolerates clay and chalky soils (*see pp.12, 64*).

ALSO RECOMMENDED: *'Alba'* ♥ *has white flowers; 'Loddon Anna'* ♥ *has lilac-pink flowers.*

☼ ☀ ◊◊ ❀ ❀ ❀   **Perennial**
‡ 75cm (30in) ↔ 60cm (24in)

CHIONOCHLOA CONSPICUA

The plumed tussock grass is grown for its strong, elegant shape and attractive flowerheads, which are ideal for dried flower arrangements if cut before they are fully mature. It forms tussocks of stiff and arching, red-brown-tinted leaves, and from midsummer, strong, tall stems emerge bearing droopy, feathery, creamy brown flower clusters. Choose a sheltered site protected from excessive winter wet, and cut out old, flowered stems at the base in early winter. Grow as a feature plant in a border or as a specimen on its own.

☼ ◊◊ ❀ ❀   **Perennial**
‡ 2m (6ft) ↔ 1m (3ft)

CHRYSANTHEMUM
'Mary Stoker'

Above a bushy clump of dark green leaves, this chrysanthemum bears single, rose-tinted, apricot-yellow, daisy-like flowerheads from late summer to autumn. The centres of the flowers turn from green to yellow as they open fully. It is a reliable border plant, and the flowers last well when cut. It can be container grown (see p.110).

ALSO RECOMMENDED: *'Clara Curtis'* *has clear pink flowers; those of 'Duchess* *of Edinburgh' are rich coppery red .*

☼ ◊ ❀ ❀ ❀   **Perennial**
‡ 75cm (30in) ↔ 60cm (24in)

CROCOSMIA ×
CROCOSMIIFLORA
'Star of the East'

An orange-flowered crocosmia that is valuable as a border plant for its late summer to early autumn display of bright flowers. They are borne on arching spikes over the fans of mid-green leaves. It is suitable for coastal gardens (see p.166). Plant corms in spring and cover with a dry mulch in winter. Tolerant of clay soils (see p.12).

ALSO RECOMMENDED: *'Jackanapes'* *(syn. 'Fire King') has orange-red and* *yellow flowers; C. 'Lucifer' ♀ (see p.184);* *C. masoniorum ♀ has orange-red flowers.*

☼ ☀ ◊◊ ❀ ❀ ❀   **Perennial corm**
‡ 70cm (30in) ↔ 8cm (3in)

DELPHINIUM GRANDIFLORUM *'Blue Butterfly'*

This delphinium makes an excellent border plant with bright blue flowers that are lovely for cutting. Unlike the tall hybrid delphiniums, this one has open spires of elf-cap-shaped flowers in early summer. They appear amid the five-lobed, divided foliage. It tolerates clay and chalky soils (*see p.12, 64*) and seldom needs staking. Cutting and removal of dead flowerheads will induce further flowering.

ALSO RECOMMENDED: D. grandiflorum *(syn. D. chinense) has blue, violet, or white flowers;* D. tatsiense *(see p.81).*

☀ ◊◊ ❀❀❀   **Perennial**
‡ 20–50cm (8–20in) ↔ 23–30cm (9–12in)

DORONICUM PARDALIANCHES

A vigorous colonizer for a woodland garden or wildflower border (*see p.494*), the great leopard's bane bears wiry-stemmed, daisy-like, light yellow flowerheads from late spring to early summer. They appear above narrowly oval, softly hairy leaves and last well as cut flowers. It grows in most moist, humus-rich soils, including those on chalk (*see p.64*).

ALSO RECOMMENDED: D. *'Miss Mason'* ♀ (see p.83); *'Frühlingspracht' (syn. Spring Beauty) has double yellow flowerheads.*

☀ ◊ ❀❀❀   **Perennial**
‡ 90cm (36in) ↔ 60–90cm (24–36in)

ERYNGIUM GIGANTEUM ♀

Miss Willmott's ghost is a steely blue-green perennial with spiny leaves along its stems. In summer, clusters of flowers rise above the foliage; each flowerhead is ringed by a spiky ruff of silver bracts. Shelter from excessive winter wet. It is short-lived, but it may self-seed. Suitable for coastal and hot, dry sites (*see pp. 166, 190*), and tolerant of sandy and chalky soils (*see pp. 39, 64*). It can be used for fresh or dry displays.

ALSO RECOMMENDED: *Silver Ghost* ♀ has very silvery bracts; E. bourgatii (see p. 208); E. × oliverianum (see p. 186); E. × tripartitum ♀ (see p. 56).

☼ ◐ ◊ ❀ ❀ ❀   **Perennial**
‡ 1.5m (5ft) ↔ 60–90cm (24–36in)

GEUM *'Red Wings'*

This sturdy plant forms a clump of hairy, fresh green, divided leaves. In early and midsummer, it produces bowl-shaped, semi-double, bright scarlet flowers, which last well when cut. It also looks good in a mixed or herbaceous border, especially one with a hot-coloured theme.

ALSO RECOMMENDED: *'Lady Stratheden'* ♀ has semi-double, rich yellow flowers; *'Mrs J. Bradshaw'* ♀ has semi-double scarlet flowers.

☼ ◊◑ ❀ ❀ ❀   **Perennial**
‡ 60cm (24in) ↔ 40cm (16in)

IRIS CHRYSOGRAPHES ♀

This iris has a sheaf of narrow, greyish leaves and bears fragrant, deep red-violet flowers with gold-streaked fall petals in early summer. It is an elegant border perennial, making an exquisite cut flower. If flowers cannot be removed from garden displays, grow several in a cutting border; the clumps can be increased by division in late summer. It tolerates chalky soils (*see p.64*).

ALSO RECOMMENDED: I. bucharica (see p.86); I. ensata (see p.400); I. foetidissima *var.* citrina (see p.233); I. forrestii ♀ (see p.382); I. innominata (see p.112); I. pseudacorus (see p.401); I. 'Shelford Giant' (see p.516).

☼ ◊ ❀ ❀ ❀   **Perennial**
↕ 40–50cm (16–20in) ↔ 30cm (12in)

KNIPHOFIA *'Royal Standard'* ♀

A classic red hot poker that bears tall, conical flowerheads from midsummer. Its bright yellow, tubular flowers open from red buds, from the base up. The clumps of arching, grass-like leaves die back in winter. Provide a thick mulch in autumn to protect from winter cold. An architectural plant for coastal and hot, dry sites (see *pp.166, 190*); it tolerates sandy and chalky soils (see *pp.38, 64*).

ALSO RECOMMENDED: *'Jenny Bloom'* *has pink flowers;* *'Percy's Pride'* (see p.187); *'Shining Sceptre' has yellow flowers;* K. caulescens ♀ *has red flowers that turn yellow with age.*

☼ ◊◊ ❀ ❀ ❀   **Perennial**
↕ 1m (3ft) ↔ 60cm (24in)

LEUCANTHEMUM × SUPERBUM
'Phyllis Smith'

This Shasta daisy is a robust, clump-forming plant with glossy dark green basal leaves. From early summer to early autumn, its tall, strong stems bear single, daisy-like flowerheads with golden centres and narrow, twisted white petals. They are ideal for cutting. It tolerates exposed sites (*see p.118*).

ALSO RECOMMENDED: *'Aglaia'* ♥ *has fringed, semi-double flowerheads; 'Wirral Supreme'* ♥ *has double flowers.*

☼ ☀ ◊◊ ❄ ❄ ❄   **Perennial**
‡ 90cm (36in) ↔ 75cm (30in)

LIATRIS SPICATA

Gayfeather is an upright perennial with leafy stems, which bear fluffy spikes of bright mauve-pink or white flowers in late summer and autumn. They open from the top of the spike downwards and are long-lasting when cut. This plant is ideal for late colour in a mixed or herbaceous border.

ALSO RECOMMENDED: *'Alba' has white flowerheads; 'Kobold' (syn. Goblin) has deep bright purple flowerheads.*

☼ ◊◊ ❄ ❄ ❄   **Perennial**
‡ 1.5m (5ft) ↔ 45cm (18in)

LILIUM *'Journey's End'*

A stout oriental lily that produces a number of large, broad, turkscap flowers in late summer; the spreading petals, which curve back on themselves, are deep pink with maroon spots and white margins. Choose a site in full sun, preferably with the base of the plant in shade. Plant bulbs in autumn; it can be container-grown (*see p.412*).

ALSO RECOMMENDED: *'Star Gazer' has large, star-shaped red flowers;* L. candidum ♀ (see p.490); L. regale ♀ (see p.433); L. superbum ♀ (see p.113).

☼ ◊ ❁ ❁ ❁　　　　　**Perennial bulb**
‡ 1–2m (3–6ft)

LIMONIUM SINUATUM 'Iceberg'

This stiff, papery plant bears tightly packed heads of white flowers from summer to early autumn; they are very long-lasting in a vase, keeping their colour well as a dried flower. It has upright stems with narrow wings and dark green leaves and suits a sunny border or a gravel garden. Like other statice, it is usually grown as an annual. Grow in sandy soil; it tolerates dry, stony, and chalky sites (*see pp.38, 64*).

ALSO RECOMMENDED: *Forever Series have a mixture of blue, pink, and yellow flowers;* L. platyphyllum (see p.56).

☼ ◊ ❁ ❁　　　　　**Perennial**
‡ 60cm (24in) ↔ 30cm (12in)

MALVA SYLVESTRIS
'Primley Blue'

A spreading, almost ground-hugging perennial producing upright spires of funnel-shaped, pale blue-violet flowers with darker veins. They appear from late spring to mid-autumn, which gives many opportunities for interesting associations with cut flowers from different times in the season. It is useful in a mixed or herbaceous border, it tolerates chalky soils (*see p.64*).

ALSO RECOMMENDED. *'Brave Heart' is upright, to 90cm (36in) tall, with large, dark-veined purple flowers.*

☼ ◊◊ ❉❉❉   **Perennial**
‡ 20cm (8in) ↔ 30–60cm (12–24in)

MISCANTHUS SINENSIS
'Silberfeder'

This tall grass forms substantial clumps of arching, bright green leaves, which look good in a mixed or herbaceous border, or as a screen. In early and mid-autumn, it bears straight-stemmed, silvery to pale pink-brown flowerheads. They can be dried for indoor display if cut before the spikelets are fully open. It is also sold as Silver Feather.

ALSO RECOMMENDED. *'Rotsilber' has red-tinted, silvery plumes; 'Zebrinus' has maroon-tinted spikelets and creamy-yellow-banded leaves.*

☼☀ ◊◊ ❉❉❉   **Perennial**
‡ 2.5m (8ft) ↔ 1.2m (4ft)

Morina longifolia

This prickly whorlflower forms evergreen rosettes of aromatic, glossy bright green leaves. Whorls of tubular, two-lipped, waxy white flowers arise on sturdy stems in midsummer, turning pink after fertilization. They are ideal for cutting, and the seedheads are useful for drying. Grow in a herbaceous border in poor to moderately fertile, gritty, well-drained soil.

☼ ◊ ❀❀❀❀ *f*   **Perennial**
‡ 90cm (36in) ↔ 30cm (12in)

Narcissus *'Bridal Crown'*

A highly scented narcissus that bears heads of several, double white flowers, each with clustered, orange-yellow petals at the centre. It makes a beautiful cut flower and can be grown in a spring border or container (*see p.412*). It tolerates chalky soils and coastal sites (*see pp.64, 166*). Plant bulbs in autumn.

ALSO RECOMMENDED: *'Cheerfulness'* ♀ *has double white flowers with creamy centres; 'Tahiti'* ♀ *has double yellow flowers with bright red-orange centres.*

☼ ◊ ❀❀❀❀ *f*   **Perennial bulb**
‡ 40cm (16in) ↔ 15cm (6in)

PAEONIA LACTIFLORA
'Sarah Bernhardt' ♥

With its large, fragrant, fully double flowers in early summer, this peony is indispensable in a herbaceous border. Its flowers are light pink with ruffled, silver-margined inner petals. Mulch with well-rotted organic matter in autumn. It tolerates chalky soils (*see p.64*).

ALSO RECOMMENDED: *'Bowl of Beauty'* ♥ *has carmine-red flowers with creamy centres;* *'Karl Rosenfield' has double, deep red flowers.*

☼ ◑ ◊◊ ❀ ❀ ❀ *f*   **Perennial**
↔ 1m (3ft)

PANICUM VIRGATUM
'Heavy Metal'

This metallic-looking form of switch grass is valued for its light and airy, weeping, bronze to purple-green inflorescences, which can be cut and dried for indoor flower displays. These appear in early autumn, above stiff clumps of blue-green leaves; the foliage fades to yellow in autumn. It suits a mixed or herbaceous border.

ALSO RECOMMENDED: *'Hänse Herms' has red-purple autumn foliage and a fountain-like habit;* *'Rubrum' has red-tinted leaves, red in autumn, and brown inflorescences.*

☼ ◊ ❀ ❀ ❀   **Perennial**
↕ 1m (3ft) ↔ 75cm (30in)

PENNISETUM SETACEUM ♥

The fountain grass forms deciduous mounds of rough-textured green leaf blades to 30cm (12in) long. It flowers from midsummer to early autumn to produce fluffy, tail-like, pink or purplish spikes; they can be used in both fresh and dried flower arrangements. It is often grown as an annual border plant as it may not survive cold winters; it tolerates hot, dry sites (*see p.190*). Cut back dead top growth by early spring. Also known as *P. rueppellii*.

ALSO RECOMMENDED: P. alopecuroides *has yellow-green to purple inflorescences;* P. orientale ♥ *has pink inflorescences.*

☼ ◊ ❀ ❀   **Perennial**
‡ 1m (3ft) ↔ 45cm (18in)

PHLOX PANICULATA *'Eventide'* ♥

Perennial phloxes are upright plants, well-suited to herbaceous borders. They are grown for their clusters of bright, flat-faced, lightly fragrant flowers in summer and autumn above mid-green foliage. 'Eventide' has lavender-blue flowers, and it may need staking for support. Larger flowers can be encouraged by removing the weakest shoots in spring. Cut back after flowering.

ALSO RECOMMENDED: *'Bright Eyes'* ♥ *has pink, red-eyed flowers;* 'Starfire' *has crimson flowers;* 'White Admiral' ♥ *has white flowers.*

☼ ☀ ◊ ❀ ❀ ❀ *f*   **Perennial**
‡ 90cm (36in) ↔ 45cm (18in)

RUDBECKIA *'Goldquelle'* ♥

A tall but compact perennial that bears large, fully double, bright lemon-yellow flowers from midsummer to autumn. These are carried above loose clumps of deeply divided, mid-green leaves. The long-stalked flowers are ideal for cutting. It tolerates chalky soils and exposed sites (*see pp.64, 118*).

ALSO RECOMMENDED: *'Herbstonne'* ♥ (*see p.90*); R. fulgida *'Goldsturm'* ♥ *has large, golden yellow, daisy-like flowerheads with dark centres.*

☼ ☀ ◊◊ ❋ ❋ ❋   **Perennial**
‡ 90cm (36in) ↔ 45cm (18in)

SCHIZOSTYLIS COCCINEA *'Sunrise'* ♥

A strong-growing, clump-forming plant with a stiff and upright habit that bears gladiolus-like spikes of salmon-pink flowers. They appear in late summer and autumn above the narrow, almost floppy, mid-green leaves and last well in water when cut. In the garden, it is good near the front of a sheltered border; it tolerates permanently moist soils (*see p.372*). Divide congested clumps every few years.

ALSO RECOMMENDED: *f.* alba *has white flowers;* 'Jennifer' ♥ *has pink flowers;* 'Major' ♥ *has large red flowers.*

☼ ◊ ❋ ❋ ❋   **Perennial**
‡ 60cm (24in) ↔ 30cm (12in)

× SOLIDASTER LUTEUS

This upright, branching perennial with relatively large leaves is grown for its attractive clusters of small, daisy-like flowerheads, which appear in profusion from midsummer to early autumn; they have pale yellow petals and golden centres. It is good for late colour in a mixed or herbaceous border. The flower clusters attract beneficial insects (*see p.494*) and last well as cut flowers. It is also known as *S.* × *hybridus*.

ALSO RECOMMENDED: *'Lenmore'* ♀ *has light lemon-yellow petals.*

☼ ◊ ❄ ❄ ❄   **Perennial**
‡ 90cm (36in) ↔ 30cm (12in)

TULIPA *'Purissima'* ♀

Also sold as 'White Emperor', this tulip has pure white flowers in mid-spring, and they make for a bold indoor display. In the garden, group them together with other tulips in a spring border, or grow in a large container (*see p.412*). Plant bulbs in autumn. Lift the bulbs after the foliage has died down and store them in a cool greenhouse. It tolerates sandy and chalky soils (*see pp.38, 64*), and coastal and hot, dry sites (*see pp.166, 190*).

ALSO RECOMMENDED: *'Keizerskroon'* ♀ (see p.439); *T. hageri 'Splendens'* (see p.63); *T. praestans 'Unicum'* (see p.214).

☼ ◊ ❄ ❄ ❄   **Perennial bulb**
‡ 35cm (14in)

DIPSACUS FULLONUM

The teasel is an architectural plant (*see p.472*), but with its prolific self-seeding, it is best confined to a wild garden, where goldfinches will enjoy the seedheads in winter (*see p.494*). The gardener can harvest them for dried winter arrangements in midsummer. It has a basal rosette of prickly dark green leaves; the branching stems above bear thistle-like, pink purple or white flowerheads from midsummer. Sow seeds in autumn or spring where it is to grow, and it will flower the year after. It tolerates clay soils (*see p.12*). Also known as *D. sylvestris*.

☼ ☀ ◊◊ ❄❄❄   **Biennial**
‡ 1.5–2m (5–6ft) ↔ 80cm (32in)

ONOPORDUM ACANTHIUM

This architectural biennial (*see p.472*) forms a basal rosette of large, densely white-hairy, spiny leaves in its first year. The massive, candelabra-like, white-woolly stems of thistle-like, pale purple or white flowerheads arise in the summer of the second year. They are good for cutting and drying. Grow in a sunny border or in a gravel garden. It self-seeds freely; transplant seedlings to the flowering site when small.

ALSO RECOMMENDED: *O. nervosum* ♀ *(syn. O. arabicum) has bright purple-red to purple-pink flowerheads.*

☼ ◊ ❄❄❄   **Biennial**
‡ 3m (10ft) ↔ 1m (3ft)

AMARANTHUS CAUDATUS

Love-lies-bleeding is a bushy, upright annual with red, purple, or green stems clothed with broad, light green leaves. It is valued for its drooping, tassel-like clusters of crimson-purple flowers, which appear freely in summer. They suit fresh or dried cut-flower displays. It tolerates poor soils, but it needs plenty of water. Sow seed where it is to grow in late spring, after the last frosts. Use to add height to a summer border.

ALSO RECOMMENDED: *'Viridis' has bright green tassels, which age to cream; cultivars of* A. hypochondriacus *have plume-like flower clusters in different colours.*

☼ ◐ ❄ ❀   **Annual**

↕ 1–1.5m (3–5ft) ↔ 45–75cm (18–30in)

BRIZA MAXIMA

Greater quaking grass is an upright annual that bears green, red- or brown-tinged flowerheads from late spring until the end of summer. They hang from hair-fine stalks and ripen to a beautiful straw colour. The green leaves fade to the same colour. It is suitable for a mixed or herbaceous border, or in a rock garden. The flowerheads are popular in dried flower arrangements. Sow seed where it is to grow in spring or autumn.

ALSO RECOMMENDED: B. media *is a perennial;* B. minor *is shorter.*

☼ ◐ ❄ ❄ ❄   **Annual**

↕ 45–60cm (18–24in) ↔ 25cm (10in)

CALLISTEPHUS CHINENSIS
Ostrich Plume Series

These sturdy, partially wilt-resistant, variably coloured, fast-growing annuals are ideal for summer bedding and sunny pots (*see p.412*). They have feathery, rounded flowerheads from late summer to late autumn in shades of pink and crimson; their long stems make them ideal for cutting. Choose a sheltered, moist site and remove dead flowerheads to extend flowering. They tolerate chalky soils (*see p.64*). Sow seed in spring.

ALSO RECOMMENDED: *Compliment Series have pink, light blue, and white flowerheads with quilled petals.*

☼ ◊◊ ❀❀   **Annual**
‡ 60cm (24in) ↔ 30cm (12in)

DAHLIA *'Fascination'* ♀

This dwarf dahlia has large and showy, daisy-like, purplish pink flowerheads above dark bronze, divided leaves. The flowering period lasts from midsummer to autumn; flowers removed for cutting will soon be replaced. It is useful for filling gaps in a border display or in a sunny container (*see p.412*). Dwarf bedding dahlias are usually raised each year from seed and discarded at the end of the season.

ALSO RECOMMENDED: *'Border Princess' freely bears strong-stemmed, golden bronze, spiky, rounded flowerheads; 'Yellow Hammer'* ♀ (*see p.442*).

☼ ◊ ❀❀   **Annual**
‡ 60cm (24in) ↔ 45cm (18in)

LAGURUS OVATUS ♥

Hare's tail is an annual grass, which bears fluffy, oval flowerheads in summer. These are pale green, often purple-tinged, and fade to a pale creamy buff. The flat, narrow leaf blades are light green. It is effective in a border. The flowerheads can be cut for either fresh or dried arrangements; for drying, pick the heads before they are fully mature. Sow seed where it is to grow in late spring.

ALSO RECOMMENDED: *'Nanus' is much more compact, to 12cm (5in) tall.*

☼ ◊ ❀❀   **Annual**
‡ 50cm (20in) ↔ 30cm (12in)

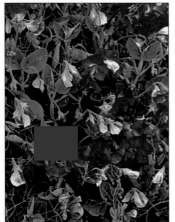

LATHYRUS ODORATUS
Bijou Group

Sweet peas are annual climbers. Cut them regularly for a long display of beautiful flowers, which are available in most colours. This selection has pink, blue, red, or white flowers; its bushy growth is more-or-less self-supporting. The widely grown Spencer sweet peas are tall-growing and the best for cutting with their long stems and sweet scent. Most types will need to be trained on a pyramid of canes or trellis, or allowed to scramble among larger plants. Sow seed in spring.

☼☀ ◊◊ ❀❀❀ *f*   **Annual climber**
‡↔ 45cm (18in)

LAVATERA TRIMESTRIS *'Pink Beauty'*

Annual lavateras are excellent bushy plants for grouping in a summer border, flowering continuously from midsummer to autumn, which makes them an excellent source of cut flowers. 'Pink Beauty' has purple-veined, very light pink flowers, complemented by the soft green leaves. Water young plants well until established, and check for aphids. It tolerates chalky soils and coastal sites (*see pp.64, 166*). Sow seed in late spring.

ALSO RECOMMENDED: *'Silver Cup' has bright rose-pink flowers. 'White Beauty' and 'White Cherub' have white flowers.*

☼ ◊ ❀ ❀   **Annual**
‡ 60cm (24in) ↔ 45cm (18in)

MALOPE TRIFIDA *'Vulcan'*

The annual mallow is a bushy plant with hairy stems and round-lobed, mid-green leaves. It flowers from summer to autumn, bearing magnificent magenta-pink, trumpet-shaped flowers in abundance; flowering is further stimulated by regular picking. It is best in full sun and thrives in coastal gardens (*see p.166*). Grow in the middle of a summer border. The flowers last well when cut. Sow seed where it is to grow in mid-spring.

ALSO RECOMMENDED: *'Rosea' has rose-red flowers; 'White Queen' has white flowers.*

☼☀ ◊◊ ❀ ❀ ❀   **Annual**
‡ 90cm (36in) ↔ 23cm (9in)

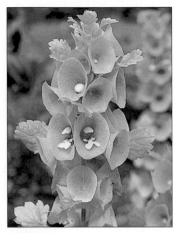

MOLUCCELLA LAEVIS

The shell flower is named for its unusual flower spikes, which are up to 30cm (12in) tall and appear in late summer; each small, fragrant, white to pale pink, two-lipped flower is enclosed by an expanded, pale green calyx, which has the shape of a limpet shell and becomes papery with age. The pale green leaves are deeply scalloped. Grow in a mixed or summer border. The flower spikes are useful for dried arrangements. Sow seed where it is to grow in late spring.

☼ ◊ ❀ *f* **Annual**
‡ 60–90cm (24–36in) ↔ 23cm (9in)

PAPAVER SOMNIFERUM 'Peony Flowered'

The opium poppy (*P. somniferum*) has attractive blue-green seed pods, which are good for dried flower arrangements. This double-flowered form has frilly flowers in red, purple, pink, salmon-pink, maroon-red, or white. It is a spectacular, upright annual for a summer border. All parts of the plant are toxic. Sow seed where it is to grow in spring.

ALSO RECOMMENDED: *'Hen and Chickens' has very large seed pods with clusters of baby pods.*

☼ ◊ ❀❀❀ **Annual**
‡ 1.2m (4ft) ↔ 30cm (12in)

SALVIA VIRIDIS *'Claryssa'*

The annual clary is an upright and bushy plant for summer bedding, with hairy green foliage. It bears upright spikes of insignificant flowers in summer, but these are enclosed by very colourful bracts. 'Claryssa' has bracts in shades of pink, blue, purple, or white, available in mixtures or single colours. These are long-lasting as cut flowers, and they also dry well. It tolerates chalky soils (*see p.64*), and it can be container-grown (*see p.412*).

☼ ☀ ◐ ❉ ❉ ❉   **Annual**

‡ 40cm (16in) ↔ 23cm (9in)

XERANTHEMUM ANNUUM

The immortelle is named for its everlasting flowers, which keep their colour indefinitely when dried. It is an upright plant with silvery green leaves, bearing its pink-purple flowerheads on long, wiry stems in summer and autumn. It is suitable for an annual border. The cut flowers can be used fresh; for drying, cut them before they have fully opened, then hang them upsidedown in a cool, dark, well-ventilated area until dry. It tolerates chalky soils (*see p.64*).

ALSO RECOMMENDED: *'Snow Lady' has single white flowerheads.*

☼ ◊ ❉   **Annual**

‡ 25–75cm (10–30in) ↔ 45cm (18in)

INDEX

Acknowledgements

Picture Research: Marie Osborn
Picture Library: Romaine Werblow, Richard
Dabb, Neale Chamberlain, Denise O'Brien
Index: Dorothy Frame

The publisher would like the thank the
following for their kind permission to
reproduce their images:
(key: t=top, b=bottom, c=centre)

Heather Angel: 399t, 408b. **A-Z Botanical
Collection:** 400t; Michael Jones 398b. **John
Fielding:** 64c, 64-65, 216c, 216-217. **Garden
Picture Library:** 387t; Howard Rice 399b; Ron
Evans 470t. **Andrew Lawson:** 38c, 38-39, 394c,

394-395. **N.H.P.A.:** 411t. **Clive Nichols:** 211b.
Photos Horticultural: 75b, 83t, 118c, 118-119,
123t, 141b, 160t, 165b, 209t, 272t, 279b, 314b,
403t, 443t, 551t. **Howard Rice:** Beth Chatto
190c, 190-191. **Harry Smith Collection:** 148b,
162b, 282b, 414t, 440b, 502b, 536t, 545t, 545t.

Dorling Kindersley would also like to thank the
following for editorial assistance:
Candida Frith-Macdonald, Louise Abbott, Pam
Brown; at the Royal Horticultural Society,
Vincent Square; Barbara Haynes, Susanne
Mitchell, and Karen Wilson.

Visit the RHS on the internet at **www.rhs.org.uk**